Marketing for Engineers, Scientists and Technologists

Marketing for Engineers, Scientists and Technologists

TONY CURTIS

John Wiley & Sons, Ltd

Copyright © 2008   John Wiley & Sons Ltd,
                     The Atrium, Southern Gate, Chichester,
                     West Sussex PO19 8SQ, England

                     Telephone   +44 (0) 1243 779777

Email (for orders and customer service enquiries): cs-books@wiley.co.uk
Visit our Home Page on www.wiley.com

Other Wiley Editorial Offices

John Wiley & Sons Inc., 111 River Street, Hoboken, NJ 07030, USA

Jossey-Bass, 989 Market Street, San Francisco, CA 94103-1741, USA

Wiley-VCH Verlag GmbH, Boschstr. 12, D-69469 Weinheim, Germany

John Wiley & Sons Australia Ltd, 42 McDougall Street, Milton, Queensland 4064, Australia

John Wiley & Sons (Asia) Pte Ltd, 2 Clementi Loop #02-01, Jin Xing Distripark, Singapore 129809

John Wiley & Sons Canada Ltd, 6045 Freemont Blvd, Mississauga, ONT, L5R 4J3

Wiley also publishes its books in a variety of electronic formats. Some content that appears in print may not be available in electronic books.

Library of Congress Cataloging-in-Publication Data

Curtis, Tony (Anthony)
   Marketing for engineers, scientists and technologists / Tony Curtis.
     p. cm.
   Includes bibliographical references and index.
   ISBN 978-0-470-05709-4 (pbk.: alk. paper)
  1. Marketing.   2. New products.   3. Product management.   I. Title.
   HF5415.C79 2008
   658.8–dc22
   2007046840

A catalogue record for this book is available from the British Library

ISBN: 978-0-470-05709-4

Typeset in 10/12 Palatino by Aptara Inc, New Delhi, India.
Printed and bound in Great Britain by Bell & Bain, Ltd, Glasgow.
This book is printed on acid-free paper responsibly manufactured from sustainable forestry in which at least two trees are planted for each one used for paper production.

Contents

Preface

This book has been written as a result of 17 years' experience of teaching marketing to undergraduate and postgraduate engineering and science students. Increasingly employers are expecting their technical staff to be multifunctional and understand not only their science but also the organisations' customers and markets. New product development is more than just making products that work. In competitive international markets they have to be what customers want, at a price they are prepared to pay: technology in a marketing business context.

This book has four main parts. The first part defines marketing, current marketing issues and marketing contexts. The second provides a structured overview of the powerhouse of marketing, the seven elements of the marketing mix. To apply the concepts of marketing, certain marketing skills (e.g. negotiation skills) are required. These are presented in Part Three. Part Four provides a review of three key areas where technical staff are often involved in marketing: new product development, market driven quality and marketing plans.

The book is intended for undergraduate and postgraduate engineering, technical and scientific students taking a one- or two-semester programme in marketing or management. The material has also proved useful for engineers, technicians and scientists taking an MBA. A strategic and international perspective is provided as well as further reading references to mainstream marketing and corporate strategy texts.

Acknowledgments

The models in this book have been developed over a number of years with final year undergraduate and postgraduate engineering and science students. Their contribution in refining the models is appreciated. Sharon Heard (University of Plymouth) assisted in the preparation of the draft manuscript. Helpful discussions and input, to revise and considerably improve the draft, were contributed by Ali Green (University of Exeter), Lorraine Kirby (University of the West of England), Mandy Burns (University of Plymouth), Jocelyn Letts, Alex Janes, Andrew Reece-Pinchin and John Ayres.

Tony Curtis
October 2007

PART ONE

Introduction to the Context of Marketing

CHAPTER 1

What is marketing and why do it?

Learning objectives

After studying this chapter you will be able to:

- Define marketing and explain the importance of a marketing orientation
- Describe the marketing system and explain the individual elements

Introduction

In the 1960s, architects were implementing a vision of the future to replace the slums of an earlier century. The vision was of a new utopia with cities in the sky. Small squalid terrace houses were demolished to make way for high-rise flats: cities in the sky. In the event, an old nightmare was replaced with a new nightmare. The new cities in the sky were not fit for purpose. At the social level, their implementation destroyed the social fabric of existing communities. At the technical level, they did not provide safe, warm accommodation. A comparatively minor accident at 'Rowan Point' led to the partial collapse of a multi-storey building. After 50 years, authorities across the UK have had to demolish (in some cases simply blow them up) these monuments to failure to replace them with housing that is fit for purpose. How could this past disaster have happened? Could history repeat itself?

Some years later, the new town of Milton Keynes was conceived and built. Much open space was provided, with more trees than residents. Unemployment is low and people want to live and work there. However, even this success story has a downside. Milton Keynes is said, in some ways, to resemble a US city. This is true to the extent that Milton Keynes is, as are many US cities, built for the car. It could have been built with public transport as the arteries, but 40 years ago global warming and carbon footprints were not an issue.

Applied scientists, engineers and technologists are engaged in the development of products and services to satisfy the needs and wants of real people. To be successful the technologist must understand:

- What are the needs and wants of the target market?
- How will people use the product?
- How much are people prepared to pay?
- How do you provide an effective technical solution at an economic cost?

Often the question is asked: 'Should new products be technology driven or market driven?' The answer is simple. If you have a product and people do not want it, you do not have a product. If you have an idea for a product that people need and want but the product itself fails to perform you do not have a product. It is necessary to move on from a two letter word, 'or', to a three letter word, 'and'. Products must make the best economic use of technology *and* satisfy the real needs and wants of customers. On Valentine's Day when a young man proposes to his girlfriend he does not give her an uncut diamond. The boy presents a cut diamond in an engagement ring. Our technological skills are the uncut diamond. To be successful we must know how to cut the diamond and set it in a ring. The assertion, on which this book is founded, is that there is no such thing in the real world as a purely technical problem. There is, in fact, a 'business problem' that has technology as part of the total solution. The technologist who fails to take into account the broader context will not come up with the most elegant, cost-effective solution.

MICRO CASE STUDY   **HOW TO MAKE MONEY SAFE**

Consider the problem of keeping paper money safe. An early solution was to build safes. As criminals got more sophisticated, the 'simple' technical solution was to build bigger and better safes. However, a smart technologist remembered that stolen money is of no use if it can be identified. A potential solution was to have a lightweight 'safe' with a computer key. If the safe is 'hacked' or attempts are made to cut it open, the notes are covered in a dye mixture. The dye identifies that the money is stolen and the dye (here comes the technology) can be, in effect, 'watermarked' so that each device has its own fingerprint. So, on recovering just one note the police can not only identify that the note was stolen but they also have a unique link to the original theft. Furthermore, if the thief gets contaminated with the dye, life is even easier for the police.

The simple, direct 'technical only' solution is to make bigger and better safes with ever more sophisticated locks to 'keep the money safe'. The second solution demands that the technologist looks further and takes on a new view. Let us not make the money safe, let us make the money worthless and identifiable. Then a new range of technology provides an innovative solution.

Consider the case of a construction engineer faced with a transport problem across a tidal river (Figure 1.1). The first stage of the project is not technical: What is the nature of the transport problem? Who and/or what (freight) has to be transported? What is the means of transport: road, rail, boat (canal)? What are the volumes of traffic going to be and how might they change during the lifetime of the bridge? This is, in effect, a purely business environmental analysis.

The next stage is to consider the physical environment:

- What is the nature of the river (e.g. depth, tidal range, flood levels, river traffic etc.)?
- What is the nature of the ground (clay, sand, slate, granite etc.)?
- What is the nature of the weather conditions (temperatures, snow, rain, wind speeds etc.)?
- What other conditions may affect the construction? For example, is it to be built in an earthquake zone?

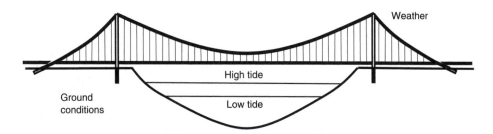

Figure 1.1 Factors affecting the construction of a bridge. *Source:* Based on Curtis, T., *Marketing in Practice*, figure 2.1, page 38, © Elsevier 2006.

After the investigation of the general physical environment and determination of the transport objects (nature and volume of traffic), the strategic options can be considered. These might include ferry, tunnel and bridge. For the purposes of discussion, we will consider that a bridge is the solution selected. Then the next stage is the selection of the specific bridge technology (strategy detail): should it be a box-girder bridge or a suspension bridge? This decision will be affected by technical issues (e.g. new techniques and materials of construction such as composites) and commercial issues (e.g. relative costs). Then the detailed design of the bridge can commence, followed by the construction.

Marketing and business projects follow much the same type of process. The first stage is to determine the broad aims of the organisations and the project. The strategies to be developed will depend on the environment. In business situations, the business external environment is divided into the macroenvironment and microenvironment. Figure 1.2, which is reproduced later, shows the organisation in its macro- and microenvironment. Strategic options can then be developed (e.g. what new products should be developed). Just as with the bridge's construction, business technologies change (e.g. nature and costs of business communications options). Then detailed plans can be formulated and effected.

The purpose of this book is to provide the technologist with the marketing insight to ask the key environmental questions and formulate commercially successful solutions. Projects that fail provide little satisfaction; marketing and business skills are a critical part of the survival kit for an engineer, scientist or technologist.

What is marketing?

In less-developed countries, millions of people do not have enough money for food, clean water and healthcare. Here, the need facing technologists is not for the manufacture of 'designer' styled bottles for French mineral water bottled at source. The need is solely for adequate supplies of clean, safe water. In a five star international hotel, there will be a range of mineral waters (sparkling, still, etc.) and these are supported by extensive marketing effort. In developed countries tap water is entirely safe and will satisfy the core benefit need (i.e. stop you dying of thirst). However, consumers in advanced economies have moved beyond the core benefit of survival to other non-core benefits such as flavour and lifestyle associations. In the post-industrial society, products have to do more than satisfy core benefits. (More development of benefits is given in Chapter 4.)

Organisations can be considered to have three orientations. The first is **product orientation**. This assumes that what customers want is the best quality product providing the core benefit – the 'build a better mouse trap and the world will be ours' attitude. This strategy can be successful when the product is in short supply. However, it can be very risky when this view is taken by technologists who love and understand their product but do not really know the needs and wants of their customers.

Second is **sales orientation**. This assumes that people are reluctant to buy the product and all that is needed is heavy advertising, sales promotions and an aggressive sales force – the typical evening call: 'Do you want some double glazing?' This orientation tends to be forced on product-orientated organisations when the market becomes saturated. Demand is in balance with supply and possibly supply is beginning to outstrip demand.

Third is **marketing orientation**. This has at its heart the belief that for an organisation to be successful in the long term, it needs to understand the needs and wants of its customers. Moreover, the organisation develops an offering, the so-called marketing mix (which is covered in detail in Part Two), to satisfy these needs and wants economically, providing value to the customer and profit to the organisation. To be marketing orientated, the organisation has to make the satisfaction of customers' needs and wants the focus of the organisation. Profits flow from satisfied customers.

The word 'marketing' is used in a number of ways:

- As an adjective, it describes a type of organisation (a marketing organisation) that undertakes the activity called marketing – developing and supplying the customer offering (marketing mix).
- As a verb, it describes something people and organisations do.
- As a noun, the word acts as a label for a department: 'Marketing'. However, if all the people in the organisation have a marketing orientation there may not be a need for a formal 'marketing department'. This is particularly true of small organisations in a technical market where the new product development team and the technical sales support may be all that is needed, so long as they understand marketing.

The UK Chartered Institute of Marketing has defined marketing as:

... the management process responsible for identifying, anticipating and satisfying customer requirements profitably.

The US marketer Philip Kotler has an alternative definition:

The marketing concept holds that the key to achieving organisational goals lies in determining the needs and wants of target markets and delivering the desired satisfaction more efficiently and effectively than the competition.

The activity of marketing provides the understanding of the needs and wants of the customer. The technologist will be heavily involved in the new product development and logistics to provide the offering (marketing mix) to the satisfaction of the market segment. The technologist must be able to understand and interpret the results of marketing (e.g. market research) and provide innovative, cost-effective solutions (application of technology).

MICRO CASE STUDY

BOEING AND AIRBUS

Some major international airport hubs, such as Heathrow, are operating at near full capacity. On some routes, such as London to New York, major airlines operate several flights a day. Airbus has taken the view that to address this issue what is needed is a 'bigger and better' super jumbo jet.

An alternative view is that, for a significant number of major regional airports, it might be feasible to run point-to-point and cut out some of the costly short-haul feeder flights to the hub. Why take hours to travel to Heathrow from Manchester when you could fly direct from Manchester to Jacksonville? What is needed is a super-efficient, medium-sized long-haul airliner that can economically fly point-to-point and cut out the time and cost of the 'regional airport–hub–long-haul flight–hub–regional airport' business model.

These are two visions of the future. To design the next generation of aircraft requires more than just answering a range of technical questions (e.g. how much lighter can we make the aircraft by the use of advanced composites in place of heavy metal?). The designers have to take a view of the pattern of demand for travel in the future. The business analysis is every bit as important as the technology. Although Concorde and the Channel Tunnel were technological triumphs, both of these projects were financial disasters.

Marketing involves an exchange process. Customers pay money for goods and services in a free process. The customer gains benefits (e.g. travel) that they then perceive to have value (worth what they have paid). The supplier receives money, which for long-term stability of the business must exceed the costs of production. To make long-term profits the organisation must achieve two key objectives:

1. create and provide perceived value for the customer
2. reduce the costs of production and delivery of the product

The implications of these simple rules are profound. It is easy for the technologist to decide to design the best possible product. This approach can produce an over-engineered product with features not wanted (not valued) by the customer. The low-cost airlines perceived that there was a market for a low-cost service with no frills. This developed a new market for air travel. The clients do not get the best possible product but they get value for money and they are satisfied; and the airlines are profitable.

How this book is structured

The book is divided into four core sections:

1. Introduction to the context of marketing
2. The tools of marketing – the marketing mix
3. Skills and tools for implementation
4. Bringing it all together – the application of marketing

The marketing system

Organisations take inputs and through a series of internal activities create offerings (products and services), which customers buy. These processes take place in a context. If we consider the movement of a Mars Explorer, the trajectory is affected by the gravitational forces of the sun and other planets. Other factors such as the solar wind may have an effect. There is always the possibility of a catastrophic effect such as the impact of a meteorite. During the time the space craft is moving to Mars, checks will be made on its progress and, if necessary, adjustments made with the control motors. At the end of the trip motors will again be fired for a soft landing of the explorer vehicle. The business process, such as the launch of a new product, is very much the same. The plans are affected by the business environment, the so-called macro- and microenvironments. The organisation has to take account of these ever-changing forces and take corrective actions to keep the plan on track. Then the delivery of the product can be effected successfully. The succeeding chapters of this book cover the various elements in some detail. The general overview is given in Figure 1.2.

The path 'suppliers–organisation–channels–buyers–users' is often known as the supply chain. It operates in the context of the micro- and macroenvironment. Although, in a two-dimensional diagram, this process looks simple, it is not. A major organisation (e.g. a car manufacturer) will have thousands of suppliers and may have thousands of distributors around the world, supplying a variety of different customers (market segments). In their turn, the suppliers have their own suppliers (e.g. a manufacturer of GPS systems will be buying memory chips). The total supply chain is a complex network and supply chain management is a vital element of the overall management required for the success of an organisation.

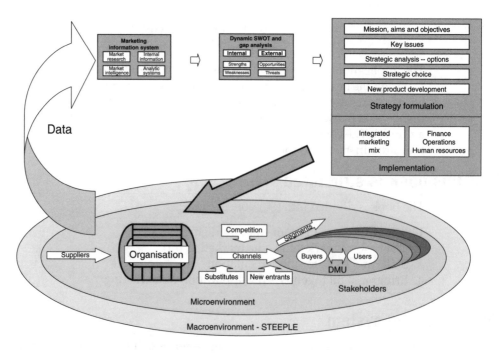

Figure 1.2 The business system and environment.

Where the supply chain operates in the context of the macroenvironment, there are a number of aspects to consider and the STEEPLE model provides a framework for analysing them (other versions include PEST: see Chelsom, Payne & Reavill and Wilson & Gilligan):

- *Social/cultural*
- *Technological*
- *Economic*
- *Educational*
- *Political*
- *Legal*
- *Environmental*

Within the microenvironment, closer forces act on the supply chain. A major aspect here are the forces of competition and these are explored using the five components proposed by Porter:

- direct competition
- supplier power
- buyer power
- substitute products
- new entrants

The Porter competition model does not, though, provide full cover of all the potential forces having an impact on the organisation. Consideration must also be given to stakeholders. Stakeholders may be defined as:

> People, groups of people and organisations who have a stake in the organisation and may affect its plans and operations. Stakeholders may have a positive or a negative effect.

The owners, suppliers, customers and employees of an organisation are obvious stakeholder groups. However, every business situation has its particular context of stakeholders. A civil engineer involved in the construction of a new supermarket will need to take account of the concerns of local residents. Local residents will influence their local politicians, who have considerable power through the mechanism of local planning regulations. Neither one of these stakeholder groups is in the organisation's supply chain yet failure to understand and manage their impact could seriously jeopardise the project.

It has been said that there are three types of companies:

- those who wonder what happened;
- those who watch what is happening; and
- those who make things happen.

To avoid the first situation, the organisation must have good information on the marketing environment. The marketing information system provides this flow of information.

In the conduct of our lives, we do not rely on one source of data, we have different sources of data, such as sight, touch, hearing, smell, taste and temperature. In cooking a meal for a dinner party we will use all of these sources of data. However, data do not help us make decisions. We need information.

We can define data as a collection of single elements of information (e.g. the temperature of a joint of meat when cooking a meal). The information we need is: 'Is the joint cooked?' This may involve the integration of a set of data elements, such as weight of the joint, colour, aroma, temperature, time cooked at that temperature, texture, etc. The expert chef instinctively processes these inputs and using past experience arrives at a single conclusion: 'Time to eat.' Just as we have a variety of mechanisms for collecting and processing data, so do organisations. The marketing information system (MkIS) has the following elements:

- market research
- market intelligence
- internal information
- storage/retrieval process and systems
- analytical systems (decision support systems)

The application of the above processes provides an explosive amount of data and information. However, information and data do not of themselves enable managers to make decisions such as:

- which products/markets should we exit?
- which products/markets should we enter?

To aid the manager, various tools and models (e.g. SWOT, portfolio analysis, product life cycle) provide appropriate frameworks for decision making.

It has been said: 'Plans are nothing but planning is everything.' The meaning of this is that plans need continual adaptation in the ever-changing business environment. In adopting a good planning process, the insight is developed to respond to environmental turbulence. No plan is worth the paper it is printed on or the computer memory it occupies if there is not sound execution. There are four key elements to the execution of business plans:

1. the offering (the marketing mix)
2. finance
3. operations
4. human resources

This book concentrates on the marketing aspects but explicitly recognises the need to integrate the marketing aspects with the other three elements. The most wonderful product is not going to be a business success if there is not a profit margin, if the product is not delivered on time and if the field staff are not well trained. A full treatment of the marketing system is given in Chapter 2.

Contemporary issues and contexts in marketing

The development of business and management theory does not take place in a vacuum. A century ago, factories were built and processes developed with only modest consideration of their environmental impact. In Chapter 3, the issues of consumerism, environmentalism (green marketing) and corporate social responsibility are presented.

Much of marketing was originally developed in the area of consumer product marketing. Every day we see advertisements across the whole spectrum of media stressing the virtues of one detergent or another. The word 'soap' for a genre of TV series originates from the early days of television advertising when they were sponsored by detergent (soap) manufacturers. However, the techniques of marketing soap powder are very different to selling steel to a car manufacturer. There are core skills to engineering and science, such as mathematics. However, there are differences in the skill set and application of skills between a chemical engineer and a robotics engineer, even if they are both very concerned with the practical mathematics of control theory.

Chapter 3 continues with an examination of a range of marketing contexts and frameworks, including consumer marketing, service marketing, business-to-business (B2B) marketing, international marketing, not-for-profit and social marketing, entertainment marketing, relationship marketing, internal marketing and marketing on a limited budget.

The tools of marketing – the marketing mix

To be successful, organisations must develop a package. The best product in the world is of no use if the customer is unable to find it or unable to pay for it. An automobile engineer considers different aspects of a car (engine, transmission, etc.) in the development of a new vehicle. Different groups of engineers and different organisations may be involved in developing the various elements (e.g. GPS and gearbox). All these elements must converge and integrate to provide the driving experience desired by the ultimate customer. For convenience, the marketing offering to the customer – the marketing mix – is divided up into various elements. Just as with the car, these elements must be integrated to provide the experience that is required for the target market segment. The seven elements of the marketing mix are: product, price, place, promotion, people, physical evidence and process. Part Two (Chapters 4–8) provides detailed consideration of these elements, which have to be integrated to provide the desired customer experience.

Skills for implementation

Cute concept pictures on a designer's computer are no substitute for the physical product. We do not live in a virtual world just yet. To convert the concepts of a design into a physical reality, a whole range of skills will be needed. Without those skills, it will not be possible to realise the desired marketing mix. An engineer designing a car will want to know the conditions of use: driving around an African safari park is different to a school run. Information is needed to draw up the specifications and design parameters. The collection and management of marketing information is covered in Chapter 9.

Organisations need to operate profitably or they run out of cash and go out of business. Chapters 5 and 10 outline the key aspects of financial management needed to develop and implement marketing plans. The emphasis is on finance rather than accountancy. Detailed consideration of the balance sheet and taxation policy are best left to the professional accountant. However, the technologist is expected to produce profit-optimised solutions and this demands an understanding of aspects of financial management such as costing, cash flow, budgets, performance and investment analysis.

Safety, quality, customer care and environmental responsibility are dependent on people working in appropriate ways with appropriate values within organisations. The first work experience of a technologist will be working within a team. As the technologist develops he/she will take responsibility for team leadership and co-operation with other teams. Often the implementation of development (e.g. change in materials of manufacture) will involve process changes affecting people. Technologists need to understand the issues of change management. Chapter 11 provides the foundations on people management skills.

Project management is a key aspect of the technologists' work with marketing. The development of a new product and its successful launch will have a range of sub-project elements, such as developing the advertising copy, etc. The control and co-ordination of projects is covered in Chapter 12. Events associated with a product launch, such as press conferences and exhibitions, are important in marketing. Special cover is, therefore, given to events management because this is often not covered in standard project management texts. Many technologists act as external consultants or as an internal consultant to project teams. This is covered in Chapter 13.

Bringing it all together

The first three parts of the book cover the background and foundations of marketing. Part Four brings these elements together into some of the key marketing activities that technologists are involved in. New product development is discussed in Chapter 14 while Chapter 15 covers market driven quality. Highly technical aspects, such as statistical process control, have not been included because there are many texts that discuss the technical aspects of quality management. A significant aspect of market driven quality is the identification, and development, of effective communications with the relevant publics. An important aspect of effective quality management is internal marketing to develop a 'quality culture'.

The heart of an organisation's marketing is the ever-evolving marketing plan. The formulation, implementation and control of the marketing plan needs a holistic integration of the total company resources to the effective and efficient satisfaction of customer needs and wants. This process takes place in a turbulent macro- and microenvironment which at times may involve the company reinventing itself – such as the transition of HP from a scientific instrument company to a computing brand. The marketing planning process is covered in Chapter 16.

How to use this book

It is not possible to build a radio transmitter without understanding how the individual components perform and an understanding of radio transmission and antenna design. Thus, Parts One and Three provide the background theory and context for marketing while the key components of marketing – the marketing mix – are given in Part Two. It is recommended that these units should be covered before considering the broader issues, such as new product development, which are covered in Part Four.

The glossary provides a quick guide to marketing and management terms when clarification might be required.

Throughout the text, case studies and examples provide illustrations of the various concepts and theories. Marketing is similar to technology as a career. Success depends on knowledge, understanding and application of theoretical concepts. The process is creative, requiring the ability to formulate innovative solutions to problems. Even the definition of a problem needs insight and creativity; technology is rarely the total solution. Practice is needed to develop skills. You do not learn how to win a Formula 1 race simply from reading a text book.

Review

In this first chapter, the importance of marketing and marketing orientation has been discussed. The elements of the marketing system have been briefly reviewed, including the macro- and microenvironment, marketing information systems and strategic processes. The general four-part framework of the book has been explained.

Further reading

Chelsom, V., Payne, A. & Reavill, L. (2005) *Management for Engineers, Scientists and Technologists*, 2nd edn, John Wiley & Sons.

Curtis, T. & Williams, W. (2001) *An Introduction to Perfumery*, 2nd edn, Micelle Press.

Porter, M. (1980) *Competitive Strategy: Techniques for Analyzing Industries and Competitors*, The Free Press.

Wilson, R. & Gilligan, C. (2005) *Strategic Marketing Management: Planning Implementation and Control*, 3rd edn, Elsevier.

CHAPTER 2

The marketing system

Learning objectives

After studying this chapter you will be able to:

- Complete a macroenvironment analysis using the STEEPLE model
- Complete a microenvironment analysis, considering competition, segmentation and stakeholders
- Complete an internal environment analysis using the augmented value chain model
- Focus the results of an environmental analysis by performing a SWOT analysis
- Describe the major elements of a marketing plan and its information needs

Introduction

Consider a system of electrically charged iron particles suspended in a fluid. The particles are subjected to electrical and magnetic forces. As a physicist, you are assigned the task of calculating the movement of a given particle. The particle will respond to the forces acting on it (electrical, magnetic). It would be possible, with the right data set, to predict the ultimate force vector. The speed of movement would be restrained by viscous drag. The magnitude of this would depend on the viscosity of the fluid and this, in turn, would be influenced by temperature. The electrostatic and magnetic forces will be influenced by the dielectric constant and permeability of the fluid. The local forces experienced by the given particle will be influenced by the magnetic properties and electrostatic charges of other particles around it. This physical system is similar to that of a business organisation.

A business organisation, just like the charged iron particle, is affected by its environment and the variety of forces operating on it. This is the so-called macroenvironment. The STEEPLE model provides the marketer with a tool to identify and estimate the magnitude and effect of these forces. Just as the charged iron particle is affected by other charged particles, the organisation is affected by its immediate competitive environment. The 'Porter Five Forces of Competition' model provides the lens to appraise these influences. The immediate competitive environment is known as the microenvironment. These two models and their practical application are covered in the following sections of this chapter.

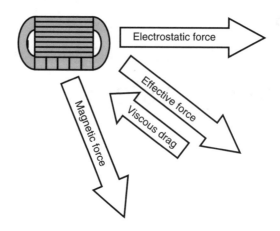

Figure 2.1 Movement of a charged iron particle.

STEEPLE analysis

In the analysis of motion of a body the physicist will seek to identify the force set and will use vector analysis to determine the resulting vectored force. In considering a typical three-dimensional environment, it may be possible to use the normal orthogonal x, y, z coordinate system.

The acronym STEEPLE stands for:

- Social/cultural
- Technological
- Economic
- Educational (training)
- Political
- Legal
- Environmental

The elements in this 'vector' set are not orthogonal (Figure 2.2) and the various elements interact. An environmental issue may be discovered (global warming); people may be concerned about the impact on endangered species (a social issue); they may express their concerns with parliamentary pressure (a political issue), which may result in laws (a legal issue) to change taxation (an economic impact) and make people aware of the ecological impacts (an educational issue). The vector analysis of the physicist is following fixed 'laws of nature' (e.g. Newtonian dynamics). In some textbooks, STEEPLE is presented as a 'model' but it is not a 'physical theoretical' model. Business academics are still a long way from formulating the Newtonian dynamics of business. STEEPLE is a convenient acronym to prompt the marketer to ask a series of questions in order to direct research. The application of the STEEPLE model needs practice and some engagement of common sense.

Social/cultural

Our attitudes and social structures affect how we live, how we work and what we buy. In the UK, an area of concern is the use of 4 × 4 vehicles, the 'Chelsea tractor', for the school

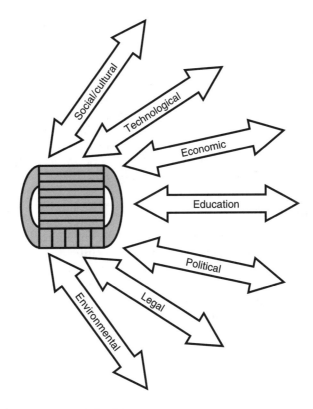

Figure 2.2 STEEPLE forces on an organisation.

run. Fifty years ago the majority of children made their own way to school on foot, by public transport or by bicycle. In the USA thousands of yellow school buses are the norm. Two key factors to be considered here are social attitudes and demographics.

Social attitudes, structures and behaviour

Social attitudes, structures and behaviour change with time. In the 1950s, marketers would be targeting the 'normal' family of mum, dad and two children. The husband would work and the wife would keep house. The typical family holiday would be taken at a UK holiday camp. In the dot-com age, there are many more singles and DINKY (double income, no kids yet) couples. Family holidays will involve flights around the world. The low-cost airlines provide an infrastructure for mini-breaks. The weekend cottage may now be in France and weekend commuting a practical option. This type of social change affects both infrastructure (new international airports) and more personal items of consumption (the widening range of 'exotic' foods now accepted to be part of everyday life). A US citizen, on his/her first holiday in the UK, might do the 'Shakespeare experience' and gain the impression that the English live off 'the roast beef', whereas in reality, they are more likely to be down the curry house tucking into a chicken tikka masala.

Different social groups (e.g. national and/or religious) have different social attitudes and structures. The changing landscape of social/cultural behaviour is not confined to the UK but is a global trend. Social/cultural issues are vitally important and these are covered more in Chapter 3.

Demographics

The shapes of populations change with time and vary from country to country. In the nineteenth century, European life expectancy was relatively low; in the twenty-first century it is relatively high. The result is that there are many older people in the twenty-first century population. However, this is not true of some less-developed countries, where life expectancy is relatively low. It is important to understand the structural makeup of populations in formulating marketing plans.

Technological

Many of the social changes interact with technological issues. The desire for the inexpensive family holiday in Tenerife depends on the infrastructure of mass air transport. The invention and mass adoption of the contraceptive pill provided a context for change in family structures and roles (many more working professional women as a consequence). For convenience, technological issues may be considered under four headings: (1) discoveries, (2) inventions, (3) technological advances and (4) infrastructure.

Discoveries

A major factor in the advance of human kind has been an ever-developing understanding of the world. The invention of accurate chronometers was vital for improving navigation at sea but none of this was possible without the discovery that the Earth was round and not flat. Massive changes in human existence can result from these deeper understandings. The discovery and appreciation of the significance of bacteria changed the shape of medicine and contributed to the improvement of health and life expectancy. A parallel step change is taking place now with the discovery of the structure of DNA and the resulting science of molecular biology. The impacts are often unexpected and diverse. It is doubtful if Watson and Crick would have predicted their work would result in GM agriculture on one hand and a complete new tool for forensic science with genetic profiling on the other.

Inventions

With a better understanding of the world, new opportunities exist to create new devices and other inventions. Here a distinction is drawn between discoveries and inventions. Discoveries are new insights into the nature of the world, (e.g. discovery of superconductivity, discovery of ozone depletion). Inventions take the ever-growing body of knowledge and understanding and utilise it to synthesise new products and devices. For example, developments in the understanding of semiconductors provided the theoretical basis for the invention of the transistor. However, inventions do not necessarily depend on new discoveries. They can come from a creative process where innovative solutions are found to problems. The interaction of discoveries and inventions can form a loop. The invention of the jet engine needed alloys that would perform at high temperatures. This demanded better understanding of high performance alloys. This, in turn, made the design of still better engines possible. The key issue for the analyst is to spot when a new device will have a major impact on the organisation's business. More consideration of this creative process is given in Chapter 14.

Technology advances and integration

Many products we use, such as the car, are very complex systems. In the last section, the synthesis of knowledge into the creation of new devices was discussed. In the same way, the integration of some disparate technologies is vital to the design of a modern car. Developments in new composites may enable the replacement of heavy metal components with lighter versions, as has taken place in aircraft manufacture. Advances in the understanding of catalysts and fuels are vital to the development of low-emission internal combustion engines. Sensing devices such as solid-state gyroscopes and control mechanisms are required for better engine management and braking control.

Success can be dependent on spotting the opportunity to synthesise a new offering. The last decade of the twentieth century saw the development of a multimillion pound industry in sandwiches. This advance only became possible with the development of appropriate packaging which extended the shelf-life of a sandwich from a couple of hours to a few days. The key issue is for the marketing analyst to spot when a new convergence is possible.

Infrastructure

The modern car depends on roads to be effective. The smart sports car is consequently not much use in the Australian outback. An argument can be made that part of the problem of the first dot-com revolution was that the process could be cumbersome if people were reliant on dial-up access. With the majority of households having access to broadband, the second dot-com wave has an entirely better infrastructure and is proving much more successful. A key skill for the analyst is to decide when the infrastructure is not appropriate and what action may be taken (if any). In less-developed countries the electrical power supply can be unreliable and 'dirty'. High-voltage spikes can damage electronic equipment and sudden interruptions can cause the loss of data. In such situations, the installation engineers will specify UPS (uninterruptible power supply) systems able to cope with these conditions. Another key skill is to decide when the infrastructure can support new applications. We can see such an exploitation in the UK development of fibre-optic networks. A relatively simple device was invented that could wind a fibre-optic cable around the earth line on high-voltage electrical transmission systems. This enabled a complete complex optical network to be built in record time. Many new HT cables have fibre-optic capability built into them.

Economic

It serves no purpose to make products if they do not provide value or if customers are not able to afford to buy them. When the first nuclear power stations were built, some analysts forecast a future where electrical energy would cost so little it would be almost pointless to meter it. In the year 1900, it would cost an average person's weekly wage to send a modest message from the UK to Australia by telegram. Nowadays, once a household has broadband access, communications become effectively cost-free.

Taking a broad view, it costs a bank around £1.00 to service a face-to-face transaction in a high street branch. It costs around £0.10 to service a transaction from a call-centre in India (the low cost of communications making this option possible). It costs around £0.01 to service an internet transaction (made possible by the availability of broadband access). A wide range of issues needs to be considered, including: the business cycle, inflation rates, interest rates/credit, disposable income/wealth distribution, credit, employment levels/cost of labour, exchange rates, taxation, raw material and other input cost drivers.

Business cycle

There are cycles of activity in all aspects of life. In the UK, the early 1990s were a time of stress for some home-owners. Many of them had negative equity when their house values plummeted below the amount of their mortgages. Such cycles also affect business activity. Consequently, as recession looms, investment in new capacity falls. Spotting when the upturn will arrive is important: invest too early and you have unused capacity; invest too late and potential market opportunities will be lost to the competition. This is the classic economists' business cycle. The time-scale of such cycles can be a few years but some economists believe there are longer fundamental cycles measured in decades.

For convenience, we will consider another major business cycle: seasonal structure in demand. In the UK, the example used to illustrate this by some accountants is the firework manufacturer, where the majority of sales are in October and November. A vast range of products and services need good seasonal planning. Similarly, electricity demand can peak in very cold weather (heating) or very hot weather (air conditioning). The demand for water peaks in the summer, just when the natural supply is low, which has profound implications for the related technological infrastructure. Time series analysis and statistical forecasting techniques can help the analyst in such instances.

Inflation rates

Inflation rates affect a number of issues, one of the most important being interest rates (which are considered in the section below). However, another key issue with inflation rates is that they influence the demand for products. If inflation is high, people may find that bank savings provide a negative return in real value. In such circumstances people may find investment in metals (gold, silver and platinum) could provide a better investment and inflation hedge. This will fuel the demand for the metals and stimulate further exploration and capacity expansion. The increase in prices may affect industrial costs (e.g. costs of catalysts for chemical processing).

Interest rates/credit

In capital investment plans, the climate of interest rates has a major impact on target rates of returns and pay-back periods. This issue is considered in more detail in Chapter 10. Here we simply note that high interest rates force short-term views, with short pay-back times required and high operating profits needed (to service the high cost of capital). High interest rates affect the primary demand from consumers, negatively affecting the complete supply chain. With easy credit and low interest rates, consumers can enjoy retail therapy and fuel demand. It is important to note that some activities are counter-cyclical. When interest rates are high and people are reluctant to buy more, then they are forced to 'make do and mend'. Companies that provide repair and renovation services may then benefit. There is nothing like a wave of bankruptcies to bring a smile to the face of the insolvency practitioner!

Disposable income/wealth distribution

In considering the costs of manufacture, two types of costs need to be considered: fixed costs and variable costs. (Chapter 10 discusses these in detail.) The family budget has a similar structure. In simple terms, there are three types of costs for households:

1. fixed costs (mortgage, rates, etc.)
2. semi-variable costs
3. discretionary costs

There are certain things we may have to buy, such as food. However, if times are tight, the fillet steak and champagne may have to be replaced with fish 'n' chips and a pint of beer. Other costs may be more discretionary. High-cost Gucci might be out and a raid on the old wardrobe and retro-dressing are going to be in. In short, when fixed costs increase and the disposable income decreases (what is left after the fixed household expenses), the pattern of consumer spending may change. This may be bad news for the up-market restaurant but good news for the 'cheap and cheerful' takeaway.

In international marketing (covered in Chapter 3), wealth distribution may be an important issue. The average income given in a UN handbook may conceal the wide variations in wealth that could be present in countries where there are, in fact, substantial segments of the population with high disposable income (e.g. China and India).

Employment levels/cost of labour

Poor employment levels also affect disposable income. There are associated social effects: in areas of high unemployment, there tend to be higher levels of crime, with related security issues (e.g. South Africa). This can be good if you want to sell surveillance systems but high murder rates can deter tourists.

A major concern for companies is the availability and cost of labour. The building boom in the UK would not be possible without a substantial number of immigrant workers because there is a skills shortage in the UK labour market. A UK company wanting to outsource and offshore its computer department will find India an attractive option because of the lower pay rates and the rich supply of well-trained graduates from excellent universities.

Exchange rates

Many products have to be imported. When a country's currency falls, the costs of imports (e.g. oil, etc.) are forced up. This can cause the perceived costs (i.e. costs in local currency) to rise. When a currency appreciates, then the costs of imports decrease. This will then allow import penetration of lower cost manufactured goods.

There is also an impact on global competitiveness. If a major exporting country's currency appreciates it can lose market share as its competitors in other countries may then have lower costs in export markets. More consideration of this is given in Chapter 3.

Taxation

Taxation has an effect on personal disposable income and, therefore, affects what people buy and what they do. High fuel taxation and other motoring taxes (e.g. congestion charging) governs the type of car people buy (the purpose being to encourage people to choose low and zero carbon emission vehicles) and how they use them. In capital projects, taxation may have profound effects with the ability to offset investments against taxable profits. Investment grants and assistance (e.g. EU assistance in less affluent areas of Europe) and subsidies may affect capital and running costs. Care must be taken to ensure that the taxation class of a product has been correctly identified for taxes such as VAT. In the UK, food products are zero-rated. Although a fresh orange is zero-rated, some fruit-based processed consumer products do carry VAT. A company that decides to produce freshly squeezed orange juice for sale in the chilled cabinet needs to establish if this product will or will not carry VAT. The extra cost of VAT may make the product too expensive for customer acceptance.

Raw material and other input cost drivers

As discussed above, commodity process can change with demand patterns and interest rates. These effects are not small. The cost of oil or gold, for instance, may double or halve in the space of a year. The impact can vary for different countries and companies. In France, a substantial proportion of electrical energy is based on nuclear generation. In the UK a higher proportion is based on gas. Thus, UK electricity generation is sensitive to commodity process in a different way to a French-based generator. Countries basing energy needs on fossil fuels now have high energy costs, giving a differential advantage to countries based on hydro-electric and/or geo-thermal sources (e.g. Iceland).

The input cost of labour has two major effects. First, it can affect the location of manufacture (e.g. clothing and consumer electronics moving to China). Second, it can drive the elimination of labour by automation (e.g. ATMs replacing bank tellers).

An increasing effect is also now coming from the impact of the cost of services. On the one hand, the falling costs of communication are driving costs down. On the other, costs are being driven up by the increasing price of insurance resulting from perceived higher risks and higher claims payouts.

Educational (training)

The availability of a well-trained and skilled workforce is a major issue in locating facilities. The level of education may affect what is marketed and how it can be marketed, (e.g. levels of literacy can affect packaging instructions and forms of marketing communications). With the introduction of new technologies and processes, there is the need to re-train the workforce. A particular problem for complex products is to ensure agents and distributors' staff are fully trained (e.g. advanced electronic systems in cars necessitate highly trained field technicians).

Political

National politics has an impact on all organisations and individuals. There is a fairly free market for personal firearms in the USA that does not exist in the EU. The USA gun lobby is a major political force in the USA. The political climate affects the nature of legislation and the way it is enforced.

Often underestimated is the impact of local politics. A key issue for organisations is the need to gain local planning approval. Two current controversies in the UK involve the location of wind farms (green energy equals good, but not in my back yard) and supermarkets. Part of the UK commercial success of Tesco is building up a bank of suitable sites for future expansion.

Legal

Legislation against smoking in public places is rapidly covering the whole of Europe. This will have an impact on pubs and clubs. In countries where the ban is in place people have complained about the level of body-odour, which was masked in the past by the smell of cigarette smoke. Clubs are considering how to meet this unexpected challenge from the changed legal environment.

Legislation covers many activities including employment, safety, consumer law, environmental, taxation, etc. Some selected discussion is given below but each of these headings has the scope of a full degree and there are professionals who spend their whole time operating in a single area of law. It is essential to consult experts in these areas because legislation is far-reaching and ever changing. Failure to comply may result in both civil and criminal penalties.

Employment

The whole employment life cycle is heavily regulated. Advertisements for positions must conform to a range of laws, many of which are associated with ensuring equal opportunity. These also apply to the selection and appointment process. Almost all aspects of working life are regulated, including holiday entitlement, leave of absence (e.g. maternity leave), hours of work, conditions of work (e.g. temperature), reward systems (e.g. equal pay, minimum wage, etc.), disciplinary procedures and dismissal procedures, (e.g. redundancy).

Safety

The whole product life cycle is covered by various aspects of legislation. Materials must be procured and stored safely before use. The manufacturing/service operations must be conducted safely. Effluents must be disposed of safely. The distribution and use of the product must be safe (e.g. distribution and use of gas, transport of hazardous materials, etc.). Specifically in marketing terms there are issues in ensuring that consumers can use products and services safely (e.g. installation by accredited and well-trained field staff).

Consumer law

Yet again, there is a whole raft of issues to be considered. The product must be fit for purpose and properly described. This may involve questions of simple fact: what does 'gold' as a descriptor of materials of manufacture mean and imply in terms of conformance? More diffuse concepts such as 'organic' and 'free range' need definition. Key consumer issues include terms of trade (e.g. controversies in 'illegal' bank charging) and performance claims (e.g. how do you defend a claim of 'beneficial to health' for a food supplement?).

Environmental

The political view is that 'the polluter pays'. Much research is directed at the reduction of environmental impact in production processes (e.g. the reduction of VOC – volatile organic compound – emissions). In marketing terms, 'green' credentials for a product in manufacture and distribution are becoming a factor in the marketing mix (e.g. the 'greening' of the major supermarkets). Environmental issues may affect what can be offered to the marketplace (e.g. the banning of lead-based paint; emission standards for vehicles). A more recent legal requirement is that manufacturers must have facilities and processes for the safe and environmentally acceptable disposal/recycling of products (e.g. legislation for safe recycling/disposal of refrigerators containing chlorofluorocarbons). These laws not only apply to products but also to services (e.g. the restrictions on heavy vehicles in residential neighbourhoods and night flights from airports). More consideration of environmental issues is given below.

Taxation

Some general consideration of taxation has been given above in reviewing some of the economic impacts on the macroenvironment. It is impossible in a text of this nature to give comprehensive cover of this topic – the government's explanatory notes to current UK taxation run to thousands of pages. Here it is appropriate to note some impacts. VAT has an important impact and, as discussed above, it is vital to determine early in the development of a new product or service just what the VAT situation may be in target markets. Taxation law may have significant implications on manufacturing processes (e.g. excise duty with bonded facilities for brewing and distilling alcohol) and distribution (e.g. motor fuel carrying an excise duty). Conformance to these laws may not only involve the payment of the taxes but also place significant requirements on how operations are conducted and records kept. These requirements may have significant cost implications.

Environmental

As with safety, the starting point for the environmental impact audit is the product life cycle analysis. This is covered in detail in Chapter 4. Issues to be taken into account are consumer concerns, VOCs (volatile organic compounds, such as petrol fumes and solvents), POPs (persistent organic pollutants, e.g. DDT), environmental fate, ozone depletors (CFCs and other organic-chlorine compounds), greenhouse gases (e.g. CO_2, methane etc), GM crops, sustainable products and processes. In some areas such as GM crops and treatment of animals, the environmental issues have further dimensions with ethical concerns.

How to conduct a STEEPLE analysis

The above discussion and Table 2.1 provide a starting list of questions to be asked. Many of the issues may not be relevant to a given context. There may be issues that are relevant and not included in this brief review and these should be added. A key tool in the conduct of a STEEPLE analysis is the 'So what?' test. If the answer is nothing or very little, just move on. The purpose of the STEEPLE analysis is not to produce a laundry list but to identify critical issues to be considered for the decisions to be made (e.g. in selecting the material of construction for a new product). The suggested process is to set out the analysis in an Excel spreadsheet. This can allow additional tools to be used, such as assigning weightings to factors and then sorting the identified forces. A simple structure for analysis is to set up a table with four headings:

1. STEEPLE element and sub-element
2. issue
3. potential impact and implications (apply the 'So what?' test)
4. comments and potential actions for consideration

This file can become a 'living document' and it can be revised from time to time as issues change and new events have an impact on the business.

Further help in understanding issues can be colour coded. There is a wealth of legal and political issues that have an impact on environmental issues. These need not be repeated in full in the section 'environmental'. Issues that have an environmental impact can be colour coded green and not repeated in full.

Segmentation, targeting and positioning

Not all customers want the same product. Take cars, for example: some people want to travel fast and want a sporty image whereas others may want a town run-around. The outdoor enthusiast and farmer will need a four-wheel drive vehicle with an off-road capability. It is not by accident that there are a large number of offerings catering for a rich diversity of needs.

People can be segmented by their gender, age, lifestyle, where they live, profession, religion, etc. Industrial customers can be segmented in a parallel process by variables such as size of company (e.g. global, national, regional, small), industry (manufacturing, banking, healthcare, etc.) and location. Figure 2.3 outlines the generic type of segmentation situation. A typical example is that faced by the manufacturer of car tyres. Two key segmentation variables are the new-fit (when the tyres are fitted to the new vehicle in the factory) and the refit replacement market. Within these two segments there are a series of sub-segments (e.g. tractors, lorries, vans, cars, etc.). Each of these sub-segments may need further sub-segmentation (e.g. sports cars, as opposed to town run-arounds).

Not all the segments that can be identified have to be targeted by the company. Rolls Royce and Ferrari both make expensive cars but appeal to different market segments on which they focus. For each market segment the company has selected, it will be

Table 2.1 Selected STEEPLE elements

STEEPLE element	Selected key issues	Examples and discussion
Social/cultural	Demographics	The structure of populations (e.g. ageing population of European countries)
	Lifestyle	How people live (e.g. involvement in sporting activity as opposed to couch potatoes)
	Culture	People's values and behaviour (e.g. religion)
	?	
Technological	Discoveries	Ozone depletion in the upper atmosphere
	Inventions	New products (e.g. transistor, laser, etc.)
	Technological integration	Integration of various technological elements (e.g. merging of different functions in mobile telephones)
	Infrastructure	Can be new infrastructures (e.g. broadband networks) or, in international context, different infrastructure elements (e.g. 240 V, 50 Hz in the UK but 120 V, 60 Hz in the USA)
	?	
Economic	Business cycle	Levels of economic activity follow cycles (long term). Other demands may follow other cycles (e.g. seasonal demand for heating and air conditioning)
	Interest rates/credit	High interest rates affect consumer spending; this is linked with the availability of sources of lending
	Disposable income/wealth distribution	Disposable income is the income left after essentials (i.e. after taxes and bills have been paid). Wealth distribution is a form of demographics: the shape of disposable income (e.g. UK has few very poor people; India has many poor but more super rich than in the UK as well)
	Employment levels/cost of labour	Level of employment affects free income of the unemployed. Availability of labour is important for organisations (e.g. skilled engineers). Costs of labour differ vastly (e.g. USA vs China)
	Exchange rates	With a high £ and a low $, UK people holidaying in the USA will find their holidays cheaper and US people find UK holidays expensive. With a high $ and a low £ the reverse is true
	Taxation	The nature and rates of taxation affect business. In the EU, we are familiar with VAT; other countries have sales taxes. High EU fuel taxes have made small cars more popular in Europe than in the USA
	Raw material and other input costs	Different raw materials and other costs can affect competitive balance (e.g. with low-cost oil it was economic to make industrial alcohol from ethylene; now industrial alcohol is made by fermentation)
	?	

Table 2.1 (*Continued*)

STEEPLE element	*Selected key issues*	*Examples and discussion*
Educational (training)	Education	Do people have the knowledge needed (e.g. levels of literacy)
	Training	Skills development does not stop after university (e.g. a new system may necessitate training if the skills do not exist, such as the switch from analogue to digital technologies)
Political	International	The general conditions are determined by the political outcomes of multinational political bodies such as the EU and WTO (World Trade Organisation)
	National	Different political climates can exist (e.g. US political attitudes to stem cell research compared with the UK)
	Local	Local politics can affect local implementations (e.g. attitudes to business development – welcomed in brown field areas but discouraged in the UK green belt)
	?	
Legal	Employment	Recruitment (equal opportunity law), employment conditions (e.g. minimum wage), termination (redundancy rights)
	Safety	Vast range of health and safety issues such as REACH, COSH, etc.
	Consumer	Strict liability for defective products, concerns for product claims, etc.
	Environmental	Increasingly, environmental concerns are being reflected in law – a selected range of issues is given below. A typical example is the legal limits on the quality of water discharged from industrial processes
	Taxation	This clearly links with the economic issues but the law has a major impact as to if tax may be due (e.g. taxation of fuel can vary by classification – 'red' diesel for use for agricultural machinery and tractors vs standard diesel)
Environmental	Sustainability	Use of sustainable materials (e.g. paper rather than plastic bags)
	Recycling	Recycling of packaging, cars, electrical and electronic products, etc.
	Reduction	Reduction in environmental impact (e.g. reduced packaging, high-efficiency light bulbs)
	Pollution	Reduction in the levels of pollutants such as VOCs, POPs, etc. and green house gases

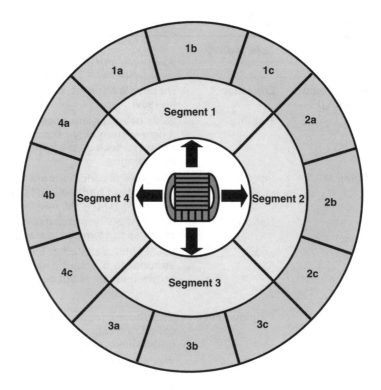

Figure 2.3 Market segmentation: segments and sub-segments.

making a different proposition that is relevant to that segment. A key issue for the town run-around will be economy, whereas the Ferrari driver will be more interested in the performance rather than a 2% reduction in fuel consumption. Companies such as Ford make cars that are positioned in both these segments. The process is outlined in Figure 2.4.

The first stage is to identify the relevant segmentation variables. This is not a mechanical process with a single 'right' answer. New variables may come into the picture (e.g. internet sales) and standard variables may need adaptation. Once the segments have been identified their characteristics can be evaluated (e.g. size, accessibility, profitability, etc.). Segments may vary in attractiveness to the firm. A UK publisher, specialising in education books may find India (where much education is taught in English and UK professional exams taken) more attractive than France (different language and different syllabi). Next, the positioning of the product can be considered. For F1 racing, tyre performance is a key issue. For the town run-around tyre, life and economy is a key factor (grandmother is not looking for a hot start at the lights to get out of the Tesco car park). Having decided the product positioning in the market, the full offering (marketing mix) can be developed. Full consideration of segmentation, targeting and positioning is given in Chapter 4. Further consideration of the marketing mix is given at the end of this chapter and there is detailed cover in Chapters 4 to 8.

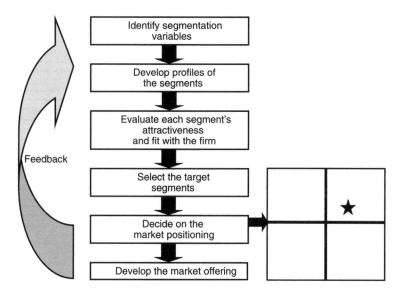

Figure 2.4 Segmentation, targeting and positioning process. Adapted from: Curtis, T., *Marketing in Practice*, figure 1.11, page 26, © Elsevier 2006. Reproduced by permission.

Stakeholders

Stakeholders are defined as people, groups of people and organisations that have an interest in and an impact on the organisation. Customers and users of the firm's products are key stakeholders but not the only ones. Figure 2.5 shows a simplified generic stakeholder structure for an organisation. To aid the discussion we will consider the situation facing a formulation chemist working for a cosmetic company. Just as with customers (segmentation), there may be structure within other stakeholder groups. In a manufacturing company there will be management and the production employees. Production employees may have substructure (e.g. day workers, shift workers, etc.). The owners are a key stakeholder group.

The company may supply products to the professional market (e.g. beauty salons) and to the general public for home use via supermarkets and chemists. For simplicity, the possibility of direct B2C sales via the internet has been excluded from Figure 2.5. Cosmetics are covered by the EU Cosmetics Directive and products must comply with the relevant safety standards set by the regulatory bodies. Cosmetic products often make claims such as 'anti-wrinkle performance' and the technologist must be able to substantiate these claims to appropriate regulatory bodies such as the Advertising Standards Authority. Pressure groups take a keen interest in organisations and can exert considerable influence (e.g. by 'blogging'). Green pressure groups may be concerned with packaging, animal welfare groups with 'cruelty-free' formulations and consumer groups with product performance claims.

Suppliers' needs must be considered (e.g. wild changes on supply demands can cause problems down the supply chain). In the day-to-day market, competitors fight for market share. However, competitors within an industry also collaborate (e.g. in sustaining the

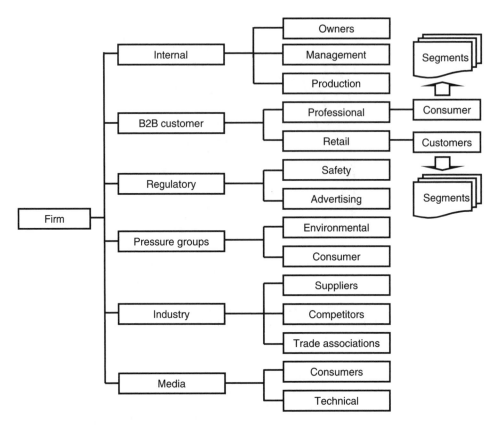

Figure 2.5 Generic partial stakeholder analysis. Adapted from: Curtis, T., *Marketing in Practice*, **figure 1.4, page 9,** © **Elsevier 2006. Reproduced by permission.**

system of bar codes). Often this collaboration will be co-ordinated through an industry association. The media provide information to all the stakeholder groups. The 'broadcast' media (e.g. TV, daily press, fashion magazines, etc.) provide information to the consumer and generalised stakeholder groups. The 'narrow-cast' press (e.g. *Soap Perfumery and Cosmetics*) distribute information to the industry stakeholder groups.

A parallel approach to STEEPLE analysis may be used. A table with four headings can be drawn up:

1. stakeholder group and sub-group
2. stakeholder agenda
3. company objectives/agenda
4. comments and potential actions for consideration

Like the STEEPLE table, this file can become a 'living document' and can be revised from time to time as issues develop.

SURFACE COATINGS

Paints and surface coatings are an important market in which major firms such as ICI operate. Below is an outline partial analysis of the STEEPLE environment, segmentation and stakeholders for surface coatings from the point of view of a surface-coatings technologist engaged in new product development.

Table 2.2 Partial STEEPLE analysis for surface coatings and paints (domestic segment)

STEEPLE issue	Issue	Impact/implications	Comments/actions
Social/cultural			
Social attitudes	People wanting a wide range of co-ordinating colours for their dream room 'make-over'	Vast range of colour options potentially required	Need to develop a range of in store colour matching options
Technological			
Nanotechnology	Potential to develop a new generation of pigments	New research required	Review technology and initiate R&D if review indicates potential in the new technology
Economic			
Rising costs of oil-based solvents	Increasing costs may reduce demand	Need to formulate low-solvent systems and/or aqueous-based systems	R&D into low solvent and/or aqueous based systems
Education/training			
Consumers	New systems may need new application methods	Demand will be restricted if consumers do not understand the issues	Marketing effort to inform consumers. Training of in-store staff to give consumers advice at the point of sales
Political			
National	General concern for environmental and safety issues	Covered in other sections of the analysis	
Legal			
Safety	Ban on toxic materials – e.g. lead and organic-tin (anti-fouling paint for dinghies)	Need to find non-toxic formulations	R&D to re-formulate products with safer and legal alternatives
Environmental			
Concern over VOC (volatile organic compound) emissions	Need to reduce or eliminate VOC solvent use	Need to formulate low-solvent systems and/or aqueous-based systems	R&D into low-solvent and/or aqueous-based systems

Table 2.3   Selective partial segmentation analysis for surface coatings and paints

Market area	Segments	Sub-segments	Comments
Industrial markets (B2B)			
	Motor vehicles		
		Primers and anticorrosion layers	
		Surface finish	Wide range of colours, specialist finishes (e.g. metallic) needed
	Marine		
		Above waterline	Good anticorrosion and wide range colours needed
		Below waterline	Good anticorrosion and anti-fouling performance needed
			Only two segments considered but there are other segments – e.g. aircraft, white goods (cookers, refrigerators, etc.)
Domestic (B2C)			
	Type of surface	Plaster	Wide range of colours and finishes needed
		Wood	Wide range of colours needed
		Metal	Wide range of colours needed
	Special situations	Damp and condensation	Finishes suitable for areas such as bathrooms
		High temperatures	Central heating radiators and pipes
			Again only a few selected segments are reviewed

Table 2.4 Partial stakeholder analysis for a manufacturer of surface coatings/paints

Stakeholder group	Sub-group	Selected stakeholder agenda issues	Company objective and issues
Internal			
	Management employees	Maintaining profitability and developing new products for a changing environment	Effective management co-ordination and team motivation
	Production employees	Concern that new products and manufacturing processes will change working practices	Effective change management
Business to Business (B2B)			
	Industrial customers	New systems will need new application equipment and major investments	Need to provide good technical service to industrial customers. Need for staff with good specialist industry knowledge
	Retail channels (e.g. B&Q)	Need for a range of value own-brand products	Difficult window of opportunity. Need to supply quality products under contract for own-label but also a need to maintain premium brands for extra margin
Regulatory			
	Safety	Concern with compliance (e.g. levels of heavy metals in paint)	Good QA procedures and records to demonstrate compliance
	Advertising	Concern that claims are realistic	Good testing procedures and records to demonstrate that claims such as 'quick drying' can be substantiated
Pressure groups			
	Environmental	Concern with heavy metals in paint	Good information on green credentials available (e.g. on website)
	Consumer	Concern that claims are realistic	Good information on consumer issues available (e.g. on website)
Industry			
	Suppliers	Pigment manufacturers must move from heavy metal-based systems (e.g. white lead) to more environmentally and safe systems	Partnership arrangements to develop new pigments and formulate new products. Supply chain partnerships

(Continued)

Table 2.4   (*Continued*)

Stakeholder group	Sub-group	Selected stakeholder agenda issues	Company objective and issues
	Competitors	All firms active in the segment are concerned that new regulations are realistic and that compliance will be possible	Collaboration to share relevant information where necessary (e.g. REACH)
	Trade associations	Industry faces common problems (e.g. preparation of old surfaces contaminated with lead-based products)	Collaboration on guidelines for contractors on safe industry working practices.
Media	Consumer	Latest news on innovative products for old problems	Good public relations to gain favourable product reviews in the DIY consumer press
	Technical	Latest news on innovative products for old problems	Good public relations to gain favourable product reviews in the narrow-cast trade press for the various specialist industries

The supply chain

In the above consideration of stakeholders, supplier and channels were included in the analysis. There is a complete chain of organisations from the primary industries to the ultimate customers and users. Issues deep down the supply chain can rapidly be transmitted and affect end users. In 2007, demand for bio-ethanol, coupled with droughts, affected the price of corn and wheat. This had impacts on the price of processed foods and drinks.

Figure 2.6 shows a schematic supply chain for the manufacture of shampoo, with a specific focus on the creative perfumery house. The primary perfumery materials are manufactured from normal chemical feedstocks or from natural sources. The plant materials for production of natural aroma materials are farmed or in some cases collected from the wild. The products are processed by local distilleries and sold on to the creative perfumery houses either directly or by a network of brokers and blenders. Personal care products may be made and marketed by brand leaders or produced by the contract manufacturers for the distributors' own-label brands. Here, all the components – such as surfactants, active ingredients, colours, packaging, etc. – must converge. The product is blended, filled and labelled. The logistics systems then deliver the final packed product to the supermarkets and other outlets through regional distribution centres.

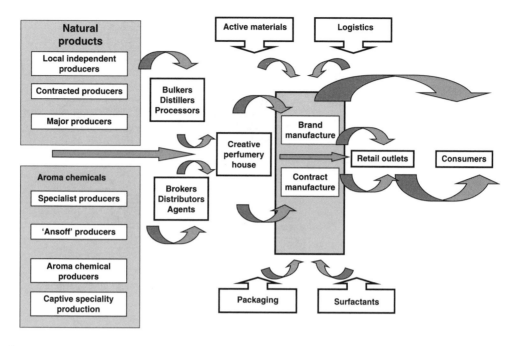

Figure 2.6 Outline supply chain analysis for a shampoo.

An engineer or technologist in completing an environmental analysis needs to consider not only the firm but also evaluate if there may be key issues affecting any part of the supply chain. Some of the issues affecting the supply chain are discussed further in the next section.

The competition environment

Earlier, in the discussion of the business environment, the physical model of an iron particle in a fluid was discussed. Here we noted that the macro-forces in this environment (e.g. the externally applied magnetic field) would be modified by the microenvironment (e.g. the magnetic properties of the other particles around our particle under observation), as represented in Figure 2.7. The effects would be different for the various forces. It is possible to have a positive or a negative electrical charge on a particle. It is not possible to have a magnet with only a north pole.

The same is true of the competitive environment of an organisation. There are different forces and they have different properties. Michael Porter developed a model to allow the evaluation of these different forces. He identified five forces of competition (Figure 2.8):

1. in-sector
2. substitutes
3. suppliers
4. buyers
5. new entrants

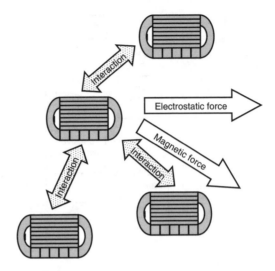

Figure 2.7 Forces acting on a charged iron particle interacting with other particles.

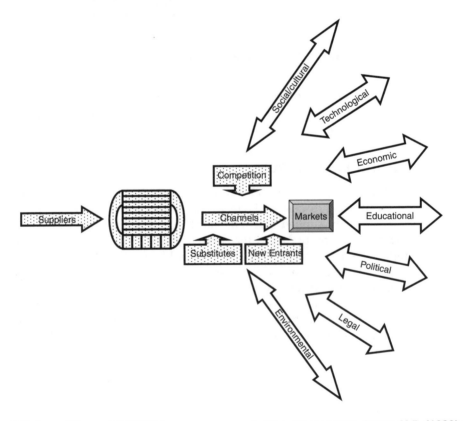

Figure 2.8 Competition and STEEPLE forces on an organisation. Adapted from: Porter, M.E. (1980) *Competitive Strategy: Techniques for Analysing Industries and Competitors*, Free Press, figure 1.1, page 4.

In the following sections we will consider the nature of these forces and the way in which macroenvironmental forces and other issues can affect (modify) the forces of competition. These 'modifiers' may be considered in a similar way to the dielectric properties of the fluid in our physical model. The dielectric constant modifies the electrical forces between charged particles. After this general review of each of the elements of competition, the final section provides an overview of how the model may be applied to practical business situations with some worked examples.

In-sector competition

This is the simple competition we discuss in our every day conversation. It is the direct competition of organisations working in the same business area and competing for the same customers. Tesco and Sainsbury compete in the same retail environment. Virgin and Vodafone compete in the same area of mobile communications. What we are evaluating is the balance of power and the potential motivation of the players.

If the sector has equally balanced competitors, then fierce competition would be the expected outcome. Two examples have been given above. Another example is competition for transatlantic air passengers (e.g. Virgin and British Airways). Where there are lots of providers, we have the street market type of situation. Another example of this is the provision of university education in the USA and Europe. There is a wealth of varied providers and competition between universities is intense. The universities illustrate another key factor affecting competitive behaviour. The marginal cost of adding one more student to a course on marketing is very low (the cost of providing an extra set of handouts for each lecture, etc.). The fixed costs of staffing all the various lectures are very high. It is essential to gain the required numbers to recover the fixed costs. To fall below the required numbers is fatal and the pressure is on for all in the marketplace. More consideration of fixed costs and break-even analysis is given in Chapter 10. The issue may be reduced or magnified according to the exit costs. If it was decided to withdraw a course in marketing, the lecturers involved could be redeployed to teach on other courses such as general business studies. The teaching facilities are very much standard and can be freed-up for other courses. The situation is very different for a specialist course in technology where redundancies and conversion of laboratory facilities would cost a large sum of money.

A key concept is that of 'switching costs'. Most of the major supermarkets supply much the same range of branded products. You can buy a packet of coffee from one supermarket one week and from another next week and you do not then have to buy a new electric kettle. There is a range of up-market coffee makers where special 'single shot' packs of coffee are required. If you want to change from the limited range of coffee on offer in the special packs, you are faced with the need to buy a new coffee maker – an example of high switching costs.

In certain industries a key role of the regulator is to ensure that switching costs are kept low. In the past it was difficult for a company to change its telephone provider and keep its existing telephone number. A change of telephone number results in a very expensive process. All customers and contacts have to be informed and a vast range of company documentation and stationery has to be reprinted. Vehicles may even have to be repainted. A key issue in the early days of an open market in telecommunications was to ensure portability of existing telephone numbers and reduce switching costs.

It is important to pick a specific platform for the conduct of a Porter competition analysis. Different platforms will give different results. An example of this is the asymmetric nature of competition. Specialist retailers of books and music were severely affected when major supermarkets stocked these items. However, these items are not a major percentage of supermarket sales. Thus, supermarkets can provide deep discounts on best-selling books to attract customers and make profits on other items bought at the same time with higher margins. The same option is not available to the specialist bookseller whose total business is books.

Substitutes

The key issue to focus on is that of benefit, rather than that of product. In the 1960s, the medium to sell music was the LP record. This in its turn was replaced by the CD and this in its turn is being replaced by digital downloads. The tape-playing Sony 'Walkman' was replaced by CD players and now MP3 devices are taking over. The focus on benefits has the implication that the model must be run for different segments where different benefits are required. LPs are still in demand for one specific segment – for use by DJs. There is even a service to convert recent digital releases into the vinyl format for this very specific segment.

The model is equally effective for the analysis of services. Analogue TV radio signals are to be phased out in the UK. The alternative substitute products include digital terrestrial, digital satellite, digital cable and internet TV. Some of these services will provide enhancements such as video on demand for past programmes. As discussed above, switching costs may influence if people will adopt a substitute product and how quickly it will be adopted. Relatively low-cost set-top converters and no hire costs for 'Free View' set-top boxes has been one factor in the rapid penetration of digital TV in the UK. If switching costs can be a barrier, then enhanced benefits can provide the customer with the drive to adopt a substitute product. In the case of digital formats for TV, there is a vastly increased range of both TV and radio channels when compared with analogue signals.

Suppliers

A person looking for a computer will be faced by a range of options. PCs have become near commodity items so competition has become cut-throat and some major players (e.g. IBM) have exited the market. A buyer can also play the market and select excellent deals on hardware. The power balance with the operating system and office software, however, is completely different, with Microsoft having a dominant position in the marketplace.

A similar situation is played out in the supermarkets. Where a product is largely a commodity, there are many small suppliers and free supply (e.g. milk), all the power lies with the supermarkets. However, the position is different if there is more demand than supply. The demand for 'organic' products has increased more rapidly than the ability to increase production. Hence, in this situation, the suppliers hold more power thereby gaining additional margins when compared with standard commodity suppliers.

The classic response of suppliers is to differentiate their products by branding. The degree of success this strategy achieves depends on the strength of the brand and the nature of the product. Even with powerful brands available, over 50% of detergents sold in the UK are supermarket own-label products. However, with high-involvement fashion products the picture can be very different. With fine fashion fragrances, brands such as Chanel dominate the market. In this case, supermarkets have gone to considerable lengths to compete. When a brand leader refused to sell them products, in some cases, they have resorted to the 'grey' market. Here, the supermarket buys from a wholesaler in a different country and imports the product themselves. Nothing illustrates the power battle between suppliers and distributors better than this scenario. The fashion brands combat this by employing mystery shoppers to gain samples of products and then security coding on the packages will trace the wholesaler who 'leaked' the product. The brand owner will then take steps to cut off the unauthorised supply channel. Such power struggles have spilled over into the courts to establish the battlelines.

Buyers

This is similar to the power of suppliers with a mirror image reflection of the issues. If there are many suppliers and customers perceive little differentiation in the benefits, then the consumer holds the balance of power and margins will be low. The supply of petrol is a typical example. There are zero switching costs and customers do not think they will get 50% performance increase from another brand.

Perceived branding and quality can give the organisation a stronger bargaining power over buyers. These are the same types of forces as operating with supplier power. The Ivy League universities (e.g. Harvard, Yale, etc.) and their UK equivalents (Oxford, Cambridge, etc.) have many more applications than places and can charge super-premium prices for courses such as the MBA. Small regional providers (e.g. a local further education college) will not be able to charge premium prices and may have to engage in vigorous marketing activities to attract sufficient candidates.

MICRO CASE STUDY   **SUPPLIER/BUYER POWER IN A B2B CONTEXT: ENGINE MANUFACTURE**

A major cost in the manufacture of an engine is the cost of the specialist alloys used in its construction. Major manufacturers buy large quantities of these alloys and there are numerous international suppliers. If the alloys are in free supply then the bargaining power will be with the engine manufacturers. Highly specialised metal catalyst systems may be needed for emission control (and these systems may also be patented). In this marketplace, there are fewer specialist suppliers and they may also have other markets open to them (e.g. their platinum is also used in jewellery). As we can see, the power balance is different here.

The level of interest in the purchased product will depend on its impact on the business. Antifreeze and corrosion inhibitors may not be a major cost input to the total costs of manufacturing the final engine but failure of either product could cause total failure of the engine. Therefore, the buying of these items would still be a major technical concern. Just as with any company, an engine manufacturer will buy minor office consumables such as paper. This is a very small percentage of total costs and minor quality problems would not have a catastrophic impact on the quality of engines produced. Hence, there will be little management concern for the purchase of this product. Purchasing will be left on autopilot and seen as a routine minor procurement activity. If the business was different in nature and paper was a major cost driver (e.g. the printing of books and newspapers) then there would be significant management attention to its purchase.

New entrants

Another key factor in the forces of competition is the threat of new and often unexpected en-trants. In the global marketplace, international acquisitions provide a framework for major new entrants, almost overnight. When ASDA was purchased by Wal-Mart, this provided the UK with a powerful new competitor. A comparatively small national organisation, ASDA suddenly had the purchasing power of the world's largest global retailer to power its low-cost strategies.

One strategy option for organisations is to add to their product line, thereby providing customers with more products to buy (in order to increase their spend and the company's profitability). In the middle of the twentieth century, people went into a garage to buy just petrol and oil. Whole groups of retailers (e.g. florists, newsagents, convenience shops) have now faced the entry of forecourt sales as a major force in the UK retail market. Similar forces apply to the B2B sector (e.g. the move of IBM into services).

Apart from globalisation, other changes in the STEEPLE environment can provide entry pathways. A major one is new technology. An important gateway for new entrants has been the internet and the dramatic growth of high-speed broadband access in developed countries. The specialist bookseller has suffered a double blow: the supermarkets can cream off sales of the best-sellers and the esoteric titles can be purchased more quickly from Amazon. The high street betting shop also now has massive competition from online betting. Again, the impact is not restricted to consumer markets but also applies to B2B markets. Corporate travel is more likely to now be booked on-line, rather than by the use of travel agents.

At times it is not too clear what is the correct classification for a new competitive force. The rise of HP as a supplier of digital cameras and image-processing equipment could be considered as a new entrant (powered by a change in technology) or a substitute system (digital rather than film and wet processing). It is recommended that time is not wasted with such arcane debates. All this model asks us to do is to ask questions to determine the competitive environment. It is the identification of competition rather than its classification that is important.

Practical competition analysis

A spreadsheet approach provides a good framework. As with STEEPLE, a table with four headings can be used, in this case:

1. competition element and sub-element
2. threat
3. potential impact (apply the 'so what?' test) and implications
4. comments and potential actions for consideration

Care has to be taken in the application of the competition model because, as with most business models, it has some limitations. The suggestion is that suppliers and cus-tomers are potential threats and sources of competitive influence. However, in supply chain management, the view may be taken that they should not be considered as threats, but as partners. In real life, under different conditions, both situations can be true. In many cases, small suppliers to large organisations feel that there is an imbalance in the relationship. However, with the advent of 'fair trade', large organisations are becoming supportive of small suppliers. The model should be taken as indicating a potential source of competitive pressure, not indicative of such threats invariably existing. The model also has the same limitation as the basic SWOT and Boston matrix – the standard application of the model provides a snapshot in time (see Wilson & Gilligan, 2005). Just as with the macroenvironment analysis, it is important to review the potential changes over time. With limited availability of oil and increasing demand for energy, the competitive position of oil producers has become stronger and prices have increased.

Value chain

In the earlier analysis, we considered the external (macro- and micro-) environment. Returning to the iron particle model, the interaction of the particle will be influenced by the detailed nature of the particle. Its size, surface area, impurity make-up and past history (e.g. heat treatment) will all have an impact on how the particle responds to the external environment. In writing a software package, the engineer will need to have due regard to the computer's operating system and performance. In the same way, the technical business person must understand the capabilities and nature of the organisation. Two models were developed in the late twentieth century to analyse the firm's internal environment: the Porter value chain and the McKinsey 7s model. These have been fused and some additional issues that are relevant to the twenty-first century included, giving the augmented value chain (Figure 2.9).

The model has two sections: the 'primary activities' (along the top of the chain link) and the 'support activities' (below the primary activities). The primary activities (inbound logistics, operations, outbound logistics, sales and field service) are involved in the day-by-day conduct of the organisation's business. The day-by-day activities would come to a shuddering halt were it not underpinned by the support activities.

In the augmented value chain, the support activities and issues identified are:

- strategic stance and strategy
- safety, environmental, quality and ethical policies
- physical and financial structure
- information systems
- human resources
- technology development
- marketing
- procurement

The nature and use of each element of the model is explained below and the practical application of the model will be outlined with examples.

Primary activities

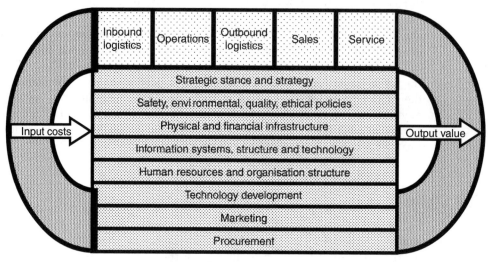

Support activities

Figure 2.9 Augmented value chain. Adapted from Porter, M.E. (1985) *Competitive Advantage: Creating and Sustaining Superior Performance*, **Free Press, figure 2.2, page 37.**

Primary activities

Inbound logistics

Containerisation and bulk carriers have revolutionised the world supply chain. Sugar and flour are conveyed and delivered in bulk, dramatically reducing handling costs and improving the environmental impact with the elimination of sacks. Oil pipelines can shift energy from one end of a continent to another. Power lines can convey electrical power from green sources (e.g. wind farms) in remote areas to centres of population and industry. Just-in-time (JIT) manufacture would not be possible without slick delivery logistics. This would be a waste of time if quality assurance then took two days to clear the delivery. Zero defect and direct onto line has to be the framework, with QA shared between buyer and supplier. This means quality has to be assured before delivery, not afterwards.

The same concepts apply to services. In some ways the long-haul telecommunications network is the simple area. The problem area is that final link – just a few miles – between the exchange and thousands of homes. So, in communications, inbound logistics is about line availability and/or bandwidth. For the airlines, it is customer check-in and security checks.

Effective and efficient supply chain management and inbound logistics are vital for both services and product manufacture. Lost calls to a call centre do not gain business. Missing components bring production to a halt. Excessive inbound logistics costs can make an operation uneconomic.

Operations

If things are not properly made, in sufficient quantities and to appropriate costs, the firm will go out of business. For the manufacture of highly standardised products required in volume (e.g. electrical components), then highly automated production lines are appropriate. For more specialised manufacture, more flexible, cell systems of operation might be appropriate. CAD/CAM (computer-aided design/computer-aided manufacture) can reduce the production cycle time even for specialised parts. Similar issues apply to other industries such as food and drink manufacture. Modern bakeries are highly automated, with very high production throughputs. Each industry has its own special sets of requirements. For the manufacture of disk drives and microchips, a particle of cigarette smoke could be a problem (thus the need for a 'clean room' manufacturing environment) and similarly for food manufacture, control of microbiological risks is also vital.

The effective and efficient delivery of operations is as important in services as with product manufacture. It is not much fun when your luggage arrives from New York at Heathrow and you are in Gatwick (or worse). In life-threatening situations, medical staff rely on rapid and accurate tests to allow appropriate diagnoses.

Outbound logistics

The dot-com revolution has made ordering products more convenient than ever before. However, no matter how great the website, that is no compensation when the product is poorly packaged and arrives late and damaged. As with the competition model, where supplier power and buyer power are in many ways just a reflection of the issues, so it is with inbound logistics and outbound logistics. In the B2B context, the supplier's outbound logistics must match up with its client's inbound logistics.

After the manufacturing operations, products must be packaged and possibly stored. When a customer's order is received, the items must be assembled and then dispatched to reach the customer safely and in good time. The whole issue of distribution logistics is complex and a whole industry provides these services. Further discussion of the marketing issues to be considered in physical distribution appears in Chapter 6. Distribution costs are often a significant percentage of the total costs. For some low-value products, such as mineral water and carbonated drinks, the costs of packaging and physical distribution may exceed the cost of production of the drink. There is no point in cutting small costs out of production if care is not taken to ensure that all the cost gains are not lost in poor distribution efficiencies.

Sales

The sales system drives the whole primary value chain. Sales provide the planning input to the production planning system. Complex materials resource planning (MRP) computer models break down a sales plan into orders for all the components and allow the development of a production plan.

In the consumer area, the competitive power that can come from good sales systems can be illustrated with supermarkets. The technological breakthrough was the mass adoption of bar codes (machine readable numbers). For the customer, this provides a faster checkout time and a complete itemised list of all the items purchased. The electronic point of sale (EPOS) system provides the input for stock control. The rate of sale of a product and subsequent reordering can then be done in real time through electronic data interchange (EDI). Using this tight stock control and sales tracking, supermarkets carry only a few days' stock. This stocking efficiency has massive advantages in working capital. In fact, goods are sold before the supermarket pays for them and the suppliers are financing the supermarkets' stock. Overall, the effect is that there is better management control for reduced operating costs. The benefits do not stop there. When the supermarket starts a new advertising campaign, the effect on sales can be tracked from the first day. Further consideration of the marketing use of sales data is given in Chapter 9.

In the B2B sector, JIT manufacture is not possible without matching needs to supply. Any mismatch in MRP forecasts will disrupt the flow of production. The whole supply chain must be integrated. A hot sunny day may trigger an upturn in sales of cola. The supermarket's EPOS system will call for further supplies of cola to be delivered to the supermarket. This demand will be reflected down the supply chain for supply of ingredients such as syrup and cola flavour.

Field service

Many products need service support. This service is not only vital to the customer, to gain maximum benefit from the product, but also provides additional cash flow. Car manufacturers earn a significant proportion of their profits from spare parts, servicing and financial services (e.g. loans to purchase a car). A computer company may offer a 'turnkey' solution to a customer, with installation, customised software and staff training. The effective provision of service may be a key competitive advantage in gaining sales.

Primary activities
Strategic stance and strategy

Different organisations have different strategic stances, even when working in the same market sector. A company may aim to be a cost leader focusing on obtaining economies of scale and ruthlessly cutting costs. This strategy has been a resounding success for the budget airlines. An organisation can focus on excellent technical performance as a strategy. In the airline industry, the fastest journey time was the competitive advantage of Concorde. In the pharmaceutical industry there are a range of companies with a market-follower strategy. The global multinational companies will spend billions of pounds on drug discovery, development, testing and marketing (market-leader stance). The market-followers lurk, waiting for the patents to expire, and then come in with low cost 'generic' versions.

In developing the organisation, different strategic approaches can be adopted. If a company intends to grow quickly, it may invest in research and marketing to grow the business from within (the so-called organic growth strategy). An alternative approach is to grow the organisation by acquisitions and mergers. A company wishing to lower costs may move its operations to a low-cost base (e.g. China) or contract out manufacture. Companies must continually appraise their strategic stance and strategies to respond to the changing macro- and microenvironments.

Safety, environmental, quality and ethical policies

At first sight, this appears to be a disparate set of issues but they have a unifying theme. They all depend on the commitment and leadership of top management and involve value changes in the whole workforce. In the nineteenth century, products were manufactured without major regard for safety (either employees or users), waste was thrown into the rivers, quality was often dubious and ethical standards (e.g. exploitation of less-developed countries) would not stand twenty-first century scrutiny.

Today, ruthless suppression of competition and establishment of cartels is, in the long run, only likely to result in heavy fines by the industry regulators. Simple maximisation of the owner's return without appropriate consideration of other stakeholder values will not work in the modern business climate (e.g. adverse publicity in the use of child labour damaging fashion brands). ISO 9000 and ISO 14000 provide formal frameworks for quality and environmental management. More detailed coverage of the issues is given in the succeeding chapters. Relationship marketing is also important since it is the identification and management of the relevant stakeholders that holds the key to success.

Physical and financial structure

To be effective and efficient, the organisation must have appropriate facilities. It is not possible to provide effective infection control in a hospital if the design and construction of the building has not been completed with this major need kept firmly high on the agenda of issues to be considered. In manufacturing operations, great regard must be paid to the physical layout of machines and assembly processes.

At first sight, it may appear that the financial structure of a company would have little impact on operations providing there is enough cash around. This is not so. For a small start-up business, it is generally bad policy to finance the business from a bank overdraft since banks can call this in at any time. A fixed-term bank loan is more likely to provide stability in the difficult start-up period. For larger organisations, similar issues need to be considered. The large limited company with many shareholders has to continually look to its share price and keep responding to the issues raised by the financial press. They can force senior management to spend too much time on the short-term issues, thereby detracting focus from the longer term strategic issues. Companies that are financed by private equity or are family owned do not have this distraction. Other special forms of ownership and finance have an impact on the formulation of organisation policy. Three types of other forms of ownership are public ownership (e.g. Civil Service), co-operatives (ownership by many members of the organisation) and trusts (e.g. universities). The key issue is that the owners form one of the key stakeholder groups. The different forms of ownership provide a varied set of stakeholders with differing expectations. The management issue is, as always, to manage stakeholder expectations and develop stakeholder value. The term 'value' is used because with some stakeholders (e.g. a charitable trust such as a professional institution) value will include non-financial elements. More coverage of not-for-profit issues is given in the next chapter.

Information systems

Early in the second half of the twentieth century, computers were introduced for fairly fixed business operations, such as payroll and inventory control. Most organisations are now completely dependent on their information and communications systems. For a manufacturing company, CAD/CAM can greatly reduce the time to market. For a retailer, the systems provide both inventory control and marketing data. There are a whole set of new organisations where computers and communications are the company (e.g. Google). It is essential that computer systems do what is intended (no bugs), are reliable (downtime kills a business), are secure to loss of data (effectively backed-up) and secure from hacking and virus attacks. This must be achieved with legal compliance to data protection regulations.

Human resources

A structured way to look at the issues is to consider the time-line: potential employee, selection process, induction, continuing personal development, motivation, discipline, and exit. No organisation will be better than its staff. The best equipment needs the best people to manage it. There are never enough good people. To attract good candidates, the organisation has to project a good reputation; just as with sales, a prior foundation needs to be laid. Appropriate potential candidates need to be attracted to the selection process, and there is more to this than just placing a few advertisements. Many good senior staff are happy in their present roles and are not scanning the appointments pages every day. In such circumstances, headhunting agencies might be employed. The interview process is not easy and professional support should be sought. Where practical skills are involved, some appropriate tests should be included in the process. The purpose of the induction process is to bring the new employee up to speed and ensure they are able to fully function in their team. The only constant of business life is continual change. The individual and organisation must practise continual professional development to ensure that skills are developed in line with changing environmental needs.

   Motivation is critical, especially for creative professional staff. The reward system is more than just appropriate pay. Non-pay elements, such as professional recognition, are also important. Where there is underperformance, it must be detected and managed. This may be supportive training but in certain cases formal disciplinary procedures may need to be invoked. There is much legislation affecting all of these policies and processes. Expert advice should be sought to ensure compliance. More consideration of human resource issues is given in Chapter 11.

Technology development

There is wave after wave of innovation in products and services. An organisation that can only provide last year's technology will soon be out of business. Chapter 14 covers the infrastructure, policies and procedures for successful product development. However, technology development can affect any aspect of the marketing mix or value chain. Radio-frequency identification (RFID) tags can help with supply chain management by tracking items with more accuracy and with less effort. New digital media are refocusing marketing communications. The view is that R&D thought should be given to all aspects of the firm's products, services and operations, not just new product development.

Marketing

Here, marketing is defined as developing the business, the sales systems providing the day-to-day power to the primary activity. The first role of marketing is to seek out and define new market opportunities. Effective marketing information systems and research techniques are vital in this phase. The role of marketing in the new product development process is covered in Chapter 14. Once the product has been developed, marketing must ensure that the product gets to the customer (Chapter 6 looks at distribution) and that customers are aware of product and persuaded to buy (Chapter 7 discusses promotion).

Procurement

This is one of the neglected areas in business schools. If sales are increased by £1 000, profits may be increased by around £100 but additional working capital may be required. However, if we make some smart purchases and reduce our costs by £1 000 we have increased our profits by a full £1 000.

The cost structures and key buying problems are very different, depending on the nature of the business. For an oil refinery, it is the cost of oil to process; for a supermarket, it is the costs of goods sold. The costs of a professional consultancy company are somewhat different, with services such as communications and travel being more important. The process is to identify the key cost-drivers for the organisation and to systematically search out better value solutions. There is little benefit in reducing the cost of the product by a few pence and then wasting large sums of money with poor physical distribution contracts.

Table 2.5 provides a summary of typical selected value chain elements.

Table 2.5 Augmented value chain: selected elements

Value chain element	Sub-elements	Comments
Primary activities Inbound logistics		
	Supply chain management, MRP	Good inbound logistics starts with good sales forecasts and then good communications with suppliers
	JIT (just-in-time) delivery and TQM (total quality management)	Inbound quality starts with supplier audits: prompt delivery is of no value if quality is poor or it takes days to clear QA to enter production
	Appropriate receiving facilities	Typical examples are bulk delivery facilities for sugar and flower at a bakery or 'online' delivery for assembly items

(Continued)

Table 2.5 (*Continued*)

Value chain element	*Sub-elements*	*Comments*
	Appropriate storage facilities	A typical example would be food ingredient production from crops that are seasonal, where stocks need to held for 'out of season' production. In a restaurant, separate facilities are needed for salads and cooked products and raw fresh meat and fish (potential microbiological contamination)
Operations	Appropriate automation	Where products are required in high volumes, highly automated systems and robots may be in order
	Flexible production	Where short runs or one-off products are needed, cell or other forms of flexible production will be appropriate
	Facility layout	For both product production or service delivery care should be taken to ensure smooth flow of the processes
Outbound logistics	Filling and finishing	Appropriate facilities for filling and finishing (e.g. labelling). For a service such as insurance it can be the dispatch of documentation
	Good documentation	Export orders need accurate documentation, even a small error can cause a major delay
	Smart delivery logistics	Effective and efficient delivery systems. This can be bulk delivery for major intermediates in the B2B context (e.g. strip steel to a car factory)
Sales	Effective order delivery systems	In the B2B context, good EPOS and EDI plus sound communications possibly with EDI systems linking MRP and stock control systems
	Effective field sales staff	Key for relationship building in the B2B context
Field service	Effective design and installation	In the B2C context a typical example would be a designed and fitted kitchen. In the B2B context it can be the provision of turnkey solutions (design, build, commission and train staff)
	Field service	Effective and efficient provision of field service with well-trained staff and free availability of spare parts

Table 2.5 (*Continued*)

Value chain element	*Sub-elements*	*Comments*
	Customer service	For many products in the B2B context, support may be needed for customers to be able to use the product (e.g. support for software engineers with the delivery of a new generation of microprocessor)
Support activities		
Stance and strategy		
	Market leader	Strong branding and high R&D effort
	Market follower	Good market intelligence, smart development and low production cost base
Safety, environment, quality and ethics		
	Safety	Safety of products (e.g. removal of toxic ingredients in products such as paints and glues) when possible. Safety of manufacturing processes. Safety in the distribution logistics
	Environment	Green buying, green production processes, green distribution logistics; environmental culture
	Quality	TQM in purchasing, manufacturing and distribution; quality culture
	Ethics	Ethical buying, ethical treatment of stakeholders, ethical conduct of financial transactions; ethical culture
Physical and financial structure		
	Physical infrastructure	Superior quality facilities for company activities
	Financial infrastructure	Appropriate financial infrastructure (e.g. appropriate balance between debt and equity funding)
Information systems		
	Data collection	Rapid collection of clean data
	Data storage and processing	Effective, efficient and secure data storage and processing capability
	Communication	Effective, efficient and secure communication capability
Human resources		
	Corporate values culture and style	Appropriate values, culture and style. The key word is 'appropriate': success in managing a rock concert venue needs a different approach to the management of a major hospital

(Continued)

Table 2.5   (*Continued*)

Value chain element	Sub-elements	Comments
	Organisation structure	Appropriate organisation structure: simple and efficient for small organisation; matrix organisation for complex project management
	Individuals	Superior process for recruitment, selection, training, motivation and rewards
	Project management	Superior process and policies for the management of project covering hard (scheduling, resource allocation, etc.) and soft issues (e.g. motivation and team building)
	Communications	Effective, efficient and responsive communications processes and systems for internal stakeholders
Technology development		*Note: technology development should not be restricted to production (e.g. robotics developments) and products (design for manufacture as well as use) but to all elements of the value chain and marketing mix*
	Research	Effective development of new enabling technologies (e.g. data compression and encryption technologies for a communications company)
	Intelligence	Effective environmental monitoring to detect when new technologies will have an impact on a business sector (e.g. move of plant protection from chemical fungicides, etc. to genetically engineered crops)
	Development	Both the above are as of nothing unless there are good systems to bring the technologies into market valued products in a timely way
Marketing	Segmentation	Effective segmentation and targeting processes
	Marketing mix	Effective development of all of the elements of the marketing mix, often (e.g. new product development) in collaboration with other value chain functions
	Good MkIS	Good environmental monitoring and data analysis. Much of what is needed is to predict the products to be developed this year required by the market next year.

(*Continued*)

Table 2.5 (*Continued*)

Value chain element	Sub-elements	Comments
Procurement		
	Production goods and services	Good buying polices for the sourcing of raw materials and production services
	Support product and services	Areas such as travel and insurance can involve significant sums, so cost control should not be restricted to production costs but extended to overhead costs as well
	Marketing	Good buying and administration of services (e.g. advertising agencies) and good buying of media to stretch the budget

FOOD AND DRINK TECHNOLOGIST: MACRO- AND MICROENVIRONMENT FOR COLA DRINKS

When people are asked to name major brands, 'Coke' and 'Pepsi' are two that will be mentioned. For 'Coke' to remain a market leader, it has to be innovative in its product development and marketing. Consider the position of a technical manager working on drink formulations and other aspects of new product development (e.g. innovative packaging). It will be essential for the new product team leader to understand the context in which the development takes place. The three models that have been reviewed (STEEPLE, five forces of competition and augmented value chain) provide the framework to do this. Tables 2.6, 2.7 and 2.8 provide a partial outline analysis of this situation. Just one element has been considered under each factor heading.

Table 2.6 Partial STEEPLE analysis for carbonated drinks in Europe

STEEPLE issue	Issue	Impact/implications	Comments/actions
Social/cultural Social attitudes	Consumers concerned about healthy eating and 'additives'	Reducing demand for drinks with high sugar content and artificial additives	Need to develop new products such as low-calorie drinks without artificial colours and flavouring
Technological Inventions	Development of new sweeteners	New formulation processes for low-calorie products	Explore exploitation of the new sweeteners
Economic Raw material costs	Demand for bio-ethanol for cars driving up the cost of invert sugars	Costs of sugar-based drinks will increase faster than other formulations	Increase marketing effort on low-calorie products with better margins

(*Continued*)

Table 2.6 (*Continued*)

STEEPLE issue	Issue	Impact/implications	Comments/actions
Educational/training			
Consumers	Consumers being educated by media and pressure groups about 'unhealthy' formulations and 'additives'	Demand for more information for consumers and changes to consumer reception of drinks	Need for changes to labelling. Full background information for consumers on website. Another driver for reformulated 'healthy' drinks
Political			
National	Concern about childhood obesity	Change in climate of acceptability for 'unhealthy' drinks	Need to lobby politicians to limit damage and change marketing (e.g. products and marketing communications) to respond to new pressures
Legal			
Safety	Changing views about the safety of flavourings and other ingredients	Need to track changes in permitted products and labelling regulations	Need to re-formulate products and change labelling as and when necessary
Environmental			
Recycling	Low levels of plastic recycling a concern	Political and legal pressures to force increasing recycling	Collaborative projects (e.g. with supermarkets) to change attitudes and increase recycling of plastic

Table 2.7   Partial competition analysis for carbonated drinks in Europe from the standpoint of a brand manufacturer

Competition element	Issue	Impact/implications	Comments/actions
In-sector			
B2B market	Pubs and restaurants have limited shelf space	Resistance of outlets to stock 'overlapping' products (e.g. likely to stock Coke *or* Pepsi)	Need for promotional activity to ensure stocking or drinking ours rather than competitive products (e.g. provision of point-of-sale material)

Table 2.7 (*Continued*)

Competition element	Issue	Impact/implications	Comments/actions
Substitute products			
Non-carbonated drinks	Increasing uptake of uncarbonated drinks such as smoothies	Carbonated drinks sector under pressure; expanding new drinks sector	Need for non-carbonated drinks in the portfolio of products
New entrants			
Start-up companies	New consumer issues and product positioning allowing market entry to new players	New entrants appearing, such as Innocent	One response is to develop matching products. An alternative might be to buy up the new company
Suppliers			
New ingredients	Some of the new ingredients (e.g. sugar substitutes) are patented	Locked into a single supplier, may be shortages if uptake grows faster than supplier capacity	Careful supply chain management, good sales forecasting and open communications with supplier about future demand
Buyers			
B2C market	Over 50% of UK grocery market in hands of just a few supermarkets	Massive buying power in the hands of the supermarkets. Supermarkets selling own-label carbonated drinks	Strong branding supported with marketing communications to ultimate customers and consumers. 'If you can't beat them join them' option to contract manufacture own-label products for the supermarkets

Table 2.8 Partial value chain analysis for carbonated drinks in Europe from the standpoint of a brand manufacturer

Value chain element	Issue	Impact/implications	Comments/actions
Primary activities			
Inbound logistics			
Raw material quality	Water	Large quantities of 'quality' water needed for manufacturing process	Availability of water (amount and quality) a major factor in site selection. Appropriate facilities needed for water purification and sterilisation

(*Continued*)

Table 2.8   (*Continued*)

Value chain element	Issue	Impact/implications	Comments/actions
Operations			
	Product diversity	Need for product changeovers in lines	Plant that is easy and quick to clean and swop product type quickly
Outbound logistics			
	Orders in transit	Need to be able to track progress of orders thorough the distribution channels	Move from bar codes to RFI tags for tracking pallets of finished product through supply chain
Sales			
	Need to replenish stock sold	Demand can be variable (e.g. hot sunny day in spring) and stock-outs cause lost sales and promote switching to other brands and/or products	Need for good EDI links to supermarkets to track sales in near real time
Field service			
	Not a major issue	Customers know how to open bottles and drink the product	Carbonated drinks are not like cars, which do need a lot of field service provision
Support activities **Stance and strategy**			
	Maintenance of brand	Strong brands need to remain market leaders and be innovative	Need to be innovative and first to market with new product concept, unlike own-brands that can follow the market
Safety, environment, quality and ethics			
	Growth in 'Fair Trade' segment	'Fair Trade' sources in less-developed countries can have variable quality	Partnership arrangements to train producers to provide consistent quality
Physical and financial structure			
	Product contamination either chemical or microbiological	Contamination control, plant sterilisation	Plant construction must be of appropriate materials (e.g. stainless steel) and access to plant controlled

Table 2.8   (*Continued*)

Value chain element	Issue	Impact/implications	Comments/actions
Information systems			
	Materials resource planning	Matching stocks to production needs	Integrated computer systems to use sales data to drive production schedules
Human resources			
	Food products need a TQM approach	Staff need to be motivated and skilled (e.g. statistical process control techniques)	
Technology development			
	New communications media opportunities	Old media not working as they did in the past (e.g. terrestrial TV). New media opportunities appearing	Tracking technical advances in media and exploiting them (e.g. product placement opportunities in computer games)
Marketing			
	Changing segmentation patterns (e.g. growth in the low-calorie sector)	Need to maintain a balanced portfolio products	Primary and secondary research feeding into MkIS to assist in new product development activity
Procurement			
	Need to maintain high advertising activity to support brand	Cost of this can be a significant part of total marketing budget for a FMCG brand	Smart buying of media essential to maximise impact obtained from the media spend

The marketing information management system

To fail to have effective and efficient information systems is like driving at 80 mph down the motorway with the windscreen misted up. The motorist needs to know the state of the road (is there black ice?). The firm needs to continually review its macroenvironment, such as interest rates. How you can drive is affected by the nature and amount of other traffic on the road. Equally, the company is affected by its microenvironment in terms of the amount

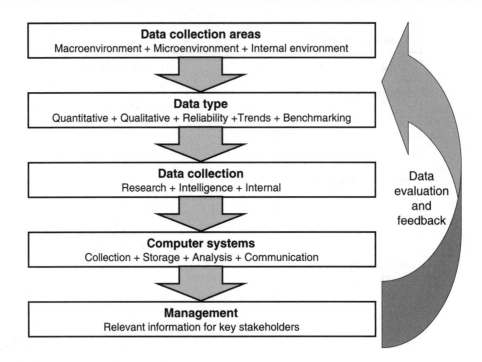

Figure 2.10 Marketing information system.

and nature of competition. The driver will also want to know the condition of the vehicle (you do not get far on an empty fuel tank). The firm needs to know the operating situation of all of the elements of its value chain. The key elements of the marketing information system are given in Figure 2.10. The major elements are briefly outlined in this section while Chapter 9 develops the detail.

Data type

There are two types of data: (1) *quantitative* (e.g. how many people buy a product) and (2) *qualitative* (e.g. why people buy the product). There are three issues to be considered in the collection and assessment of data: (1) *reliability*, (2) *trends* and (3) *benchmarking*.

These are discussed below in the context of chocolate. The food technologist working with chocolate is working in a complex environment. There are complex technical issues (e.g. the phase structure of chocolate is complicated) and consumer attitudes are multifaceted.

Quantitative data

In some ways, this is the simple part of data collection – just get the numbers. However, there can be problems. Simple facts, such as the total sales volume of chocolate, may be relatively easy to determine. Discovering how much chocolate a given consumer group eats will be more difficult. People may not want to disclose excessive and obsessive eating behaviour and it could be hard to get representative samples.

Qualitative data

Many years ago, research was conducted that concluded that the existing chocolate brands had 'feminine' personalities. The conclusion was that there was a place in the market for a 'masculine' brand of chocolate. Hence, the Yorkie bar was launched and was a major success. Quantitative data is the black and white outline of the situation (who eats chocolate and how much they eat). However, for successful marketing, the food technologist also needs to know 'why they eat it' – the qualitative aspect.

The emotional link to chocolate can be intense. When people are very young and something bad happens (say, when children have a minor fall) their mums 'kiss them better' and give them a piece of chocolate, perhaps creating the impression that chocolate is a symbol of safety, love and security. At Easter, children look forward to getting a chocolate Easter egg. Thus, at the end of a bad day, the way to happiness is a bar of chocolate. Why people do things and their relationship with products is important; it is a key factor in understanding the motivation for the purchasing decision.

Reliability

All scientists, technologists and engineers will be familiar with statistical concepts such as confidence intervals. In statistical process control, estimating the weight of a bar of chocolate leaving a high-speed packing line may need some innovative sensor systems, but it is fundamentally a simple technological problem. In marketing, some of the methods of data collection used are not applied to physical systems (e.g. the questionnaire). What people understand as 'chocolate' may differ. One person may consider an After Eight chocolate mint wafer to be 'chocolate' whereas another consumer may consider it to be 'mint confectionary'. The design and use of questionnaires is considered in Chapter 9.

To save costs, we will often use data that has already been collected (so-called secondary data). A typical problem facing the technologist is to estimate the cost of production and a key element of this will be the cost of materials. Cocoa is a volatile commodity with large price swings. The historical costs of current stocks might well not be valid for estimating the cost of production for a launch in six months' time. The second problem is often that the value of data decays with time. If secondary data indicates 50% of the population eats chocolate, we need to know when the data were collected. Consumption habits change and if the data was collected several years ago, there must be concerns about their current validity.

Trends

To stand in front of a parked car is perfectly safe. It is less sensible to stand in front of a car travelling at 70 mph on a motorway. In crossing a road, it is not only the position of the car we need to know but its speed and direction as well. There may be trends in both quantitative and qualitative data. The amount of chocolate eaten and how this divides between different segments (e.g. milk and dark) evolves with changes in the macroenvironment. How people emotionally feel about chocolate can also change, (e.g. subjective concerns about 'Fair Trade' cocoa).

Benchmarking

In overtaking on the motorway, we are not only concerned with how fast we are going but also the speed of the vehicle we are overtaking. Often it is important not only to know the magnitude and the change but also how this compares with other appropriate reference points. If we know that 50% of people eat chocolate and this is increasing by 1% a year, we might think this were the key market on which to concentrate our new product development effort. However, if we also note that 30% of people are eating healthy, high-fibre snack bars and that this is increasing at 20% a year we may come to a different decision.

Data collection

The way data is collected can be divided up into three areas: (1) *market research*, (2) *market intelligence* and (3) *internal data*.

Market research

Market research is the collection of data for specific management needs (e.g. the launch of a new chocolate confectionery). The first data to be collected should be 'secondary' data. This is existing data that has been collected before. This may be in the public domain (e.g. government reports) or from commercial sources such as Mintel. The collection and analysis of such data is not cost free but it is a lot cheaper than initiating new research.

When the secondary data has been collected, it is often found that there are gaps in the information needed. These gaps need to be filled by new 'primary' research. In the launch of a new chocolate confectionery it will be vital to determine if consumers prefer the new product to the competition. There will be a need to run consumer preference tasting trials to evaluate this. Issues in consumer product testing are developed further in Chapter 9.

Primary and secondary data may cover quantitative data, qualitative data and trends. Given that secondary data may have been collected for a different purpose, it must be interpreted with care.

Market intelligence

This is the continual collection of data of relevance to the organisation. This can cover any aspect of the macro- and microenvironment. Typical sources are the trade press and exhibitions. However, one key aspect for engineers and technologists is competitive product analysis and retro-engineering. A contract manufacturer of supermarket own-label brands will track the technical developments of the brand market leaders. Retro-engineering will enable them to copy the new product type, subject to any intellectual property restrictions (e.g. patents).

Internal data

To control the value chain, relevant information will be collected for internal management needs. However, some of this information is also of value for marketing decisions (e.g. EPOS data – see below). Sales trends indicate how well different lines are performing. A specific area of interest to engineers and technologists are customer complaints. These are often not a result of defective products but of customers using products in a way not originally expected by the development team. This may point out an opportunity for product improvement or even new product development.

Computer systems

For consumer products, electronic point of sale (EPOS) and electronic data interchange (EDI) revolutionised marketing. The foundation of this was bar coding and radio-frequency identification tags will move the possibilities still further. Linking this data with other inputs (e.g. loyalty cards) can sharpen up marketing effort.

Collection

Manual data collection is subject to human error. Electronic data collection systems are very error resistant (e.g. self-checking algorithms in processing bar code numbers can detect read errors). Further refinements on product tracking will be possible with RFID tags. Customer behaviour can be tracked with loyalty and credit card use. Mobile telephone companies even know where their customers are at any given moment. Ever increasing effort is going into more effective and efficient data capture, such as self check-in at airports, online ordering, and the like.

Storage

Once data is collected, it needs to be effectively and efficiently stored, which is why database management is so crucial. Such storage must be legal (e.g. in line with data protection legislation) and secure (both to hacking and data loss).

Analysis

One key capability of good computer information systems is to link data threads. The past purchasing behaviour of a given customer can be linked to a new product launch to direct a tailored promotional effort. It may be necessary to clean-up/adjust (not distort) data to ensure that like is compared with like. An expanding company may be increasing its number of sales outlets. In considering how effective the marketing is, stores often give annual trends on a like-for-like basis, where account is taken to adjust for the increasing number of outlets. The whole range of statistical techniques can be appropriate according to the circumstances. Typical applications are model building, times series analysis and analysis of variance.

Communication

Information is just like any other product; it is only of value if it is available at the right time and in the right place. In the supermarket, the EPOS data is the feed into the B2B communications driving the supply chain. JIT manufacturing and good MRP all rely on good clean data, rapidly communicated. However, it should be noted that the process needs to be selective and the information needs to be relevant; it can be easy to overload people with irrelevant data.

SWOT analysis

The process of completing an analysis of the macro- and microenvironment provides an explosive amount of information. Even after the application of the 'So what?' test, there can be a daunting mass of data. The suggested spreadsheet approach, with the flexibility to apply weighting factors, provides a way to review the research. The purpose of the SWOT (strengths, weaknesses, opportunities and threats) analysis is to identify the key issues that confront the business and determine the strategic imperatives. Some years ago in the UK, Marks & Spencer were losing market share and profitability was disappointing. The range of fashion products was not seen to be appealing and consumers considered them overpriced. M&S addressed these issues and has now regained its position as a star performer in the high street.

Strengths and weaknesses are internal to a company. However, they need to be linked to the external environment by benchmarking. If an engineering company has reduced costs by 20%, this may be perceived as strength. However, if the new competition is from China, with costs that are 50% less, then the cost structure is a weakness.

Opportunities and threats are external to the company. An expanding market for flat-screen TVs is an opportunity for a company manufacturing them. It is a threat to a company whose products are based on cathode-ray tube technology. Any element of the macro- and microenvironment may provide opportunities or threats.

The SWOT analysis is not a mechanical process. There is no simple formula for you to just plug the numbers into and out comes the single right answer. It is necessary to bring professional judgement and vision to the process. The SWOT analysis is a snapshot in time and a view must be taken as to how factors are developing. This applies not only to the external environment (e.g. projection of energy costs) but also to the internal environment (e.g. for a car manufacturer to develop energy efficient hybrid technology engines). The aim is to reduce weaknesses or even to develop the organisation's value chain to provide strengths. If the organisation takes the right adaptive actions, threats can be opportunities. High costs of production in Europe were a threat to Dyson. By moving to lower cost production areas, the weakness was converted into a strength; a threat became an opportunity. The SWOT analysis should be viewed as a dynamic model (Figure 2.11). The strategies and management actions that must be taken become the imperatives for the development of the organisation – SWOT has moved on from analysis to: 'This means that the key issues are a, b and c and the resulting actions are x, y and z'.

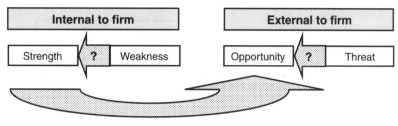

Figure 2.11 Dynamic SWOT.

The marketing plan

The environmental analysis outlined above provides the context in which the organisation operates. It does not in itself define what the organisation should be. This is defined by the managers and owners of the organisation and is often expressed as the mission, aims and objectives of the firm. These provide the sense of direction. A ship moving through a changing pattern of tidal currents may need to change heading to remain on course. Without a firm vision of the intended direction, there can be a move into strategic drift, where the organisation is moving to little purpose. Just as a ship may have to run a number of legs to complete a journey, a firm may, from time-to-time, review the mission, aims and objectives. Hewlett-Packard was founded on the supply of electronic instrumentation; it is now a computer and printer company.

Figure 2.12 provides an overview of the marketing planning process. The process looks linear and one off. This is not true. There are feedback/feed-forward loops and the process should be regarded as dynamic. A change in the environment may need the company to completely re-evaluate its mission aims and objectives. Kodak faced this with the impact of the digital camera. The BBC is reinventing 'broadcasting' in the age of the podcast and the digital download.

The mission statement should be a relatively short statement of what the organisation is – its values and its interaction with key stakeholders. Good mission statements have to be believable and the key that stakeholders must buy into. Otherwise, the statement is simply spin with no substance. A focus on what benefits the company provides rather than the internal mechanical processes is suggested. In the twentieth century, control might involve hydraulic and pneumatic systems with relays and mechanical control systems. The same company would now base its products on digital technologies. A music publisher may want to bring the best music to its customers. Technology has moved on from the vinyl disk to the CD and now on to direct digital access. The core benefit of providing entertainment has not changed; the vehicle for delivery has, and organisations must adapt or die.

The aims indicate the direction in which the organisation wants to move. These provide a general purpose but do not provide enough detail to control a plan. The aims need to be amplified into SMART (specific, measurable, aspirational, realistic and time-bound) objectives:

- **Specific** *'We aim to grow the company next year'* does not help operational management enough. *'We will launch product X within 11 months'* does provide the clarity needed.

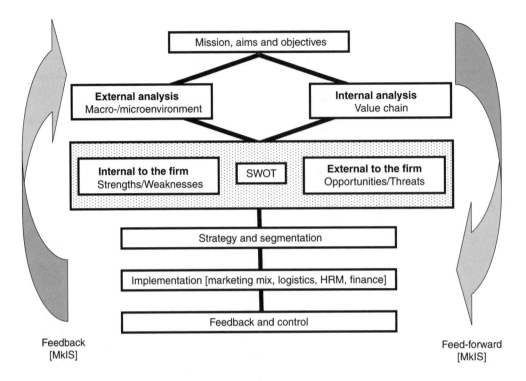

Figure 2.12 The marketing planning process. Adapted from: Curtis, T., *Marketing in Practice*, figure 11.2, page 265, © Elsevier 2006. Reproduced by permission.

- **Measurable** If reasonably practical, the objective should be framed in numeric terms, such as: *expansion by X% or by £Y*. Where it is not possible to put a numerical standard, some attempt should be made to indicate the level. *'I intend to learn German next year'* is rather general. *'Do I want to attain a sufficient level to order a meal in a restaurant, to conduct a business conversation or to be able to write a novel in German?'* provides an indication of the standard.
- **Aspirational** This term is sometimes criticised. The philosophy is that 'easy' objectives do not provide the motivation to move the organisation on in a competitive world. However, there is a window of opportunity. If the objectives are unrealistically high then they are seen as spin and have no credibility.
- **Realistic** This is a continuation of the issue from above. There must be sound foundation to the expectation that the objectives are achievable and this sound foundation must be accepted by all the key stakeholders involved in helping the organisation achieve those objectives.
- **Time-bound** Objectives that have no time limit tend never to be achieved. The company will launch the new system next month, next year or never? For complex projects, a series of milestones may be used. For the new product launch: design complete in two months, prototype testing complete in six months and launch in ten months, etc.

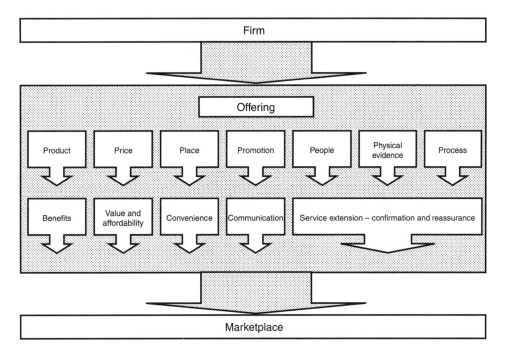

Figure 2.13 The marketing mix.

A key activity of marketing is developing the marketing mix and Figure 2.13 provides this focus. Although this is a principal role of marketing, it must be conducted in the context of all the other elements of the value chain. The launch of a new product is not going to be successful if sufficient components and materials have not been bought and production quality not assured.

The actual operation of the plan against intended standards and the changing external and internal environments are monitored through the organisation's marketing information system. The only thing certain about a plan is that it is unlikely to run 100% as expected. Just as the aircraft autopilot continually monitors deviations and makes adjustments, the company must continually adjust plans in response to business turbulence. This is why it is vital to build objectives into the plan. To run a control system you need to know what the desired set points are. Without set reference points you do not have a control system. How do you know whether you have arrived if you do not know where you are going?

The marketing mix

In the construction of a building, it can be convenient to consider the aspects of construction under various headings and different contractors may be involved with these different aspects (e.g. foundations, ventilation and air conditioning, etc.). These aspects must be integrated into a coherent whole to satisfy the client (a great building with a leaky roof is not acceptable). Marketers have, for convenience, divided up the offering made in the marketplace into seven elements: product, price, place, promotion, people, physical evidence and process (Figure 2.13). In the first development of the model only the first four Ps were proposed. However, it was found that these did not provide the full dimensions needed in the provision of services. The last three Ps are known as the service extension to the marketing mix. In the original formulation of the model it was thought useful to have each element starting with the letter 'P'. However, this is unfortunate as some of the 'P' words do not accurately reflect the true nature of the mix element.

Product

People do not want products. Too specific a focus on product can completely bypass the actual needs of the customer and consumer. This is clearly demonstrated in the consumer electronics market. The customer does not want a 32-bit, x gigahertz processor, etc. The customer wants an entertainment system: the hardware is the vehicle that provides the benefit – 'entertainment'. In 2007, portable CD players dropped out of the price index basket and were replaced with MP3 players. A full analysis of the nature of product is given in Chapter 4.

Price

In the construction of a cash flow spreadsheet, an accountant will ask what the selling price will be. Customers may ask for the price as an input to their purchase decision. However, it is not helpful in marketing to focus simply on price. We have noted before, customers want to experience benefits and products are the vehicle to provide the benefit. There are two essential factors from the customer viewpoint:

- Is the benefit value such that the price looks reasonable to the customer?
- Does the customer have the ability to pay the price – i.e. is the product (benefit) affordable?

If the answer to either of these two questions is 'no', then we will not have a sale. In the case of product, the marketer should focus on benefit. In the case of price, the marketer should focus on value and affordability. Chapter 5 provides an analysis of the nature of price in the marketing mix.

Place

This is a most unfortunate word and does not properly indicate the nature of this element of the marketing mix. Customers do not necessarily want to experience 'place', they want convenience. In fact for some services the word 'place' does not have any real physical meaning. For a mobile telephone user, convenience has two practical elements: cover and capacity.

- What is the coverage of the provider? Does my signal drop out as soon as the train speeds into the countryside?
- In the middle of a busy airport is there sufficient capacity?

Chapter 6 provides an analysis of the nature of 'place' in the marketing mix.

Promotion

This is an even more unfortunate choice of word because in marketing it has an ambiguous meaning. Promotion can be used as the label for the marketing mix element 'marketing communications'. However, it has a second meaning: 'sales promotion' (e.g. money-off offer). This is one element of the marketing communications mix, which includes other tools such as advertising and public relations. In reading marketing textbooks, you should check that you have identified the intended meaning. The details of marketing communications are covered in Chapter 7.

Service extension

The service extension to the marketing mix involves people, physical evidence and process. Services are covered in more detail in the next chapter. However, there is one key aspect of service worth mentioning at this stage: service often has elements of intangibility. When you attend a concert, you leave with happy memories. Memories are intangible: you do not have 10 kilos or 20 litres of memories. To provide indications of the nature and quality of a service, the service extension provides confirmation. Just as attractive packaging provides a pointer to the nature of the contents, the service extension of the marketing mix provides evidence where there is no physical product to convey the message. Full coverage is given in Chapter 8.

People

You can study for a MBA at a provincial university for less than £10,000 a year. However, to study at one of the top 10 international business schools will cost much more. There are not more hours of study – why, then, the cost difference? At a provincial university, the teaching staff will read and hopefully understand the textbooks to teach their subjects, whereas at an aspiring top 10 business school some of the teaching staff may write the books and at a top ten business school you will expect to learn from the people who have invented the subject and collected their Nobel prizes. The star quality of the service providers adds to the perceived value of the service.

Physical evidence

For a romantic evening you are not likely to go to the local 'greasy spoon' but to a 'posh' restaurant. In the 'posh' restaurant you do not get an extra kilo portion of soggy chips as a side order. In the 'greasy spoon' you will be lucky to get a paper napkin on the plastic table-top. In the 'posh' restaurant you will have crisp napkins on the tablecloth with sparkling glasses. Part of the eating experience comes from the physical surroundings. These provide the physical evidence and lay the foundations of a great evening (so long as the food lives up to expectations when it arrives).

Process

In the student refectory you will be happy to queue at a self-service counter for your food. For our romantic evening in the 'posh' restaurant we will expect attentive service from the waiting staff and our glasses discreetly topped up. It is not that one service is better than another but that the service is appropriate to that which is desired and expected in that context. At an expensive hotel full service will be expected for dinner. However, for that quick breakfast (in the same restaurant) at 7.00 a.m. before dashing to the airport, a self-service buffet is often provided. If you have the horror of a 5.30 a.m. checkout, a continental room service tray is fully acceptable.

Implementation and integration

The best marketing plans will not work if the other elements of value chain do not work well. Integrated consideration of the issues is vital. Three key aspects of integration are: (1) *logistics*, (2) *human resources management* and (3) *finance*.

Raw materials and components must be sourced. The products must be made and then delivered to the customer, with the required quality and at the required time. No matter how sophisticated the systems and equipment, the delivery of service depends on the quality of the people; their skills, motivation and values. All this would be comparatively easy if the organisation had infinite resources but, in a competitive world, this must be achieved cost effectively. The most motivated staff will soon get disenchanted if they do not get paid. Cash is the lifeblood of a company and if the organisation runs out of cash, then it is dead.

Logistics

There is a chain of supply that must be managed to provide effective delivery to customers and users. Many companies provide 'turnkey' computer systems for specialist users (e.g. solicitors, medical centres, etc.). The company provides the hardware, software, installation, training and maintenance of the system. The company must not only ensure that its own value chain is effective and efficient but that it links well with partners in the total supply chain. Further discussion of these issues is given in Chapters 4, 6, 14 and 15.

Human resources management

It is people who make the value chain work. The organisation must attract and recruit suitable staff. They must be trained and motivated, and they expect to be rewarded for all this effort. In most cases, people are not able to achieve their own, or the company's objectives, by their own efforts. Goods and services are delivered by teams, often working on a project basis. The people aspects are developed in Chapters 8, 11, 12 and 13.

Finance

It is not the intention in this book to cover the details of accountancy and tax planning. This is rightfully the area for the full-time expert accountant. However, all managers must be aware of the impact of their actions on cash flow and profitability. Some of the decisions are not easy. Estimating the cost of production next year is more than just entering a few numbers into a spreadsheet model. Considered estimates must be made of future materials and other costs, how much can be sold and the price that the market might accept. Technical staff do not have to become tax consultants but they do need to be financially literate. Key aspects of the financial impacts on marketing plans are given in Chapters 5, 10 and 16.

Review

In this chapter we have considered how the engineer and technologist must review the context of the organisation covering the macroenvironment, the microenvironment and the internal environment.

The STEEPLE tool provides the framework for analysing the macroenvironment. The concepts of market segmentation and stakeholders, together with the five forces of competition model, provide the framework for analysis of the microenvironment. The augmented value chain provides the means to analyse the internal environment.

To complete this process, the business analyst needs information. The nature of the information required was considered with the three investigative approaches: research, intelligence and internal information. This process is explosive in providing a potentially vast amount of data. We have considered how, by the use of SWOT analysis, this information can be distilled down to focus on the key imperatives facing the organisation.

All this analysis needs to be converted into action. The structure of the marketing plan leads us to the development of the market offering, the extended marketing mix – consisting of product, price, place, promotion, people, physical evidence and process. The need for this offering (marketing mix) to be integrated with other elements of the augmented value chain was noted.

In the next chapter we consider some of the current issues in marketing management. We have already started to discuss B2C (business to consumer) and B2B (business to business) marketing and the chapter concludes with a review of a number of different contexts that may confront the engineer or technologist.

Further reading

Chelsom, J., Payne, A. & Reavill, L. (2005) *Management for Engineers, Scientists and Technologists*, 2nd edn, John Wiley & Sons.

Johnson, G. & Scholes, K. (2005) *Exploring Corporate Strategy*, 7th edn, Prentice Hall.

Lynch, R. (2005) *Corporate Strategy*, 4th edn, Pearson.

Porter, M. (1980) *Competitive Strategy: Techniques for Analyzing Industries and Competitors*, The Free Press.

Porter, M. (1985) *Competitive Advantage: Creating and Sustaining Superior Performance*, The Free Press.

Wilson, R. & Gilligan, C. (2005) *Strategic Marketing Management: Planning Implementation and Control*, 3rd edn, Elsevier.

CHAPTER 3

Contemporary issues and contexts in marketing

Learning objectives

After studying this chapter you will be able to:

- Describe the implications of consumerism and the 'Kennedy rights' for marketing, apply the green marketing mix and appraise the ethical issues to be considered in the development of a marketing plan.
- Explain the major characteristics of consumer marketing, review the differences between the marketing of products versus services, explain the application of the service-extended marketing mix and compare and contrast the approaches to business-to-business marketing and business-to-consumer marketing.
- Describe the difference between transaction and relationship marketing approaches and understand how internal marketing can help in the management of internal stakeholders.
- Extend the application of STEEPLE and competition analysis to international market situations and evaluate methods of entry for different international market situations.
- Compare and contrast the issues in social and not-for-profit marketing with those of consumer marketing, describe the social marketing process, illustrate the special characteristics of entertainment marketing and review approaches to marketing on a limited budget.

Introduction

The basic laws of chemistry, physics and engineering do not change with the time of day. However, a key skill for the technologist is to know how to interpret and adapt the application of basic theory within given specific contexts. Figure 3.1 shows a basic electrical circuit where there is a capacitor and an inductive coil in parallel. Under DC steady state conditions, the capacitor element of the circuit will provide an infinite resistance and the inductive coil will provide a low resistance (due to the intrinsic resistance of the wire but with no contribution from the inductive properties). If we replace the DC input to the circuit with a 1 MHz radio-frequency AC input, the capacitor element of the circuit will provide a very low resistance and the inductive element of the circuit a very high resistance. The

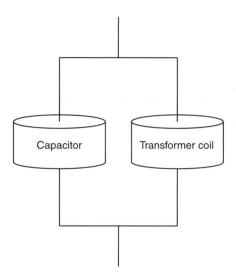

Figure 3.1 Electrical circuit under DC and radio-frequency AC conditions.

fundamental laws of physics have not changed, but, under different conditions, the application of the laws produces different results.

The same is true in marketing. Selling a cola drink costing pence to millions of customers is very different to selling a nuclear power station costing billions of pounds to a national energy utility. In this chapter we consider a selection of key marketing contexts: consumer (B2C) marketing, services marketing, business-to-business (B2B) marketing, relationship marketing, internal marketing, international marketing, not-for-profit and social marketing, entertainment marketing and limited budget marketing. For each of these contexts, different aspects of the tools and theory of marketing can become more or less important.

These different aspects of marketing are considered in the context of some important current issues in contemporary marketing (Figure 3.2). In the mid-twentieth century, radio-frequency emissions from cars were a source of interference with analogue TV signals, which was an irritation. However, today, electromagnetic interference with an engine management system when a car is travelling at 70 mph on the motorway, would very certainly be more than a mere inconvenience. In the twenty-first century, manufacturers of electrical and electronic equipment must ensure that such items do not emit excessive amounts of potentially damaging electromagnetic radiation. Manufacturers of safety-critical electronic systems must build interference resistance into their systems. Such issues would never have occurred to a nineteenth century engineer developing the first generation of electric trains. The same is true of marketing – the issues and contexts change with time.

Consumerism, environmentalism and ethics are three contemporary issues that are of vital concern to marketers. Textile scientists are now concerned with how green and how ethically sourced their cotton is. Customers not only want 'easy care' fabrics with exciting colours and finishes, but also want reassurance that their shirt has been produced from non-GM cotton, grown in an environmentally responsible way, without the inappropriate use of child labour.

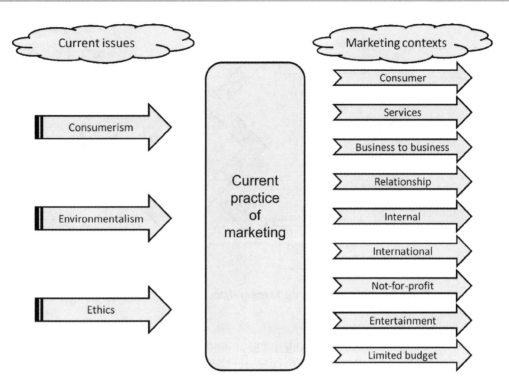

Figure 3.2 Current issues and contexts of marketing.

Consumerism

Two views of marketing have been proposed by some writers. One view of marketing is that all the ills of current society are the results of consumer marketing. The other view is that: 'We've never had it so good'. We jet off to 'dream' holiday destinations and text images back to our friends in real time. We are more aware of green issues through skilful marketing by pressure groups, thereby making the world a better place. The foundation of modern society is based on marketing. As with all 'political' issues, selective citation of examples will 'prove' the case.

The view advanced in this textbook is that both views are based on false premises. The premise is that marketing is moral or immoral (according to the standpoint of the observer). This is nonsense since theories of mathematics, science, engineering and technology have no 'ethics'. What is done with them may have positive or negative implications but, in and of themselves, theories are simply theories. Only people can have ethics. A scientist, a mathematician, an engineer or a technologist may have ethical views; theory is ethically blind. A GPS system can be used to target an atom bomb to kill millions or to provide safe navigation for ships and aircraft.

Many professional people in the UK context will be considered to have gained full professional status when they become chartered and the same is true for chartered marketers. Chartered professionals undertake to conduct their work with due regard to society, in a

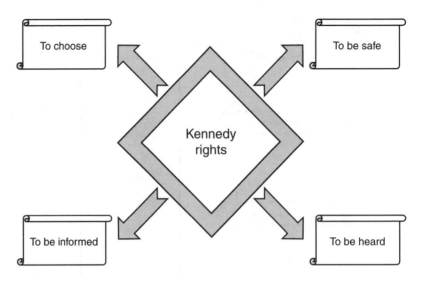

Figure 3.3 Consumerism – the Kennedy rights.

socially responsible fashion. The 'Kennedy rights' (Figure 3.3) provide a framework for the technological marketer to consider the issues.

The four 'Kennedy' rights are: (1) *to be safe*, (2) *to be able to choose*, (3) *to be informed* and (4) *to be heard*. People want to live their lives safely and do not expect to be injured by the use of products or services. People want to exercise choice: 'If I am a vegetarian I want to have a meat-free lunch in a restaurant. It is impossible to exercise choice unless I am given appropriate information.' Some years ago, a burger chain stated that their 'French fries' were vegetarian friendly. However, they used 10% beef fat in the oil to give the 'French fries' flavour. Vegetarian customers were less than delighted when the news escaped. Some 50 years ago when the 'rights' were postulated, consumers had modest practical ways to be heard. With the internet and various forms of 'blogging', consumers can now bite back if they are not happy. They can be heard around the world by millions.

To be safe

The technical manager must apply life-cycle analysis to products and services produced by the firm. The normal elements of life-cycle analysis (production, use and disposal) must be considered and all aspects of the supply chain (reviewed in Chapter 2) considered. We are not allowed to export or ignore danger. If we import raw materials such as coal, we must be assured that it has been produced by workers extracting it under international safety standards. Products must be produced safely. There is an old English saying 'Mad as a hatter'. In the nineteenth century, mercury compounds were used in the manufacture of straw hats and the description refers to the symptoms of mercury poisoning. A milestone in the development of the nineteenth century UK trade union movement was the 'match girls' strike'. Young women were employed in the manufacture of matches, which included elemental phosphorus in the formulation. The young women were not only badly paid but could suffer a disfiguring disease called 'phossy-jaw'.

The original development of the consumer movement began when people became concerned that dangerous products were being sold. Recently, a major chocolate manufacturer discovered its products had suffered microbiological contamination but decided, at one stage, the risk was 'acceptable'. Once the facts were revealed to consumers, the product was recalled and later the company faced prosecution.

Care must be taken in the disposal of products. The disposal of refrigerators is regulated for environmental reasons. However, they can also provide a safety issue if disposed of illegally. Cases have occurred where refrigerators have been 'fly tipped' into a public place where children play. An ever-inquisitive five-year-old can find this a fascinating opportunity to play hide and seek. The consequences when the lock clicks shut, with the child inside, are fatal. A very specific situation is the disposal of 'sharps' (contaminated used syringes, scalpels, etc.) in the context of a hospital. Further treatment of life-cycle analysis is given in the next section and Chapter 4.

To choose

When there is a shortage of products, we have to take what we can get. When Ford started to manufacture cars, you could have any colour you liked, as long as it was black. (It is said this colour was selected because the paint dried quicker.) A 'standard' modern car such as the Ford Fiesta has several thousand variants (number of paint finishes and colours × interior trim colours × transmission options × engine options, etc.). We have entered the age of mass customisation rather than mass production. People have cultural and lifestyle concerns. Many religions have dietary requirements. In the UK, people will pay a premium for free-range eggs laid by 'happy hens'. These are deeply held convictions and people have a right to observe their religious, cultural and lifestyle convictions.

To be informed

A major concern with consumer groups is 'confuseopoly', where information is provided in such a way that a person needs a degree to make any sense of it. A typical example is: 'what is the best credit card option?' The APR is only part of the story: to factor in all the options (credit transfers, interest-free periods, penalty payments, etc.), you need an accurate projection of all your transactions and a decent spreadsheet program to analyse the figures (a PhD in economics is also handy). What consumers and their representative pressure groups want is *transparency* – in short, 'what you see is what you get'. A public relations spin-doctor may think it is a great idea to emphasise that a breakfast food is 'healthy' because it is fat free. However, this will backfire when people realise the product is full of 'empty calorie' sugar, laced with a high dose of salt and spiced up with a good selection of artificial additives, preservatives and colouring. People want clear, 'plain English' information about the product or service offering and do not want to have to buy a microscope to read 10 pages of gobbledegook legalese in tiny print.

To be able to choose, people need information. To adhere to religious dietary requirements, consumers need to know the nature of the food they are eating. This may not be as simple as it looks at first sight. It is easy to spot the difference between a leg of pork and a fillet steak. However, consider glycerol, which can be used in some soap formulations. Glycerol is made by the saponification of animal fats as part of the process of soap manufacture and pork fat is one possible source. If people want to avoid the possibility of using pork-derived products, they should avoid products with glycerol in the formulation (or know the precise source and manufacturing process). As well as content, many consumers are also concerned with origin and process in relation to issues such as 'cruelty free' cosmetics (no animal products or animal testing), free range, organic and fair trade.

It is upsetting for a vegetarian to discover bits of bacon in their side salad but they are unlikely to die. However, a person with an allergy to nuts may die if they use or consume a product without knowing that it contained nuts. The introduction of new labelling regulations in the EU Cosmetics Directive was specifically aimed at providing more comprehensive information to enable consumers to avoid products containing ingredients that cause them physical or medical problems. It is important that organisations provide full and accurate information to their stakeholders. Lack of information may be taken to imply that the organisation has something to hide. Toll-free information lines and good websites can augment the limited information that can be given on a label. The provision of regulatory information is a major technical/legal activity in the quality assurance activities of pharmaceuticals, food and cosmetics companies, (e.g. REACH (Registration Evaluation Authorisation Chemicals), EU Cosmetics Directive, etc.).

To be heard

The Body Shop built up a very loyal base by involving and listening to customers. Now 'cruelty free' cosmetics are mainstream. It has always been important for organisations to communicate with their stakeholders. However, this has now become vital. The internet allows a single disgruntled customer to blog to the world. Communication is a two-way process. All engineers know that to control a system you need feedback. Listening to customers is a key aspect of marketing communications. The internet is not only a way for companies to flow information out but it also allows comments to flow into the organisation. In Chapter 7, the personal selling process is reviewed. The key skill, the foundation of good selling, is not being a fast talker but, rather, a good listener. How do you know what the customers want if you do not listen to them? Environmental issues have risen up the customer agenda and, hence, green marketing is covered in the next section.

MICRO CASE STUDY   **EUROPEAN UNION COSMETICS DIRECTIVE**

A small number of the population are allergic to some products they can encounter in everyday life (e.g. nuts for an allergy sufferer). Some people show an allergic reaction to some perfumery chemicals (both natural and synthetic). Dermatologists can check what chemicals a person is allergic to with skin patch tests. Over a number of years, a 'hot list' of the chemicals that tested positive most often was compiled. One of the features of the EU Cosmetics Directive was to ensure that fashion fragrances and other perfumed products gave information on ingredient materials so that people who had allergies could avoid their 'problem' chemicals. This was a major problem for the aroma trades industry, since many of these products occurred in natural essential oils (e.g. eucalyptus, orange oil, turpentine oils, etc.) and a considerable amount of analytical knowledge was necessary to determine if a given chemical exceeded the threshold limit and needed to be declared – one chemical could come from several different natural essential oils. Below is a brief review of the situation using the 'Kennedy rights' framework:

Right to be safe: sensitive people have an adverse reaction and need to avoid chemicals that give them an allergic reaction.

Right to choose: people with an allergic reaction want to select products that do not contain their 'problem' materials.

Right to be informed: to exercise their right to avoid their problem materials, they need labelling information, declaring what potential problem materials the product contains. The Cosmetics Directive provides a framework of regulation such that manufactures have to provide information on potential problem materials that exceed the statutory threshold limits.

Right to be heard: people who have concerns will lobby and can use blogs to express their views about 'dangerous' perfumes.

Note The law of unintended consequences became a problem. Well-informed and technically literate managements understood the Kennedy rules and that the aim of the regulation was to give information to a small proportion of the population with an allergy problem. They simply changed the labels (e.g. fine fashion fragrances where a perfume containing lemon oil will now have to explicitly list citral and limonene (naturally occurring in lemon oil) as being in the perfume). Some less well-informed managements demanded 'allergen free' fragrances and demanded that offending chemicals be removed. This put the pressure on to reduce the use of the natural essential oils so beloved of aromatherapists.

Environmentalism and green marketing

Earlier generations of technologists and engineers set out to tame and harness nature. Conspicuous consumption without consideration of the outcomes and fractured technology provided the route for a range of disasters such as polluted rivers, the disappearance of the Aral Sea and Chernobyl. The attitude was that we owned the world when, in fact, we have it in trust for future generations and continuation of past technologies and policies will provide a barren bequest. Organisations must 'green' their operations and marketing mix; they must move from token light green to committed dark green values (Figure 3.4).

This process provides the foundations for green success:

- the sustainability of the company's operations and marketing mix (the oil will run out – it is not a question of 'if' but 'when'
- the safety of the company's operations and marketing mix
- the social acceptability of the company
- green stakeholder satisfaction

Green science has identified a range of problems and predictions are being made about the outcomes. Greenhouse gasses such as carbon dioxide and methane are warming the world; forecasts have been made about how much sea level will rise and the rate at which this change will occur as a consequence. This effect may have been partially masked by global shading. The surface temperature of the USA increased slightly after 9/11 as a result of the disappearance of high altitude vapour trails (all flights were suspended). The

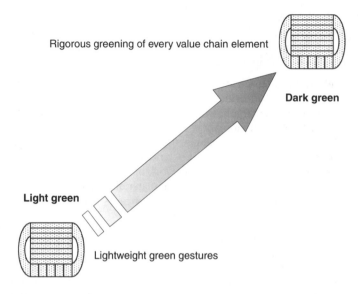

Figure 3.4 The greening of organisations.

release of stable chlorine compounds (e.g. CFCs) is causing problems in upper atmosphere chemistry with the depletion of UV shielding ozone. Though such emissions are now largely eliminated, it will take many decades for normality to be restored. The reverse problem occurs in the atmosphere at ground level. The conjunction of volatile organic compounds (VOCs), nitrous oxides (from car emissions) and sunlight produces elevated levels of ozone and photochemical smog. The burning of sulphur-containing fuels such as oil and coal releases sulphur dioxide into the environment. This, taken together with elevated levels of carbon dioxide, can cause the pH of lakes and rivers to start to drop.

Rachel Carson started to spell out the problems of persistent organic pollutants (POPs) in her book *Silent Spring* published in 1962. The insecticide DDT does not break down in the environment and minute levels can be amplified up the food chain. Penguins were a long way away from mosquitoes, but DDT could be detected in their body fat. The Chernobyl disaster affected the production of lamb in Wales because grass contamination was such that radiation levels were unacceptable in lamb for a number of years.

The depletion of resources not only includes oil and minerals but also of water, with the paradox of rising sea levels and falling water tables inland. The problems extend into the biosphere with GM crops, depletion of the rain forests and the loss of species. These forces drive the green marketing process set out in Figure 3.5, which is adapted from Peattie & Rannayaka, M. (1992).

The green stakeholders pick up the green issues in the STEEPLE environment and bring pressure on organisations and society to change. In 2007, the Australian government announced it was to ban the sale of low-efficiency tungsten filament light bulbs. The implication for the marketer is to green the marketing mix. Products must be environmentally friendly (e.g. capable of being recycled) and made with minimum environmental impact. The organisation must find ways to fund the costs of these environmental policies and this may involve additional costs to customers. Governments may punish offenders with high taxes and provide incentives (e.g. subsidising green electricity generation) to accelerate

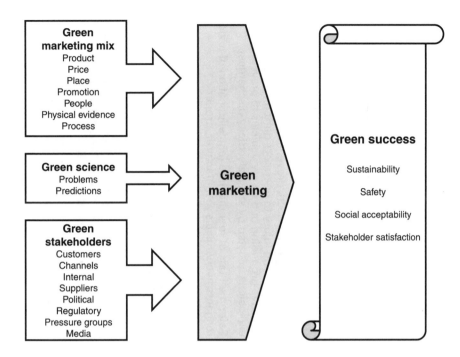

Figure 3.5 The architecture of green marketing. Adapted from: Peattie, K. & Rannayaka, M. (1992) Responding to the green movement, *Industrial Marketing Management*, 21 (2) 103–110, © Elsevier.

eco-friendly developments. The physical distribution of products should be energy efficient. However, a major challenge for some organisations is a need to have 'negative' distribution channels. Recent EU legislation is imposing a duty on manufacturers to have effective processes and facilities for the disposal of their products and packaging. Marketers have been used to selling products to people. Now, new ways will need to be found to collect obsolete products; dumping in landfill is not going to be an option. The service-extension elements are also affected. The whole effort depends on the eco-values of the company's staff. Physical evidence should be provided for green service provision and processes should be seen to be energy efficient. Table 3.1 provides a summary of some selected environmental and safety issues in an organisation's value chain and marketing mix.

Ethics

It takes decades to build up a reputation and just one ethical slip to ruin it. BP was one of the most respected companies in the world. However, when a catastrophic fire in a US facility resulted in casualties, the company's reputation suffered badly. The investigation revealed management gaps in safety and environmental policies. As in the earlier section on environmental issues, the value chain can be audited for ethical compliance. For instance, procurement should audit to ensure that suppliers have ethical policies, such as equal opportunity procedures. The marketer should review the marketing mix to ensure that this too reflects the ethical stance and values of the organisation.

Table 3.1   Augmented value chain and marketing mix: selected green and safety issues

Value chain element	Selected green issues	Selected safety issues
Primary activities		
Inbound logistics	Elimination of packaging (e.g. bulk deliveries) or recycling of packaging	Safe handling of products preventing damage to equipment and injury to operators during delivery (e.g. effective grounding of delivery vehicles to prevent explosions initiated by static electricity discharges)
Operations	Reduction of waste and use of energy-efficient processes	Safer methods of manufacture (e.g. elimination of toxic reagents in chemicals manufacture), proper maintenance and guarding of plant (e.g. drive belts and shafts)
Outbound logistics	Use of recyclable packaging. Minimisation of filling losses. Care in cleaning to ensure discharges are not polluted. Energy-efficient transport, well-routed	Full safety labelling and documentation. Appropriate transport fitted with appropriate safety features (e.g. pressure release valves on bulk tankers)
Sales	Green travel for field sales staff (e.g. bio-diesel cars)	Ensure appropriate driving hours for field sales staff (a legal necessity for HGV drivers, but tired driving is dangerous, whatever the vehicle)
Field service	Green travel for field service staff (e.g. bio-diesel cars). Make products more reliable so less servicing is required. Recycle spare parts	Full safety training and briefing, especially where external contract staff may be used for field servicing
Support activities		
Stance and strategy	Environmental leader	Safety seen as a priority that must not be overtaken by profit drives: 'Nothing is so urgent that it can't be done safely'
Safety, environment, quality and ethics	Effective environmental policies, procedures and manuals. ISO 9000 and ISO 14000 compliance	Effective safety policies, procedures (e.g. 'permit to work systems') and manuals.

Physical and financial structure	Physical infrastructure: energy efficient buildings (e.g. solar heating and natural ventilation in offices)	Proper protection of facilities (e.g. effective sprinkler systems in the event of fire)
Information systems	Data collection and evaluation of environmental performance (e.g. tracking energy efficiency)	Proper collection of data on 'near misses', not just injury-causing accidents
Human resources	Training and development of an eco-culture	Training and development of a safety culture
Technology development	Research to create a green marking mix and value chain	Research into safer ways of manufacture (e.g. automation to remove operators from potentially dangerous operations and materials)
Marketing	Green the marketing mix. Provide customers with recycling services	Clear communication of safety data. Restriction of sales to channels with appropriately trained staff and facilities
Procurement	Green audits of suppliers. Purchase from green accredited sources (e.g. Soil Association certified)	Good communications to ensure that all relevant safety information is communicated. Good clear safety documentation provided
Marketing mix element		
Product	Products made from sustainable and/or recyclable materials	Elimination of toxic materials (e.g. mercury-free batteries)
Price	Will customers pay an eco-premium?	Price levels must provide sufficient income to ensure proper training of channels
Place	Recyclable packaging or elimination of packaging with bulk deliveries. Channels developed for return of products and packaging for recycling	Proper training of channel staff. Audit channels to ensure they have appropriate facilities (e.g. storage of potentially dangerous materials)
Promotion	Eco-messages on eco-friendly media (e.g. recycled paper)	Clear safety communications (e.g. in gas distribution, an emergency phone line for leaks)
People	Eco-culture	Safety culture, appropriate protective clothing
Physical evidence	Eco-environment (e.g. in a farm shop, lots of wood rather than plastic)	A clean environment is a safe environment. Safety signage for field service operations
Process	Energy efficient processes	Safe marketing processes (e.g. appropriate tail lifts on vehicles to enable safe delivery processes)

Product

Claims for the product should be sustainable and satisfy the Kennedy rights criteria discussed earlier. This not only covers product performance but also ethical sourcing (sustainably grown wood, fair trade, organic, no use of child labour, etc.).

Price

Pricing policies should be transparent, with no hidden extras. This can be an area of considerable differences in perception. The pricing policies for Microsoft's 'Vista' can be seen as fair: premium pricing to recover a massive development investment. In the less-developed world, it can be seen as an example of American commercial imperialism, with high prices shamelessly exploiting a monopoly situation and reinforcing the 'digital divide' between the developed and less-developed nations. (In response to concerns about the digital divide, Microsoft announced in 2007 that they would sell some of their products at deeply discounted terms to the less-developed countries.) The 'Linux' open source code movement is, in part, a response to this cost of proprietary software. It will be interesting to see what proportion of PCs run on open source operating systems in 20 years' time.

The issue of intellectual property investment recovery through monopoly pricing (patent protection) is thrown into stark relief with AIDS drugs. The pharmaceuticals companies' case is that after spending vast sums of money to develop and test a drug treatment, they need high prices to recover these very substantial investment costs. A $ 10-per-day drug treatment may be fine in the USA and developed Europe but is prohibitively expensive in sub-Saharan Africa. The marginal cost of product may be comparatively low, with the company needing to recover large capital investments in R&D and testing. From the dying African AIDS patient's perspective, the high premium, over the marginal costs of production, does not appear so reasonable. Complex political agreements are attempting to 'square the circle' and allow more marginal cost-based pricing in less-developed countries.

The whole relationship between less-developed countries and the major pharmaceuticals companies is fraught with ethical complexity and ambiguity. The need in the free market model for pharmaceuticals companies to make profits directs companies to research the diseases of the rich (profitable patients). The diseases of the poor can go unresearched in this model. Charitable, not-for-profit organisations are attempting to plug this gap. Another intellectual property concern is 'intellectual colonialism'. The rainforests contain a whole medicine chest of novel drugs and these are researched by rich drug companies, which then patent their results. The indigenous populations of the rainforest area gain no profits and may find the resulting drugs too expensive for them to use.

Place

The treatment of channels and agents should be fair and consistent. 'Fair trade' polices may need to be considered when a major organisation is providing goods and services to small channels. Again, care should be taken to audit so as to check that channels are behaving ethically and safely. A particular problem exists for certain chemical, engineering and electronic products. These may be used to produce normal industrial and consumer goods but the same items can also be used to make illegal drugs and terrorist devices. This is a parallel problem to money laundering in financial services.

Promotion

As set out earlier in the 'Kennedy rights', all normal marketing communications must be true, sustainable and conform to good taste (a culturally relative term). The general rules in the UK context are set out by the Advertising Standards Authority.

Special considerations apply to specific technical segments. In the pharmaceuticals industry, there are major concerns that products should not be over-promoted and potential adverse reactions fairly reported. One mechanism of marketing communication is to sponsor research work, which is later published in the 'blue chip' academic journals. Concern has been expressed that editing pressures may have been applied in some circumstances, with favourable research promoted and discouragement of the reporting of negative findings. Some 'blue chip' academic journals are now concerned about potential conflicts of interest when sponsorship of an 'independent' research programme comes from commercial organisations. A difficult area is the partial funding of some patient pressure groups by pharmaceutical companies.

In the consideration of environmental issues, it was noted that there is now a need for 'negative' channels for the collection and recycling of products. A similar situation occurs with product recalls. Here, it is essential to get people not to buy, but to return defective and sometimes potentially dangerous products. Every ethically responsible company needs to have a disaster recovery plan that should cover product recall. This provision should include a 24/7/365 emergency helpline for the provision of urgent technical safety information. Typical examples are toxicology information for doctors (e.g. when a small child has drunk a household cleaner or when workers are exposed to a chemical in an accident) and environmental protection and safety data (e.g. after a spillage in a road accident).

People

The treatment of staff must be fair and consistent. Wal-Mart suffered considerable adverse publicity when it was considered to have unfair employment policies that discriminated against female employees. A very specific concern in the case of environmental, safety and ethical issues is the treatment of 'whistle blowers'. As the Enron case in the USA demonstrated, senior staff are not immune to temptation to commit criminal acts. There is a need for society to protect the brave individuals who take the lid off of unethical or unsafe corporate policies and procedures.

Physical evidence

The money spent on ethical, environmental and safety policies and procedures should not be regarded as a cost but as an investment. The organisation, having made this investment, needs to communicate this commitment. Ethical policies, just as with services, are in some ways intangible – you cannot say you have 23 kilos of ethical commitment. Companies should seek to demonstrate their commitment with signs and evidence. A company with good ethical employment policies may have gained the 'Investors in People' award, and be able to use the logo. Similar opportunities exist for 'organic' (Soil Association certification), 'fair trade' (Fair Trade Foundation), environmental (ISO 14000) and quality (ISO 9000) logos.

Process

The ethical value chain audit will ensure that the organisation's internal processes are sound. However, care must also be taken with the external processes. Recently, a major petrol station chain inadvertently provided a platform for identity theft. Bugged devices recorded the card numbers and miniature cameras caught the pin number entry. The reaction of the card companies was to tell customers that they should be 'card fraud savvy' and they should 'take care'. This did not play well with the financial consumer pressure groups that had been told that 'chip and pin' was going to solve credit card fraud.

A related issue is our electronic trail. As we make our transactions, there is an electronic record of our card purchases. Our mobile telephones tell the provider where we are. CCTV monitors our progress though the shopping centre. One view is that these developments provide us with better products and services and give us a more secure environment. An alternative view is that '1984' was a little premature but 'Big Brother' is with us and alive and well. We now have, potentially, a massive invasion of our privacy with possible infringement of our civil liberties.

No year will be complete without a 'shock-horror story' about poor and unfair service provision. A whole sub-set of reality television has grown out of its exposure. Poor service reflects badly on major brands. Car manufacturers need to ensure their agents are fully trained and do indeed complete the work they invoice. In the servicing of domestic appliances, the technophobic consumer may not be able to evaluate the quality of the repair but they can assess the damage from grease stains on the carpet. More consideration of service quality is given later in this chapter.

MICRO CASE STUDY   **ETHICAL MARKETING MIX FOR A PHARMACEUTICALS MANUFACTURER**

Pharmaceuticals companies operate in a fiercely competitive environment with considerable environmental turbulence. Below is an outline of some of the issues that a pharmaceuticals marketing manager might consider.

Product Are there genuine benefits to the new preparation or is it simply an expensive 'me too' of an existing remedy? Are the benefit claims sustainable with good science?

Price Is the price structure fair and reasonable?

Place Is full information provided to the agents and distributors, not only on benefits but also on potential adverse side effects?

Promotion Are the methods of promotion fair or are suspect incentives being given to prescribers to promote the product? Are marketing communications fair and honest? Is information on adverse reactions being withheld from the marketplace?

People In the event of adverse reactions, are appropriately experienced professional people available to give urgent medical advice? Are people, briefed to not 'oversell' the benefits of the product.

Physical evidence As the physical drug is involved with little direct field service, this aspect of the mix is not a major concern in this context. (Learning tip: do not over-work models).

Processes Are good processes in place should additional information and assistance be needed in the event of a problem, (e.g. accidental overdose)? Are there effective mechanisms for the reporting of adverse reactions by medical practitioners in the field?

Consumer marketing (B2C)

This is marketing as the general public know it. It covers the vast range of products and services that are a part of our daily life. It is in this sector that the science of marketing was originally developed and standard mainstream marketing texts devote the majority of their coverage to this area. However, this is rather like saying that computers were developed for accounting so we will only consider this and forget applications such as computer games, based on high-speed processors and high-definition flat screen displays. Marketing, as with the computer, has moved on from its original application into other areas. The sector covers a number of recognisable sectors including fast-moving consumer goods (FMCGs), durable goods and services.

FMCG marketing

A major supermarket may have over 20,000 lines. Most of these fall into the FMCG class. There is little need in a textbook to describe them; you experience them every day. We start the day by showering down and using a range of personal care and cosmetic products. We eat our breakfast, consisting of a range of branded foods and drinks. During the daytime we graze our way through the hours with snack foods (confectionery, savouries, etc.), and wash them down with a rage of drinks (mineral water, carbonated drinks, etc.). We use a range of products to keep our homes and clothes clean. (The word 'soap' in the TV context was coined because such programmes were originally sponsored by the fabric care companies.) As we watch our favourite TV programmes we are bombarded with exhortations to use the latest variant with new fresher fragrance and improved green specs.

Durable goods

We buy FMCG products regularly because we consume them. Durable products are products that we buy less frequently. Important areas are: clothing, electrical (for convenience taken to include electronic and computer products), entertainment goods (e.g. music, films, computer games on CD and DVD formats), furniture (including carpets and soft furnishings), white goods (refrigerators, freezers, washing machines, dish washers, cookers, etc.), equipment (cooking implements, DIY tools, etc.) and major capital goods (house, car, etc.).

Service products

In the less-developed world, where people have to survive on $1 a day, the major proportion of family expenditure is on food. In the post-industrial society of the developed world, the major proportion of family expenditure is not on goods but on services; these include:

- utility services (gas, electricity, water, refuse collection, etc.)
- communications services (telecommunications – traditional land line, mobile, e-mail, internet – and even snail mail)

- radio and TV (terrestrial, satellite, cable, internet)
- maintenance (car and appliance servicing, etc.)
- leisure and entertainment (tourism, sports, cinema, theatre, museums, theme parks, night clubs, home entertainment, digital downloads, etc.)
- eating out
- travel (taxi, bus, train, ferry, airlines, etc.)
- personal care (medical, gymnasium, health spa, etc.)
- financial services (mortgages, credit cards, banking, insurance, etc.)

More consideration of service products is given in the next section.

The key linking theme for consumer goods is that there are many millions of customers and that most communications messages are relatively simple, such as 'Drink more Coke and avoid that inferior Pepsi'. Communications messages can be more complex for high-involvement goods (e.g. home furnishing, fashion goods, computer games) and major complex purchases (e.g. house, car, etc.). The key communications channel for FMCGs and many other consumer products is mass advertising in all its variants. This area is developed in Chapter 7. Personal selling is important for high-involvement purchases.

Services marketing

The primeval foundations of marketing were laid down in the marketing of FMCGs such as detergents. These consumer items are almost pure 'product' and do not need much supporting service element. Other products such as washing machines (installation and maintenance) and cars (maintenance, insurance, financial services for purchase) need service elements. Some services such as insurance have very little product element (e.g. cover documentation) in their delivery to the average customer. The 26-hour flight to Australia is going to be a bit of an ordeal if there is no food and drink available. Services such as restaurants need products as part of their delivery to customers. One way of viewing the operation of a supermarket is as a shopping service. Is internet shopping a product or service? It is both. Figure 3.6 illustrates the product–service continuum. If you want to add value to a product, consider whether you can include service elements. If you want to add quality to a service, consider if it is appropriate to improve the product elements.

Academic marketers have identified five key differences between pure products and pure services: intangibility, inseparability, heterogeneity, perishability and ownership. Figure 3.7 outlines the differences between products and services marketing.

Intangibility

This is possibly the most important difference. When you buy a computer you can see it; it has weight; it is a physical entity. When you go to the doctors for a medical examination you do not take away 25 litres of diagnosis and 20 kilos of compassion. There is no physical

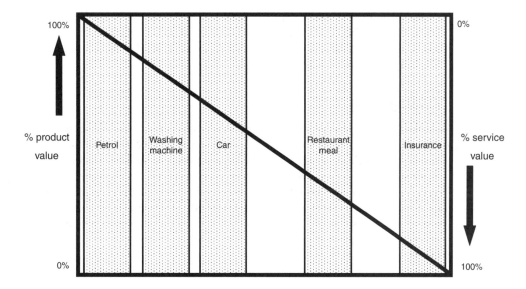

Figure 3.6 Product–service value continuum.

entity in the diagnosis. The purpose of the service-extended elements of the marketing mix is to provide physical confirmation of that which is intangible: the service.

Inseparability

Many services require us to bring the service provider and the consumer together (the age of the robotic hairstylist has yet to arrive). The mechanic and the car must come together for the car to be serviced. However, this aspect was given considerable weight in the original development of service marketing, which was before the internet age. An advanced laser photocopier/printer may have onboard intelligence and communications. This can make remote fault-finding and software upgrades an option. Internet shopping and internet banking allow us to enjoy these services without all the drag of the journey into town, with

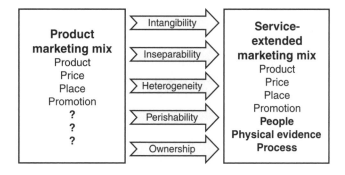

Figure 3.7 The differences between product and service marketing.

all the problems of parking. This rule is now better expressed as 'Often services need to bring the supplier and consumer together' since although many services need providers and consumers to come together, some such as e-marketing do not, which is changing the rules in some circumstances.

Heterogeneity

One of the foundations of the industrial revolution was the standardisation of items such as nuts and bolts. In the medieval age such things were craft manufactured and each item was hand-produced. A Whitworth nut made in the UK will fit a Whitworth bolt made on the other side of the globe. One characteristic of many services is that people are a key element in the provision. We have not yet entered the age of cloned restaurant waiters and diners. It should cause us little surprise that sometimes the fit is perfect and sometimes the fit is not. If it is a case of the latter, then the service encounter can be a disaster. This provides problems with the delivery and quality assurance of services. There is more discussion of this in Chapter 15.

Perishability

This is a major influence on the provision and delivery of services. Last night's empty table in the restaurant, empty room in the hotel or empty seat on a train or aircraft has no value. A key problem for the service provider is to match supply and demand. It is easy to fill a restaurant on Valentine's Day or the rooms in a city-centre business hotel midweek. The commercial imperative for the restaurant is to gain diners on a wet Wednesday lunchtime in the middle of winter. The business hotel may have theme events at weekends (e.g. a *Star Trek* convention) to fill up empty rooms with leisure customers rather than business people. This need to manage supply and demand is a major area of concern for technologists. Communications engineers must ensure there is sufficient bandwidth for peak demands and work with marketing to find background services to fill empty bandwidth in non-peak times. This is the classic network management problem that also faces utility engineers in the management of electricity, water and gas supplies. It is important for the technical and marketing staff to use the marketing mix to manage demand. Premium pricing can be used at peak times and incentives given for people to make use of the service at off-peak times.

Ownership

This is another facet of intangibility. When you have bought a product you have a physical object. After the honeymoon holiday, you do not own the hotel. The physical evidence element of the service extension of the marketing mix provides a mechanism to give some confirmation of the service. A typical example would be the rock concert souvenir sweatshirt.

Service marketing is not some special backwater of marketing. As a sector, it exceeds FMCG products in value by a large margin. The service extension of the marketing mix provides the tools to address the additional complexity of service marketing. This is covered in Chapter 8. The management of service quality is covered in Chapter 15. Service marketing is important in business-to-business marketing, which is discussed in the next section.

TECHNICAL TRAINING SERVICE

Below is an outline of selected marketing mix issues that might be considered by a company providing technical computer training from their own training facilities.

Product The benefit is imparting skills. For the employer, paying for the training, the outcome is a more skilled and effective (and hence more profitable) employee. For the employee, it is development of a personal skill base and increasing market worth (more pay?). Intangible aspects are involved such as increased self-worth and self-confidence.

Price Does the price match the 'going' rate? Is the pricing transparent or are there hidden extras? For residential courses, who will pay incidental expenses (e.g. bar bills) and how will these be settled?

Promotion Is the message clear and are key decision makers targeted effectively? Does the training organisation have a good brand perception in the marketplace?

People Are the trainers professionally competent in the computer technology? Are the trainers trained to train? (It is one thing to know; it is another to teach.) Are the trainers empathetic to participants' needs and concerns (e.g. fear of change on migrating onto a new system)?

Physical evidence Are the training manuals clear and well produced? Do participants get a professional-looking certificate of completion? Are the training facilities of an appropriate standard?

Process Are the training processes varied and appropriate? For instance, all lectures as an approach is not likely to work in the imparting of practical skills.

Business-to-business (B2B) marketing

No item gets onto the supermarket shelf without going through a B2B process. Procter & Gamble does not get millions of one pound coins for its detergents; it gets great fat cheques from Tesco, ASDA, etc. The supply chain structure, discussed earlier in Chapter 2, explains how there is a web of B2B activities, such as raw materials, components and services that are marketed up the supply chain. B2C marketing is the visible tip of the marketing iceberg. Down the supply chain is a vast labyrinth of marketing activity. In total, this activity exceeds the value of consumer marketing. The nature of B2B marketing differs from that of B2C marketing and this is reflected in the B2B marketing mix. A summary of these issues is given in Table 3.2.

Derived demand

For raw materials and components, the demand is driven by the ultimate demand for the consumer product. The manufacturer of aroma chemicals to fragrance detergents must study consumer trends with as much skill and interest as Unilever, Procter & Gamble and Tesco. A change in consumer tastes implies a changed balance in the range of aroma chemicals required. The environmental monitoring system of a company somewhere down the supply chain must monitor the environment for the *whole* supply chain. This will include the ultimate driving force – the domestic consumer. There are other issues down the supply chain that need monitoring. The maker of a fragrance containing orange oils will watch the

Table 3.2   Differences in B2B marketing compared with consumer marketing

Issue	Comments
Derived demand	Many industrial products have a derived demand depending on the supply chain from primary producer to consumer. If the price of chocolate is reduced, consumers may eat more. The number of gearboxes needed is fixed by the number of cars sold, so a 20% drop in the cost of gearboxes does not push up the demand
Stakeholders	Many consumer purchases are made on impulse: 'I feel thirsty; I will have a cola.' A car manufacturer sourcing a satellite navigation system for a new range of cars will have a fair number of stakeholders involved in the decision-making process – the decision-making unit (DMU)
Knowledgeable customers	The average car driver does not have a PhD in automotive engineering; a design engineer working for Ford may well have
Level of risk	If you do not like the new low-calorie cola, you have lost less than £1. If the gearboxes do not turn up, the automated car production line comes to a shuddering and very expensive halt
Segmentation	A different framework of segmentation is needed – e.g. type of industry, purchase process (commercial, public sector tender etc.), size of organisation and so on
Marketing mix	
Product	Products and services may be critical to the survival of the company. Branding is still important as it lowers perceived risk
Price	Terms of trade may be very different to cash over the counter for consumer purchases; 30 days' credit is normal for many business goods and services
Place	Often specialised delivery requirements (e.g. bulk deliveries) and tight delivery windows (e.g. JIT manufacture)
Promotion	Different range of stakeholders. Communications mix often different with more personal selling and less advertising
People	Professional staff required (e.g. a field engineer may visit two competing companies on the same day and must respect company confidentiality)
Physical evidence	Has a special place as some members of the DMU stakeholder group may not be in direct communication with the company
Process	The purchase systems and processes are often more complex. A supermarket may place its orders direct by EDI, driven by EPOS data. A major public sector construction project will be put out to competitive tender under strict rules

international weather reports like a hawk watches its prey. A hurricane or frost in Florida may halve the availability of Florida orange oil and drive the price up several hundreds of percent in a matter of days rather than weeks. The marketing information management system for a B2B company context needs to be functioning well or the firm will get caught out with changes that have an indirect impact through the supply chain. Although indirect, this impact can still have potentially disastrous results.

Stakeholders

At the fundamental level, there is nothing new to be considered here. As in every business situation, the need is to identify the stakeholders and manage the relationships. In the typical B2C FMCG purchase, the purchase may be made on impulse by an individual and the transaction completed in a few seconds. In the purchase of new carbon composite components for an aircraft in design development, there will be a range of people concerned with the purchase in the buying organisation. This situation is so important that marketers have given this group of customer stakeholders a special label, 'DMU' (decision-making unit), and have identified some standard roles (stakeholders) in this unit: initiators, users, influencers, deciders, approvers, buyers and gatekeepers. In the practical operation of this concept, it should be noted that one person can act in more than one role during the purchase process and negotiations. For complex purchase decisions, there may be a number of people active in the same role (e.g. a number of engineers evaluating the materials options for a new component).

Initiators

In the development of a highly complex industrial product, the initiator (in some marketing texts called the specifier) will typically be the design engineer or the formulation scientist. For manufacturers of OEM components or raw materials suppliers, a key marketing communication concern will be to build good relationships between technical support and the technical initiators in the client company. More consideration to this aspect is given in the section on relationship marketing later in this chapter.

Users

These are the actual users of the product or service. After the new product development (NPD) team have specified the component/material, production will need to know how to use the product. This may involve special requirements for deliveries and packaging. There may be special conditions for the application, (e.g. preparation of a surface for painting) or handling of the product, (e.g. grounding of staff handling microchips).

Influencers

These are the contacts of the inner core of the DMU who may not have a direct influence on the micromanagement of the purchase but set the purchasing climate. A key area is the climate in the company regarding environmental and ethical issues. For instance, the chief executive officer (CEO) who states that the company will go green and pursue fair trade sourcing may not be involved in the day-to-day negotiation of contracts for the purchase of raw cocoa but the corporate culture and values he or she engenders will certainly colour the attitudes of the core DMU members. In most cases the B2B supplying organisation will not be in direct contact with the influencers. This is why B2B organisations (e.g. suppliers of semiconductor components) still advertise and engage in brand building activities so as to influence the influencers.

Deciders

These are the people who actually make the final decision. They would typically be a NPD team leader (e.g. project engineer, senior formulation scientist, etc.). These people can also be part of the specifier group.

Approvers

The approver (in some texts called the authoriser) is the person who holds the budgetary authority and will 'sign off' the order. For major capital goods this will often be a member of the main board of directors (e.g. technical director).

Buyers

In most organisations there will be a buying department (purchasing and procurement are alternative names), which administers the day-to-day management of purchases. For small, routine, non-critical items, they may be the complete DMU (e.g. buying paper clips for a computer manufacturer). With increasing use of e-commerce, they may set up systems and arrangements that users then use to make their purchase directly over the internet (e.g. for business travel).

Gatekeepers

The individuals in the DMU are busy and are often senior staff. They could spend all their day talking to sales representatives but, if they did, they would not be effective managers. Companies have layers of protection – e.g. PAs (personal assistants), secretaries and receptionists – who guard the time of these key people. This is why communications opportunities when such staff are 'unprotected' by their time-guards form part of the B2B communications mix (e.g. presence at professional meetings, conferences and exhibitions).

Level of risk

If the TV blows up one weekend, this is irritating. If all the visual displays go down at a busy airport, this is a lot more than an irritation for passengers and staff: the airport grinds to a halt. A major manufacturer may have many hundreds of suppliers of goods and services. If any one of them fails to deliver, the operation faces shutdown. A service level of 99% for the supply of electrical power is not acceptable. The high cost of supply or quality failure makes the DMU very risk averse. It is important in the delivery of the product and in marketing communications, in the B2B context, to build the reputation for providing a secure and consistent service.

Segmentation

Segmentation needs to be reinvented and reinterpreted for B2B marketing. One segmentation variable for consumer markets is user status, usually expressed as non-user, occasional user, regular user and heavy user. In B2B marketing a variant of this is used in directing the marketing effort. In attempting to sell a product to a company it is this: a new buy (the item has never been purchased before), a modified rebuy (the same item but with new features – e.g. new release of Vista) or a straight rebuy (same item bought over and over again). In the case of a new buy, the marketer can expect full scrutiny from the members of the DMU stakeholders. For a straight rebuy situation, the purchase may be on autopilot (e.g. a supermarket purchasing a standard item via EDI). The modified rebuy provides an intermediate situation. Other segmentation variables include size, location, purchase rate, purchase systems, industry type, and criticality to end product and/or company operation.

Size

Typical structures might be: global (e.g. Microsoft), national (e.g. UK Railtrack), regional (a UK county council), local (e.g. a local university), SME (a small organisation with *under around* 100 employees), sole trader (e.g. technical author).

Location

A company may provide its products on a number of different geographic parameters: global, national, regional. Other types of geographic specification are also possible (e.g. city, countryside).

Purchase rate

What is the purchase rate and pattern of off-take? In the consumption of electricity, an aluminium smelter will have the power consumption of a town. A communications centre will have the same need for secure 24/7/365 supply but with a much reduced off-take. An international football stadium may have a fair demand, but only when a night game is on and the floodlights are in use. The utility companies have to provide secure supply at all times. However, other B2B suppliers may specialise on occasional event purchases (e.g. services for outdoor events such as floodlighting and sound systems for the Glastonbury festival).

Purchase systems

Different organisations have different policies, procedures and systems for buying. The sole trader has an effective DMU of one and can write the order there and then. For new capital purchases in a major organisation there will be a need to communicate with a complex DMU. A supermarket or a JIT manufacturer may consider the ability to call off orders electronically via EDI to be essential. Public institutions (e.g. trust hospitals) and defence purchases (e.g. Ministry of Defence) may have complex tendering processes.

Industry type

A company selling electronic equipment to hospitals and food processing firms may find that ease of cleaning and microbiological decontamination are an issue. The same supplier selling products for use on oil rigs may find corrosion resistance, intrinsic safety and resistance to dust and vibration critical parameters. A whole industry of VARs (value added resellers) exists who will provide turnkey computer systems for various different customer groups (e.g. a group medical practice, a busy firm of solicitors, a farm, etc.).

Criticality

Many of the products and services we use come from operations that are potentially very dangerous (e.g. coal mining, oil extraction, nuclear power station, blast furnace, etc.). Failure of a part of the plant could cause a catastrophic accident. The highest levels of quality assurance and ability to comply with GMP (good manufacturing practice), GLP (good laboratory practice) and other audits (e.g. ISO 9000 and 14000 series) may be essential to being considered a viable supplier for these situations. Suppliers of raw materials and components into these situations need to work under the same strict TQM conditions. Two typical examples are suppliers of speciality steels into the fabrication of valves and pressure vessels used in nuclear power plants and manufacturers of intermediates into pharmaceutical manufacturing operations. More consideration of these issues is given in Chapter 15.

Marketing mix

Issues about product quality and criticality have been covered above. In the average buying situation for consumers, the price negotiation process is more or less 'take it or leave it'. You will not make much progress by going to the supermarket checkout and asking if they will take £0.80 for a loaf rather than £0.95. How prices are arrived at (e.g. bulk discounts), periods of credit, level of credit and methods of payment (e.g. electronic funds transfer) can be important areas of negotiation in the B2B context. These, especially for capital goods and projects, may be spelt out in immense detail in complex legal contracts. Marketing communications will tend to use less advertising and use more personal selling. There is a need to set up a web of relationships (which is covered in the next section) and key account management is vital. Detailed consideration of the communications mix is given in Chapter 7.

The product or service must be consistently delivered, and within a tight time window with JIT manufacture. Physical distribution is a major cost and key issue. Some companies do nothing but specialise in logistics and physical distribution, (e.g. container lines, communications network operators, power transmission companies). In building, the relationship between the DMU and the service-extended marketing mix is important. Some of what is being marketed is intangible (e.g. security) and some members of the DMU are not in direct contact with the organisation; the service extension provides this mechanism to project the company to people it does not meet (e.g. physical evidence).

MICRO CASE STUDY **UNIVERSITY COMPUTER LEASING PROGRAMME**

Many universities are finding it more cost-effective to lease their computers with bundled services (e.g. maintenance) rather than purchase large numbers of individual computers. There are economies of scale in a large purchase. In place of hundreds of individual purchases and maintenance contracts, there is only one contract. This provides an internal administration cost saving. Consider a university that has decided to seek providers to tender for the supply of new PCs. (For simplicity we will exclude laptops, mainframe and file server aspects.) The contract will also include the removal and disposal of the existing PCs. Areas to be covered are computers for student access plus access for academics and administration staff. Table 3.3 below is a partial stakeholder analysis that the project engineer would need to complete as part of preparing for the project.

Table 3.3 Partial stakeholder analysis for university hire contract for PCs

Stakeholder group	Sub-group	Selected stakeholder agenda issues	Project leader's objectives and issues
Selected 'standard' DMU stakeholders			
Initiators	Finance management	Need to reduce the costs of computer service provision in terms of hardware costs, maintenance services and administration costs	Need to agree with finance the contract details
Users	Academic administration	Reliability, migration of data and data security (computer students hacking in to change their results is not good)	Determine needs and reflect these into contract. A key issue (not repeated again but true for many users) is safe disposal of existing computers (data on the hard drive)
	Students	Easy-to-use with good range of popular software	Need to know what student use is: surveys and internal analysis of existing use. Possible reducing demand with student ownership of laptops. Possible need to improve wi-fi
	Academics (technical)	Wide range of different needs (e.g. mathematical and statistical packages needed in maths and science departments)	Need to involve users to determine their future needs
	Academics (arts)	Many arts and graphic design professionals prefer Apple computers	Need to involve users to determine their future needs
Influencers	Computer professionals at other institutions	Professional network sharing experiences	Need to tap into past experience; at least make new mistakes
	Faculty IT committees	These consolidate faculty group needs	A key channel to provide user needs data

Table 3.3 (*Continued*)

Deciders	University IT committee	In a university context, the final recommendation will probably have to be approved by the IT committee as a collective decision	Need to keep the committee fully informed and on side
Negative deciders [people with compliance responsibilities]	Safety and environmental	Is the new equipment safe and will the disposal of existing equipment be according to university and legal requirements	In many B2B situations there are a series of decision hoops to jump through. Failure to clear any one of these will disqualify the contractor from the race for the business. Typical filters are safety, environmental, ethical (e.g. only source from equality opportunity suppliers), quality (only source from ISO 9000 sources), etc. The project manager must ensure that such 'must haves' and 'must not haves' are clearly set out in the brief to intending bidders
Approvers	Vice-Chancellor and board of governors	This is a major decision	Need to ensure that the final recommendation of the IT committee is clearly and succinctly tabled to the approvers
Buyers	University buying department	Physical order would be placed through the standard systems	Need to ensure proper day-to-day administration of contract
Gatekeepers	Personal assistants and general security	Need to prevent senior staff time being wasted	Need to control external sales contacts or they can take over the project leader's diary
'Normal' stakeholders			
	Internal	Largely covered in DMU analysis	
	Regulatory	The key aspects of these are likely to be managed via the 'negative approvers'	

Table 3.3   (*Continued*)

	Pressure groups	External concerns (e.g. green issues) will again be largely covered by roles of the 'negative approvers'. Internal pressure groups will be largely covered in the DMU influencers group	Note special issues such as trade unions and groups with concerns for special access (disabled access – e.g. visually impaired)
	Industry suppliers	Need to ensure compatibility of proprietary software	Universities use specialist software systems (e.g. complex timetabling systems). The project engineer will need to liaise with these to ensure new system is compatible and that a smooth migration to new computers will be possible
	Media	Always looking for news, this is often 'bad' news	Project is likely to be sensitive as drop in administration costs may involve job losses. Need to keep open channel with university PR. Disaster PR framework needs to be in place (e.g. 'University dumps computers with personal student records in landfill')

Relationship marketing

Relationship marketing takes a long-term view of marketing relationships rather than a short-term, transactional view. A privately owned café in a tourist trap has 'passing trade'. People will visit once and then never return. In this circumstance, transaction marketing is fine. However, when we are flying business class, airlines will devote a lot of effort to build a relationship with us. Business people travel often and they spend lots of money – they are profitable customers. The organisation needs to build strong relationships with long-term, profitable customers. Key accounts need to be managed well.

Relationship marketing holds in the B2C area. A classic example is the work that a major football club will engage in to build and maintain the relationship with its loyal fan base. In the B2B situation, the position is more complex. There is a need to build relationships with the entire key DMU group. Many of these contacts and relationships may not be with sales and marketing. It is imperative for applications engineers to build relationships with the R&D people in their client organisations. This concept forms one of the key foundations of relationship marketing: marketing may be viewed not as an activity that only marketers do, but as an attitude and value system that puts customer issues high up the agenda. As such, much marketing is done by part-time marketers (receptionists, application engineers and chemists, field installation staff, etc.). In effect the 'selling DMU' is building relationships with a 'buying DMU'. Every contact between people in the selling organisation and people in the client organisation is a moment of truth and an opportunity to practice relationship building. The 'people' word is important. The view advanced in this text is that organisations do not build relationships with organisations; people in organisations build relationships with other people in other organisations. These are real three-dimensional people. Often for the multinational organisation, they may come from completely different cultures. (More consideration of culture in international marketing is given later in this chapter.)

In the majority of cases, a manufacturing company will buy a number of components from a variety of sources. These products will then come together to form the complete system the customer manufactures. They all have to work and a product innovation in one component may interact with other parts of the system. Many consumer products were sold in metal or glass containers. However, plastic may now be considered better in many applications. This provides an application challenge to a completely different supplier, the fragrance manufacturer. Fragrances do not migrate into glass; they can into plastic. In this migration they can interact with plasticisers used in the plastic formulation to give flexibility to the container. This migration can cause loss of fragrance from the product and might cause embrittlement and failure of the package. Thus, in the development of a fragrance, the fragrance company will need to be involved in partnership with the packaging company, with which it has no selling or buying relationship, to make certain the final entity works in the consumer situation (e.g. accelerated storage tests on full packs). Thus, in the B2B environment, all parties in the supply chain interact with each other, forming a complex network of relationships. This complex network model forms another premise of relationship marketing. It is easy to count the money in the bank but part of the long-term value in an organisation is in the strength of the relationships it has built in its industry supply chain, from the source to the ultimate consumer. The practical implementation of this has been likened by some writers to a ladder of loyalty (Figure 3.8). The focus moves from transaction marketing to building long-term win–win relationships – relationship marketing.

The final aspect of relationship marketing to be considered in this text is management of the internal stakeholders. Just as some of the people in the buying DMU may not be in contact with the selling organisation, some members of the selling DMU may not be in direct contact with the buying organisation. A typical example is a prototyping or sampling department that provides prototype samples to the development team in the customer's DMU. Internal marketing is covered in the next section.

Internal marketing

Both marketers and personnel managers have come to the same conclusion: the internal publics need to be managed. Personnel professionals tend to talk about communications;

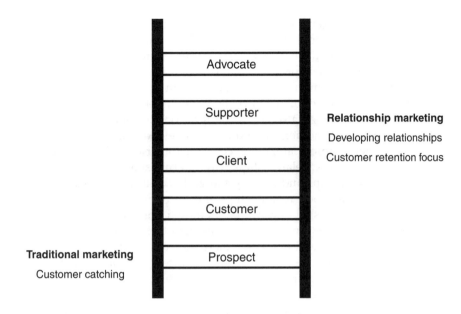

Figure 3.8 The relationship ladder of loyalty Adapted from: Smith, P. R. & Taylor, J. (2004) *Marketing Communications: An Integrated Approach*, 4th edn, Kogan Page, page 400.

marketers talk about internal marketing. Part of the driving force of marketing is the complexity and size of modern organisations. Large workforces are often out of direct contact with senior management and this implies that some of the techniques of normal marketing communication are also applicable to communication within the company, to the internal stakeholders. In the previous section on relationship marketing, we noted that it was necessary to build relationships and that some of the people within the organisation were not in contact with the customer (e.g. a shift process worker).

The process of internal marketing is much the same as for external relationship marketing. The first phase is to review the key stakeholders. For the customer, this was analysing the DMU. All we have to do is identify the support providing unit stakeholders. This is just a special application of the more general process of stakeholder analysis covered earlier (Chapter 2). We will consider the situation where a new generation of a component is to be fabricated from novel materials for an existing application but to provide better performance and extended life. The design engineers will be working with the design team in the client. Good field marketing staff will have briefed the design team about existing business, past history with the client and the personalities in the client DMU. Production will need to be kept in the picture about production volumes, any new tooling that will be required and to discuss the impact on existing business (e.g. how work in progress on the existing component is to be 'worked off'). The component is made from a novel material, so procurement must be in the loop to co-ordinate the sourcing schedule for the new production. The handling of the new material may involve new hazards and safety will be involved in a hazard assessment. In some ways, the task of the project manager is like that of the conductor of an opera. Some people are very visible – the singers – whereas the orchestra is largely hidden in the orchestra pit. However, they had better be playing to the same tempo, even if the audience can't see them. When the opera is complete the house lights come up, the orchestra get a chance to take their bow and have their performance recognised by the audience. The problem is that the production operative who worked weekend overtime to get that larger-than-expected order out will not get a round of applause from the client. However, the skilful and responsible project manager will ensure the 'unsung heroes' also get their appropriate recognition and reward.

Internal stakeholders should not be shielded from bad news; they should be informed and, where appropriate, involved in customer complaints investigations. Here the value of open and good relationships with internal stakeholders comes to pay off in a big way. Poor relationships and a 'hang the guilty' culture will result in a cover up and a failed investigation. Good relationships and an open communication can quickly identify the problem (e.g. a skill gap can be identified and the operator given training). Back-room people in poorly run companies talk about 'mushroom management', where people are kept in the dark and every few days someone opens the hatch and throws another lot of manure on them. Feedback on performance to all contributors to the team is vital; if they are not given this, it is the team leader's fault that the team member underperforms and is not fully integrated.

The detailed process is the same as for all stakeholder analysis. Identify the internal stakeholders. Identify their agenda and attitudes (e.g. in our example, the machine operator may need new training and could be a little apprehensive about working with the new material). Then consider what management objectives are needed to develop the relationship and implement actions and communications to ensure that these objectives are attained. This is not always easy because there may be resistance to change or even hostility. (More consideration of this is given in Chapters 11 and 12.) The mechanisms used can be traditional (briefing sessions, notice boards and the like) or e-based (intranet, e-mails). Opportunities should be taken to involve the back-room people in team-building events such as 'away-days'. Special issues arise in multicultural and multinational organisations. The next section considers some of the issues involved in international marketing.

MICRO CASE STUDY　　　　　　　　　　**SPECIALIST SOFTWARE COMPANY**

Consider the situation of medium-sized company (employing a few hundred people) developing specialist software for high-performance applications. Below is a partial internal marketing analysis for this type of situation. The internal publics would include: senior management, finance and administration staff, R&D, design, marketing, fields sales, production, buying, logistics. (Hint: use the value chain as a checklist to see if you have covered all the internal stakeholders for a given situation.)

Communications and internal marketing activities might include the following.

Company staff intranet General company news on performance, new contacts, interesting product applications. This should be accessible for most staff. It might be an important channel for remote (e.g. overseas based) field sales staff. Some staff may not have easy access (e.g. shop-floor production technicians).

Notice boards May be old hat but still have a value for very local news and where staff (e.g. shop-floor production technicians) do not have ready access to staff intranet.

Company newsletter Rejected in this case. You may not agree. If so, justify your standpoint. Business situations do not have one unique right solution. Justification for rejection: likely to duplicate what could be done on the staff intranet. Desktop publishing could be time consuming and printing expensive. There is a lack of control over where hard-copy newsletters could get to; confidential information could leak out. This is less of a problem with on-screen information.

Off-job company events Carefully considered away-days can promote team building between members of the extended team who are not in daily contact (e.g. marketing and production). This can be an opportunity to recognise achievements (e.g. outstanding performance at a local college by one of the apprentices).

E-mail Can be a useful way to distribute breaking news (e.g. a promotion or new appointment). However, too much can amount to internal spam. As with the intranet not all employees will be in daily e-mail contact.

International marketing

Most organisations operate in an international environment. A rise in demand can force up the cost of copper, affecting the costs of a domestic producer of copper fittings. A manufacturer of components may find they have joined the global market when one of their customers exports the final product. Many countries (e.g. UK, USA and Australia), have multicultural domestic workforces and markets. The background of international marketing is therefore handy, even in the domestic market. The good news is that there is not much new theory to learn, just a different context. International marketing is just marketing but across an international border. This implies that the macro- and microenvironment of the destination market and the international trading environment must be considered as well as the domestic environments. Figure 3.9 outlines the international business environment. A key aspect is that cultural issues become more prominent and some expansion to the STEEPLE model is helpful to the international marketer.

International social/cultural issues

Just as domestic social attitudes change, so do social attitudes in other cultures. It is useful to consider broad social groups and patterns of culture but care must be taken not to stereotype people. Tea may be considered the UK's national drink but many people prefer coffee. With these two reservations in mind, a brief outline of the issues that the international marketer needs to consider is given below with some selected examples.

Language

Language is not just about communication; it is about culture and cultural identity. A culture's literature and music is part of its heritage. In moving to a new country, the languages used in the country need to be identified. Some countries (e.g. Canada) have more than one 'official' language. Labelling and documentation need to be translated. Local native

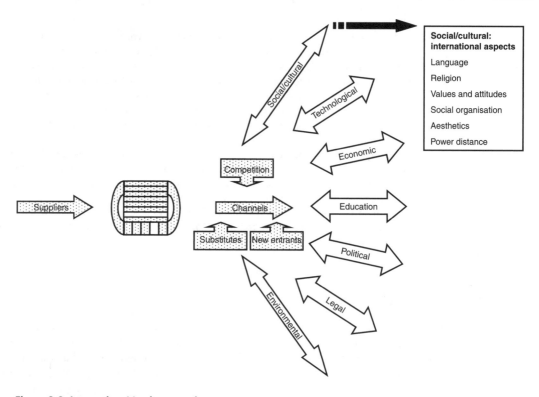

Figure 3.9 International business environment.

speakers should be used to at least proof the final versions. Language evolves and words take on different meanings and identities with time. In different countries, this may happen in different ways. US English and UK English are so different that they are considered different languages in a word-processing package. English may be the official language in the USA, but a substantial proportion of USA inhabitants have Spanish as their first (sometimes their only) language.

Religion

Religion is one of the key values that a person may hold and religious observances can affect all parts of the marketing mix. A major area is food and drink, where different religions have different practices on what food may be eaten (e.g. Muslims and Jews with pork). In certain countries, the use of alcohol is not allowed so European fragrances diluted with alcohol may have to be reformulated into an alcohol-free version. A fast-growing sector of banking is with products conforming to *Sharia* law. With these financial products, the payment and receipt of interest is forbidden. In marketing communications, due regard should be taken in imagery not to offend religious groups. In setting meetings and conferences, consideration must be given to accounting for different national and religious holidays. In the UK, we have become accustomed to the 24/7 hours of trading in major hypermarkets. In other countries, religious and other cultural reasons may restrict hours of opening.

Values and attitudes

Apart from religious reasons, different cultures have different attitudes to products. In some countries, a pony steak might be a treat; in another, dog meat. In parts of Africa 'bush meat' is part of the local culinary tradition. Non-UK citizens can be amazed about the passion and hostility that can be aroused by fox hunting: 'What is all the fuss about with people in funny clothes chasing a little furry animal?' Equally, a European might be a little surprised to find strict laws on the sale and consumption of alcohol in parts of the USA when it is fine to pop into a shop and buy a gun. The type of clothes we wear and the designs and colours we select are also affected by our cultural traditions.

Social organisation

The way society is organised and how people interact can differ from country to country. In the UK, part of the pressure on housing is the large and increasing number of single-person households. In other countries the extended family, with several generations living in the same home, is normal. In the UK, the daily commute has become part of life; in rural India, the traditional village sets the pattern. However, the urbanisation of culture is a global phenomenon and the majority of the people in the world will soon be living in cities.

Aesthetics

What people find beautiful and aesthetically pleasing can also be different. Language is one facet of cultural identity. Visual art, architecture and music are also influenced by culture.

This is important in the design of products and affects imagery that is appropriate for different countries. An important area is in personal grooming and fashion products. Black African hair is physically different to European hair. Different skin colours demand the formulation of different cosmetics. Different cultural fashions (e.g. Bollywood, Caribbean, Indian, Chinese, European, etc.) demand different offerings.

Power distance and cultural norms

After studying employees in a major multinational company, Geert Hofstede identified four cultural dimensions:

1. *Individualism versus collectivism.* In cultures such as America and the UK, people are more individualistic than in other places, like Singapore and Indonesia, where people view themselves much more as part of a group.
2. *Large or small power distance.* In small power-distance cultures (e.g. USA and UK), business relations are fairly democratic. In large power-distance cultures (e.g. China and Russia), the processes are more authoritarian.
3. *Masculinity versus femininity.* In some cultures the values and attitudes favour fairness and equality (e.g. Sweden). This is a so-called feminine culture. In other cultures (Japan

and Germany), there is less equality. (There are even a few places left in the world where women are not allowed to drive motor vehicles.)
4. *Risk aversion*. Within some cultures there is an acceptance of risk (e.g. USA and UK) whereas in other cultures (e.g. France and Russia) there is considerable aversion to risk.

The key issue is that to run the same operation (e.g. construction of an airport) the manager must be sensitive to local cultural norms or role conflicts will develop and performance will suffer.

Technological issues

Cultural differences can affect attitudes to technology. In general, the Japanese love technology and will adopt the latest gismo with enthusiasm. However, one group in the USA, the Amish, reject modern conveniences such as the internal combustion engine and electric light.

A key issue is the availability and quality of infrastructure in different countries. In developed Europe, we are used to high-quality motorways and consistent power supplies. In less-developed countries, many of the roads may be unmetalled and the electricity supply may also be dirty (brown-outs, spikes, interruptions), which can destroy microprocessor-based equipment. Here the use of UPSs (uninterruptible power supplies) may be essential, not only to maintain service but also protect the equipment.

A second issue is that of clashing standards. There is a major problem with differences between the USA (largely 'imperial' – feet, US gallons, etc.) and Europe (largely metric). Furthermore, there are odd infrastructure issues such as:

- Road vehicles, which are left-hand drive in most countries but right-hand drive in others, including the UK and India
- Light fittings (screw or bayonet) and power plugs (two or three pin; round or rectangular pins)
- Electrical power supply (240 V, 50 Hz in the UK; 120 V, 60 Hz in the USA)
- TV transmissions standards

The key issue is to check the standards for all aspects of the product or service in the target destination and check that the product can conform. This may be a major undertaking and rather expensive (e.g. safety testing of a European car for the USA market).

Economic issues

There are over 150 different countries in the world, each with their own currencies. If you walk into a typical high street bank, only some 25 to 30 are easily convertible. A number of questions need to be asked:

- What is the local currency in use?
- How stable is it? What are local inflation and interest rates? (In 2007, the inflation rate in the UK was around 3%; in Zimbabwe it was over 1 500% and rising.)
- What is the conversion rate and what are the trends? (In 2007, the UK pound reached a 20-year high against the US dollar.)

■ Is the currency freely convertible? Some currencies are not and that can make it difficult to get profits out of the country. (A potential solution is to barter or engage in other forms of counter-trade.) However, in many cases, international trade will be conducted in a major international currency (e.g. US dollars or euros).

Average income can be a misleading statistic. What has to be considered is wealth distribution. The average income in China and India is still low but there are many millionaires and there is a market for high-technology and luxury products. However, there are still many hundreds of millions of people attempting to exist on less than £1 a day. The ability to spend will be affected by availability of credit and local taxation rates. Local taxes (e.g. sales taxes and corporation tax) will affect the profitability of overseas ventures. In the EU, we operate in a free trade zone but more generally the nature and size of any import duties and taxes must be considered.

A vast range of general population issues needs to be considered, such as ownership (e.g. degree of product penetration and ownership of cars, computers, etc.) and consumption patterns (e.g. in the USA, consumption of carbonated drinks is higher than in Europe, although both are wealthy economies).

Education

In the developed world, the majority of people can read and write. In less-developed countries, many people still do not enjoy a good, basic education. Even when the level of education is high, the structure may differ. Bear in mind that the French, UK and US systems of education are very different.

Political

There are organisations that shape global trading – such as the World Trade Organisation (WTO) – with the setting of tariff rates and intervention in trade disputes (e.g. between EU and US trading blocs). The political climate can affect attitudes in given countries. In 2007, a key issue in the French presidential election was the preservation of the French 'system' rather than being dragged into global American or British attitudes (e.g. to job security).

Legal

In the review of the national STEEPLE model, we noted that the law was most complex issue. Now we multiply the complexity. A person working for a US company in France drafting a contract may find that aspects of American, French, European and international law might all apply. Some selected issues are briefly reviewed below, using the marketing mix headings.

Product

What it is legal to sell differs from country to country (e.g. guns in the UK and USA). Other issues include standards (e.g. UK beer is sold by the pint; Germany by the litre, etc.), product liability rules, labelling regulations, safety and environmental standards.

Price

Some products and services have prices regulated (e.g. water, telecommunications, electricity, etc.) and such regulations differ from country to country. The forms of contract, including credit frameworks, also differ between countries. How prices are given is affected by local law (e.g. in the UK, pricing is by the kilogram, not the imperial pound). A key issue is price setting. Care must be taken so as not to be seen to be 'price fixing'. Equally, care must be taken to ensure that discussions with competitors about general industry issues cannot be viewed as an attempt to set up an international cartel. It is highly dangerous to share cost or price information with competitors.

Place

Hours of opening may be restricted and local planning regulations may determine where facilities can be located. Some products have specified distribution requirements (e.g. prescription pharmaceuticals). Physical distribution may be regulated (e.g. night flights at airports and restrictions on deliveries in city areas).

Promotion

Different countries restrict advertising in different ways. What may be advertised, how it is advertised, when it may be advertised and the imagery and messages are all subject to regulation. These regulations are not even standard within the EU. Other aspects of communications may be affected. For instance, a great promotional campaign may simply be illegal in another country. An example would be the regulations on competitions, which differ in various countries. In 2007, problems were highlighted in the UK with badly managed TV phone-in competitions.

People

A key specific aspect for engineers, technologists and scientists is what it is that makes someone a 'qualified person'. People signing off technical documentation (e.g. safety certificates, certificates of composition) must be suitably 'qualified'. Chemists and engineers may become chartered – and other professions (e.g. in medicine) have parallel frameworks – to certify full professional competence.

Physical evidence

There can be specific requirements about product documentation in different countries. This is something that must always be checked when marketing internationally.

Process

Careful checks need to be made to ensure certain processes are legal. For instance, an area still not fully settled is the law regarding international internet transactions: which countries' law applies to the transaction; which courts will have jurisdiction in the case of dispute (e.g. defective product quality)?

Environmental

There are varying attitudes to environmental issues. Some countries (e.g. Germany) are truly green and have comprehensive environmental policies and infrastructure. In less-developed countries, it is understandable that if you do not have enough to eat, global warming may be less important to you than concentrating on where your next meal is coming from.

There must be due regard for local needs. 'Save the elephant!' may seem to be a great cause for well-fed, middle-class Europeans. However, if elephants from the reserve are eating your crops, tensions will arise with the 'green' European lobby. Eco-tourism can provide an income for local populations and give them a stake in green issues, but too much eco-tourism can destroy the environment that people want to see and have preserved. A few specific environmental issues with international dimensions are given below.

Energy

In 2007, China was commissioning new electrical power stations, with sufficient capacity to supply the total UK demand, in a single year. The majority of this capacity was based on coal. Various options are being proposed to reduce carbon dioxide emissions. In Europe, consideration is being given to capturing the carbon dioxide and injecting it into suitable geological structures (e.g. depleted oil fields). However, the drive is now on for true green energy sources. Bio-fuels (e.g. ethanol) in some countries can be significant (e.g. Brazil). However, overall the issue is complicated. Cutting down the rainforest to grow bio-diesel crops is not very eco-friendly and may not actually save any carbon dioxide emissions. In the UK, wind and wave power are viable options. In other areas, solar power may become viable. Where the geology permits, geothermal energy can provide the solution (e.g. Iceland). Hydroelectric power, on the other hand, may have mixed environmental impacts.

Water

Possibly the greatest environmental challenge to the world will come from the lack of water available where it is most required. Vanishing lakes (e.g. the Aral Sea in Asia and Lake Victoria in Africa) illustrate the problems of over-extraction of water for irrigation of crops. In some countries, the water table is dropping alarmingly, (e.g. India). In China, pollution and over-extraction are causing water supply problems and reducing the flow of major rivers.

Bio-risks

The UK's foot-and-mouth epidemic and the Irish potato famine illustrate the great harm that animal and plant diseases can cause. The introduction of rabbits to Australia was an ecological disaster. Strict regulations now exist to attempt to limit the importation of problem diseases, insects, plants or animals.

Pollution exporting

A major problem exists with old ships. These contain toxic materials (e.g. asbestos) and appropriate facilities for the safe recycling of super-tankers do not exist in Europe. There is an insatiable demand for scrap steel in India and current practice is to beach the ship and cut it up on the beach with minimal protection for the workers or the environment. Increasingly, producers of products will have to provide safe and effective recycling facilities; simply burying them in landfill or exporting the problem to a less-developed country will not be an option.

Environmentalism is an international issue: pollution and disease do not recognise international barriers. However, these environmental pressures are also creating new business opportunities, such as the generation of green energy (wind power, for instance) and water management consultancy.

International market segmentation

International market segmentation needs to be completed in two stages. There are over 150 countries in the world and these can be segmented by various approaches, including: state of development, national language, religion, culture, and climate. Within a given country, local market structures may differ and alternative segmentation approaches may be demanded. In the UK, one useful consumer segmentation approach (an example of a geo-demographic segmentation) is called ACORN (a classification of residential neighbourhoods). This is based on the UK's postal codes. Such an approach will not work in a less-developed country, where there are no postcodes. (More consideration of consumer segmentation is given in Chapter 4.)

Competition

Just as with the STEEPLE model, there is no need to invent a completely new model. Figure 3.9 shows the international STEEPLE (macroenvironment) and competition (microenvironment). The competition model discussed in the previous chapter is still fully effective. The nature and properties of local competition can be very different. A US clothing retailer moving into the UK will have little experience of Marks & Spencer as a competitor. The same is true of new entrants. Potential new entrants may vary in different national markets. The nature of the channel structure can be different. In the UK, over 50% of grocery sales are through just a few major supermarket chains. In less-developed countries, the channels are much more fragmented. The nature of substitute products can also be different. In India, elephants are still used – a form of substitute product for the small van. A key problem is the changed nature of the supply chain. Things that can be taken for granted in a developed country may not prevail in less-developed countries (e.g. there may be problems in sourcing parts, materials and services). The final aspect is to take care to identify the benefit use. In most of Europe and the USA, a bicycle is more for recreational use; in China it is still a major form of transport (although this is starting to change as motorbikes and scooters are becoming more popular). The model still works but new research and careful consideration of the changed context is needed to extract full insight into the given national business situation.

Market entry

Once an international market has been identified and the company has decided to enter it, the next consideration is what mechanism to use. Some products must be exported. For instance, in Australia it is possible to make champagne (here defined as a sparkling wine) that is almost identical to 'real' champagne. However, it is only legal to call sparkling wine 'champagne' if it has been produced in that particular geographic region of France. Hence, exporting is the only option. Low-value, high-weight goods or short shelf-life goods need to be manufactured in the destination market. The decision tree for market entry is given in Figure 3.10.

If a company has underutilised capacity, then exporting may be a key option. Commodity products (oil, cocoa, tea, coffee, metals, etc.) are extracted and marketed on a global basis. Specialised distribution systems (e.g. supertankers and bulk carriers) can move massive amounts of raw material around the world at low unit cost. Overseas production can lower

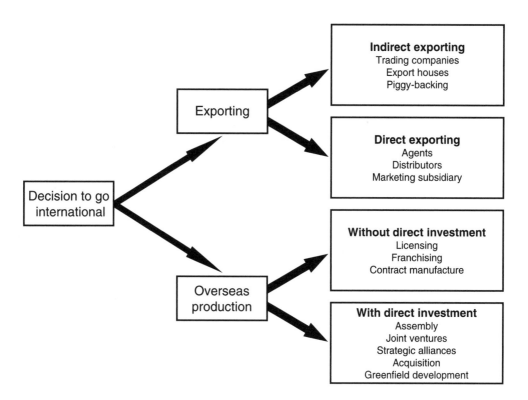

Figure 3.10 International market entry decision tree.

distribution and total costs of getting to market. In trading in less-developed countries, labour costs may favour local production.

The next decision is the level of commitment. This, with the first decision, gives us the following four major options (within which there are sub-variants).

Indirect exporting (low export commitment)

Export houses can be commissioned to market (at a cost) the firm's products. For the producers of many OEM (original equipment manufacture) components, 'piggy-back' exporting happens almost by accident. A company may make gearboxes that then go into cars, which then are exported. The gearbox manufacturer does not actively get involved in the physical process of exporting. A parallel situation happens when a major contractor (e.g. builder of an airport) subcontracts out aspects of construction or fitting out.

Direct exporting (higher export commitment)

Agents take orders and pass them on to the firm. The firm then pays the agent a commission on the value of the business they have gained for them. Distributors tend to take the process further and take control of local stocks (e.g. a car distributor in the UK). They tend to provide more local marketing and technical support (e.g. field technical support for local manufacturers in a B2B context and maintenance for cars in the B2C context). However, if a company wants full control and has the resources, they may set up a full marketing subsidiary to market and distribute their products.

Overseas production without direct investment (low commitment)

A company may have intellectual property (brands, designs, copyrights, patents, etc.) that it may not want to use in a given market. The company can then simply sell (license) the intellectual property to another company. This can often happen with books and copyright material. For example, some books sold in Europe may have a note on the cover: 'Not for sale in the USA and Canada'. In this case, the copyright has been sold to another company for sales in the North American market. Having sold the property, the company has little direct control of the business.

If the company does not have the capital but still wants to retain a greater measure of control, then the business can be franchised. This has been a notable success in some services (e.g. hotels) and retailing (e.g. The Body Shop). This option costs more than licensing because the franchiser needs to have field control requiring an inspection system to ensure franchisees are operating to the parameters and standards of the franchise agreement.

A hidden universe is the world of contract manufacture. Few retailers are also producers. Tesco, Marks & Spencer and similar companies do not make anything; they work with contract suppliers for the manufacture of their branded products. A major brand of a consumer product might wish to enter a new expanding market with full control but without the money for a greenfield (see next section) development. Contract manufacture provides good control without capital needs and reduced risk. A related activity is outsourcing, where a company making branded products (e.g. digital cameras, printers, etc.) may out-source assembly to a low-cost production region (e.g. China) for sales and distribution around the world.

Overseas manufacture with direct investment (higher commitment)

It may be more cost-effective for a company to complete the final assembly in the target market. A typical situation occurs in consumer products such as cola. The high-technology, high-value component (the flavour) may be made at a key central location while the low-value, heavy parts (water and the packaging) are sourced locally and the final product assembled in the destination market.

Two companies may come together to produce and market a product or service: a *joint venture*. These can be difficult to manage because the two partner organisations may evolve different priorities over time, thereby putting a strain on the original joint venture philosophy. A related form of collaboration is where companies may effect strategic alliances without setting up a new trading entity. A typical example is alliances between airlines (e.g. where a European airline makes arrangements with a US airline). Each partner of the alliance then gets access to the domestic networks of its strategic partner.

The maximum commitment and control is where the firm has ownership of the entire entity (production and marketing). Acquisition (if a target exists) provides a quick method of entry. Moreover, it can provide entry when other methods of expansion would be difficult. Wal-Mart, in its takeover of Asda, would have found it difficult to grow a business by greenfield development in the UK; there are just not the sites where planning permission would be granted for a chain of 1 000 new stores across the country.

Greenfield development provides the maximum control. Here, the organisation builds a new facility on a virgin site, hence, the description 'greenfield' development. There are two key problems with this: (1) the capital costs can be very high and (2) the time from developing the original business planning concept to completion may be years.

No business is fully insulated from the forces of globalisation. Increasingly, multicultural societies are becoming the norm (USA, Europe, South Africa, etc.) and these, in effect, provide a domestic 'international' market. In working within global organisations, the engineer and technologist must not only understand the implications in the marketplace but also the impact on the workings of the firm's value chain and the workings of multicultural project teams.

MICRO CASE STUDY   **INTERNATIONAL MARKETING OF DOMESTIC COOKING EQUIPMENT**

We will consider the situation facing the design engineer of a company marketing kitchen equipment and intending to start exporting. For this micro case study, we will focus on one sector of kitchen equipment: cookers, ovens and hobs. At present, the company manufactures electrical and gas variants of its products. Table 3.4 reviews some of the international STEEPLE issues this design engineer may need to consider.

Table 3.4   International marketing issues to be considered by a design engineer working on cooking equipment

STEEPLE element	Issue	Comments
Social/cultural	Language	Instructions need to be translated and displays may need to be modified. Use of internationally recognised icons may minimise this
	Religion	Not likely to have a major effect
	Values and attitudes	In some countries, the kitchen is the temple of culinary delight; in others it is just a place to microwave the frozen TV meal
	Social organisation	In countries with extended families, larger ovens, etc. may be the norm; in countries with many single households, small units would be more common
	Aesthetics	Different countries may need different colours and designs
	Power distance	Likely to be an issue if manufacturing in the destination market
	Other	Food and its preparation are very culturally sensitive. In some countries, oven cooking is important (the English roast, Italian pasta bakes). In others, stove-top methods are popular (e.g. Japanese cuisine)
Technological	Local technical standards	What is the local electrical power supply? Are local kitchen units designed to imperial or metric measurements? What are local standards for gas and electrical fittings (e.g. thread sizes for gas fittings)
Economic	Disposable income distribution	If a less wealthy nation: a range of basic products with no frills but possibly still also a luxury market (e.g. India)
	Fuel costs and availability	In some locations, mains gas is not available and bottled gas can be expensive. In some locations, alternative fuels may be economic, such as oil, coal or wood. New designs may be needed with technical developments for the company to diversify into these alternative fuels
Education	Training	Maybe there is a need to train local agents' staff for efficient and safe fitting of the appliances
Political	Not likely to be a major issue	However, note that political risk may deter entry to some markets (e.g. it would probably be sensible to give Afghanistan a miss for a few years)
Legal	Safety	Need to make certain that appliances and their fitting comply with all relevant local safety regulations
Environmental	Packaging	Arrangements for local recycling of packaging

Not-for-profit and social marketing

Many organisations do not have maximisation of profits as their primary objective. These include:

- Charities (e.g. National Trust, universities, trust hospitals)
- government bodies (e.g. Ministry of Defence)
- professional bodies and learned institutions (e.g. Royal Society of Chemistry, Institute Engineering and Technology, Royal Society)
- pressure groups (e.g. Greenpeace)
- NGOs (non-governmental organisations such as Oxfam)
- political parties
- religious organisations

What all these institutions have in common is that their core objectives are non-financial (e.g. for the National Trust, it is the preservation of heritage; for the Royal National Lifeboat Institution, it is the saving of lives). A 'normal' for-profit organisation may have the objective of 'providing maximum profits to its owners, subject to the legitimate expectations of other relevant stakeholders'. This definition needs to be modified for a not-for-profit organisation to: 'The organisation seeks to achieve the best possible outcome for its not-for-profit objectives, subject to satisfactory financial outcomes and subject to the legitimate expectations of relevant stakeholders.' The 'subject to satisfactory financial outcomes' is important. A museum funded as a charity needs to generate income; a charity can still become bankrupt. In the title of this section we have included a second aspect: *social* marketing. A charity may have special customers (patients and clients) who have special needs such as drug and material dependency. Such an organisation is attempting to give people knowledge, change actions and transform the individual's value system. In a sense, marketing theory has gone full circle. Classical marketing theory has been developed to provide effective tools for the social marketing sector. However, key aspects of modern management, such as quality, environmental, fair trade and ethical aspects, involve 'value change' as a vital aspect. The leading edge of value change marketing is being formed in not-for-profit and social marketing and these new developments are finding uses in areas such as internal marketing in the commercial sector.

One key aspect of social and not-for-profit marketing is the complexity of the stakeholders. The normal rules apply; there is just more work to do to get a complete analysis. However, it is worth noting that there are some special stakeholders for the social and not-for-profit marketing context: volunteers, owners and donors.

Volunteers

Some of the rules of management have to be rethought because much of the frontline effort of major charities depends on unpaid volunteers. The reward package, for instance, has to be rethought for this context. Often the commitment is for some altruistic motive, such as concern for humankind and the world (an environmental charity). Internal marketing takes on a special relevance in this context: 'How is what we are doing changing the world?'

Owners

A firm may be owned by an individual, a group of individuals (private companies) or by shareholders (a public company). However, a charity's physical assets are often held in 'trust' and the 'owners' are the trustees. They have different legal obligations and motivations to profit-hungry shareholders.

Donors

A significant amount of the capital and revenue needed to sustain a not-for-profit organisation may come from corporate or individual sponsors. This is not to imply that the people do not expect a 'return', just that the return is not directly financial (e.g. a dividend). Trade union members and commercial companies who donate to a political party are seeking a return: a more favourable political climate.

The basic rules of stakeholder analysis are not violated in not-for-profit and social marketing. The approaches developed earlier are valid. However, just as with B2B marketing and international marketing, some additional thought and insight is needed for this context. Some of the issues to be considered in social and not-for-profit marketing are discussed below.

Sensitive issues

There are numerous not-for-profit organisations working on healthcare and associated issues. These areas can be extremely sensitive and this sensitivity can be greatly heightened in different cultural contexts. Is a women's rights organisation practising moral colonialism or does it have legitimate health concerns in campaigning against female circumcision? Is an AIDS trust behaving acceptably in promoting the use of condoms in a Catholic country? Is a free needle exchange programme for addicts a sensible move to prevent AIDS infection or a ridiculous activity to support material abuse? Is it right that a sexual health charity should give contraceptive advice to underage adolescents without their parents' consent? Should a state health service provide a free abortion service? These complex areas are associated with very strongly held personal views, based on core values, (e.g. religious belief).

Public scrutiny

In the renovation of an old castle for a heritage charity, the civil engineer will need to provide the site with signage (e.g. 'To the keep'). If poor quality signage is used, the charity is perceived to be unprofessional and a well-meaning bunch of amateurs that should not be left with such a responsible task. Too much 'marketing' expense and 'lavish' signs can be perceived as the charity having no respect for other people's money. What is needed are professional signs but without too many frills. In this sector some stakeholders will have a suspicion of marketing: 'It is capitalist stuff just for soap powders. What we want are more nurses, not to waste money on marketing.' However, you only need a nurse if you are ill. Health education is social marketing to persuade people to eat better food, not to be ill and therefore not to need a nurse.

Poor data

The UK crime statistics are a problem area. The police records only hold reported crime; many crimes such as 'date rape' are under-reported. Care has to be taken to check the basis of reporting. In the design of questionnaires care must be taken to ensure that the questions are not driving the answer.

Negative issues

Most of consumer marketing is about 'drink more coke' or 'eat more burgers, especially ours' whereas in the not-for-profit area we are asking people to use less (water, energy) and eat less (fat, sugar and salt). The age of consumption is the age of instant gratification. You have fries and a burger, you feel satisfied. If you don't eat a burger, you do not feel fit enough to run the London Marathon 30 minutes later. The benefits are often distant and largely intangible. It is easy to see the burger and fries, but more difficult to get over the concept of a 30% reduction in the risk of heart attack in 25 years' time. Environmental issues can be even more difficult to sell: 'What has me leaving the computer on got to do with a one metre rise in sea level in 50 years' time? What do I care: I might be dead by then!' This is similar to a technical manager with safety procedures who might consider that accidents always happen to 'other' people.

Difficult to modify the mix

An engineer participating in the eradication of stagnant water as part of antimalaria programme is not able to dial up the marketing department and order some nice mosquitoes that do not bite humans. The biology and behaviour of the mosquito is fixed. We can change the colour of a car; we can change the operating system of a computer; we cannot change the greenhouse properties of carbon dioxide.

The impact of the issues above is that social and not-for-profit marketing is somewhat more challenging than traditional commercial marketing. There is one additional complexity. In B2C marketing we take people along a road of awareness, interest, desire, action (action is purchase). Figure 3.11 shows the social marketing process. In the case of 'drink driving' in the UK, the process has largely been successful: people now know that drinking impairs driving skill (knowledge) and they do not drive over the limit (action change). Many people are moving to the attitude: 'Either drive and drink nothing or drink and don't think about driving'. There is a long way to go with cutting out the use of mobile telephones in cars. Many people can be seen every day talking on their mobiles while driving. It is comparatively easy to get people to buy a product. In an AIDS awareness programme, it is not too difficult to impart the knowledge of the disease and its transmission mechanisms. There are considerable problems in action change (e.g. wear a condom) and vastly more problems in ultimate value change (one partner for life).

Marketing of entertainment

In the post-industrial world, entertainment is a significant proportion of the average family expenditure. There are three additional points to consider above the two obvious

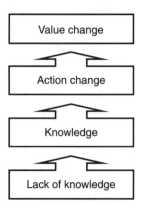

Figure 3.11 The social marketing process. Adapted from: Curtis, T., *Marketing in Practice*, figure 2.7, page 68, © Elsevier 2006. Reproduced by permission.

ones: entertainment is a service and relationship marketing (RM) is most important (e.g. maintaining viewing figures for a TV channel). The three issues are that the place has to be marketed (e.g. tune into Film 4), the performance has to be marketed (e.g. all the PR support for soaps such as *Eastenders* and *Coronation Street*) and the 'stars' have to be marketed.

Marketing the location

Theatres, cinema complexes, TV and radio stations all spend significant marketing effort promoting the channel. If you go to Stratford-upon-Avon, the visit is not complete without an evening at the theatre. Radio channels such as Classic FM actively promote the channel and use RM activities to gain a commitment from their audience and get them to consider themselves part of an extended social network. One of the most successful areas is illustrated by the level of commitment and identity that football supporters give to their chosen club – not so much entertainment, but part of their lives.

Marketing the performance

The specific performance/performances need to be marketed. A lover of ballet may look out for a new performance of Swan Lake. A radio channel may market a '100th anniversary day' for a major composer. The local cinema complex will market the specific films on release that particular week.

Marketing the star

Over a given weekend in the UK, many thousands of people play football. If we consider that the normal laws of economics apply, then there is a vast oversupply of people who want to play professional football. Elasticity of demand then tells us that, with oversupply, the wages in football should be rather low. The same is true of singers and 'wannabe' musicians. Thousands of them perform each night in small local venues and people pay just a few pounds for admission. To see the performers at Glastonbury on the other hand, the tickets are expensive and vastly oversubscribed (hence, considerable efforts have been devoted to prevent a second market developing on eBay, etc.). Why? The answer is the 'star' quality of the performer(s); the celebrity factor. It does not matter if it is opera, sport, popular music or TV drama, part of the product mix is the 'star' quality of the people involved in the delivery. Again, this will involve relationship marketing (e.g. the rock group's fan club and skilful PR in the celebrity magazines).

INSIGHT

MARKETING EDUCATION

The same concepts can apply to other contexts. Consider a person deciding to go to university. The university will take great care to market their brand (Oxford, Harvard, etc.) with skilful PR, etc. They will market the course: 'Best course on biochemical engineering in Europe.' Individual professors will be promoted thorough publications, media appearances and individual websites, etc. The invitation is: 'Come and learn from the person who invented the subject'. A new university will struggle to fill its places while the 'blue chip' universities, such as Cambridge, will have many more applicants than places. Similar concepts can apply to the marketing of other creative services such as design and architecture.

Marketing on a limited budget

In the technical arena, there are many small and medium-sized enterprises (SMEs). Technical service and design consultancies are examples of such companies. Many of these operations will have a total turnover that is less than that devoted to an advertising campaign for a high street brand. Mass TV and press advertising is just not an option for most SMEs (a single full-page advertisement can cost £ 20,000). A sound, functional website can, however, be a key element in the marketing strategy. It can contain considerable amounts of core information. However, having a website does not imply that you are in international marketing. Most PCs have an excellent word-processing package but this does not imply every owner is a great novelist. The trick is to create awareness and to lead people to the website. Very limited advertising may be appropriate (e.g. in a specialist trade directory). Skilful use should be made of PR with press releases and media appearances where possible. In the technical arena, developing the personal network is valuable. Opportunities include attending exhibitions (you do not have to exhibit; that is expensive), technical conferences and professional meetings.

A full market research programme for a single issue may cost many thousands of pounds. Often SMEs will have to place more reliance on secondary sources, with only limited primary field research. This can be augmented by skilful market intelligence. Overall the message is simple: marketing works but how it has to be done has to be reinvented. It should be regarded in the same light as energy efficiency: not that things are impossible, but ways have to be invented to get the maximum effect from a minimum budget.

Review

In this chapter, contemporary issues in marketing have been examined. The Kennedy rights model was used to provide a framework for the organisation to respond to consumerism developments in the external environment. The green marketing mix was described and illustrations given as to how this can be used to make the marketing mix more environmentally friendly and address the concerns of the green stakeholders. Corporate governance and ethical marketing are important aspects of modern marketing and a range of current aspects were presented.

Much of traditional marketing was developed by brand manufacturers of FMCGs. The characteristics of this were discussed and then differences were noted in the marketing of services and B2B marketing. The need to develop value chain links was noted and the way in which relationship marketing can be used to develop strong profitable networks was described. No organisation can succeed without the motivation and empowerment of its internal stakeholders. The role of internal marketing was presented as an approach to help in the management of internal stakeholder relationships. The globalisation of business has an impact on most organisations. The nature of international marketing was explored and aspects of market entry considered. Not all organisations have profit maximisation as their principal objective. The nature of not-for-profit organisations has been reviewed. The differences between traditional consumer marketing and not-for-profit and social marketing have been assessed. The marketing of entertainment and marketing on a limited budget have special challenges. These particular needs were explored and marketing solutions proposed.

In this first part of the book, the nature of marketing has been outlined. The tools for exploring the macro- and microenvironment have been reviewed and their application illustrated with examples. Current issues having an impact on marketing managers have been reviewed and the various marketing contexts explored. To respond to these needs, the marketer has to tailor the market offering – the marketing mix. In the next part, the practical implementation tools of marketing are explored, namely, the seven Ps of the marketing mix. In Chapter 4, we consider P = *product* and provide a range of tools to analyse the architecture of products. This lays the foundation for later development, in Chapter 14, of the new product development process.

Further reading

Carson, R. (2000) *Silent Spring*, Penguin.

Swayne, L., Duncan, J. & Ginter, P. (2005) *Strategic Management of Health Care Organizations*, 5th edition, Blackwell Publishing.

Hoffman, K. & Bateson, J. (2001) *Essentials of Services Marketing*, Dryden Press.

Hofstede, G. (2001) *Culture's Consequences*, 2nd edn, Sage.

Hutt, M. & Speh, T. (2004) *Business Marketing Management: A Strategic View of Industrial and Organisational Markets*, 8th edn, Thomson.

Kotler, P. & Scheff, J. (1997) *Standing Room Only: Strategies for Marketing the Performing Arts*, Harvard Business School Press.

Peattie, K. & Rannayaka, M. (1992) Responding to the green movement, *Industrial Marketing Management*, **21** (2), 103–10, Elsevier.

Sargeant, A (2004) *Marketing Management for Non-profit Organisations*, 2nd edn, Oxford University Press.

Usunier J. & Lee, J. (2005) *Marketing Across Cultures*, 4th edn, Financial Times Publishing.

PART TWO

The Tools of Marketing

CHAPTER 4

Product

Learning objectives

After studying this chapter you will be able to:

- Explain how a product can be considered as an input–output device, evaluate the product life cycle characteristics of a product and illustrate the differences between basic, expected, potential and ideal products in benefit terms
- Apply the Plymouth model of product architecture to existing and proposed products, link product features to the provision of intangible and tangible benefits and explain the importance of setting standards and test protocols for the evaluation of product performance
- Analyse the customer use of a product in a systems context and the role of supporting products in delivering satisfactory benefits to the user, analyse the product mix options for a given firm's context, review the contribution of packaging to product success and understand the importance of branding and describe the major branding approaches
- Evaluate the balance of forces for product standardisation versus product adaptation for international markets

Introduction

A successful product is an entity that customers perceive to meet and provide their benefit needs and wants. The entity may be a physical product, a service or a mixture of both (the product–service continuum discussed in Chapter 3). In the marketing of make-up, it is said that 'in the factory we make cosmetics; in the shop we sell hope'. Products have features that deliver benefits and we can view a product as an 'input–output' device. The inputs are the features that are designed or formulated into the product. The outputs are the benefit sets that the customers and users need, want, expect, value and pay for (Figure 4.1).

Not all customers are the same and different groups demand different benefit sets. In personal care products, manufacturers formulate different products for men and women. This process of dividing a market into subsets is called market segmentation. Effective segmentation is the foundation to formulating the marketing mix (see Figure 2.4).

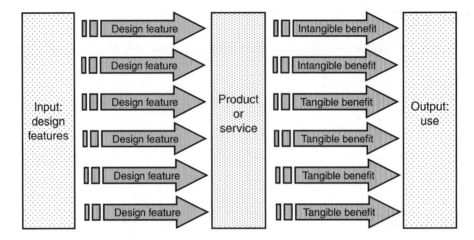

Figure 4.1 Product as an input–output system.

Market segmentation

The aim of market segmentation is to define a group of customers who have similar needs and are different to other groups. The process has to be practical and the resulting segments should be meaningful. It is easy to apply several segmentation processes and end up with a large number of small segments. In most cases, it is not practical to market to too many small market segments. The process of segmentation is not to be regarded as analytic and convergent. It is an open-ended process without a unique single right solution, just as in product design. The process does need analytic skills but these need to be directed in a creative problem-solving framework.

Consumer market segmentation variables

Gender Many products need different variants for males and females (e.g. clothing, cosmetics, magazines etc.).

Age People have different needs and wants at different stages of their lives. An undergraduate student has different financial needs to a retiring scientist.

Race Different cosmetics are required for different coloured skins (e.g. pale skinned Europeans are more sensitive to UV radiation than people with dark skins).

Religion Religion affects a whole range of products, including clothing, food, drink and financial services.

Geographic This not only includes issues such as country of residence but other approaches (e.g. city dweller as opposed to rural residence).

Geo-demographic segmentation Where people live gives an indication of their lifestyles. In the UK, each small residential area has a postcode and these have been classified (e.g. ACORN) according to the nature of the housing. People in small, city-centre studio apartments have different lifestyles to commuters living in the suburbs in a detached house, with a large garden.

Personality and lifestyles Lifestyle affects the range of products people want (e.g. sports enthusiasts).

Socio-economic groups Professional status and income affect some purchases (e.g. the more educated and higher earners tend to be more frequent customers to arts events).

Purchase occasion Some products are purchased at specific times of the year (e.g. Easter eggs, perfumes – duty free on holiday, Christmas and birthdays – and fireworks). This can provide interesting problems for technologists to ensure availability of products with short periods of high demand (e.g. flowers for Valentine's or Mothers' Day, cold storage of Easter eggs etc.).

Benefit sought A computer may be used by one person to write a book and another to play games.

Consumption behaviour A typical classification would be heavy, medium, light and non-user for a service or product (e.g. use of the internet).

The above is a starting prompt list. Variables may need to be interpreted for any given situation and novel segmentation approaches will need to be devised. Figure 4.2 shows the process. Sometimes the segmentation variables are simple and provide just a few relevant variables. In providing restroom facilities in a university teaching block, only three variables might be considered: male, female and disabled. In risk evaluation for car insurance, the systems will work down to a segment of an individual: a personal profile for a given driver. Variables likely to be built into the risk algorithm are postcode (measure of risk of theft), type of car, age of car, driver's gender, age, past accident record, occupation etc. This is an example of the application of multiple segmentation variables. Table 4.1 shows the range of products devised and issues considered by a fabric-care formulation scientist. B2B segmentation is different and these issues have been considered in the previous chapter.

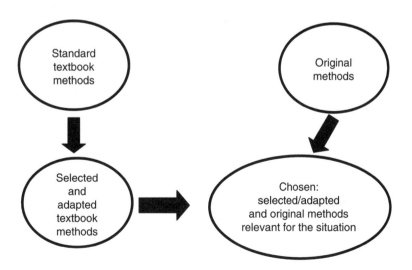

Figure 4.2 The segmentation process.

Table 4.1 Some selected segmentation of detergents

Standard variable	Interpretation	Comments
Geographic	Hard water and soft water area	In hard water areas (water from chalk and limestone sources), washing machines need to be protected from scale build up
	Out-of-town use	In rural areas, with septic tanks in use, formulations may need modification
	International	The popularity of various types of washing machines varies from country to country (e.g. top-loaders vs front-loading automatic)
Consumption	Singles in studio apartments are lighter users than large families	Different size packs
Benefits	**Cleaning:** food stains etc. are different to other soil	Biological and non-biological products
	Cost: heavy users on tight budgets (e.g. large families) need to have economy of washing; professional singles not so concerned	Premium products such as branded detergent pods and economy generic powders. Low temperature washing reduces costs
	Allergies: concern for allergic reactions	Low allergy, non-biological formulations, possibly without perfume
	Appearance: maintenance of appearance of fabric: colour	White products may need bleach and optical brighteners. Coloured products may need 'colour-care' formulations. Black fabrics can show powder streaking (specially formulated liquid products)
	Appearance: maintenance of appearance of fabric: nature of fabric	Cotton is different to wool and silk. Different products needed for different fabrics
Personality	Some people just want to clean their clothes; others want to save the planet. Low temperature saves energy and carbon dioxide emissions	Low temperature and eco-friendly formulations
Other segmentation issues		
Method of washing	Hand washing, automatic machines, top-loading machines	High-foam detergents, formulated for hand washing, will be a disaster in an automatic washing machine (it can flood the kitchen with suds). Low-foam products are needed for automatics

Table 4.1 (*Continued*)

Standard variable	Interpretation	Comments
Ease of use	Some people find measuring out a quantity of detergent irritating	Detergent tablets and liquid pods
Place of wash	Home, launderette and open air	In developed countries, small vending packs may be needed for launderettes. In less-developed countries, washing is often done by hand with bars of laundry soap
B2B applications	Laundries form a different market	Bulk deliveries

Product life cycle

Products have a life cycle. They are introduced to the market and, if successful, grow to maturity. After a time, the product will decline and be replaced. In the 1950s, the music enthusiast would listen to 'micro-groove' long-playing (LP) records. In the 1980s, the LP was replaced by the CD. In its turn the CD is now being replaced by downloads and MP3 players. The actual time for this process can vary from a few weeks ('England for the World Cup' sweatshirt) to a lifetime. Wet film technology served the amateur photographer for over a hundred years. When the end came courtesy of digital photography, it was quick. Within a few years most mobile telephones had an embedded digital camera.

Figure 4.3 shows some of the typical life cycle patterns. Care has to be taken in the analysis because different market sectors may exhibit different product life cycle characteristics. In the UK, the bicycle as a primary form of transport is largely extinct except for a few sturdy Greens. However, in the form of the mountain bike, it is alive and well as a leisure/sports item. Chanel No. 5 has remained among the top-selling fine fragrances for generations by careful relaunching with the new 'face' of Chanel every few years.

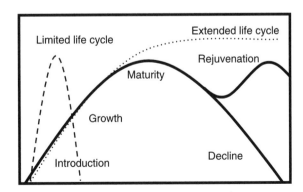

Figure 4.3 Product life cycle patterns. Adapted from: Tony Curtis, *Marketing in Practice*, figure 3.1, page 80, © Elsevier 2006.

The message for the technical company is that it must maintain a balanced portfolio of products. Polaroid and Kodak were highly linked with specific photographic technologies and when the life cycle of their expertise was ended by digital technologies they were in difficulties. Companies in turbulent technological markets must exist with challenging life-cycle demands. Wave upon wave of new technology rapidly makes last year's cutting edge product look dated. Domestic entertainment manufacturers had to move seamlessly on from cathode-ray technology to liquid crystal and plasma displays. The organisation needs to ensure that there are new products to replace those in decline. More consideration of portfolio analysis is given in Chapter 16.

MICRO CASE STUDY

THE REJUVENATION OF HARLEY DAVIDSON

Harley Davidson was founded in 1903. At the height of the American motorcycle industry, there were 114 bike manufacturers in the USA. In 1977, Honda was the leading motorcycle brand in the USA, with Harley Davidson (the only remaining major US manufacturer) down to less than 6% of the market. The Harley had become associated with less reputable members of society (*The Wild One*, starring Marlon Brando, was a portrayal of the situation). The Honda was positioned as 'nice', 'easy going', 'friend' and 'family'. Hondas were largely low-powered bikes and were marketed to a different section of the community. One advertisement read: 'You meet the nicest people on a Honda.' This was a bleak period for Harley, who regularly featured in the 'what went wrong stories' in business texts.

Fast-forward to the 2000s: Harley has become one of the most iconic and powerful international brands, with a decade of growth and strong profitability to show for it. The products sell for more than some cars. Harleys are fashion icons, many being bought by 'born again baby boomers' for leisure and as a personal lifestyle statement. They use the Jaguar for the daily commuting but at the weekend the grey suit comes off and the leathers go on. Loyalty is such that owners form themselves into 'chapters'. Purchase of a Harley is not so much about owning a bike, but ownership of a classic and entry into a worldwide club. Great products and brands can sometimes be rejuvenated if the right segment is identified and attacked with the right product positioning and inspirational marketing.

The nature of products

Products have a range of features and benefits. These can be defined into hygiene features and motivating features. If the product has all the required hygiene features, it has the possibility of entering the race. However, this is like a 'fun-runner' in the London Marathon; there is not much likelihood of winning the race. Hygiene features are the core benefits provided by the basic product (Figure 4.4). They are expected and, if supplied, no notice is taken of them. If they are not provided, the customer will disappear. A hotel will not advertise 'All our rooms have beds'; this is expected. If the hotel advertised 'Our rooms are very cheap, bring your own bed and sleeping bag', they are not likely to gain much business. A person does not buy a given car because it has four wheels, has an engine and provides

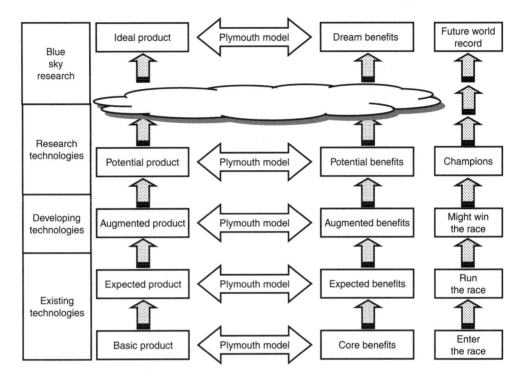

Figure 4.4 Levels of product: basic to ideal.

transport. People expect more: air conditioning, in-car entertainment, satellite navigation, smart engine management system, good styling, etc. The goalposts are always moving: last year's augmented product will be this year's expected product. If we want to be champions we had better be developing the technologies to create the potential product. If we want to be a world-beater, blue sky research will be needed to invent the technologies for the ideal product of the future. In a short time, the mobile telephone has evolved from a wondrous one-kilo brick, costing hundreds of pounds, into an entertainment and communications centre that fits in your shirt pocket.

MICRO CASE STUDY   **THE HISTORY OF THE GLASS WINDOW**

The Stone Age hut had a hole in the mud wall, with an animal skin curtain and a gap in the roof to let out the smoke from the wood fire. In brick and stone buildings, a hole in the wall was fine to let in daylight, but could be rather draughty in the winter. What was needed was something that kept out the cold air but let in the daylight; what was needed was window glass.

   In medieval times, one way to make window glass was to blow a glass sphere. With the glass still hot and soft, the end of the sphere, opposite the blow-pipe, could be cut off. The pipe and the soft glass could then be spun and the soft bottomless sphere opened out and flattened into a glass disk. Where the blowpipe was attached would be a 'bulls eye' surrounded by concentric ridges. There were four problems with this process: the process was slow, the process was expensive, only comparatively small sheets of glass could be made and the surface of the glass was far from perfect. This type of glass provided light but not good vision.

The next process was to 'draw' the glass and this provided larger sheets and the surface was much more even, although not optically flat. The subsequent great revolution was the Pilkington float glass process. Here, the molten glass is allowed to cool over a large tank of molten metal. According to the rate at which the molten glass is added to the tank and drawn off, the thickness of the glass can be varied. The surface of the molten metal is a perfect flat, with no surface imperfections. The resulting glass is of good optical quality and the overall process is cheaper than the old process. Perfect window glass had arrived. Actually, no, not yet!

One of the fun jobs of owning a house is cleaning the windows. It's just what a Sunday morning is made for. Who wants to read the paper over a lazy breakfast on Sunday? Better to be up with the birds and get scrubbing. When you are driving a car and it starts to rain you turn on the wipers and squirt a jet of cleaning fluid onto the windscreen. The detergent in the cleaning fluid reduces the surface tension of the water, allowing the windscreen to be cleaned.

The next step in the development of glass windows is to build a surfactant into the glass surface and you have self-cleaning glass. Add a silver oxide catalyst to oxidise, under the influence of sunlight, stubborn bird contributions and they too can be removed. There we are – perfect window glass. Well, no!

It is a hot sunny day; we want the glass to become more reflective. In the evening, for privacy, we might want the glass to become opaque. Developments are in hand to produce electro-chromatic glass. This will change its properties by application of suitable electrical voltages to the glass. We can have intelligent windows for our intelligent house. These are today's research technologies.

What is the ideal window? Will it also become the room lighting in the evening, providing us with a substitute for natural daylight? The ideal window is limited only by our imagination. The ability to provide it depends on new technologies not yet discovered.

How could the nineteenth century communications engineer, criss-crossing the oceans with telegraph cables, have envisioned today's network of digital optical communications. The Morse code, a method of transmission of characters for radio and cable transmission based on 'dots' and 'dashes' (short and long pulses), can be considered as an early digital communications code, at a few bits (sic) per second. We now take 8 Mb per second to be normal for domestic broadband access and send megabits of pictures home from the holiday beach in the Bahamas. Ultimate products will depend on blue sky research providing the enabling technologies. Transistors, lasers and fibre optics provided the foundation for the early twenty-first century potential products. What will be the new technologies, taking us closer to the ideal product?

There is an interaction between the benefit needs of society for the ideal product and the enabling technologies. The new product development question is the 'chicken and egg' problem. Which comes first, the technology or the market identification of the benefit need? Which is more important? If we have a benefit need and no technology we do not have a product (e.g. there is not yet an effective vaccine for AIDS). If we have a product but no need, we do not have a product. To have a successful product, we need enabling technologies and real demand from the market for the benefits. Consider it a double gate situation, as found in some electrical circuits (e.g. relay logic systems): both gates have to be open for success. The creative process can start from either platform. A perceived market need can set off a search for the technology (e.g. the search for an effective AIDS vaccine) or a technology developed for one purpose can be implemented to produce entirely new products. What is needed is the way to link the benefit needs to the technical or engineering definition of the product. This is provided by the Plymouth model (shown later in Figure 4.6).

Plymouth model for the architecture of product

The Plymouth model provides a framework for the analysis of an existing product or a template to draw up a product innovation charter definition for a new product. The treatment below is given in the context of new product development. Prior to the application of the Plymouth model the segmentation process should be completed. The needs of dissimilar segments are different and these variations need to be reflected in the marketing mix for each of the selected target market segments.

Market positioning

Returning to the fabric-care example earlier in this chapter, we note that for white cotton clothes the proposition, the positioning statement, for a detergent might be 'washes whiter.' For a low-temperature product, designed for coloured, special-finish fabrics, the positioning statement might be 'colour care, easy iron' (see Figure 4.5). The formulation of the product will need to be different to reflect the different functional (benefit set) needs and product positioning.

Although this model is simple it does allow the product proposition to be compared with that of other products in the marketplace. It is one tool for new product visioning.

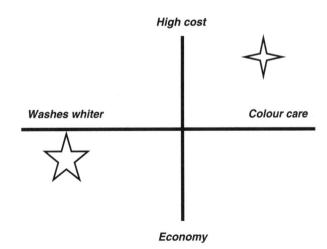

Figure 4.5 Brand positioning map. Adapted from: Tony Curtis, *Marketing in Practice*, figure 1.11, page 26, © Elsevier 2006.

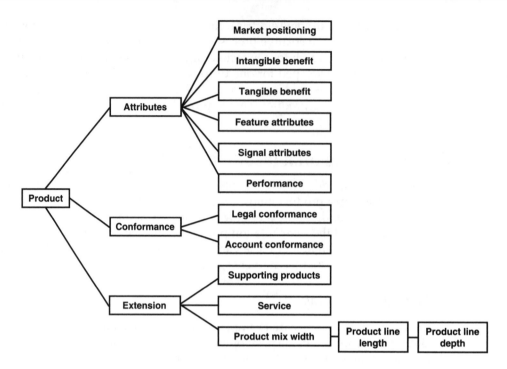

Figure 4.6 Plymouth product model. Adapted from: Tony Curtis, *Marketing in Practice*, figure 1.11, page 26, © Elsevier 2006.

If the spread of products leaves a hole in the cover of the domain of all possible market positioning, then this might indicate that there was a gap in the market. Market leader companies are always attempting to find good market gaps and then be first to develop products for them. Another strategy, followed by the market followers, is to create 'Me too' products. Here, the engineer or formulation scientist re-creates a product with very similar or even identical market positioning. The trick to this process is to find the 'right' variables for the product positioning variables. Figure 4.5 shows this process in two dimensions but segmentation variables form a multidimensional space and products should be mapped in a multidimensional space. In the detergent example, two additional vectors might be ease of use and degree of eco-friendliness.

Having defined the market segment and the positioning of the product in the segment the next stage is to complete the attribute analysis. For a market-driven process this should begin with the analysis of the benefit set. There are two types of benefits: intangible and tangible (see Figure 4.6).

Intangible benefits

Many of the products we buy have an aesthetic component. The textile technologists, working with the fashion designers, are creating clothes that are fashionable and make people feel good. We buy a Chelsea football shirt because we want to belong to the Chelsea fellowship, not just because we want to keep warm. A generic shirt of the same quality might be available for a few pounds in Primark, but we are happy to pay considerably more for the intangible benefits of it being a Chelsea shirt (the Chelsea colours do not make it warmer or last longer). In the levels of product model (Figure 4.4) we largely concentrated on physical features and performance. However, for many products, a significant proportion of the benefit set is in the intangible benefits. It may be on these intangible benefits that the business is won or lost. The flowers purchased for the candle-lit romantic dinner for two are about creating a sense of occasion. Much the same is true for the scented candle. The product packaging will not announce 'As effective as a 20 watt electric bulb but only 10% as efficient and a great fire hazard'. It is more likely to say 'Relaxing and romantic scent of tropical yang, jasmine and sensual sandalwood'.

It is easy to think that intangible benefits are not important for prosaic products such as car lubricating oil. However, the owner of a £50,000 car wants reassurance that this liquid component is looking after their prized possession. Often, successful marketing communications will be focusing on the intangible benefits. The old slogan of 'the Colgate [toothpaste] ring of confidence' was focusing on self-assurance, coolness and social acceptability. Deep in the small print you might find 'kills the bacteria that cause bad breath'. Marketing it as 'disinfectant for the mouth' is not likely to hit the success button. Although we are not able to measure 21 litres of confidence, 12 kilograms of love, 33 metres of reassurance, or 60 decibels of compassion, these are some of the most important things in our lives. Products that deliver these benefits are more likely to be purchased.

Tangible benefits

These are the actual physical things we wish the product to deliver. In some ways the process can be regarded as mission, aims and objectives for the product innovation charter. The mission is the delivery of the intangible benefits and the aims and objectives of the product are the explicit, measurable outcomes needed. As such, tangible benefits should be expressed as measurable outcomes. This is important, as we need to evaluate performance; performance evaluated against the tangible benefit objectives we have set ourselves. In the design of a car, one of the intangible benefits might be a sense of well-being for the driver. A sweltering hot driver in a summer heat wave is suffering a lack of well-being. Freezing to death on a frosty winter morning is not a lot better. This could be translated to the tangible benefits of 'Maintain an even car temperature of 20°C to 25°C for ambient temperatures from minus 10°C to plus 40°C'.

For some products, imagination and ingenuity are needed to define tangible benefits and their estimation. For a low-calorie drink product, a beverage technologist might have the brief 'should taste sweet'. Unfortunately we do not have a pH meter for sweetness. For sensory perceptions the use of trained panellists can assist. (More consideration of panel selection and training is given in Chapters 14 and 15.)

Feature attributes

Having defined what the product has to achieve, the engineer and technologist can use these as design parameters for the product innovation charter. The creative process can then be sought to find the most effective and efficient design and formulation solutions. To maintain the car temperature, the engineer might consider that a heater with x heat output was needed and an air-conditioning unit of y output. The flavourist, devising the low-calorie drink, will go to the spectrum of artificial sweeteners. The nuts and bolts of product specification and design can now get underway.

Signal attributes

For many domestic and personal care products a desired intangible benefit is 'well-being'. We do not associate well-being with the aroma of half-eaten pizza and stale beer in the party room the morning after our shindig. Concepts of 'fresh as an Alpine spring meadow' are more likely to be the order of the day. A detergent is odourless and in any case it is rinsed away (we hope) at the end of the cleaning process. The vast majority of household and personal care products are fragranced. How do we know the room is clean and get the sense of well-being? Because it smells clean, just like an Alpine meadow in spring.

Many technical products are not very interesting in themselves. That is a great microchip, just look at the sexy terminals on that! How do we know that it is a very good TV? Because it looks good, not that we have a PhD in communications engineering and have just spent three hours with a signal analyser checking out the circuits. In our earlier consideration of services, we learned that the service extension of the marketing mix was needed to make the intangible service tangible. We labelled the process as confirmation. Packaging and product design can convey intangible aspects of products and product performance. An important factor, in the purchase selection of a motorcar, is its design styling; it not only has to be aerodynamic but also look good. A TV is not just an electronic device, in the home it is functional furniture and must look good. The iPod was simply a clever technical gismo; part of the reason for its success was its design styling. The iPod will join such products as Concorde as a design icon, capturing the *zeitgeist* of the time. Watches and mobile telephones should be considered as functional fashion jewellery. Good styling and design is not an alternative to good engineering or technology. Great products marry form and function to produce iconic market beaters.

Performance

One important rule of engineering and technology is: *to control, you have to measure*. In setting the desired tangible benefits we should express them in ways that can be quantified or assessed. Simple parameters such as temperature can be easily measured but products often throw up more challenging issues. For a vast range of products, including food, cosmetics, surface coatings, printing inks and textiles, colour matching is a significant issue. That Chelsea shirt better be just the right colour. Wherever possible, instrumental methods should be developed. Instrumental methods have been developed for colour matching of difficult materials such as textiles. They are more consistent and panel testing, with highly trained personnel, is expensive.

A hair conditioner may claim the benefit 'easy to comb'. Just what does this mean and how do you measure it? Cosmetic chemists have come up with a solution. Wash standard swatches of hair under standard test conditions with the test formulations and the control standard. Attach the test swatch to a frame and insert a comb connected to a force-measuring device. Then measure the force needed to move the comb through the hair. The cosmetic scientist then has a set of benchmarked figures to support the claim 'easy to comb' and can set about improving the product performance even further. The feedback loop is completed.

What are needed are measures and estimates of performance which indicate the product's performance in the customer's end-use situation, with methods that indicate the probable level of customer satisfaction. To set a tangible benefit aim without setting standards and devising methods of estimation is a complete waste of time. More consideration of the measurement of product performance is given in Chapter 14.

Legal conformance

Consumers demand products that are safe. They want to exercise choice and need information (the Kennedy rights). To satisfy these public demands, there is a tangle of laws. These may be specific about materials that may not be used (e.g. colours no longer regarded safe for food use) or testing standards (e.g. collision performance of a car and fire resistance tests for fabrics). Regulatory compliance is a major demand on technical staff and specialist testing facilities may be needed. Product descriptions have to give specific information, often using very prescribed and detailed protocols (e.g. food and drink labelling). In the UK a small specialist craft producer of 'home made' ice cream ran into legal problems with their 'Rum-n-raisin' ice cream, made with real rum. As this contained over 0.5% alcohol, a licence to sell alcohol was required. The licensee had to attend a specified training course (normally designed for publicans) and the product could only be sold to people over 18 (bring your passport to buy an ice cream). This is a particular problem with new classes of products and considerable legal/technical judgement may be needed; just when does a food become an alcoholic drink?

Account conformance

Many companies have generalised supplier conformance issues such as employment policies (e.g. equal opportunity, international supplies, no inappropriate use of child labour etc.). These are generalised management issues and not covered further in this text. Issues for international customers (e.g. Kosher conformance for food and drink products) were outlined in Chapter 2. However, individual companies may have their own specific requirements. Some cosmetic companies want to make the claim that their product contains no animal derived products, so this may restrict the use of some ingredients (e.g. should bees wax be classified as an animal derived product?). A key area for food technologists is the concern with healthy eating. 'Junk' food is perfectly legal. Simple rules can be perverse (e.g. 'ban all high-fat foods' clears the cheese counter for you). Some considerable debate is needed between the supplier and the customer company to get sensible interpretations and suitable reformulated products (e.g. 'bad' hydrogenated fats eliminated, low-salt recipes etc.).

In discussing product performance it is essential that buyer and seller agree methods of test. Old methods of testing density used to measure the weight of a given volume of liquid. With modern instrumentation, it is possible to measure density to a high degree of accuracy – sufficient precision that the density of the air displaced by the liquid could be a significant error (should you note the atmospheric pressure to make this correction as well?). If a chemical 'beam balance' is employed, with the use of weights, changes in gravitational acceleration (g) in various parts of the earth will not affect the result. If a load-cell approach is used, then changes in g in different parts of the world will give slightly different results. A common way to measure density is to measure the frequency of vibration of a U-tube filled with the liquid under test. The frequency of the vibration depends on the mass (not the 'weight') of the liquid. Transnational bodies help with testing procedures (e.g. European Standards) and can provide international testing protocols (e.g. measurement of fuel efficiency of an engine). Learned bodies or trade associations can set standards (e.g. communications standards for digital signals). However, where such standards do not exist, it is part of the new product development brief to define the product innovation charter, to not only specify performance standards but also the protocols and reference standards to be used in their measurement.

INSIGHT

WHAT IS DIFFERENT TO MASS WHEN COMPARED TO LENGTH AND TIME?

A vital aspect of good laboratory practice (GLP) is that all measurements should have an audit trail that links the measurement to agreed international standards. The international standards for length and time depend on physical properties of atoms and light. The definition of one kilogram is still a platinum weight in France. (More consideration of GLP is given in Chapter 15.) The message is clear. To give a measurement you need to also specify the reference standards used and the detailed test protocol. In the above discussion of density, no reference was made to temperature. Liquids change volume with temperature (which is how a liquid-in-glass thermometer works) so the temperature of the measurement needs to be specified.

Supporting products

In the context of B2B marketing of components and ingredients it is essential that the components marry up precisely on the production line. It is not much use if one component has left-handed threads and the other right-handed threads. It is essential that all the components combine to function perfectly. A special case of this exists where the 'components' have to integrate in the customers' end-use situation. A washing machine is, in this sense, not a complete washing system. To function, the machine has additional needs: electricity, hot water, cold water, detergent, bleach (in some countries liquid bleach is added in washing whites) and fabric conditioner. When liquid detergents were first introduced to the UK market the machines were not designed for this type of formulation. The improvised solution was the 'detergent ball', to be filled up with the liquid formulation and added into the wash in the drum. The same situation applies to a car: you do not get far without fuel, lubricants, glycol coolant, screen-wash and insurance.

In the development of new products and in moving into new international markets, it is essential that the customer has access to the supporting products that are necessary for the actual performance of the product to deliver the benefit. Poor quality in any part of the system will cause problems.

> ### MORE IS NOT NECESSARILY BETTER
>
> Some fuels have a tendency to foam and this can cause fuel to froth out of the car fuel tank during the filling operation. This is unpleasant (who likes a shoe full of diesel?) and dangerous. Very small quantities of silicones (antifoaming agents) are added to minimise this problem. In 2007, there was an error in dosing and high levels of silicones were added to a large batch of petrol. Motorists found, to their dismay, this interfered with a sensor in the engine management system and the damaged part had to be replaced.
>
> **A fuel for all seasons**
> A diesel engine functions differently to a petrol engine. The diesel fuel is injected into the engine and has a higher boiling point than gasoline. Diesel can contain a certain amount of waxy materials. These are no problem in warm, summer weather but in a severe winter frost, waxy sludge can precipitate out of diesel fuel and clog the fuel lines. As the leaves begin to change colour in the autumn, companies start to deliver winter grade diesel fuel. The winter grade fuel is formulated to have a lower waxing temperature.

Service

Looking at the product–service continuum (discussed in Chapter 2), we note that many products need services and these may be provided by another company. In the latest case, they should be considered under supporting products (e.g. electricity and water supply for the washing machine). Services can be an important profit source. A car manufacturer can make more profit from selling car maintenance and financial services (insurance and car purchase loans) than on the original purchase of the vehicle. Effective service is part of the package needed by the customer (e.g. a car where it is difficult to get spare parts becomes a nightmare).

Product mix

Originally, the Model T Ford had a restricted product mix: one product line, a car, and one variant, black. Ford now makes a whole range of products, from commercial workhorses (B2B market) to cars (consumer capital goods), in a diverse product mix. Cars (one product line) are available in a number of different categories serving different major consumer market segments: there is a considerable product line length (e.g. luxury (Jaguar), saloon, town run-around, 4 × 4 etc.). Ferrari makes some good sports cars but they do not offer a town run-around or a range of commercial vehicles. They have a narrow product mix width and a very short product line length. A key decision for a manufacturer is to decide the appropriate product mix for their target markets and business strategies. Diversity allows tailored products to better fit a wider selection of target segments. However, diversity comes with costs and drains on management energy. The product mix decisions are linked to the segmentation and positioning strategies of the organisation. A summary of the Plymouth model is given in Table 4.2.

Table 4.2 Summary of the Plymouth product model

Plymouth model element	Comments and selected examples
Attributes	
Market positioning	What is the proposition being made to the customers and users in the target segment (e.g. up-market, down-market, easy to use, advanced eco-friendly etc.)? This process must be repeated for each market segment
Intangible benefits	Love, security, status, self-confidence, freedom, well-being, belonging, excitement, comfort, relaxation etc. are things that are important to the buyers and users but may not be measured in the normal sense (we have yet to devise the sex-meter). When we buy a lock we are marketing security not hardware
Tangible benefits	These include temperature control (air conditioning), transport (vehicles), access time (broadband), hair shine (hair conditioner), shelf life (UHT milk), economy (refilling ink cartridges), etc. The acid test is whether there is a physical method of measuring or estimating the parameter. The fuel economy of a car can be measured. The sweetness of a product can be estimated with panel tests. If it is a tangible benefit you can measure or estimate it; if you can't it is an intangible benefit. The skill is translating intangible benefits into the supporting tangible benefits. Comfort and well-being in a car is slightly intangible but the tangible benefits can be developed – e.g. temperature (not too hot or too cold), air circulation (not stale but not a blast from hell), leg room etc.
Feature attributes	The precise formulation or product design elements. Can include materials of construction, manufacturing process and sources of raw materials etc. Sometimes features may link directly to intangible benefits. A 'fair trade' cotton shirt does not keep you warmer than a standard cotton shirt
Signal attributes	Colour, texture, odour, sound, shape etc. can all signal properties. Strawberry ice cream will be pink, not green. These are elements that are designed or built into a product to allow the product to communicate (e.g. the aesthetic design of a game console is important as a contributor to product success). For services the service extension of the marketing mix acts in a similar way to signal attributes for products, making the intangible tangible
Performance	The methods of test to measure the products ability to deliver the tangible benefits (e.g. stain removal measurements for a detergent, distortion measurement for an audio amplifier system etc.). If you do not have a method of testing, your tangible benefit has become a pseudo-intangible benefit
Compliance	
Legal conformance	Labelling: 'must not haves' (e.g. banned food additives, banned heavy metals pigments in paint), 'must haves' (e.g. tamper-evident packs for food), safety standards, emission standards etc.

Table 4.2 (*Continued*)

Plymouth model element	Comments and selected examples
Account conformance	Issues that are not legal requirements but have become demanded by specific accounts. Sometimes these are rather specialist (e.g. Kosher compliance for a manufacturer of food products for the Jewish market) or more general (e.g. ISO 9000 compliance for suppliers as a quality audit requirement). In the briefing process it is important these account conformance requirements (e.g. 'must haves' and 'must not haves') are known to the NPD team. A good understanding of the purchasing company's DMU is essential
Extension	
Complementary products	It is essential to take a systems view of a product. Most products are used in conjunction with other products and services. The complete system must deliver the expected benefits to the required standard or you do not have a product. That new computer is a bit of a dead duck if the power supply does not plug in and in any case will not take the local voltage. That great program is not a lot of use if most people still do not have Vista.
Service	Typical services are: design, technical support, installation, training and maintenance. Remember the product–service continuum
Range and depth	*Product range:* the number of different lines that the company decides to make. Does a manufacturer of locks (benefit definition of business: security) also make burglar alarms, smoke and carbon monoxide detectors? *Product depth:* the number of different subvariants of the product that the company decides to offer: sizes, thickness, flavours, colours, materials (e.g. nut and bolt manufacturer: mild steel, high tensile steel, stainless steel, brass etc), power ratings (e.g. range of electric motors), functions etc. Note: these decisions are linked to the segmentation and targeting strategy of the firm

---

| MICRO CASE STUDY | **MOBILE PHONES FOR TEENAGERS** |

One of the most competitive markets is that for mobile telephone handsets. These have become 'must have' functional fashion accessories. From time to time, fashion magazines will feature 'this season's mobiles'. Table 4.3 outlines an analysis for the teenage market.

Packaging

Packaging gets a very bad press. Hardly a week goes by without the Green lobby launching an attack on 'over-packaged' products. This section is not setting out to defend the UK addiction with free carrier bags at the supermarket checkout. However, packaging is a

Table 4.3 Outline application of the Plymouth model to mobile telephone handsets for the teenage market

Plymouth model element	Comments and selected examples
Attributes	
Market positioning	Advanced, funky
Intangible benefits	Connected (belonging; my friends only a text away), security, status, self-confidence, excitement (e.g. games features)
Tangible benefits	Capabilities (e.g. images as well as text and sound communications), value (cost of ownership and use), battery life, sound and display quality, easy to carry, robustness etc.
Feature attributes	Built-in camera, memory size and media, display quality, battery type, chip set, material of case construction (plastic, metal), size and weight etc.
Signal attributes	Design, case colour, material of case cover etc.
Performance	Images: pixel density, brightness, colour range and contrast etc. Sound: volume and distortion. Value: cost of purchase – affected by cost of manufacture. Battery life: hours of performance under different use conditions (e.g. talk time, stand-by time etc.). Physical: easy to carry, small size and low weight, robustness (drop tests)
Compliance	
Legal conformance	Power levels for transmission etc.
Account conformance	Precise requirements of network providers and channels that retail the product to end users
Extension	
Complementary products	Radio network, power supplies, software, content providers, insurance etc.
Service	Technical advice from website and call centre for problems and questions (e.g. will my unit work on my holiday in Mongolia?) Other services such as insurance are likely to be provided by the channel
Range and depth	*Product range:* hands-free 'Bluetooth' headsets to provide hands-free use, range of MP3 players (note one trick in the industry is to provide multifunctional products combining what were different products before) etc. *Product depth:* range of different colour covers; specialist versions (e.g. adapted for visually impaired people)

vital aspect of products and poor packaging will cause problems. We would not accept a computer with dents and scratches. Above all else, packaging protects.

Protection

Computers, printers and the like are packaged to protect them from mechanical damage. Without the packaging, it would not be possible to stack 500 computers onto pallets and load them onto a flat-bed lorry. Packaging can do more than just provide mechanical protection.

In medieval times, more soldiers would die from disease and hunger than from wounds suffered in action. Knowledge of nutrition (e.g. importance of vitamins) and innovative packaging (e.g. tin can) changed this. Packaging protects products from contamination, including microbiological contamination. The exclusion of light and oxygen can also extend the shelf life of the product. Certain microorganisms need the right atmospheric conditions to thrive. Selecting the right atmospheric environment (mixture of gases) with multilayer (gas impervious) packaging can extend the shelf life of products such as meat. The toothpaste tube also protects the unused product. Packaging can still go on working, even after the product has arrived in the customer's hands.

Communication

The shape of the packaging can be an important part of the brand image. What would Perrier water be in a square bottle or Marmite in a cylinder? In the marketing of fashion products, perfume bottles are the pinnacle of commercial art. Old perfume bottles are collectors' items. The labels on the packaging not only convey brand imagery they convey factual information (e.g. how to use the product), much of it a statutory requirement (e.g. ingredients, amount of contents etc.). Bar codes and RFID chips convey the information that allows modern inventory systems to work. The modern supermarket could not exist without bar codes.

Dispensing

Packaging can assist customers in using the right amount of product. This can be single dose units (e.g. liquid detergent pod) or providing a measured amount of product. A life-critical example of this is aerosol inhalation medication systems for people suffering from asthma. Consistent dose delivery is not for convenience, but for life preservation. More prosaic examples are pump action dispensers on bottles of liquid hand-wash and measuring caps built into fabric conditioner screw tops (designed so fabric conditioner does not run down the outside of the bottle). Where would breakfast be without the upside-down ketchup bottle to add that final relish onto our egg and bacon? Innovation in packaging creates whole new brands and product types. How did we live without the toilet duck?

Point of sale

The supermarket shelves are crowded, so products have to sell themselves off the shelf. Innovative packaging, good graphic design and powerful branding are all essential ingredients to survive and thrive in the supermarket shelf jungle. This can present technical design requirements to ensure that products fit the displays and do not fall over. One criticism is that this can cause products to be over-packaged: 'Why do I need a blister pack for 12 little nuts and bolts when I can go into the local DIY store?' In the nineteenth-century hardware shop, a sales assistant would have gone to a wall with hundreds of little drawers, count out the required nuts, repeat the process for the bolts and then pop the items into a paper bag. (Just how did they keep track of inventory?) In the modern, post-industrial society, the time and cost of this labour may exceed the value of the item. Such packaging is thus a feature that is required to make our low-cost super-efficient distribution systems work.

Branding

Branding is a use of images, colours, shapes, words and symbols etc. used to differentiate the brand from its competitors. Brands are a form of intellectual property that may be registered for protection and traded (sold or licensed). Figure 4.7 shows a structure for branding.

Manufacturers may use a variety of branding strategies. A family brand may be used for a whole range of products. The Heinz brand, for instance, is used for products ranging from ketchup to soups. In some conditions, a brand manufacturer may decide to market products under individual brands (e.g. P&G with Bold and Daz detergents). A third option is to use a common name for different ranges. Ajax is a range of cleaners produced by Colgate-Palmolive. Their toothpaste products are marketed under the Colgate brand. An owner of a good brand may consider that it would be appropriate to offer some additional ranges under the same brand (brand extension). A typical example is a range of skin-care products marketed under the brand name of a successful fine fashion fragrance.

Supermarkets and other retailers (e.g. Staples, B&Q etc.) market products under their own labels. They may also create sub-brands for specific ranges (e.g. Per Una for M&S and George for Asda (fashion clothing)). At the other end of the spectrum, they stock 'no frills' basic products in generic packs, the proposition being adequate performance at the lowest price in town.

A problem confronts the OEM making 'prestige' materials and components. A related issue is when products are produced or sourced under 'prestige' conditions or processes (e.g. 'free range', 'organic', 'fair trade', 'ISO 9000', 'ISO 14000', etc.). Manufacturers of such intermediate products and raw materials develop their own brands and 'license' their logo and branding to end-use producers. The brand producers gain street credibility by using only the best in their production. The upstream producers encourage the ultimate consumers to seek out the best products; those that carry the seal of quality. Examples include 'Dolby

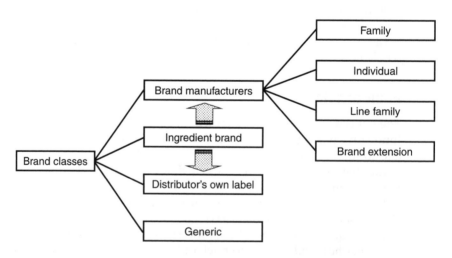

Figure 4.7 Structure of branding strategies. Adapted from: Tony Curtis, *Marketing in Practice*, figure 3.6, page 92, © Elsevier 2006.

sound' (feature films), 'Intel inside' (computers), 'NutraSweet' (low-calorie, non-sugar sweetener), 'Lycra' and 'Harris Tweed' (fabric brands made up into fashion clothing).

An important value of a brand is to reduce risk: 'I may not have bought this particular product before but if HP, M&S and the like are selling it, then I know it is OK.' In Chapter 2, in reviewing B2B marketing, the risk-adverse nature of the DMU was discussed. Thus, branding is still an important factor in B2B marketing. Many companies – such as HP, Ford, Lloyds and BA – operate in both B2C and B2B markets. Indeed, the same person may be both a B2B customer and B2C customer. A technical service engineer may fly BA to service a customer one week and next week fly BA on holiday with the family. This can be a double-edged sword: a bad holiday experience can discolour the brand later in a B2B context. People do not always stay in the same market segment: they can pop up in more than one context. Brand consistency with continual observance of the brand proposition and brand values is essential.

International

Should the offering be standardised or adapted? There may be cost reductions if products can be standardised but there can be macro- and microenvironmental restraints on this. Many technical products are relatively standardised. It would be a difficulty if the USB flash-drive only worked in France. However, even here, manuals may need to be provided in various languages. This is when the CD can come to the rescue: give them all the instructions in all the languages and they can then pick what they want. And we only have to supply one standard disk.

Some consumer products, such as fine fashion fragrances, tend to have the same formulation in all their markets. However, here too some difference may be needed (e.g. a switch of solvent away from alcohol for some countries). In most cases, changes will be necessary to the labelling and packaging of the product to reflect not only the local language but also other aspects such as the local STEEPLE and cultural environment. More consideration of product adaptation issues is given in Chapter 3.

Review

The basis of product analysis is to understand the market segments. Different market segments may have different benefit needs and the product positioning may need adaptation. This may involve changes in the product features. Users take the basic product and core benefits for granted. They have higher expectations. Market leader, innovative companies need to continue to climb the product ladder; to continually find new ways to engineer and formulate approaches to the ultimate ideal product, providing the dream benefit set. Markets evolve and the product life cycle concept was presented. The need for a balanced product portfolio was discussed.

The Plymouth model provides a tool to analyse how the input features provide the customers' desired benefit set – market driven design. Many products are parts of a system used by customers and this system context needs to be managed so that poor performance will not be experienced by the customer, even if our product component of the system is perfect. Packaging provides more than just physical protection and the additional dimensions of packaging's contribution to product success have been reviewed, as have the various approaches to branding strategy. The need, in international markets, to appraise the right balance for standardisation and adaptation was explained.

Further reading

Chelsom, J., Payne, A. & Reavill, L. (2005) *Management for Engineers, Scientists and Technologists*, 2nd edn, Wiley.

Crawford, M. & Di Benedetto, A. (2006), *New Products Management*, 8th edn, McGraw-Hill.

Curtis, T. & Williams, D. (2001), *An Introduction to Perfumery*, 2nd edn, Micelle Press.

Wilson, R. & Gilligan, C. (2005) *Strategic Marketing Management: Planning Implementation and Control*, 3rd edn, Elsevier.

CHAPTER 5

Price

Learning objectives

After studying this chapter you will be able to:

- Review the role of customer valuation in the formation of pricing strategy, explain the difference between customer value and affordability, illustrate with examples elastic and inelastic product demand contexts and assess the impact of the macro- and microenvironments on pricing decisions
- Apply the concepts of fixed and variable costs to calculate the break-even point for a given context, evaluate the alternative pricing strategies that can be used to exploit the strategic pricing gap and explain the range of options for setting prices
- Describe the concept of transfer pricing between strategic business units in a large company, review the impact of legal and taxation forces on prices, illustrate with examples the issues to be considered with pricing in international markets and discuss the options available for countertrade

Introduction

Customers are not impressed with 'price' as such. Their first concern is 'value'. If their perception of value is less than the price of the product offering, they will not buy it. Even if we have provided value, we are not home and dry because the customer must have the funds to purchase the product; so, therefore, it must be affordable. Customers must have the cash or have access to other sources of finance for the purchase to be possible. People concerned with controlling their telephone bills may prefer to use a 'pay-as-you-talk' mobile telephone contract rather than a direct debit, monthly account. In formulating the pricing strategy, consideration needs to be given to the acceptable methods of payment.

In a capitalist society, with free trade policies, the purchase transaction should be an exchange process. On one side of the exchange process, the buyer should consider that the purchased product provides value for money. The seller should consider that they have received a fair payment that will yield a fair profit; the second side of the exchange process. If the buyer considers the price is excessive they will feel 'ripped off' – a situation many bank customers found themselves in during 2007, with 'excessive' penalty bank charges on unauthorised current account overdrafts. If the supplier does not make a long-term profit, they will go out of business. Profit is the difference between sales revenue and the

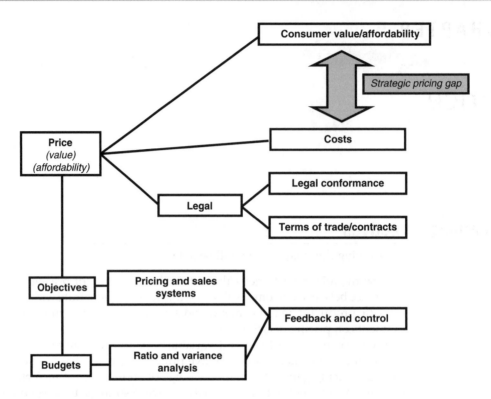

Figure 5.1 The architecture of price. Adapted from: Tony Curtis, *Marketing in Practice*, figure 4.1, page 112, © Elsevier 2006.

organisation's costs. The difference between product costs and customer value is called the strategic pricing gap. An implication of the model is that costs should not necessarily set the selling price. In the auction of a work of art, a free exchange process takes place. If the art form is popular (e.g. Picasso), the selling price may be many times the original purchase price. What costs do set is the minimum price (customers' perceived value) that a firm will consider acceptable. The other implications of the model are for the firm to work to increase the value of the offering (e.g. by marketing activities such as branding and celebrity endorsement) and to drive down the costs associated with the organisation's value chain (e.g. smart procurement policies). Figure 5.1 provides an overview of the architecture of pricing.

Customer value and affordability

A customer can walk into a shopping centre and pay less than £10 for a pair of jeans from Primark or go to a designer boutique and pay over £100. Both types of outlets thrive and are profitable. It is likely that the jeans are both made in the same type of low-cost manufacturing facility, in a low-wage economy, such as China. The additional price in the boutique is justified by the customer's perceived additional value of the designer jeans provided by the branding and celebrity endorsement of the product; not any massive

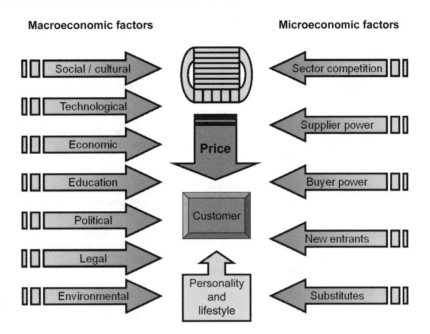

Figure 5.2 Environmental factors affecting price.

improvement of the quality or costs of manufacture. The high disposable income, fashion-conscious DINKY (double income, no kids yet) professional will happily pay the high price so as to join the elite set wearing the right styles for this season. The single parent family still has broadband and is well aware of fashion trends. They want cut-price trendy clothes and that is what Primark, Matalan and TK Maxx provide, but without the chic, celebrity endorsed designer label. Any of the macro- and microenvironment forces can affect how an individual consumer reacts to price. Additional internal factors, such as the consumer's personality, are considered in Chapter 7 under the heading of 'Buyer behaviour'. Figure 5.2 shows the factors affecting price. Table 5.1 illustrates the nature of these forces with some examples.

Elasticity of demand

When consumers perceive that the value of the product offering is relatively high, when compared to the purchase cost, then common sense would suggest that they will buy more of the product. The way in which people respond to changes in price with purchases is called *elasticity of demand*. Figure 5.3 schematically shows some demand curves. Elasticity of demand is the rate of change (in calculus terms, the derivative) of sales volume with change of price, $d_{[demand]}/d_{[price]}$. For schematic convenience, all the demand curves except 'fashion' have been shown as straight lines (in real life they are curves).

The elasticity of demand is a vital issue for services as it is often used as a method to attempt to regulate demand. Rail tickets in commuter hours are very expensive, attempting

Table 5.1   Selected examples of macro- and microenvironment forces on prices

STEEPLE element	Issue	Comments/examples
Social cultural	Fashion products are culturally sensitive	Last year's fashion is being remaindered; the skill is to predict today what people will want in six months' time
Technological	Obsolete technology becomes unsaleable	Who wants a cathode-ray TV when you can get those nice stylish flat screen sets that do not take up half of the room?
Economic	High interest rates	These cut into disposable income and force people to trade down and look for bargain prices. Attempts to edge prices up may be met with brand switching
Education	Lack of cost knowledge and understanding on complex products	Good advice being given by pressure groups such as the Consumers' Association to inform people on the total costs of ownership of items such as freezers
Political	Dumping	Low cost imports can cause job losses. This can lead to political pressures with demands for punitive duties and/or quotas to protect jobs
Legal	Role of regulators	In monopoly type conditions (e.g. utility services) the regulator has legal rights to enforce prices
Environmental	Landfill and recycling	Landfill is becoming scarce and expensive. Companies will not only have to make provisions in prices for distribution but also for recycling at the end of the life of the product
Competition forces		
In-sector	Overcapacity	The chip market swings from boom to bust. Demand is difficult to predict and new capacity comes on line in large chunks
Supplier power	Supply and demand effects	In the past, metals went in demand cycles. However, with some exotic elements with less than 50 years' proven reserves (e.g. indium), supplies will become more problematic and raw material prices will increase. Power will shift from buyers to suppliers
Buyer power	The promiscuous customer	Customers are becoming more price savvy (e.g. with the help of internet help sites) and will move to other brands to get better deals. This is keeping prices very competitive in segments such as consumer electronics
New entrants	The emerging superpowers	India and China have already provided severe levels of competition for industries such as European apparel manufacture. However, countries that can make nuclear bombs and put satellites into orbit are not just going to sit around making cheap sweatshirts. Fierce competition can soon be expected in advanced areas such as pharmaceuticals and aviation
Substitute products	Lower price alternatives are always interesting to consumers	As metal prices increase, a move to substitute plastics will be observed in such areas as domestic plumbing

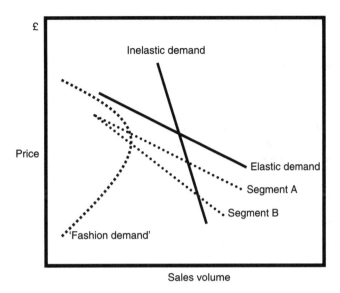

Figure 5.3 Elasticity of demand curves.

to discourage unnecessary journeys at this time. In the middle of the day, when core demand is low, rail operators will use off-peak pricing to lift the demand when there is spare capacity.

Elastic demand

If the demand for a product is strongly influenced by its price then the demand is said to be elastic. The rise of the low-cost airlines attracted many more travellers. The demand for air travel proved to be elastic: lower the price and gain more business.

THE COST OF WATER

In the UK, most water is unmetered and, once the water tax is paid, the marginal cost of water to consumers is zero: consumers can have unlimited baths and wash one shirt at time. Industry has to pay for water that is used because it is metered. Industry has to reduce water waste in manufacturing to minimise production costs. Government pressure is on to move domestic users over to meters as a method of driving down the waste of water as these resources get scarcer.

The cost of road use
For the vast majority of car journeys in the UK the cost of road use is free once car tax is paid. The continual rise in demand for road use is not sustainable. The congestion charge in London is a major experiment in pricing, which is attempting to manage a potentially out of control demand situation.

Inelastic demand

If the demand for a product is not strongly influenced by its price then the demand is said to be inelastic. Table salt is a part of every kitchen. However, if you reduced the price of table salt to 10% of its present price the demand would not go up tenfold. A 10% change in the price of table salt has very little effect on the volume of use. The use of table salt is much more influenced by healthy eating forces than price.

The same product in two different segments may have different demand curves (illustrated as segments A & B in Figure 5.3). In the purchase of a computer, most people do not look at the energy consumption; the use of electricity in powering computers is relatively inelastic. However, in the purchase of a water heating system, gas may be favoured if the cost of electricity is high, the electric elements in the hot water tank being only held as an emergency reserve in case of mechanical breakdown of the gas boiler. This example illustrates a second point about the elasticity of demand. Often the demand may be relatively inelastic in the short term. If the price of electricity rises 30%, people have modest options the next day. However, in the longer term, when they modify equipment, they can make changes.

The cost of a car is not just the purchase price of the car. There is a cost to the ownership of a car (e.g. insurance and road tax); there is a cost in the use of the car (fuel costs, etc.). When a person buys a new car they want to sell the old car. The resale value of the vehicle is an important factor in the total cost of the lifecycle of ownership of the vehicle. In looking at the elasticity of demand, it may not be just the purchase cost that the consumer is factoring into the purchase decisions, but also costs of ownership, costs of use and lifecycle of ownership costs.

Fashion pricing

With fashion and luxury products, there can be a special demand curve for a premium market segment product. If the designer perfume costs £1 000, not many people will purchase it, but if the price is in the £50 region, many people will. If it is £10, it ceases to be a premium market product and people in this segment will not purchase. There has to be some element of exclusivity in the pricing to position the product as a premium fashion product.

Customers wish to gain value and can only exercise their right to purchase if they have the necessary money or access to credit. The above discussion has provided an overview of how the macro- and microenvironment may have an impact on customers' perceptions of value. The elasticity of demand concept provides a framework for marketers to consider the potential impact of price changes on sales volume. This provides an understanding of the upper boundary of the strategic pricing gap. In the next section the lower boundary of cost is explored.

Costs

In the manufacture of a product or service there are three types of costs: fixed costs, variable costs and semi-variable costs. For the sake of illustration, we will consider a company making high-performance gas turbine components.

Fixed costs

These are the costs that do not change with the volume of production of components. Typical fixed costs are rent and insurance. If the company does not produce a single component, it still has to cover these costs. If the company is working at full capacity, the fixed costs still do not change.

Variable costs

These are the cost elements that vary in direct proportion to the volume of production. Typical major components of variable costs are the raw materials costs. In our case, it will be the cost of purchase of the metal blanks for machining and the costs of disposal of the swarf and waste cutting oil.

Semi-variable costs

Life can become a little more complicated when some costs do not fit neatly into the two boxes described above: fixed and variable. In our machining case, two costs may have slightly more complicated patterns. The cost of electricity to light and ventilate the workshop is not much affected by production intensity. However, the amount of electrical energy to drive the lathes, computer-aided manufacture (CAM) systems, etc. does depend on the level of activity. In this case, the single cost may be split into its fixed and variable components to facilitate analysis. At first sight, labour costs may be fixed – the employees are on the payroll and need to be paid irrespective of the level of activity. However, if production increases to a point where all normal hours are being effectively used, it may be possible to expand production with overtime and weekend working at different pay rates. This illustrates a second problem where there are break points in the cost structure. In the discussion of break-even analysis below, only fixed and variable costs will be considered. A more complete treatment of the issues in costing is given in Chapter 10.

Break-even analysis

For this analysis, we will consider a simple case of a workshop that only produces one component. The fixed costs will be the costs of renting, insuring, lighting and heating the workshop. The raw materials costs can be calculated from the bill of materials (list of parts and raw materials needed to make the component). At zero production volume, the costs are simply the direct costs. As production increases the total costs are:

$$\text{Total cost} = \text{fixed costs} + (\text{volume} \times \text{unit variable costs})$$

The sales income is:

$$\text{Sales income} = \text{volume} \times \text{sales price}$$

Profit is:

$$\text{Profit} = \text{Sales income} - \text{total costs}$$

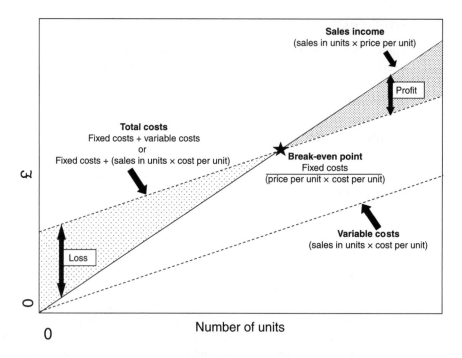

Figure 5.4 Schematic contribution break-even chart. Adapted from: Tony Curtis, *Marketing in Practice*, figure 10.7, page 254, © Elsevier 2006.

At low volumes, a negative profit is made: a loss. At high volumes, a profit is made. The point at which the firm makes a zero profit is called the break-even point. In some cases, the costs can be largely concentrated in the fixed costs. The cost of flying an airliner from the UK to the USA is much the same if the aircraft is full or half empty. In other cases, the costs are centred on the variable costs. A company manufacturing specialist components from platinum may find the raw materials costs to be the major proportion of their total costs. A project with a high break-even point is very vulnerable to any issues that may cause sales volumes to drop below target. Although break-even analysis is simple in concept, it does provide insight to the business issues (e.g. the need to contain fixed costs). Figure 5.4 provides a graphical presentation.

Care has to be taken in the input figures used. Historical costs are the costs that were actually incurred in the manufacture of the past batches. Current costs are the costs that will be incurred if production was in progress today. Future costs are the estimates of the costs of production at some defined time in the future. In our case of a specialist component manufactured in platinum (e.g. for the chemical industry where corrosion resistance is vital), the cost of the metal can double or halve in the space of a few months. The historical, current and projected costs could therefore be very different. Another complication is to decide the appropriate treatment of direct and indirect costs. Further consideration of the intricacy of costing is given in Chapter 10.

HOME INFORMATION PACKS

In 2007, the UK government faced a major problem with the introduction of 'home information packs' (a set of documents to be assembled by the seller of a house). One of the key documents, the 'Energy performance certificate', related to the energy efficiency of the house (e.g. level of insulation). There were not enough trained inspectors to meet demand. A consultancy and training company perceives that there is a market opportunity in providing a course to train inspectors for this work. The type of costs and break-even analysis are given in Table 5.2.

Table 5.2   Break-even analysis for training programme

Fixed costs	£	
Preparation of manuals	6,500	
Fees and expenses to trainers	8,500	
Hire of training room in hotel	2,000	
Marketing	4,500	
Total fixed costs	**21,500**	
Delegate variable costs		
Reproduction of manuals	125	
Stationery and other consumables	75	
Hotel day delegate rate	175	
Total Variable costs	**375**	
Break-even number @ rate of	1,000	34.4
Break-even number @ rate of	1,500	19.1
Break-even number @ rate of	2,000	13.2
Break-even number @ rate of	2,500	10.1
Break-even number @ rate of	3,000	8.2

Strategic pricing gap

Having created the strategic pricing gap by driving up value and driving down costs the next issue is to decide how to exploit the gap. This will depend on the organisation's business objectives motivating the policy. There are three aspects to be considered: the company's business/marketing objectives, the selection of strategy and the method used to set the price.

Pricing objectives

At different stages of product life cycle and in different conditions, organisations may need to operate various pricing objectives. In the entry into a new market, the objective may be to gain market share. With a mature product in a recession, the objective may be pure survival. A review of major objectives is given below.

Market share

Here, the company's key objective is to penetrate the market and gain market share. Pricing is not the only weapon to do this and an integrated mix approach needs to be adopted. Aggressive activity to gain market share will normally also include marketing communications and distribution strategies.

Maximum profit

In some cases the company may have a long-term position (e.g. with patent protection). The company may take the view that the best return is to maximise the profit over a longer term and sacrifice some short-term profitability to maximise the long-term returns.

Cash flow

Where there is a short-term opportunity, the need may be to extract the maximum cash flow in a short period.

Survival

Adverse macro- and microenvironment movements may put the organisation onto the defensive and the objective is maintaining the business's viability. Most businesses have long-term survival as an implicit, if not an explicit, factor in their pricing strategies.

Return on investment (ROI)

This is a general issue for business and an organisation will not wish to enter into a market without the long-term probability of obtaining a satisfactory return on the capital employed. Discounted cash flow (DCF) analysis provides a tool to assess the impacts of various strategies on long-term return on investment. The detailed methods are covered in Chapter 10.

Once the firm's objectives have been considered, then the precise pricing strategies can be determined. If the company has launched an innovative new product with high customer value then a skimming strategy (the analogy is with skimming the cream off milk) may be appropriate. In another situation the innovation may be a new way of working the value chain, such as reducing costs (e.g. low-cost airlines). Here, the lower costs can be used with a penetration pricing strategy.

Skimming strategy

High prices are charged and high profit margins gained. However, the sales volume may be limited. A typical situation would be with computer firmware. The company may well target the professional users with deep pockets and high benefit valuation with a first wave of skimming. When this market has been harvested, the company can drop the price and bring in domestic users with lower spending power. Over the long run, the company may make more profits, but some of these may be delayed.

A version of this is used with film releases. A blockbuster film will be released to the cinema market exclusively for a number of months before being released in DVD format for domestic viewing.

Penetration strategy

Where a company enjoys a market cost advantage over the competition, then low prices can be used to buy market share. For many years Chinese exports of textile products to Europe were limited by a fixed quota system. When these were removed, the Chinese entered the market with low prices that could not be matched by European-based garment manufacturers.

A version of this is used with 'buy now, pay later' strategies. A typical example is that very cheap, excellent quality, ink-jet printer – just wait until you need to buy the replacement cartridges! Another version is the 'free' mobile telephone. The profit is made over the length of the mandatory contract that comes bundled with it. Thus, the entry costs to the customer are low when the seller is using a penetration entry strategy. The profits are harvested on the later purchases that are needed. This version of the strategy is sometimes called 'captive pricing'.

Differential pricing

Here, the organisation may want to operate different prices in different markets. A typical example may be office software where professional segments may be suitable targets for skimming prices. More price-sensitive markets such as the student market may need different versions with a penetration price. This is often the strategy in international markets where higher prices will be charged in developed countries and low prices are required in developing countries. However, this can be difficult to maintain because people will arrange their own exports from the low-cost areas.

INSIGHT

EVERYDAY LOW PRICES – PROMOTIONAL PRICE

'Everyday low prices' is a pricing strategy. As it suggests, the same pricing strategy applies all year.

Promotional pricing is an invitation to buy now and the prices will not be available in a few weeks. This is a typical situation for a product launch where a launch offer will be used to build volume quickly.

Setting the price

Organisations have to have mechanisms to implement their pricing strategies. There is no single 'one size fits all' that applies to all situations.

Cost plus

Here, the seller examines the costs and then adds a margin. This has the advantage of being simple and can, if the prices can be sustained, provide a secure return on investment and profit margin. Earlier we discussed a company fabricating specialist corrosion-resistant components in platinum. With the volatile price for the metal, long-term contracts may have the cost of raw materials as a defined element. Distributors may work on fixed margins either as a mark up (cost + fixed percentage) or operating a fixed margin (a fixed percentage of profit on sales). The philosophy is the same; the arithmetic a little different.

Value-based pricing

Here, the price charged is based not on costs, but the perceived value to the customer. In fashion products, we have noted that a key aspect of the value is in the brand and low prices in this market can be counterproductive.

Going-rate pricing

In competitive markets with customer price awareness there may be a need to stay in line with the prevailing market prices; if you do not, the customers will switch. With some products (e.g. cosmetics), branding can be a defence. However, with petrol, people will drive the extra mile for 5p a litre off.

Product line pricing

In areas such as cosmetics, companies may operate a product line pricing strategy. They may have a budget (modest profit) brand line and have a second, premium (high profit) brand line.

Bundled or à la carte

When you buy your next computer system it is likely you will be offered a competitive price bundle for hardware, firmware and software. In the purchase of a car the customer may be offered a range of optional 'extras'.

By-product pricing

This often happens in B2B contexts. In the manufacture of paper, a by-product is turpentine oil. This is used in the manufacture of aroma chemicals. The turpentine price obtained by the paper mills is the going rate. This depends on the balance of by-product supply and manufacturing demand.

Some processes produce a range of co-products (e.g. oil refinery). Here, the pricing issues are most complex (e.g. demand for heating oil depends on the time of the year) and sophisticated cost and pricing models are required (e.g. linear programming). These are particularly valuable when there are complex constraints (e.g. fixed amounts of different grades of crude oil to be processed). Detailed discussion of this is outside the scope of this text; leading references for further reading are given at the end of the chapter.

Psychological pricing

For many consumer products there are perceived price breaks and prices should be in these bands. A particular issue is around the price break to match the brand. For organisations providing value for money, a £100 product will be priced at £99.99 (after all, this is less than £100). However, for products that may be considered premium, such as designer clothing, the price may be expressed as £100.00, £99.99 being considered downmarket. The £99.99 strategy is often known as 'odd pricing' and the £100.00 strategy as 'even pricing'.

A related approach is 'bait' pricing. Here, a particular product line is priced very low to attract customers and drive footfall. The profit is made on the range of other goods sold. The retail margins on petrol and diesel are modest but garages make up profits on the range of products on sale in their forecourt shops.

B2B pricing

In major contracts there may be considerable negotiation in the setting of prices. In other contexts, particularly for contracts in the public sector, a bidding process may be used.

Transfer pricing

This is a special situation in B2B pricing. Many companies operate a divisionalised structure. Often these divisions are considered as sub-business and profit centres. In business texts such entities are often called strategic business units (SBUs). A car manufacturer may make engines in one plant. The engines may be sold to other car manufacturers and also used in the production of the firm's own cars in another plant, possibly in a different country. In the perfume and flavour industry, companies make aroma raw materials. These are sold around the industry and also used for captive use for the creative house to make its own compounded flavours and fragrances. The question arises as to what should be the transfer price between the SBU producing the raw materials/component and the SBU producing the assembled product. There are four popular formats for setting the transfer price:

1. at cost
2. at cost plus a fixed additional percentage
3. at market price minus a fixed percentage margin
4. at arm's length, charging the internal SBU the same price as other customers

The practical implication of the first policy is that the materials manufacturing SBU is supporting the final assembly SBU with a subsidy. The lower costs provide the assembly SBU with a cost competitive advantage when compared with other firms operating the same sector. The arm's length policy forces the assembly SBU to stand on its own feet, with no internal cost cross-subsidy. There is no single 'right' policy. It all depends on what the objective of the overall company is. If the company wants to maximise total profits of the group, then the arm's length policy may be best. If the parent company wants to grow market share with its assembly operation, then the at-cost policy may be appropriate. Pricing is a key aspect of business policy and it is too important to be left to the accountants; they can be left to count the beans. In technology-rich contexts (e.g. computers, chemicals, pharmaceuticals, etc.) such decisions have to be made by engineers and technologists who are financially literate and strategically orientated; an engineer must be able to drive a financial spreadsheet as well as a CAD/CAM system.

Legal conformance

For a free exchange process to take place, consumers must be able to enter the exchange process freely. If competitors were to collude, to set up a price fixing ring, to hold up prices, the free market would be distorted. In 2007, BA had to set up a provision of over £300 million to cover expected fines for inappropriate communications with competitors on the subject of fuel surcharges. The regulatory bodies have to be ever-vigilant to ensure that organisations and companies do not attempt to 'rig' markets to the detriment of customers. The implication for the individual professional is that it is usually unwise to discuss costing or other issues related to pricing strategy with staff from competitive organisations. It is all too easy for regulators to interpret this as an attempt to establish a pricing cartel.

Many businesses exist in monopoly type situations. It is not possible to have 10 rail lines from Bristol to London; all trains have to use the same infrastructure. The same is true of electricity and gas supplies. Each house down the road does not have 10 pipes or cables entering the house. Prices charged in utility markets are watched over by the regulators, who can enforce prices and if conditions are violated they can levy penalty charges.

Another minefield area is the sale of marginal production and predatory pricing. In predatory pricing, a major company may move into a market (e.g. a supermarket into a new geographic area) and sell at very low prices (in extreme cases, at a loss) to undercut local small competition. When the competition has been driven out of business, prices are restored to more normal levels. A similar situation exists where a company is not able to sell its entire product into one market and then sells excess production on a marginal cost basis. Where this can be clearly proved to be predatory and/or uneconomic this marginal pricing is called 'dumping'. One person's fair low prices can be perceived by others as dumping or predatory pricing. In the international context this can spark off trade wars where the 'injured' country may impose punitive import duties. The World Trade Organisation (WTO) has a difficult time holding the ring and attempting to bring good order in the midst of such disputes.

Taxation may have a profound effect on prices. Different taxes apply to different situations. The term situation is used because the taxation for the same product may be dissimilar in different circumstances. Fresh salad purchased at the supermarket is a food and in the UK has zero VAT. Eat the same salad as part of a meal in a restaurant and it is subject to VAT. The tax on diesel for agricultural use (e.g. tractors) is different to that levied on fuel supplied for domestic diesel car users.

WHEN IS COOKING OIL NOT COOKING OIL?

After a certain time, the oil in deep fat fryers (in fish and chip shops, burger bars, etc.) has to be replaced. It is illegal to dump such material down the sewers (it has a high biological oxygen demand) and it has a significant value. Just a little clean up, and a little tweaking of your engine, and you have the ultimate bio-diesel.

A local supermarket discovered it had very high sales of discounted cooking oil, when compared with sales in equivalent outlets round the country. It was discovered that some of the customers were topping up their diesel tanks with cooking oil. With diesel at around a £1 a litre, low-cost cooking oil is an attractive proposition. There is only one problem. Using it in your deep fat fryer is fine, but tip it into your diesel tank and you have committed an offence, unless you pay the appropriate duty and tax.

Note: It was rumoured that the authorities had no problem in detecting the offending motorists because their exhausts had a typical 'frying tonight' odour.

Taxation is a complex area and the advice of experts should always be sought; the issues are not only intricate but also ever-changing. An area of special concern to technologists is revenue approaches to green issues. Increasingly, governments are using taxation and other revenues to penalise ungreen activities and products (e.g. gas guzzling 4 × 4 'Chelsea tractors') and to promote green activities and products (e.g. electricity from wave power).

Terms of trade and contracts

The pricing details of sales contracts are vital (e.g. extended periods of credit represent, in effect, a price reduction). The contract must clearly spell out the rights and obligations of buyer and sellers (e.g. period of credit, acceptable methods of payment, etc.). A particular issue affecting engineers and technologists is disputes about fulfilment of contracts (e.g. disputes regarding product performance or quality). Most of the major chartered professions have panels of experts who can assist with arbitration in such disputes. Again, as with taxation, contract law and payment conditions are complex areas and expert advice should always be sought in problem areas.

Pricing and sales systems

An important area for developing competitive advantage has been in sales systems. Electronic point-of-sale (EPOS) and internet buying greatly reduce transaction costs and provides secure payment in the B2C context. This effect has been seen in 2007 with the first major retail chains moving to refuse cheque payments (not a significant problem as so few transactions are now conducted by cheque, in this context). The 'Oyster' system, in use in London for tube fares, is an example of a move to an 'electronic purse' for cash-free conduct of small transactions.

Effective linking of materials resource planning (MRP) systems with electronic data interchange (EDI) provide efficiencies down the supply chain in the B2B context. Quill-pen, hard copy, order and invoice systems are slow, error prone and costly to operate.

Some of the approaches of pricing and costing have been discussed above. In the case of volume consumer products, the day-to-day implementation is a relatively standard process, once the policy has been set. Decisions are made and monitoring takes place but little effort is needed to maintain the system. However, there are some B2C contexts where the pricing system is a vital element of the business model. In simplistic terms, there are only three factors to be considered in running a successful insurance company: correctly identify the level of risk, reduce the transaction cost of administering the policy and manage the costs of claims. Smart systems backing a good website can help with all three. Sophisticated algorithms convert the customers' information to an individually assessed risk profile, providing the correct pricing of the policy in real time. The web-based format provides the mechanism for cost-efficient conduct of the transaction. Smart systems can even prioritise claims for investigation by detecting potential anomalous elements to a claim (e.g. excessive valuation of an item). This is one example of the bespoke B2C pricing situation. Other examples are the maintenance contract situation (e.g. to re-paint a house) or the bespoke product/service (e.g. carpet a room).

A major activity for engineers and technologists is participating in the costing and pricing of major contracts for B2B customers. The cost of building a bridge will depend on the nature of the subsoil and the type of foundations needed. For a computer maintenance contract, costs will depend on the nature of the hardware and firmware to be maintained. The cost of bidding for a major contract (e.g. build an electrical power station) may in itself cost millions of pounds. Failure to complete this process properly or a failure to consider contingencies can involve costly mistakes (e.g. the overrun with the new Wembley stadium). Profitability in these types of situations involves good cost estimation at the bidding stage and rigorous project and cost management in the implementation stage.

Control of pricing

This aspect follows on from the objectives set in the pricing strategy review. In short, has the organisation achieved the objectives it set itself? If profitability is down, is it because the sales volume is down or have there been problems in containing costs? What is the situation with bad debts and overdue accounts? If costs have risen, is it because the cost of materials has risen or have there been quality issues requiring excessive rework? Ratio and variance analysis are important financial tools to analyse the performance of the organisation. Further consideration of this is given in Chapter 10.

International pricing

Costing in international markets is somewhat complex, major issues are adaptation costs, duty, currency, local market situation, and risk.

Adaptation costs

For most products, some form of adaptation may be needed. This may be modest, such as revised labelling, or it may be major, such as left-hand/right-hand drive vehicles. Other costs need to be considered. The cost of freight and insurance are volatile. The calculation of 'cost, insurance and freight' (CIF) delivery needs to be researched and calculated for each delivery and for a specific delivery time. Allowance must be made for the costs of the preparation and production of export documentation, including relevant safety sheets.

Duty and taxes

Care has to be taken, particularly for new products, to ensure that any export and/or import duties have been determined. In the EU, we have become used to VAT as a key taxation process. In some other countries, sales taxes may operate. Other specific taxes may operate (e.g. excise duty on alcohol and tobacco products).

Currency

In 2007, inflation rose above 1 500% in Zimbabwe. The pound, dollar and euro all float against each other. That good contract may be a disaster if the currency has moved in the wrong direction or inflation is out of control. Various hedging methods can be used to insure against this risk (e.g. forward currency contracts). Many currencies are not freely converted and care must be taken to ensure that profits can be remitted back.

MICRO CASE STUDY | **ZIMBABWE A BUSINESS OPPORTUNITY FOR E-COMMERCE**

Inflation galloping at thousands of per cent, people unable to buy the necessities of life and 25% of the population having fled the country – this does not look like a good context to start a new e-business.

Many countries such as Mexico and the Philippines have a major international cash flow from their nationals working abroad. Special provisions have been made by UK banks for Polish workers to remit money back to parents and other family members remaining in Poland. However, this only works if the exchange rate is fair and the currency reasonably stable. Neither of these conditions was true in 2007 for Zimbabwe.

A number of entrepreneurs realised this presented a unique business opportunity. One model was for the Zimbabwean in the UK to buy the required goods (e.g. food and cooking oil) on-line in the UK. Delivery was made direct to the Zimbabwean address; in effect an electronic food parcel. Another entrepreneur sold a 10-digit code number (each number being unique) that could be texted to the recipient in Zimbabwe. On banking the code, to the agent in Zimbabwe, the recipient was given a voucher for ten litres of petrol.

Quick-thinking entrepreneurs had recognised that the unique currency problems provided an exceptional e-business opportunity.

Local market conditions

Macro- and microeconomic conditions may be different in the destination market (e.g. there may be strong local competition). It is essential to check these conditions.

Risk

Physical risks can be insured for (e.g. goods in transit). There is an enlarged risk of non-payment in some international markets, when compared with the domestic market. This can be managed by using an irrevocable confirmed letter of credit on a home bank. Here, the home bank pays on completion of the contract and then gets its payment in turn from the customer's bank. This is a form of payment insurance and has costs associated with it.

Counter-trade

A special problem exists with developed countries trading with less-developed countries. A less-developed country may need advanced products (e.g. veterinary products) but not have a convertible currency. In such situations there may be very little 'hard' currency (e.g. £, $, euros) available. There may be a demand for luxury products, such as cosmetics, and people with local currency prepared to buy the products at premium prices. How then do you do business in a context where you are not able to convert local currency and there is no source of 'hard' currency to finance the transaction? The answer is counter-trade, and three common approaches are given below.

Barter

Here, there is no exchange of money in any stage and no third party is involved. In the case of veterinary products the company may be paid in frozen meat. A company producing agrichemicals might be paid with an agricultural commodity (e.g. coffee, cotton and the like). The company will then sell on the product into the developed world markets. There are typically two major problems for the developed world buyer. Commodity prices are volatile and what is the appropriate conversion rate for one kilo of fertiliser in terms of coffee beans? There is financial risk and buffers must be built into margins to provide reasonable provisions for the potential risks. Given the less-developed world production context there may be quality problems. For the producer, the two problems are reflected back and the result is likely to be a poor rate of exchange for coffee beans for fertiliser. It is of advantage to both the buyer and seller to improve the quality of the coffee beans.

Offset

A problem with barter is that the transaction has to be back to back. In an offset arrangement, the money is paid into an account and then the money is later used to buy compensation products. The overall effect is similar to barter (over the two paired transactions, no hard currency is used) but the transactions do not have to be back to back as they do with simple barter. The time problem is removed and there may be more flexibility on the compensation product package. However, many of the problems of barter are still present.

Buyback

Returning to the example of the agrochemicals-for-coffee transaction, the shipping costs of the raw coffee beans are relatively high. Moreover, the less-developed country is a low-cost economy where processing into premium instant coffee would be potentially cost attractive. However, the companies in the less-developed countries do not have the capital or the expertise to build and run the advanced plant.

The solution is for the developed world partner to provide the capital to finance the project. A key aspect for the engineer and technologist is that technical assistance is needed to build and commission the plant. The last phase is the training of the local staff and management. The advantage for the developed world partner is a more valuable, more saleable product. The advantage for the less-developed world partners is more locally added value and the acquisition of new technology. The role of engineers, scientists and technologists in this technology transfer process is vital. Buyback is one of the stepping-stones that can assist a less-developed country to emerge into the community of developed nations. The process involves not only capital equipment but also the transfer of intellectual property, manufacturing know-how and skills.

Review

Customers will only purchase products if they perceive value. Customers must also be able to afford the price; they must have the cash or access to finance. Equivalent changes in price, in different contexts, do not change demand in the same extent. With inelastic demand conditions, demand is not sensitive to price changes; with elastic demand, demand does change freely with price. Value, affordability and elasticity of demand are affected by the macro- and microenvironment. Special consideration has been given to legal issues and the impact of taxation on prices.

In this chapter, the various strategic pricing options, such as penetration and skimming, have been reviewed and options for price setting described. The additional issues to be considered in international marketing were presented. Counter-trade was presented as an option for non-cash trading with less-developed countries.

Further reading

Atrill, P. & McLaney, E. (2000) *Accounting and Finance for Non-specialists*, 3rd edn, Pearson Higher Education.

Chelsom, J., Payne, A. & Reavill, L. (2005) *Management for Engineers, Scientists and Technologists*, 2nd edn, John Wiley & Sons.

Wilson, R. & Gilligan, C. (2005) *Strategic Marketing Management: Planning Implementation and Control*, 3rd edn, Elsevier.

CHAPTER 6

Place

Learning objectives

After studying this chapter you will be able to:

- Define convenience in terms of 'who?', 'where?', 'when?', 'what?', 'how?' and service, describe why some customers may have special delivery needs, explain the special challenges of ensuring safety in the physical distribution of hazardous goods and review key factors to be considered in the management of physical distribution networks
- List the various physical distribution options for goods and services, give examples of situations requiring different levels of physical service level provision and describe how queuing theory can assist in the design of physical distribution.
- Explain the issues that a firm needs to consider when developing its geographic strategy for physical distribution and review how the nature of outlets needs to be tailored for different distribution situations
- Discuss what levels of service provision are required at the point of sale and explain the range of legal issues that apply to physical distribution

Introduction

One problem with the original dot-com bubble was that some companies forgot that a birthday present is not a birthday present when it arrives broken, a week later, at the wrong address. No matter how fun and whizzy the web page, the products have to be delivered. Distribution is often not given much prominence in traditional marketing texts. Much of the physical activity of distribution is out of sight to marketers. International supply chain management and logistics remains in the hands of specially qualified professionals and is one of the major hidden industries. It is a long and complex path from a hole in the ground in Nigeria to the filling of the fuel tank at the local hypermarket.

In the seventeenth century, travelling minstrels brought music to the masses and there was no other option but to physically bring the performer and audience together. In the nineteenth century, mechanical contrivances such as the 'punch card' fairground organ could distribute music to the masses and there was no longer the need to bring performer and audience together. In the twentieth century, a series of refinements moved though the shellac and vinyl disk and other essentially mechanical systems to sophisticated analogue electrical systems. In the final decades of the twentieth century, delivery and recording moved from analogue electro-mechanical to digital CDs. Now we can hear that new track on our mobile communications, office or entertainment system.

The birth of industrial revolution was founded on the close proximity of coal and iron ore. In the age of the horse and cart, moving millions of tonnes of commodity products was not economically viable. It was fine for spices and silk from India but not for mountains of coke to smelt iron ore. The canals provided a first breakthrough, followed by the railways. The clipper for tea is now replaced by air freight for high value goods and bulk carriers now move base commodity products around the world in 100,000-tonne quantities. Some ill-informed people talk about food miles. A bulk container carrier can move products from China to Felixstowe for less effort than it takes to distribute them in the UK. Food miles are rather like estimating the amount of money you have in your pocket by the number of coins you have. That gold £1 coin is worth 100 of those little brown penny coins.

Developments in logistics are every bit as important as developments in products. Customers do not see product or place, they want to experience an integrated offering, provided through the integrated marketing mix. Moreover, for many consumer products, some 30% of the total cost is made up of logistic costs. Having effective and efficient logistics is not an option, it is vital for profitability.

Figure 6.1 provides an overview of the architecture of place (i.e. distribution). The customer wants to experience convenience. The need is to define what the customer demands are and then work out how to satisfy them.

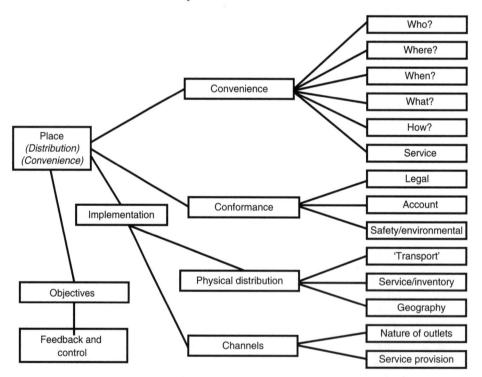

Figure 6.1 The architecture of place (distribution). Adapted from: Curtis, T., *Marketing in Practice*, figure 5.2, page 128, © Elsevier 2006. Reproduced by permission.

HOW TO DISTRIBUTE ENERGY

In the Middle Ages it was necessary to bring materials for processing to the source of energy. For hundreds of years, grain was brought to the windmill or the watermill. Below are some of the ways we move energy around.

Coal Physical movement by bulk carrier, canal, rail and road. (In some areas wood and peat are still important.)

Oil and gas Physical movement by pipeline. Even processed products can be distributed by pipeline (e.g. aviation fuel to Heathrow), bulk tanker, canal, rail and road.

Water Pipelines and tunnels for hydroelectric projects.

Electrical power Electrical high-tension distribution. (Note the move to combined heat and power (CHP) and more local generation to reduce transmission losses and to gain thermal efficiency with heat and power systems.) Also note that for a few difficult situations (e.g. replacing power supply cables in existing cable space where there has been a major increase in demand), superconducting cables are in commercial use. Still the philosopher's stone of energy transmission is room-temperature superconductors. For 'independent' electrical supply, batteries and fuel cell systems provide viable solutions.

For local energy distribution within a factory complex Steam lines, drive shafts, drive belts, compressed air and hydraulic systems provide a range of solutions.

For transmission from a few metres to around the world and from a fraction of a watt to megawatts, a whole range of approaches provide energy where and when we want it.

Convenience

The regular questions need to be asked. Who wants the product or service? Where do they want it? When do they want it? What do they want? How do they want it delivered? Does the product need additional service? These elements of convenience are considered below.

Who?

In the B2C context, this involves looking at the segmentation and stakeholders. The buyer is not always the user (e.g. children's toys). This analysis should have been completed when considering the mix-element product and the results of this analysis just need to be re-examined in the context of distribution. In the B2B context, the general issue is the same: a re-examination of the segmentation and stakeholders. However, in the B2B context, explicit consideration needs to be given to the decision-making unit (DMU).

Where?

For many consumer products, the awkward answer is 'anytime they want it'; we are in the 24/7/365 society. Cans of drink are available from every possible outlet and just in case the customer gets caught between outlets, automated vending machines can fill the gap. Who wants to go to the CD store on a Saturday afternoon of the big match when you can download music on your wi-fi enabled laptop on the way home? Interestingly, people's wants and expectations are changing. Many people do not want to go to the butchers, greengrocer etc., they just want to run round the hypermarket once a month and get the pain over quickly (or, better still, order on line and never stand in the check-out line again). Any top-ups can be picked up in the forecourt shop when filling up the tank.

The need is to get thousands of products to thousands of outlets effectively (stockouts are not acceptable) and efficiently. For the manufacturer of consumer products, this is the delivery to the retail outlets or their distribution centres. Down the supply chain, it is the delivery to the manufacturing facilities. In either case, just-in-time (JIT) delivery will often be needed. Two days early or three hours late are not acceptable. For a major manufacturer of consumer goods (e.g. processed foods, personal care products, etc.), the decision of where to locate manufacturing facilities, distribution centres and the formulation of drop-off schedules are complex aspects of logistics management. Full treatment of this is not possible in a marketing text. References to key texts in operations, logistics and supply chain management are given at the end of this chapter.

When?

The general demand from consumers for 24/7/365 service and the needs of JIT delivery have been noted above. Seasonal demand for products may need ingenuity (e.g. deep freezing Easter eggs manufactured months earlier) but the most difficult problems occur with services. Wind energy is not much use on a frosty Christmas day with no wind. People can forget that everything from gas central heating to water supply and sewerage are all vulnerable to a general failure of the electricity supply. Each year a major black-out will take down a major area such as London, Italy and New York (all victims in the past). Sitting in the cold when the central heating is down is not pleasant, and it is a lot worse if you are stuck in a lift for several hours.

MICRO CASE STUDY   **WATER SUPPLY**

A major problem exists in the UK with the supply of water. Many of the pipelines are over a hundred years old and water leakage is a serious problem. There is a parallel problem with sections of the sewer system, also of a venerable age.

In the early hours of the morning water demand is fairly low. If action was not taken, pipe pressures would rise and sharply increase the rate of water loss through cracked pipes in the crumbling infrastructure. At around 7.00 a.m. everyone is getting up and going into the bathroom to freshen up for the day. If action is not taken, the water pressure could drop sharply. In extreme cases, the water pressure could become negative. If this happened, contaminated ground water (from the cracked sewers) could enter the system with serious health implications. Considerable management and engineering skills are needed to manage water distribution networks under fluctuating demand conditions.

What?

The detailed nature of 'product' has been discussed in Chapter 4. However, different customers may want the product delivered in different forms. In the food industry, some customers may want their product delivered fresh while others may need to have the product delivered frozen. Normal vegetables may be delivered trimmed of root and well washed. Organic produce may have some root left on with earth still clinging to the vegetables – a clear signal that this produce is 'organic'. The 'what?' question links distribution back to the segmentation issues considered in developing the range of product variant offerings.

How?

How does the customer want the product delivered? This is often vital in the B2B context and detailed specifications may be written in the contract. In the shipment of liquids, different drums may be needed for delivery by 'roll-on, roll-off' ferry as opposed to air shipment, where a different set of regulations apply. Some companies may want bulk delivery; others may want specific pack sizes.

MICRO CASE STUDY

50 Kg OR 1 Kg

A company manufacturing hop extract was given an opportunity to buy 20 tonnes from an overseas source at a very advantageous price. The buyer assumed that the product would be delivered in the normal type of 50 kg packs. There was considerable consternation when it was discovered that the delivery was in 1 kg tins. Repacking for sale involved a trip to the hardware store for some tin openers and a few days of hard work. It is always good practice to ensure that contracts specify how the product will be delivered.

Service

In our discussion of the product–service continuum (Chapter 3), it was noted that some products also include service. In the B2C sector, kitchen appliances are often sold as part of a package when a complete kitchen is installed. Such manufacturers offer directly, or in partnership, design and installation services. Similar situations apply in the B2B sector. Companies manufacturing cables will also offer cable-laying services for customers wanting a 'turnkey' solution. The ability to provide a good design and installation service may be a significant factor in the selection of a supplier.

Conformance

In the consideration of convenience, a range of issues was identified. However, some of these issues are more than just about convenience. Some products and services have important legal constraints as to how they are offered, what is offered and where they are offered. We noted above that lack of clarity can cause problems when products are not delivered in the way the customer needs them. A major concern for engineers and scientists is safety in the distribution of hazardous materials: explosive gas into millions of homes and litres of highly flammable petrol into millions of cars.

Legal

The supply of electricity is regulated. The supplied voltage and frequency are only permitted to vary from the norm by very small tolerances. These tolerances must be maintained even in turbulent demand conditions, which is a major headache for network management. There is a wide range of laws that affect the delivery of products. The tachograph and related driving-hours limitations must be factored into the planning of product distribution. Many cities have restrictions on the hours that commercial vehicles may enter an area (e.g. night-time restrictions on heavy commercial vehicles in residential neighbourhoods). Many airports close to populated areas also have restrictions on night flights. In the UK we are used to 24/7/365 trading, but in many countries there can be regulations affecting the hours and days of opening. Different countries have different patterns of closing so the logistics manager needs to keep to hand the checklist of national holidays around the globe.

Different forms of travel (road, rail, air, sea) can have their own regulations and a major issue here is with documentation, labelling and packaging. This can become a logistical nightmare when distribution between the manufacturer and the customer involves a variety of transport methods. There is a final twist of complexity in international distribution, which entails ensuring that all relevant export, import and customs documents have been correctly completed and authenticated. This is a complex area that can consume a significant amount of technical effort (e.g. cargo inspection and certificates of analysis). That brilliant bit of route planning and that slick transfer from container ship to dock is of no value if the container gets held up in customs. All insurance documentation must be in order. Shippers will insist on this, not to protect your interests, but theirs. A leaking drum can contaminate other products and produce a third-party liability claim.

Account

Just-in-time (JIT) delivery is increasingly being demanded. Here, the end of the supply chain, the manufacturer, must deliver the product within a fairly tight time window. There must be supply chain integration and tracking systems between the supplying and buying organisation must be compatible (e.g. bar codes). In some manufacturing situations, the delivery can be direct to the production line.

Safety/environmental

As with manufacture, the distribution processes must be environmentally friendly. There is an argument that large central electrical power stations, where two-thirds of the energy goes up the cooling tower, are not green efficient. If transmission losses are factored in, the picture is even worse. Looked at in this light, local combined heat and power (CHP) systems are much more green efficient.

A major concern is the environmental impact of an accident. After some 20 years, an oil spill in Alaska is still causing pollution problems. A major concern of engineers and technologists is in devising systems that are resistant to catastrophic failure with consequent pollution problems. The second line of defence is that, should catastrophic failure occur, the escape can be contained and environmental damage minimised.

The escape may also cause death, injury and physical damage. Companies transporting hazardous goods must first identify the hazards, according to international and national agreed standards. Precise instructions can then be given to the emergency services on the information cards attached to road tankers and containers. In the event of an accident this provides vital information (e.g. some materials react explosively with water). This information must be provided in a standard format understood by all emergency services. For international transport, this may have to be provided in several languages. Hazard assessment and preparation of transport hazard documentation may consume significant technical resources.

The 'flash point' is a measure of how easy it is to ignite a flammable liquid. A low flash point is a high risk; an elevated flash point is a lesser risk. How materials may be distributed, types of containers and warning labels are different for different flash point bands. A company, making a range of compounded products that are inflammable (e.g. solvent-based paints) needs to measure the flash point of each product in order to know the flammability hazard classification and, hence, the necessary safety labelling. Even a simple issue such as density can be important. In the event of a spillage it is important to know if the oil is less dense or denser than water – in one case, the oil floats; in the other, it sinks.

A major danger time is during the transfer of the product. Appropriate provision must be made by suppliers, customers and transport contractors for proper earth bonding during transfers. Transferring liquids or powders can create a build-up of static electricity and without earth bonding this can cause sparking and explosions. When filling a petrol tank, petrol saturated air is displaced, creating an explosive mixture. It takes just one spark.

The final aspect of this is the provision of safety advice and data. Major companies maintain special 'toll free' 24/7/365 technical help lines. When a drum ruptures and contaminates workers in Australia, an answer-phone message saying 'Sorry, we are not available at the moment; ring back at 8.00 a.m. UK time' is not acceptable.

Physical distribution

There is an old adage in marketing: 'When is a refrigerator not a refrigerator? When it is in New York and the customer wanted it in California.' Customers want and expect an efficient delivery service; companies that fail to provide that pay the penalty and lose customers. Take your mobile telephone as an example of the distribution challenges associated with today's consumer staples. Raw materials (e.g. indium for LCDs) are mined around the world, processed through the supply chain into manufactured products and supplied to customers throughout the world.

Transport

A few minutes spent observing any major motorway brings home the vast range of goods that have to be moved to support society. Containerisation and palletisation speed up the process and minimise the risks of damage in transit. Goods are moved around the world by super-container ships with computer-controlled loading and unloading ensuring optimal turnaround times. Specialist ships dedicated to specific cargos include frozen meat, oil, gas, iron ore and coal. Higher value goods can be delivered throughout the world in hours by air freight. Water, gas and oil are distributed by pipelines and electricity by cable.

Communications services are similarly supported with complex networks of copper, fibre optic, microwave and satellite systems. This has enabled global outsourcing of services, such as call centres. Hybrid systems can now be used. Newspapers can be typeset centrally and printed in regional centres. This cuts costs but also shortens delivery times, allowing later printing with more up-to-date news. National and international content can be merged with some regional content to provide tailored editions for the regions.

The majority of homes in developed countries now have broadband access. This has revolutionised the way in which radio, television, films, games and information can be made available and accessed. Digital cinema projection technology and broadband distribution will allow simultaneous worldwide release of a new film and even make distribution to smaller cinemas an economic proposition. Each print of a conventional film is expensive and physical distribution is slow and expensive.

The evolution of distribution systems and technologies creates new business opportunities. For example, mass air travel has opened up new long-haul holiday destinations. As always, the need is for the engineer and technologist to read the developments in the macro- and microenvironment and respond with innovative responses.

Service and inventory

For a given market situation, the firm must decide the level of service that is required. If you go to the shop and they are out of milk, it is mildly irritating to have to drink your coffee black. A failure in the oxygen supply in the middle of surgery is life threatening.

Queuing theory can help in this situation and the petrol station is a classic form of the problem. If the company has too many pumps, the capital and running costs are not recovered in sales. If the company has too few pumps, people will avoid the station because queuing is not one of their favourite pastimes. Detailed mathematical treatment of the subject is given in standard texts on operations.

From the marketing point of view, some key information is needed. To plug in the numbers, an analysis of traffic density and arrival rates is required. Some assumptions may be made to fit a distribution to the arrival rates (e.g. Poisson). Information is needed to build a model of how long a person occupies a pump space (a normal distribution fit might be used). These are relatively standard statistical issues with well-defined tools. Mathematical models and simulations can then be run to look at service levels with different numbers of pumps.

Changes can be made to queuing rules. Many banks and some airline check-in systems operate one queue with many service desks. First-class passengers are directed to a separate fast-track section as a reward for the premium price they have paid. In a supermarket most outlets operate a separate queue for each service station. Some of these checkouts will be express, reserved for people with less than a certain number of items. The overall procedure is relatively simple, even if the mathematics can be demanding at times. First, do the required research to be able to build models of aspects such as arrival rates. In the case of the supermarket queuing problem, analysis of checkout records will give the distribution of number of items purchased by a given customer. This allows many 'what if?' simulations to be run. How many express checkouts? Should the number of items for the express checkout be eight, nine or ten? Run the model with different numbers and analyse the results. Terminal Five at Heathrow was one of the largest construction projects in Europe. How the building has been designed and how elements are configured (e.g. baggage transport and reclaim systems) hinges on the engineers and architects working with statisticians and market researchers. Too many check-ins and you have a white elephant; overloaded systems and you have Terminal One on a bank holiday weekend all over again.

The next key aspect involves psychology and a judgement of buyer behaviour. It is not the actual time of queuing that matters, but the perception of time. Many banks now have a TV screen above the queuing area, tuned to one of the 24-hour news programmes. Stand in line for two minutes with nothing to do and it can feel like 10 minutes; catch up on the latest test cricket score and it appears like no time at all. The check-in time one hour before the flight is not too bad if you can have a coffee, surf the net and do a little duty free shopping. It is not enough to analyse the physical time in the service experience. The team must also understand how to manage the customer's perceptions during that time.

The design, construction and management of networks are important activities for engineers in communications, water, gas, power and transport systems. The carrying capacity may be litres per second or megabits per second, but the basic problem is the same: too much capacity and the company will lose money; too little capacity, the company will lose money and customers are not happy. The widely fluctuating network demands add to the technical challenge.

A related problem for both the B2B and the B2C situation is optimal stockholding for products and components. The simplest system is to consider a deterministic system where units are ordered in fixed periods in fixed quantities against a steady demand. This is shown in Figure 6.2.

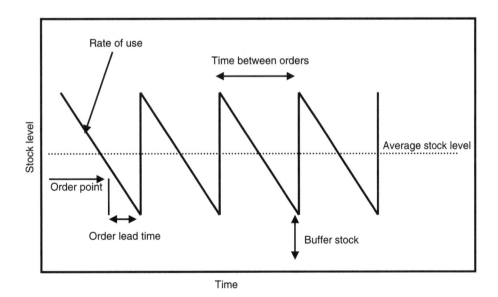

Figure 6.2 Schematic outline of a simple stock-cycle model.

We can calculate the total annual cost as: annual purchase cost + annual ordering cost + annual holding cost. This can be put in equation form:

$$TC = D \times C + S \times (D/Q) + H \times (Q/2)$$

where:

TC = total cost of purchase (or manufacturing), ordering and holding
D = the total annual demand
C = unit cost
S = cost of ordering and delivery (purchase situation) or
S = set-up costs for line change (production situation)
Q = Quantity to be ordered or manufactured
EOQ = the economic order quantity (the quantity where the overall costs are minimised)
H = cost of holding

By the normal techniques of differential calculus it can be shown that the economic order quantity is given by the equation:

$$EOQ = (2DS/H)^{1/2}$$

There are many deficiencies in this simple model. For example, demands are rarely certain and susceptible to random changes, and it may be more convenient not to order fixed quantities, but to order at fixed periods. There are many approaches to modelling stock and these are covered in texts on operations, logistics and stock control. Here, we just note that there is generally an optimum region (region of minimum total costs) for trading off service levels and costs (Figure 6.3). For any given situation, sound technical and management analysis and decision making are required. For example, in some production cultures the setup time was regarded as fixed; in flexible manufacturing cultures, the challenge for the production engineers is to get the setup time and costs down, thus making smaller batches economic. As always, business equations need skill, intelligence and technical expertise to extract the best understandings.

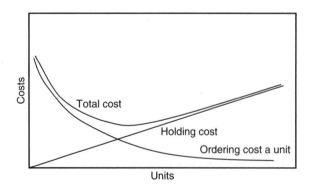

Figure 6.3 Schematic outline cost of stock holding and ordering.

Geography

This simply links back to the segmentation strategy. What are the geographic segments to be served? A local motorcycle courier service may just restrict its activity to a single city such as London whereas DHL and its partners operate on a global scale. Sometimes the areas of activity are licensed on a national rather than a continental basis (e.g. a mobile telephone service). Geographic is not to be taken just to apply to 'political' boundaries. The speed of broadband over copper-based telecommunications networks degrades with distance. Isolated villages need alternative solutions.

An important aspect for products such as computers, photocopiers and motor vehicles is field service; technical staff have to be trained and spare parts stocked. Just as with the network problem, too many service staff equals high cost, too few service staff equals poor service. Again, the engineer and technologist must take a holistic view of the problem. It may be financially more profitable to build diagnostics into the equipment. Most software fixes are downloaded, not shipped slowly and expensively by disk. Providing field service in a densely populated country such as the UK is relatively easy. In a country such as Australia, with vast distances and with low population densities in many areas, it is a much more difficult issue.

INSIGHT

HOW DISTRIBUTION HAS CHANGED: ELECTRONIC FIELD SERVICE

In the 1950s, electronic amplifiers used in laboratory instrumentation were based on valves and were relatively unreliable, needing constant servicing to replace the valves, which had restricted working lives. The field service engineer would almost be a member of the laboratory. By the 1970s, the field technician would occasionally plug in a diagnostics board, identify the problem circuit board and replace it. Now, systems will have built-in diagnostics and/or internet access. Software fixes will be downloaded. Hardware board exchanges will be made customer friendly with the customer effecting the exchange. Drivers can be downloaded from the internet to connect new hardware to PCs.

Channels

In this section, the situation of a company manufacturing products for consumer use is considered. Figure 6.4 shows the typical range of channel options for getting a manufactured product to customers. Where sales outlets are to be a part of the distribution strategy, the firm must decide the nature of outlets to be used.

Nature of outlets

The decision is linked with the segmentation strategy. A continual stress exists with fashion houses wishing to maintain exclusive distribution in 'status' outlets and then there are the Wal-Marts and Tescos of this world wanting some designer items to spice up their broad range. In the developed world, more and more business is conducted through the hypermarket-type outlet and less and less through specialist outlets. Major supermarket outlets, for example, already have an in-store pharmacy. The traditional, small high-street shop is being encircled by the supermarkets on one side and by e-purchasing on the other.

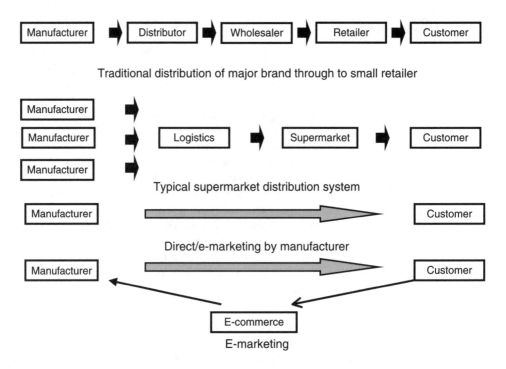

Figure 6.4 Some channel models. Adapted from: Curtis, T., *Marketing in Practice*, figure 5.1, page 126, © Elsevier 2006. Reproduced by permission.

One way to view a shop is as a 'selling service'. In this context, the service-extended marketing mix elements should be reviewed. The 'physical evidence', the ambiance, of the shopping experience is vital. If people are to make that irritating journey to the shopping mall, they must be rewarded with a proper shopping experience. People go to 'shop' rather than just to 'buy' – the two hours of browsing around the options, with a one-hour gossip over coffee, turns mere 'buying' into a 'shopping experience'. Architects, engineers and technologists combine in the teamwork to ensure that the full experience – physical, visual, auditory and olfactory – is tailored to cocoon and tempt the customer. The shopping mall is the twenty-first century cathedral of consumerism.

Service provision

Many years ago Marks & Spencer opened their first store in Paris. In the UK they had operated their stores without the provision of fitting rooms. No self-respecting French woman would purchase clothing without checking the fit. This was not a major problem; they just converted the whole floor into an impromptu fitting room.

For some products, such as prescription spectacles, professional service provision is mandatory. For clothing, the options can range from 100% self-service to the full-service experience of the tailor-made garment. The firm needs to decide the level of service support needed at the point of sale. The budget 'Wash-n-go' shampoo will have to sell itself off the shelf; the prestige perfume will be sold with a lot of one-on-one attention from a skilled fragrance consultant.

Negative distribution

For the past 200 years, developed countries have been building up sophisticated supply chains and distribution systems. After the consumer had finished with the product, the ultimate resting place was the landfill site. There is no way that this model can continue. Europe is running out of suitable sites. Moreover, we are fast depleting finite stocks of oil, metals, etc. It is now a case of recycle or run out (Figure 6.5).

In the UK, there is no satisfactory recycling infrastructure. The age of mass production has fine-tuned a system to make millions of the same products and get them into millions of homes. What is required is a parallel change:

- a change in value systems for people to reduce, reuse and recycle
- the development of systems and infrastructure to make this possible

This is an immense challenge. We have to find a way to reverse engineer the process. Small amounts of mixed recycle items (paper, cans, bottles, plastic, computers, refrigerators,

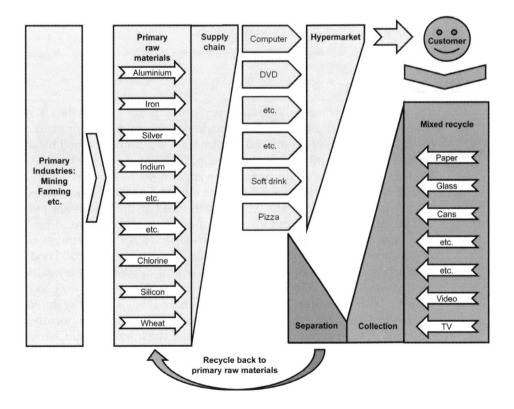

Figure 6.5 Recycle distribution.

etc.) have to be returned from millions of homes to be collected, separated and processed to be next year's products. We have yet to fully invent the negative supermarket where a vast range of recycle elements flow in and are converted into sorted streams fit for recycling. Just how do we sort that PET (polyethylene terephthalate) bottle out from the low-density polythene items? Just how do we pluck out the individual components from a circuit board and recover the tin, lead, gold and other valuable items? At the moment there is a – largely illegal – trade in recyclable material going to low-wage countries (e.g. India and China), where primitive, by-hand methods are used. Often these methods (e.g. incineration of circuit boards to recover metals) are dangerous to the workers. The infrastructure for recycling and reusing toner/ink cartridges is one small example of the way in which things have to develop.

MICRO CASE STUDY

BATTLE OF THE WHEELIE-BIN

The UK has a dismal record of developing the 'reduce, reuse, recycle' habit. Some local authorities are experimenting with systems where wheelie-bins are microchipped. The collection vehicle can then identify the owner of the bin and the weight of rubbish. People could then be moved to a 'pay for what you throw' system. The credit/debit card system in the shop has become 'chip and pin'; the negative process of disposal may be seen as 'chip and bin'. As a consequence, people have reportedly started to engage in negative burglary – dumping unwanted items into other people's bins. It is potentially going to be as important to have as secure a space to park your wheelie-bin as to park your car.

International aspects

The world has become truly global. Over 50% of the toys sold in the UK now originate from China. Such globalisation has been made possible with development of containerisation for a diverse range of products. Even frozen food can be shipped by container. Specialist bulk carriers move oil, liquefied natural gas, coal, iron ore and the like around the world. High-value products as diverse as flowers and microchips are air freighted around the world. Logistics managers with a multicultural perspective are needed to manage these global supply chain networks. Vendor rating and quality audits are a vital aspect of this.

If the physical process of movement of goods around the world has become more and more streamlined, the documentation aspects have not. The regulations for the transport of goods are complex and a plethora of documents are essential. Food and other natural products (e.g. wood) may need certificates of health. Customs entry will require documents such as pro-forma invoices giving the customs classification of the goods and the value for customs purchases. Smaller organisations are well advised to use the services of a freight-forwarder who can advise on export documentation. Just one document out of line may leave the goods stranded. The implications of the International Chamber of Commerce's International Commercial Terms (the so-called 'Incoterms') such as FOB (free on board) may necessitate cargo inspections.

Around the world, there are vast differences in the standards and quality of physical transport infrastructure. In Europe, we are used to an infrastructure of excellent railway and motorway networks. These do not exist in less-developed countries. Another factor that it is easy to overlook for Europeans is the distances involved in other countries. Your flight to Australia from Europe soon demonstrates this reality. You enter Australian airspace and you might think: 'Just time to have a quick coffee and we will be landing'. But no: it's still a few more hours until you get to Sydney. Vladivostok is further away from Moscow than London. Another factor that can be easily overlooked is the influence of climate. Winter in Alaska can involve temperatures below minus 20°C. Shade temperature in New Delhi may reach over 50°C and a container in exposed sunlight can be 20°C hotter. Emulsion products (e.g. food, cosmetics, paint, etc.) may suffer disruption of the emulsion system if they freeze. Food and cosmetic products often do not react well to periods of exposure to temperatures of 50°C (typical accelerated storage tests will use temperatures of around 35°C, assuming normal ambient storage temperatures of 15°C to 25°C).

The nature and roles of channels varies in different countries. In Europe, we are used to large supermarkets and shopping malls. Major retailers, such as Tesco, hold large percentages of the market in the UK, where the top-five supermarkets hold more than 50% of the market share. In other countries, retailing can be much more fragmented and involve many more intermediaries (e.g. local agents and wholesalers) in the supply chain.

As always in international marketing, there is no substitute for good local knowledge and understanding of the regional trading conditions.

Review

In this chapter the approaches to defining convenience in customer-orientated terms has been presented using a series of questions: 'who?', 'where?', 'when?', 'what?', 'how?' and 'what service?'. The legal aspects of physical distribution have been reviewed. Special attention has been given to the safety requirements in the physical distribution of hazardous materials. There are often different options for the delivery of goods and services. Various approaches for different situations have been explored: different situations require different levels of physical distribution service. Some specific technical aspects such as queuing, optimal stock control and network management have been described. In the B2C context, the concept of the retail outlet as a 'sales service' has been discussed and the impact on how engineers and architects build airports, shopping malls, etc. reviewed. The need for appropriate service at the point of sale was noted.

Further reading

Chelsom, J., Payne, A. & Reavill, L. (2005) *Management for Engineers, Scientists and Technologists*, 2nd edn, John Wiley & Sons.

Swift, L. (2001) *Quantitative Methods for Business, Management and Finance*, Palgrave.

Waller, D. (2003) *Operations Management: A Supply Chain Approach*, 2nd edn, Thomson.

Wilson, R. & Gilligan, C. (2005) *Strategic Marketing Management: Planning Implementation and Control*, 3rd edn, Elsevier.

CHAPTER 7

<hr>

Promotion

Learning objectives

After studying this chapter you will be able to:

- Review the communications task in the context of the organisation's stakeholders and identify issues in the macro- and microenvironment that have an impact on marketing communications for given situations
- Describe buyer behaviour and illustrate how this helps direct marketing communications, describe the communications mix options and construct an effective communications mix
- Formulate a personal selling strategy, brief an agency, set out the criteria for agency selection and explain the importance of budgets and schedules in effective communications programmes

Introduction

The design of a communications programme embraces many of the basic issues that have to be considered by a communications engineer in designing a communications network. What types of information have to be sent (images, data, voice, etc.) and who needs to receive the information. In the marketing communications context, the targets are the communications stakeholders. In the environment of marketing communications these are sometimes called 'publics'. For each of the communication stakeholders, the organisation will have specific communication objectives (e.g. in a new launch situation, to make customers aware of the new product). The actual messages are the propositions that are being made to the buyers, users and customers (e.g. for a provider of a broadband service, faster speed, more content, lower cost, etc.).

Marketing communications is a regulated environment and legal issues need to be carefully considered. A particularly challenging area for engineers and technologists is in supporting product performance claims. Different media have conformance requirements. These may be 'house' rules (e.g. your advert for the 'Sizzling Steakhouse' is not likely to be overwhelmingly welcomed by *Vegetarian Monthly*). For technical staff, there may be precise formats for the delivery material (e.g. acceptable file types for images being sent to printers).

For a major purchase, such as a new car, people do not cut out a coupon from the daily paper and send it off with a cheque for £20,000. Before making a purchase, buyers often have to be taken on a journey that will include collection of information from various communications sources – a test drive and some negotiations in the personal selling process.

The typical steps in the buyer's journey are:

- *Recognise there is a problem*. My downloads are slow.
- *Information searches*. What are the options?
- *Evaluation of alternatives*. What speeds? Which service? What costs?
- *Action*. Sign contract and log on
- *Post-purchase evaluation*. Is what is being provided up to the quality promised?

To take them along this journey, they may need various messages delivered in diverse ways. The marketer has a good range of options in the communications mix tool kit. These are given in Figure 7.1.

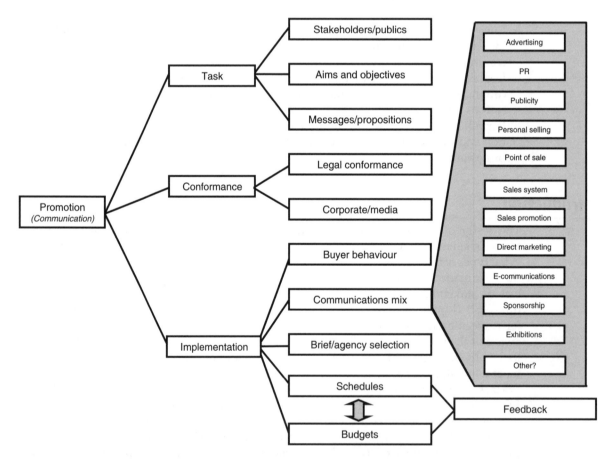

Figure 7.1 The architecture of marketing communications. Adapted from: Curtis, T., *Marketing in Practice*, figure 6.1, page 134, © Elsevier 2006. Reproduced by permission.

The technical marketer should not try to become a graphic design artist or a TV producer. An architect does not install the drains; a plumbing contractor is appointed. Just as with a construction project, when appropriate, subcontract out the work. The scheduling of communications is important. There is no point in advertising a product to the consumers unless the necessary personal selling has been done to get the retail outlets to stock the new product. A communications programme is just another project to be managed and that implies managing to budget: cost overruns are all too easy when subcontracting.

Task

There can be a temptation to set out by deciding what advertising to do and which exhibitions to attend. This is like erecting the steelwork before the foundations have been built. The key to a successful communications programme is sound groundwork and answers to the following three questions:

1. Who do we have to communicate with?
2. What do we want to achieve by this communication and what are the objectives?
3. What are the messages and propositions that will achieve the objectives?

The communications environment

The nature of the task and the communications activities are shaped by the macro-, micro- and internal environments (Figure 7.2). The nature of the organisation and its competitive strategy will affect the communications publics and the communications objectives. Innovative market leader companies, such as IBM, will stress their innovation. Market follower, 'me too', companies will stress same quality, but lower price. Market nichers may stress their specific competence (e.g. a vendor of computers for laboratory information systems (LIMS) may stress solutions for the good laboratory practice (GLP) environment). The level of activity will be affected by the nature and intensity of competition. In 2007, there was intense competition to gain market share in broadband services with much communications activity from Sky, Virgin Media and BT. How the message is received will depend on the nature of the individual, their personality and motivation. In the B2B context, this necessitates consideration of the DMU roles; the culture of the company and the personalities and motivations of the individuals making up the decision-making unit. Further consideration of buyer behaviour is given later in this chapter.

All elements of the STEEPLE environment can affect marketing communications (Table 7.1). Changing social habits are moving from mass viewing of broadcast TV to more time on the internet and picking up programmes on demand. The ability to do this is provided by the advances in technologies such as transmission speeds and disk storage capacities. Social change may be direct or may come from the pressure of other stakeholders, like the influence of the media on people's perceptions and values (e.g. media interest in endangered species has changed social attitudes). The message to be given can be affected by the economic climate: in boom times, 'spend'; in times of recession, 'value for money'. In the early days of the internet, the systems were a little clunky and e-mails were a favoured medium for just a relatively select group of academics. Nowadays, 10-year-olds are web-savvy and have the educated competence to surf the net for the material to complete their latest school projects. One of the major issues for formulation chemists and food technologists has been

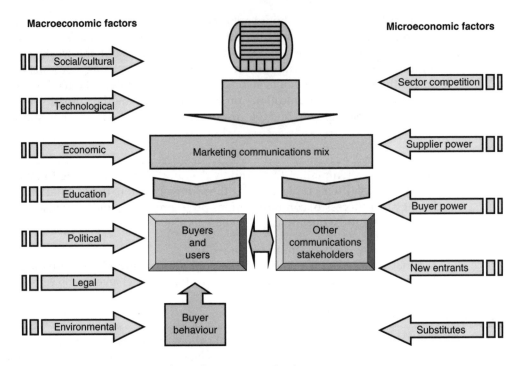

Figure 7.2 Environmental factors impacting on communications.

the political concerns with safety and labelling (e.g. nutritional information, declaration of sensitisers). The environmental agenda influences communications; products will promote their green credentials and proclaim the smallness of their carbon footprint.

Conformance

Conformance issues for marketing communications can arise directly as a result of legislation (e.g. the ban on tobacco advertising and health warnings on cigarette packs) or from industry regulation (e.g. the Advertising Standards Authority). Some companies may have internal restrictions on imagery and messages. This is usually encoded in the organisation's house-style manual, which will provide guidance on a range of issues (e.g. colour(s) to be used in reproducing the corporate logo). The media have similar requirements (e.g. file formats for artwork acceptable to a printer).

Legal

There are restrictions on consumer advertising for a wide range of products. A major industry affected is the pharmaceutical industry. In the UK context, there is little scope for advertising directly to patients. There is large communications expenditure, but it is directed at personal selling and promotion to medical practitioners and pharmacists. PR effort can stimulate media coverage and activities with patient pressure groups. Marketing communications claims must be substantiated with relevant evidence. Experiments to evaluate performance must be properly conducted by qualified persons with appropriate

Table 7.1 Selected examples of macroenvironment forces on communications

STEEPLE element	Issue	Comments/examples
Social/cultural	Changing social attitudes	The first 'gay kiss' on TV was major news. Social attitudes are continually changing. Communications must be culturally sensitive. This is particularly important in international markets
Technological	New technologies provide new opportunities	When 'scratch and sniff' technology was developed, it allowed perfume manufacturers to sample perfumes in fashion journals
Economic	Economic cycle needs to be reflected	More emphasis on value for money may be appropriate in a recession
Education	People being better educated about issues such as nutrition	Ensure that claims can be substantiated: what does 'healthy living' mean? In 2007, the famous comic TV advertisements 'Go to work on an egg' could not be rerun on their 50th anniversary because, today, more emphasis on a balanced diet is deemed necessary
Political	Public health concerns on smoking and healthy eating	Smoking and healthy eating have become political causes
Legal	Political health concerns are reflected into legislation	The increased political concerns about health have resulted in legislation strengthening the health warnings to be placed on tobacco products
Environmental	Increased concern about the environment has provided a communications platform	Organisations are promoting their products or services as 'carbon neutral'

documentation and validation (e.g. fuel consumption performance of a car). Care must be taken in the use of words and symbols (e.g. logos) that these do not infringe other organisations' intellectual property rights. The situation is similar to technical advances where care must be taken not to infringe patents or to seek appropriate licences. An interesting example was when Apple computers got into a dispute with the Beatles over the use of the name 'Apple'. 'Apple' for a computer is fine. 'Apple' for music is fine. However, when Apple computers move into iPods and 'downloads', does this become an infringement of the Beatle's use of 'Apple' for the intellectual property in music? The issue for the technologist moving a company into a new market segment is that intellectual property rights that were fine in the original segment may not be so in the new segment. As always, if in doubt, check with the appropriate legal experts.

A special area is where people are producing a countertype product (e.g. distributor's own brand, 'me too' product for perfume, cosmetics, clothing, etc.). The formulation approaches for a 2-in-1 anti-dandruff shampoo/conditioner are not a major industry secret. Just how close can an own-label get in terms of pack style and label design? On one side, there is fair countertyping. On the other side is deliberate counterfeiting. In the middle is an area where countertyping is getting too close and intellectual property rights are infringed. A key aspect for the lawyers is the question: 'Is the product communication and packaging such that a normal consumer might be confused?' If the answer is 'Yes', then it is likely that the countertyping has positioned the product too close to the original and a case may have to be answered.

Corporate and media

The corporate issues can be considered as hard and soft. The soft elements relate to things that are important but are not easy to allocate a precise number. Companies have a culture and the communications must conform to that culture. A company selling academic textbooks is not likely to use the same provocative imagery that might be used by a lads' magazine. Different brands have different personalities and the marketing communications must stay true to the brand values and character.

The hard elements are those that can be given precise terms. These include typeface, point sizes, and colours as Pantone numbers. The range of items to be considered is large. For an airline, it can range from a ticket to the livery of a jumbo jet. These are formulated in the house-style manual and one role of marketing is in the maintenance of the corporate identity. Particular areas that affect engineering and technical staff are instruction manuals, transit packaging, technical reports, laboratory documentation and certificates. All of these convey brand values to the decision-making unit and must reflect the corporate values and culture; they must also conform to the corporate house-style manual.

Implementation

Having defined the task, the next stage is implementation. As was discussed, in segmentation, not all buyers are the same; not all stakeholders are the same. It is essential to consider how the individual will respond because people with different motivations may need different approaches and messages (e.g. one person may be concerned to reuse cartridges to save money; another may be motivated by green concerns and an overall culture of reuse and recycle). One of the individual characteristics, sometimes a segmentation variable in its own right, is the media habit of the communications targets (e.g. do they read a newspaper; if so, what paper(s)?). Moreover, different media have different characteristics. In general, a poster can contain only modest amounts of information; you can have the world on a website. Graphic design, media buying and the building of exhibition stands are all specialist skills so here it is often a wise policy to use consultants. (In marketing, these are often called agencies.) However, it is essential that the briefing process is sound, or the firm will not get the right bids and clear criteria should be set for bid acceptance. Communications programmes for projects, scheduling and budget control are vital to ensure that everything remains on track.

Buyer behaviour

Earlier, we noted that the buyer has to be taken on a journey and that different media and messages may be needed to progress people successfully through the course. These transitions are influenced by the internal nature of the buyer: their personality, motivation,

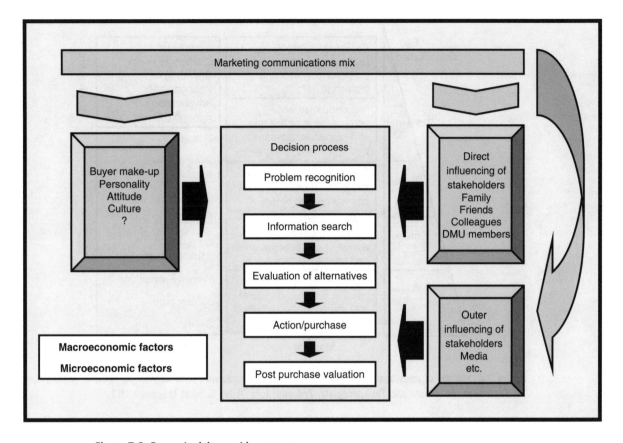

Figure 7.3 Buyer decision-making process.

attitudes and social values. External factors – the macro- and microenvironments – are also important. Figure 7.3 shows a more detailed view of the overall issues outlined in Figure 7.2. The make-up of an individual is partially genetic and partially nature (i.e. the influences of family and culture). Stakeholders close to the buyer such as family, friends, and colleagues are vital. The members of the DMU interact with each other, sharing values and attitudes. These inner stakeholders are influenced by an outer ring of stakeholder groups such as religious organisations, pressure groups, professional institutions and the media.

A significant factor affecting buyers is the level of perceived risk. Performance risk is where there is concern that the product is not 'fit for purpose' and will not perform to expectations, potentially producing problems. This is the way most people seem to feel when they get the latest upgrade on their software. Financial risk is the sinking feeling, the week after the purchase, that the product is available for £100 less or that an alternative represents better value. Social risk is where using a given supplier or source is seen to be being associated with activities that are not acceptable (e.g. the European campaigns in the past for cruelty-free personal care products).

In Chapter 4, the concept of hygiene was discussed in the context of the core product not being enough in itself and more benefits were needed to motivate the purchase of our firm's product rather than a competitor's. This is in some ways a reflection of people

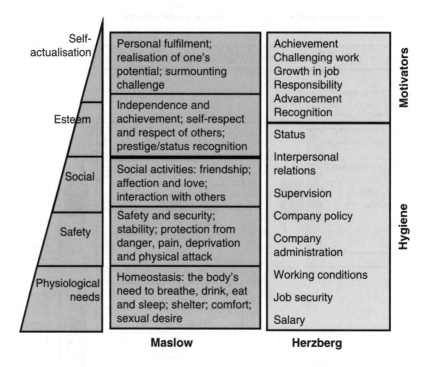

Figure 7.4 Models of motivation. Adapted from: Chelsom, J., Payne, A. & Reavill, A. (2005), *Management for Engineers, Scientists and Technologists*, **2nd edn, John Wiley & Sons Ltd, page 163.**

always wanting more (e.g. 'I want a job' soon becomes 'I want a better job'). As each level is satisfied then the goalposts for needs and wants move on. Figure 7.4 shows these levels and motivators as identified by Maslow and Herzberg. The model is helpful as it can help direct the communications message. A young person just starting on their career may feel the need to belong to the group. A professional with experience and a secure well-paid job will be looking for self-actualisation.

Communications mix

Figure 7.1 showed the range of communications tools that are available to the marketer. For each communications task, the appropriate kit of communications tools must be selected. This is rather like selecting a drill, then selecting the type of drill bit (for masonry, wood, etc.) and, finally, selecting the size to be used. This decision process is shown in Figure 7.5, using communications for a daily newspaper as the example:

1. The first decision level is for deciding which elements of the communication mix to use: in the example, advertising.
2. The second decision level decides what types of advertising media to use: in our example, press. (Other media will likely be used and the 'pop up' menus need to be considered for each element. Here, for reasons of length, only one is considered: press.)

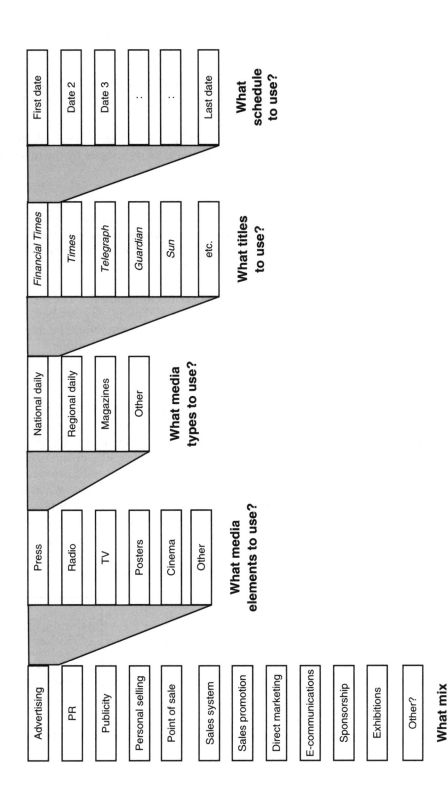

Figure 7.5 Levels of communications mix decisions (daily newspaper). Adapted from: Curtis, T., *Marketing in Practice*, figure 10.5, page 252. © Elsevier 2006. Reproduced by permission.

3. The third level is used to decide what type of press to use: in our example, national daily. (Again, other types might be used.)
4. The fourth level is for selecting the actual publication titles to be used.
5. The final level is to decide the precise schedule; those dates on which it is planned to place the advertisement.

Each of the communications mix elements has its own strengths and weaknesses and getting the right mix is a special skill that needs to be developed by the marketer.

Advertising

There are two key issues to consider in the selection of advertising media. The first is effectiveness. Does the medium have the right characteristics to convey the desired message and imagery? A poster has limited capacity to convey information. A website has enormous capacity to communicate information. Radio does not lend itself to imagery and lacks the full impact of the cinema.

The second consideration is efficiency, as shown in Figure 7.6. The ideal media should reach 100% of the target audience with 0% wastage. This is why database and direct marketing are so popular. With a good, clean database, wastage should be minimal and cover should be good. E-advertising is considered under e-communications.

Press

The range of titles is large, with circulations of millions for daily newspaper to a few thousand or even hundreds for technical and trade journals. The lifetime of a daily newspaper is short, while magazines may be kept for months. Publishers produce press packs that give the intending advertiser information about the demographics of the readership. Armed with this, informed decisions can be made as to which titles will provide effective cover with acceptable wastage. For highly targeted magazines, the cost per thousand readers may be high, but the extra cost is balanced by the selectivity of the publication in reaching

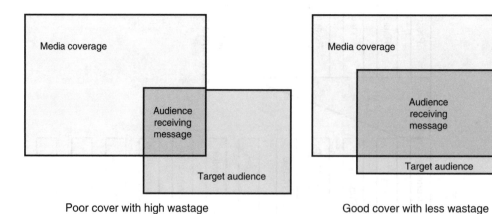

Poor cover with high wastage   Good cover with less wastage

Figure 7.6 Media coverage and wastage.

the desired audience. This is particularly important in the B2B context, where some publications are highly targeted on specific sectors and reach key members of the DMU (e.g. *Soap, Perfumery and Cosmetics*).

Radio

Radio is a highly fragmented medium, but with the use of agencies, it can be used as part of a national campaign. The fragmentation can be useful where specific targeting is wanted (e.g. only regional cover is needed). As with press, the audience demographics are available from the stations: Classic FM has a different audience to Pirate FM. In the UK, radio coverage is surprisingly high; many people listen to the radio on the drive to work.

TV

TV is in a state of flux. Analogue TV will be phased out in the UK over the next few years. People will then receive their TV by digital terrestrial, satellite, cable, internet or even mobile telephone. There are still large audiences for the major soaps, but TV has become a more flexible medium, with the proliferation of digital channels catering for minority interests. In some ways, TV is moving towards the press in this respect, with large mass audiences for some channels and targeted audiences for special interest groups. With convergent technologies, people can switch between TV and websites, so TV advertising can link into extensive information banks.

Posters

These can be very flexible. They can form part of a national campaign or be highly targeted (e.g. posters in and around exhibitions such as the Southampton Boat Show). Apart from their use in support of the general campaign, they can be very useful to remind people just before or during the shopping experience (e.g. poster near and in supermarkets for FMCG products).

Cinema

Cinema advertisements are the ultimate in ability to deliver impact: massive screen and surround sound. As with TV, the audiences for films may differ, allowing some selectivity and targeting. The audience at the arts cinema for an international film with subtitles is different to *Pirates of the Caribbean* at the local multiplex.

Public relations and publicity

Publicity is where the organisation gains coverage in the media, but has not made a payment for the media time or space. Often the publicity will be the result of public relations activity, such as a press conference. Publicity is more believable than advertising. Nobody advertises 'Rotten fish for sale'. This is a strength and a potential threat. If *What Camera* writes 'Best new camera and fantastic value', this is just great. If the test does not go well and they write 'Obsolete before it was launched and poor value for money', this is a bit of a problem. With advertising, the organisation can dictate the copy; after all, they are paying for it. With publicity, the organisation does not write the copy and there is risk.

PR activity is useful for launch events, exhibitions lobbying key stakeholders, and generating positive media cover. A special aspect of PR is disaster management (e.g. product recall). This aspect is covered in more detail in Chapter 15.

Personal selling

This is less important for minor consumer purchases but for major consumer purchases (cars, mortgages, etc.), this element of the mix is key. In B2B, the sales role is usually one of the more important elements of the communications mix, replacing advertising (which is often more important for consumer marketing). Technical staff may be directly involved or provide support for field sales personnel. There is a seven-stage model for the personal selling process:

1. prospecting and evaluation
2. preparing
3. approach
4. presentation
5. overcoming objections
6. closing the sale
7. follow-up

Prospecting and evaluation

Remember the 80:20 rule: 80% of the business tends to come from 20% of the customers. Do not overwork this rule of thumb, but the message is clear: be selective. There is a critical mass of effort needed to win an account. If you do not achieve this critical mass, there is no result. Effort spread too thinly over too many accounts results in dismal sales. The key skill is in determining which are the attractive accounts (not always the large ones; it could be a small account if we expected it might grow) and having a sense of which ones are winnable. In real life, much time can be spent chasing dead accounts that are happy with their supplier but need some other quotations to satisfy their internal purchasing system. In short, devote the sales effort to where it is likely to be profitable.

Preparing

Cold calling (arriving on the doorstep of an unprepared client) is usually a waste of time because much of the effort is spent catching up on the ground that careful preparation would have covered. Preparation of the client can be generic (e.g. advertising in the trade press) or specific (e.g. tailored mail shot).

Apart from preparing the client, the sales person should also prepare. If the client has been visited before, then details of the client DMU should be on file. A cuttings file should be kept with copies of press reports, etc. regarding the company. For both old and new accounts, it is useful to check on the website for any relevant news (e.g. expansion plans and other announcements).

Approach

Care should be taken over housekeeping issues such as parking and facilities for presentations and demonstrations. (Many of the best sales people take their own laptop and portable projector – that way they do not get software problems.) Using network contacts to break the ice or following up from an exhibition can all be useful. This element is the most important to get right; the wrong foundation here will not support the rest of the efforts. This is very much relationship marketing in action. Trust and a working relationship need to be built up. There is no 'one-size-fits-all' approach. Individuals are different and culture provides an additional layer of complexity. The working breakfast may work in the USA but not in some other cultures.

Tip: the best sales people are the best listeners. Customers want their needs and wants satisfied in the purchase. How do you know what they are? Listen and then make the sales approach.

Presentation

This is the 'show and tell' part of the process. Having identified the prospect's needs and wants and evaluated the appropriate company products, this is the presentation of the tailored offering.

Often, supporting materials such as samples and documentation will be required by the client. Making certain that all needs are identified is vital in the preparation and approach process.

Overcoming objections

This is where the sales person must know their product and full marketing mix and have a deep understanding of the client needs. This is negotiation written large. A typical objection in a B2B sale might be 'we do not have the capital budget for this at the moment'. Earlier, in pricing, we noted that affordability was a key aspect of pricing strategy. A smart company may, therefore, come up with a scheme such as a leasing option (convert capital expense into a revenue expense).

Closing the sale

This is the term used in the models given in the leading sales textbooks, but life is not always like that. Several visits may be needed to land a big contract. However, the key issue is to end up with an agreed milestone (e.g. 'We will meet in one month, after you have completed the trials on the samples I brought today'). Do not leave with 'We will meet sometime' – next month, next year, next decade? It is best to fix a follow-up date in the diary there and then.

Follow-up

Getting the first sale is not the end. In relationship marketing terms, it is another milestone in building and maintaining an ongoing partnership to the mutual benefit of both parties. Again, a good MkIS is vital. If there is to be a delay in delivery, it is best for the account manager to talk to the client immediately, before they set up a production run needing a product the supplier knew was going to miss the deadline. It is essential to build relationships that can endure, even when there are difficulties.

Point of sale

Point-of-sale support is important for many consumer purchases. This may be a simple stand to display the products to maximum advantage or more complex in-store displays. The value is that the communications is close to the sales decision. In one context, it may swing the selection from a competitor's brand. In other cases, it may prompt an impulse purchase.

Sales systems

Electronic point-of-sales (EPOS) systems and ATMs have made major impacts on how people buy goods and services. Apart from their value in the collection of payment, the capture of information and role in logistics, there is an additional marketing role – it is also an opportunity for communications. It gives the organisation an opportunity to cross-sell more products or services to the customer.

Sales promotion

The importance of sales promotion is to get the customer to act now. Take up this offer now as next week it will not be available. Competitions, money-off coupons and extra product free (by one, get one free) are all options. In the B2B context, promotional activities may still be relevant. For advanced equipment, it could be free training.

Direct marketing

The attraction of direct marketing is that with efficient and well-maintained databases, there can be minimal instances of sending the message to the wrong targets. With the merging of databases, more tailored messages may be given. There is the additional advantage that the mailing can also include product samples.

INSIGHT

INTEGRATION OF COMMUNICATIONS ACTIVITY

The promotional customer loyalty card provides the customer with incentives. It provides the organisation with a pattern of sales purchases. This allows tailored promotional offers and marketing communications based on the past behaviour of the customer.

E-Communications

The explosive growth in e-communications has transformed marketing communications both in the B2C and B2B sector. Web-based marketing has made a major impact on high street retailing. The e-mail and text message are an instant means of communication. Greater functionality in mobile telephones will give them the characteristics of baby laptops. Wi-fi is putting into public areas the broadband capabilities that are in over 50% of homes in developed Europe. There is a key qualitative difference in much of e-based communication. Unless you are a graphic/graffiti artist, there is not much scope to reply to a poster. E-communication now empowers consumers and pressure groups to respond to an organisation's activity. Care has to be taken: just having a website does not imply that you are in e-business. The strategy must be integrated. The vast information capability of the website is very useful and media with poor information content capability (e.g. posters) can direct targets to visit the website.

Sponsorship

A significant cash flow for many sporting and artistic events is sponsorship. European football and the Olympic Games have sponsorship activity as a key component of the business strategy. The sponsored organisation gains cash and also gains more publicity as the sponsor exerts leverage in its connection with advertising activity. Different patterns of sporting interest require that sponsorship should be reviewed on a region-by-region basis. Multinationals can sponsor local events and charities through their branch networks to provide a face to what otherwise could be perceived as a monolithic giant. Again, this is relationship marketing in action.

Exhibitions

Exhibitions can be useful in some B2C campaigns, with a range of events catering for specialist interests. An advantage of exhibitions is to be able to demonstrate products and engage in personal selling. This characteristic makes exhibitions especially useful in the B2B sector. The PR opportunities can make a major international exhibition an ideal platform for a new product launch. Care must be taken to ensure that the exhibition venue is appropriate (e.g. ease of access; availability of special requirements; services such as three-phase electrical supply, etc.).

Exhibitions can be expensive. Specialist services may be needed in the design and erection of stands. Staffing and travel costs can also be high. It is therefore essential to ensure that the exhibition will attract the target audiences. Exhibitions that are held on an annual basis conduct extensive analysis of their attendees. A review of this is helpful to check that a range of suitable contacts will be established at realistic cost.

Agency selection and briefing

An agency should be selected on the basis that it is best able to fulfil the brief. There should be a match in size. A major international agency is not going to be right for a small regional campaign. To assess suitability of the agency, its past clients may be an indicator and evidence of past work is valuable. Some agencies specialise in specific business sectors and for specialist B2B products this can be helpful; industry knowledge and network contacts can be vital. As always, with external contract services there is the 'x' factor: do the two organisations work together or is there a clash of cultures?

It is essential that the brief should be well thought out and complete. Poor briefing will result in a poor response – a waste of time and resources for both sides of the process. Issues that should be considered include:

- General background of the organisation, including its overall branding strategy.
- Appropriate overview of the key macro- and microenvironmental factors. This may include information on competitor activity.
- Segmentation issues and the targeting strategy.
- A review of the marketing mix to be used – all elements of the marketing mix have the capability to communicate. This should include full technical details of the product, as appropriate.
- A statement of the tasks to be undertaken (e.g. campaign elements to be developed). This should include specification of who will complete the work. There can be a danger that the best people are used to make the brief pitch, but less-experienced staff may then work on the project later.
- A full outline of the schedule and milestones for the management of the project.
- A specification of the budget and how expenses are to be controlled. Failure to do this can result in cost overruns.
- The deliverables (e.g. reports, artwork, etc.). This should also specify issues such as copyright ownership, etc.
- A list of resources available (e.g. product for consumer testing) and project management contacts.
- In the context of the learning organisation, it is valuable for there to be a debriefing review. What went well? What did not go so well? How could this be done better in the future?

Schedules and budgets

Schedules are a particular issue in communications programmes. There are two aspects. Firstly, the communications must be coordinated with the other elements of the mix. A launch programme before stocks have been built in the distributors is not going to make sense. Furthermore, some products have seasonal patterns in their sales and late marketing communications can miss the window of opportunity. The second aspect is availability. The size and complexity of a website is under the control of the organisation. However, some media are constrained. There are only so many poster sites and if they have all been booked you are not able to create more. Some media (e.g. fashion press) are planning months ahead of publication. Care must be taken not to miss copy deadlines.

As with any project, cost control is vital. It is all too easy to experience cost overruns with an agency contract or an exhibition. Some contingency flexibility should be built into the budget but only strict financial control will ensure on-budget delivery of a project.

To launch a communications project with well-considered objectives and not to attempt to measure the results is a waste of resources. In setting objectives, consideration should be made as to how achievement of these objectives can be evaluated. For an exhibition, it can be the number and quality of new contacts obtained as a result of the event. For a publicity campaign, the amount and nature of press coverage can be evaluated (agencies specialise in scanning media for coverage and can provide a valuable service).

International marketing communications

Care has to be taken with international marketing communications. How people perceive messages and the impact of images varies between different cultures. Using the structure outlined in Figure 7.1, selected key issues are discussed below.

Stakeholders

The spectrum of stakeholders may vary with different macro- and microenvironments in different countries. In some countries, the green movement is very powerful (e.g. Germany) and others less so (e.g. USA). The general stakeholder analysis needs to be reviewed and amended appropriately for each country that the organisation operates in.

Aims and messages

Products may be in different stages of their life cycle in different countries. In a country where the brand is well-established, the aim and messages will be about reminding and reinforcing. In a country where entry is new and the brand is not known, the aim and message will be about creating awareness. In different environments the message may need to be adapted because people have different needs and wants. In Germany, the recycling of printer cartridges might be given as a green message; in India, the key message might be 'Save money'.

Legal conformance

What can be advertised and how products may be promoted varies from country to country. In Europe, many countries ban the general advertising of tobacco products. Claims for performance must be substantiated. The description and ingredient labelling often are subject to complex national legal regulation.

Buyer behaviour

Motivation and influencing of reference groups differs from country to country. Celebrity endorsement from a great cricketer may go down well in Australia but leave the Germans cold.

Communications mix

The availability costs and reach of the various media differ from country to country. In the UK, there are many national newspapers and a high proportion of the adult population will read them. This is not necessarily so in some other counties. Clearly e-communication into the home depends on the local broadband infrastructure; not all parts of the world have this infrastructure in place.

Review

The need to identify and communicate with all relevant stakeholders has been reviewed. The detail of the communications mix to be used depends on the objectives and the macro- and microenvironment. Communications are to individuals and buyer behaviour provides the marketer with a framework to take the customer and DMU through the decision-making process. The characteristics of the different communications options were reviewed. The importance of scheduling and budget control was explained as part of the integration of the communications plan into the overall marketing mix.

Further reading

Chelsom, J., Payne, A. & Reavill, L. (2005) *Management for Engineers, Scientists and Technologists*, 2nd edn, John Wiley & Sons.

Hutt, M. & Speh, T. (2004) *Business Marketing Management: A Strategic View of Industrial and Organisational Markets*, 8th edn, Thomson.

Sheth, J., Mittal, B. & Newman, B. (1999) *Customer Behaviour: Consumer Behaviour and Beyond*, The Dryden Press.

Wilson, R. & Gilligan, C. (2005) *Strategic Marketing Management: Planning, Implementation and Control*, 3rd edn, Elsevier.

CHAPTER 8

Service extension: people, physical evidence and process

Learning objectives

After studying this chapter you will be able to:

- Describe the elements and sub-elements of the service extension to the marketing mix
- Apply the concepts of the cultural web to a given organisational context and compare and contrast the cultural web and 7-S models
- Explain the importance of the individual in the service provision process and evaluate the roles of various stakeholders affecting service provision
- Illustrate how physical evidence can be used to signal service quality and appraise the issues to be considered in selecting the process to be used in service provision (e.g. the level of automation that might be appropriate)

Introduction

Services are different to products; services are intangible. After the training session, you have not gained five kilos of knowledge. Often the service provider and the customer must be brought together and have a person-to-person interaction. In mass production, we can standardise components. You can, for instance, have a standard Whitworth thread. However, we do not have standard Whitworth people. Given the variability of the person-to-person interaction, there is considerable variability in the service process. Services may not be stockpiled in the way products can be warehoused. The unsold seat on last night's flight is a sales opportunity lost. At the end of the service experience, there is no transfer of ownership. The challenge is to brand a service and to indicate its nature and quality. With a product this can be achieved by package design, labelling and the use of signal attributes (e.g. perfume in personal care products). The service extension to the marketing mix performs a similar function to signal attributes in the analysis of product. The service-extended marketing mix communicates and confirms the nature and quality of the service experience. The people providing the service process are, in many cases, central to the service encounter. As with signal attributes (products), physical evidence (e.g. quality of documentation) communicates service benefits. Packaging has functional and communications uses in the marketing of products. Similarly, process has functional and communications aspects. When you go to work on a wet day, a standard taxi is fine; for the bride it will be the classic car and chauffeur. In both cases the physical benefit is transport from A to B; however, more style is appropriate in the bride's case.

People

To deliver effective performance, people must be placed in an organisational context that allows them to function. Poor communications and poor leadership destroy an organisation. Having established the appropriate context, the individual must be developed to make their full contribution to the team. In the supply-chain context, three key stakeholders are the suppliers, the channels and the customers.

Just as with an advertising campaign, it is essential to evaluate performance. It is not sufficient to say that training is good. The question is how good and by how much it improves the performance of the individual and the organisation. The architecture of the people element is shown in Figure 8.1.

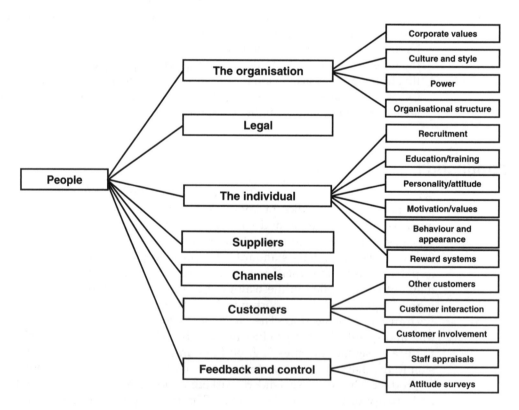

Figure 8.1 The architecture of people. Adapted from: Tony Curtis, *Marketing in Practice*, figure 7.1, page 163, © Elsevier 2006.

The organisation

Different organisations have different corporate values and cultures. The transition from public service to profit-making, privately owned companies involves more than just a change of name for the privatised utility companies. In universities and hospitals there is a power tension between the professional managers and the academics and medical practitioners. Creative solutions have to be found to structure the organisation to serve various objectives (e.g. in a university, to provide successful undergraduate courses and also do cutting-edge, 'blue sky' research).

Corporate values

The Eden Project in Cornwall is a holiday visitor attraction. There are also various commercial theme parks in the region. They have differing corporate values. Theme parks are commercial organisations: just like any others, they are concerned with visitor numbers and profitability. The Eden Project has equally compelling financial pressures (no visitors = no money for the research) but, with its educational objectives, the Eden Project not only wants to attract people and give them a pleasant day, it has the objective of educating visitors and society.

The values of the UK Co-operative Society are somewhat different to other successful high street traders. The form of co-operative ownership has an important impact on its values and the owning stakeholders are completely different to that of a company owned by shareholders. This is not to suggest that one set of values and styles are right and another is wrong, merely that differences exist. These differences express themselves in the culture and style of the organisation.

Culture, style, power and structure

The cultural web provides a tool for the analysis of culture and style (Figure 8.2). The various elements merge to provide the company paradigm. The major problem is when a paradigm shift is required. Major shifts in the business environment may make this necessary (e.g. impact of the internet on services).

Stories   Employees gossip about their work. What are the stories and what core values do they reflect? In a fast-moving technical market, there may be stories about technical breakthroughs. In a market leading company in a mature FMCG market, it may be activities to support a major advertising campaign. In a failing company it may be stories of management ineptitude.

Symbols   A key symbol of a company can be its logo. When BP needed to denote its increasing green activities it changed the company logo as part of the process of shifting the paradigm. Symbols can be important within the company; they denote status. That personal parking space near to the entrance is more than just a convenience. In a hierarchical company, there will be a separate restaurant for the directors. In a more democratic company, there will be a single-status restaurant used by all employees.

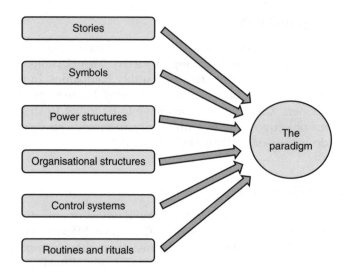

Figure 8.2 The cultural web. Adapted from: Johnson, G. & Scholes, K. (2005) *Exploring Corporate Strategy*, 7th edn, Prentice Hall, page 202.

Power structures What are the dominant power structures in the organisation? What are the core beliefs of the senior executives and what is the professional discipline of the chief executive officer? In the middle of the twentieth century many CEOs developed their careers from the finance function. In the increasingly competitive markets towards the end of the twentieth century, more marketing and sales professionals came into the top job. With increasing concerns about corporate governance and related issues, knowledge of legal matters is becoming more important.

Organisational structures Is the organisation hierarchical and arranged on a functional basis (e.g. finance, production etc.) or is a more organic matrix structure used to reflect the complexity of the management of large organisations? In a hierarchical company, there may be many layers between the front-line employees and the chief executive officer. In some companies, there has been de-layering to take out some middle management and shorten the communication path from the leadership to the front-line workers.

Control systems All companies must exercise appropriate control over money. However, what else is measured and controlled? For example, what form of time-keeping control is there? Are people allowed to work from home when preparing a report? Recent controversies in education and health services have surrounded the appropriateness of targets and their measurement. Setting the wrong targets may have perverse effects. Some medical practitioners consider the target of having very high (90%) bed occupancy rates in hospitals to be a hindrance to the control of infection because of the need for quick turnarounds between patients. They suggest that a little more flexibility is needed, with occupancy rates of around 80% being better. The key issue is that controls must be appropriate to the organisation's needs and that care must be taken to ensure perverse effects do not occur. In the service context, this problem is highlighted by *gap theory*: the gap between management's intentions and the customer service experience (covered in Chapter 15).

Routines and rituals   What are the social routines? How do people interact? Are people expected to socialise around work? What are the values being reflected in the rituals? In a hierarchical company, the rituals may be formal (e.g. use of titles in addressing senior staff). In less formal organisations, first-name terms may be the rule. What is the company dress code? What values does the dress code reflect? The dress code in a creative graphic design agency is likely to be a lot less formal than in the chambers of a commercial lawyer.

The paradigm   How does this all come together? This is often a problem in mergers and acquisitions, where two organisations with different paradigms have to fuse. This process can be difficult and there may be conflict in the transition period. Similar problems can occur as a start-up company grows. The informal, free-wheeling style that was appropriate in the early pioneering days must adapt as the organisation and the issues it confronts become more complex. The rise of Microsoft is not only a triumph of software skills, but also in evolving management systems and structures to manage a complex global organisation operating in very diverse markets.

INSIGHT

McKINSEY 7-S MODEL

The McKinsey 7-S model (Figure 8.3) provides a slightly different tool for the analysis of the firmware and people aspects of an organisation. The implications of this model have largely been built into the augmented value chain introduced in Chapter 2 for the analysis of the internal environment. The seven elements are:

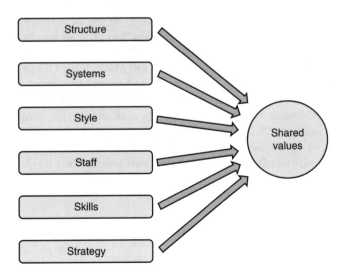

Figure 8.3 The McKinsey 7-S framework. Adapted from: Peters T. J. & Waterman R. H. (1982) *In search of Excellence***, Harper and Row.**

> **Structure**   The organisation's structure covers much the same ground as 'organisational struc-
> tures' and 'power structures' in the cultural web model.
> **Systems**   This takes the issues of 'control systems' a little further and prompts the consideration
> of systems in use for sales, marketing information, etc.
> **Style**   The organisation's style covers the way things are done and the way people behave.
> This is paralleled in the culture web model with 'symbols' and 'routines and rituals'.
> **Staff and Skills**   This covers the recruitment and development of staff. In this text, these issues
> are covered under the heading of 'The individual'. The elements are shown in Figure 8.1.
> **Strategy**   This covers the strategic values and direction of the organisation (e.g. market leader
> or market follower).
> **Shared values**   If all of the above are co-ordinated effectively then the result should be shared
> values and a coherent corporate culture.

Legal

There are many laws that affect the recruitment, employment and dismissal of staff. Equal
opportunity and trade union representation are complex areas and expert advice should
be sought. UK law is frequently amended and can be affected by EU policies. Outside the
EU, the law can be significantly different from country to country. Aspects of the law such
as Health and Safety may also apply to contractors, distributors and even customers.

The individual

There is a life cycle of employment. A key public for a company is the pool of potential
employees. There are never enough good candidates and the market for the best talent
is competitive. The selection process should be fair and should allow the organisation to
select the most appropriate candidates. To get new employees to reach full performance
quickly, there should be a formal induction process for the tasks and company (an assimi-
lation process into the organisation's cultural web). The business environment is continually
evolving, requiring new skills and ways of working. Continuing professional development
is essential if the technologist is not to become fossilised. Motivation and values must be
maintained. Part of the corporate cultural web is behaviour and appearance. For employees
in front-line contact with customers and clients, the employee becomes the face of the
organisation. All the marketing communications are as nothing if the service contact does
not live up to the experience. Reward systems are important and cover more than just
financial rewards (the basic pay structure tends to be a hygiene factor). Other aspects such as
recognition and opportunities for professional development are important for professional
engineers, scientists and technologists.

Recruitment and personality

The recruitment process involves 10 stages:

1. *Task analysis:* what has to be done?
2. *Job description:* an outline of the role and responsibilities.

3. *Job specification:* what attitudes, skills, knowledge and qualification are required of the person?
4. *Personnel specification:* what are the essential qualities and qualifications? What are the desirable qualities and qualifications?
5. *Recruitment search:* the use of advertising and/or head hunters to attract a range of suitable candidates.
6. *Shortlisting:* reducing the pool of potential candidates down to the number that can be interviewed and go through the assessment process.
7. *Interviewing/assessment:* the process of evaluating the candidates and deciding who should be offered the position(s).
8. *Formal offer and acceptance:* making the formal offer and dealing with the contractual details when acceptance is received.
9. *Induction:* initial training and introduction to the company.
10. *Professional development:* the ongoing process of developing the individual's potential.

It has been said that a company should hire for attitude and train for performance. The logic behind this statement is that it is easier to provide people with skills than to change their attitudes. In short, what is wanted is the right person for the role. The introverted genius may be fine if developing the next generation of encryption technology, but possibly not the right person for personal selling at a computer exhibition. If service staff do not have the right make-up and do not have the necessary knowledge and skills, then poor service delivery will be the inevitable consequence. More detailed consideration of the issues is given in Chapter 11.

Education and training

The selection process should have identified the ideal person profile. However, more often than not, there are some mismatches (e.g. a good project manager may have used a different software package in their last employment). Suitable tailoring of the induction package should address these immediate issues. The appraisal process should identify a mutually agreed personal development programme to maintain and develop these individuals' professional competence and ability to contribute to the organisation. Such programmes should focus on the 'hard' aspects (e.g. keeping up with technical developments) and 'soft' skills (e.g. team leadership for a project manager).

Behaviour and appearance

As discussed in the cultural web, different organisations and different situations require different behaviour and appearance. In key customer contact situations (e.g. field service for installation and maintenance), this is part of the customer service experience. Organisations will take considerable care with the design of uniforms and customer care training to ensure that these part-time marketers meet the expectations of the customer in the service encounter experience.

Motivation and values

World-class organisations require world-class performance and commitment from their staff. The need for organisations to develop shared values with their staff appropriate to the marketing context is embedded in both the cultural web and 7-S models of organisations. More coverage of motivation and leadership of people working in teams is given in Chapter 11.

Reward systems

Getting the basic pay right for the professional level is a hygiene factor. People are dissatisfied if they are not appropriately paid. If people are properly paid, that is just what they expect. The reward package can be composed of additional elements such as benefits in kind (e.g. company car), holiday entitlements and pension rights. In the context of marketing, it is important that incentives actually reward behaviour and values aligned with the company strategy and values. A simple commission system for sales staff may encourage them to milk existing accounts (the easy sales) and not go out prospecting for new accounts, where the sales are harder to win.

Suppliers and channels

In relationship marketing terms, two key partner stakeholders are the organisation's suppliers and channels. Suppliers not only include the sources of materials and parts to an organisation but also to providers of services. In world-class lean supply chains, there must be tight integration of suppliers and channels into the organisation's activity. To make just-in-time (JIT) production work, there must be precise synchronisation of operations and management along the complete supply chain.

Where the organisation is not in direct contact with the ultimate customer then the channel outlets can colour the ultimate customers' view of their product and the value of the organisation. Poor service from an agent or distributor will be perceived to be poor performance of the organisation itself. For economic reasons more use is being made of outsourcing by many firms. Where such services are in customer contact (e.g. security, call centres and delivery services), again poor service and image will tarnish the service quality perceptions and brand value. Increasingly there are demands that organisations should take care that their suppliers act responsibly (e.g. green issues, fair trade, corporate governance, etc.). That low-cost supplier may damage the company's reputation if pressure groups discover that they are polluting the environment and/or have exploitive employment policies.

Customers

In the service encounter, customers are often not passive. They also become part of the service process. In education, teachers can only teach if students also want to learn. There are three components to be considered: other customers, customer interaction and customer involvement.

Other customers

In segmentation terms, some customers may have different needs and wants from a service. On long-distance railway services, there may be one carriage designated as 'quiet' for the laptop addicts to work away. Another carriage may be designated 'family' for people travelling with children. Excited children going on holiday do not always mix well with a professional finishing off a presentation for a business meeting.

Other customers can act as a sign of quality. A restaurant frequented by 'A-list' celebrities will be perceived to be a 'quality' establishment and not just the place to eat but also the place to be seen to be eating. Word-of-mouth reports from satisfied customers can be very powerful. With customer agreement, this can be augmented in promotional material. Service providers may list their clients. The logic is that if you can satisfy the needs of a demanding international client, you must be a quality organisation. Architects, designers and agencies will maintain a portfolio of their past successful work for key accounts as evidence of their ability to deliver future exciting successful projects.

In certain cases, there can be situations where there is a perceived conflict of interests. In some services, only one customer from a given segment might be accepted.

Customer interaction

The classic example given in service marketing texts is in entertainment. People attend events (e.g. concerts, football matches, etc.) to socialise and meet other people with similar interests. In building relationships this can be used with corporate hospitability events for members of the key account decision-making units.

In the technical area, there may be other reasons to bring customers together. In the science instrumentation industry, there may be specialist segments. For example, plasma emission and atomic absorption spectroscopy are two methods of determining accurately (often at very low levels) the concentrations of metals in a sample. This analysis can be used in very different application areas. The spectrum of isotopes in an archaeological specimen (e.g. a tooth) may allow the investigator to determine if the person grew up in a region or travelled after childhood. Trace metal concentrations can assist in forensic investigations. Heavy metals can be a major problem in pollution incidents and are of key interest to environmental investigators. Determining the amount of metal and metal composition in lubricating oil can give engineers information about the wear taking place in an engine. Though the basic instrumentation may be the same, the specific needs of the different sectors are different (e.g. preparation of the sample for analysis). In such situations the instrument manufacturer can promote customer interaction by sponsoring special interest user groups where people can share best practice and develop standard methodologies. This is paralleled with learned societies (e.g. the Institution of Engineering and Technology and Royal Society of Chemistry) which have special interest groups with specialist publications and meetings so that members with a common application interest can develop their aspect of science or technology. Pharmaceutical companies have similar needs in assisting the diffusion of best practice in the treatment of various medical conditions.

Customer involvement

In the previous section, customer-to-customer involvement was explored. In many service situations, there is customer–service provider involvement. The local pub darts team may be supported by the landlord but it is run by the team members. The perfume industry developed gas chromatography/mass spectrometry to a fine art for the analysis of essential oils. However, the isolation of the essential oil from the plant altered the composition from the true odour perceived by smelling a real rose. Head-space trapping techniques (in which the volatile organic compounds in the airspace over the flower in the field is trapped in a cartridge for subsequent desorption into the analytical instrument in the laboratory) that were developed between the aroma researchers and instrument manufacturers have evolved into standard sampling technology.

In the OEM market, customer involvement in the design and development process is vital. The collaboration may be so close that the two organisations are almost fused. The design and manufacture of the Boeing 787 Dreamliner is largely outsourced, with only the final assembly taking place at the Boeing works. In consumer products, there must be intimate involvement of the end producer and its key suppliers (e.g. the design and supply of innovative packaging). In relationship marketing terms, a key competitive advantage for the OEM supplier is to be able to build and maintain the strong links with the customer's DMU: key account management in action.

Feedback and control

Staff appraisals and performance monitoring provide mechanisms for the tracking of individual development. Just as with customers, attitude surveys can be conducted on other key stakeholders, both internal and external (channels and suppliers). This provides vital evidence to management on the success (or lack of it) of current policies and strategies and may indicate where these may have to be altered.

Physical evidence

The physical environment provides evidence of the quality of the service. If the demonstration facilities are dirty and cluttered, customers may envisage similarly chaotic service. Often with a service, tangible items must be provided. For the technical marketer, a key area is customer documentation (e.g. training manuals) and certificates (e.g. certificate of analysis). To enjoy a service, there may be an opportunity to sell additional products. A golf course will generate considerable income from the shop. A telecommunications company may generate income from the sale of hardware to access the service. Figure 8.4 shows the architecture of physical evidence.

Environment

All our senses contribute to the service experience. How does the place look, what is the nature and standard of decoration of the facility? Is the place full of distracting noises? How do things feel: is the seating comfortable? Does the place smell right? All these things are important to architects and engineers in the design of buildings. How do we ensure the

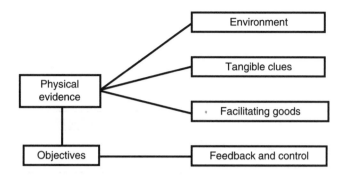

Figure 8.4 The architecture of physical evidence. Adapted from: Tony Curtis, *Marketing in Practice*, figure 7.2, page 170, © Elsevier 2006.

temperature is comfortable and the air conditioning doesn't create an irritating background noise?

Tangible clues

What is the quality of the products used in the delivery of the service? Is the documentation printed on good-quality paper, well-presented and free of typing errors? A good technical training course may lose some of its sparkle if the coffee is cold, the biscuits soggy and the buffet a disaster. Quotations and invoices are not only legal documents, they should also be regarded as marketing communications; everything used in the delivery of a service can affect the client's perception of the service quality.

Facilitating goods

These are the products that can be bought by the customer to aid the enjoyment and improve the quality of the experience. A technical museum may sell catalogues to assist people with the identification and selection of the artefacts they want to see. To generate additional revenue, they may sell posters, books and DVDs on their area of interest (e.g. 'Development of the steam engine in the nineteenth century'). This area can extend into more ephemeral areas with souvenirs (e.g. 'Steam 2008' sweatshirt and scale models of Stephenson's *Rocket*).

Process

What is the nature of the service? Is it to be highly flexible and does it need personal contact or can it be automated? In some situations (e.g. payment of fees at a tollbooth), a relatively inflexible automated system might be appropriate (with just one channel reserved for non-standard traffic (e.g. wide loads). In other situations, such as a consultation with a general practice doctor, the process may need to be highly flexible and involve a considerable amount of person-to-person communication. Figure 8.5 shows the architecture of process.

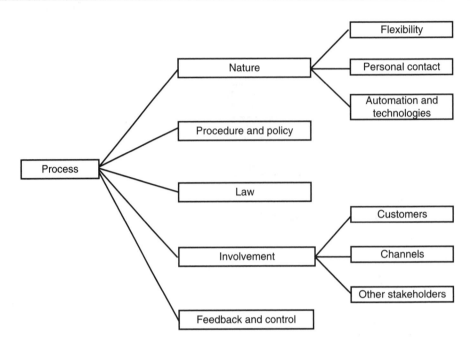

Figure 8.5 The architecture of process. Adapted from: Curtis, T., *Marketing in Practice*, figure 7.3, page 172, © Elsevier 2006. Reproduced by permission.

Nature

Flexibility

A service such as the AA and RAC has to have very flexible delivery. A wide variety of vehicle types can have a diverse range of problems occurring in any place at any time. The coin-operated turnstyle to a station toilet has only one function: let one person enter for 20 pence. With the internet and other communications, more functionality and flexibility can be incorporated into outlets such as ATMs. The London Oyster card system could develop into the long-awaited electronic purse. There is often a trade-off between flexibility and speed of service. An ATM is fine for paying out £50 in the evening, but not much use to a trader wanting to pay £3 637.27 in cheques, notes and coins into a business account. A typical large bank may have an ATM for these simple cash withdrawals, a standard set of positions for normal domestic transactions (e.g. payment of bills), a separate position(s) for commercial traders with large and/or complex transactions and usually yet further provision of positions for foreign currency transactions.

Personal contact

The question is, what is the level of personal contact that is relevant to the transaction? In the case of the OEM markets, relationship marketing theory tells us that part of the competitive advantage of the OEM supplier is developing strong personal contacts with the customer

DMU. The two organisations can fuse into one extended team for the development of the component (e.g. precision bearing) to go into a complex new product (e.g. new generation gas turbine). At the other end of the spectrum, there is little need for person-to-person contact if the organisation simply wants a copy of new European standard, etc. – internet purchase with payment with corporate credit card is fine.

Automation and technologies

Often the key concern between provider and the customer is cost-effective delivery of the service. In this context, highly automated systems are perfectly acceptable. The porter system used on nineteenth-century railways is not going to work with baggage handling in Heathrow Terminal Five in the twenty-first century. However, automation is not always welcomed. Remote call centres and a disembodied voice telling us to 'press two for balances' when you want to report your card stolen often just makes a bad day worse.

Procedure and policy

There are two apparently contradictory objectives in the provision of a service. People expect the same standard of service from all outlets at all times. However, people also want flexibility and this implies discretion. The remote call centre with an operator working from a script may be efficient and cost less, but it has limited flexibility. As insurance loss adjusters know, the one in a million does happen. No script is going to allow for all eventualities. Loss adjusters have firm guidelines but have the flexibility to apply the guidelines responsively to diverse situations.

Law

The process of delivery of some services may be governed by laws and regulation. A special area is the recording of data that may later be required in the provision of evidence in court. There must be safeguards to ensure that the data is not subsequently manipulated. Another area is safety, where there may be legal aspects as to the competence of staff and the way services are delivered and recorded (e.g. maintenance of passenger aircraft).

Involvement

Often services are delivered with the co-operation of key stakeholders such as the customers and the channels. Failure to fully consider the implications of this can result in poor service.

Customers

The internet and other technologies are providing new ways for customers to be involved with news and information services. At any major incident there is likely to be a someone there with a digital camera-enabled mobile telephone. Within minutes the image can be on BBC News 24. Thus, viewers are also becoming reporters. Information websites can involve the customers with providing content (e.g. book reviews on internet booksellers' sites). This is not only good in providing content but also develops the relationship in RM terms.

Channels

In some circumstances, the organisation may need to work through intermediary channels to the customer. A particular issue in telecommunications for new service providers has been access to historical copper landlines (the last mile to the house) owned by the heritage telecommunications companies.

Other stakeholders

Many organisations involved with major contracts will need to involve subcontractors. Any failure of the subcontractor will reflect badly on the main contractor: late delivery is late delivery. The customers are not concerned with where the problem occurred; all they care about is that they have not had delivery of the service on time. In many situations, such as tourism and entertainment, the provider is totally dependent on the travel service infrastructure to deliver the customers. A good restaurant experience starts with good food and drink supplies. The suppliers of products and services to the organisation should also be involved in the quality service partnership.

International service extended marketing mix

Both people and physical evidence are culture dependent. In one culture, a fairly formal culture of interaction between customers and service providers can be the norm. In other countries, a more informal and personal interpersonal style is acceptable. When you check out of a US hotel the final 'Missing you already' type of comment may be fine, but it is not welcomed in all situations. For some international organisations, there may be a global house style for their buildings but national companies often reflect their cultural identity in their buildings and other aspects of corporate physical evidence.

The nature of process to be used may be influenced by the various elements of the macro- and microenvironment. In a low-wage cost area, more personal service may be economic. In higher cost areas, a higher level of automation may be needed to contain costs. In the international situation, the organisation may be reliant on agents and distributors.

MICRO CASE STUDY   **MORE THAN ONE LONDON AIRPORT?**

On a journey from Jacksonville (Florida) to the UK, a traveller flew to Newark Airport on an internal flight with an American airline. The transatlantic leg was completed by Virgin Airlines. However, there were two Virgin flights from Newark to London that day: one flight to Gatwick and one flight to Heathrow. Jacksonville check-in had not considered that that there might be two Virgin flights from Newark by Virgin Airlines. The traveller was a little unhappy when he arrived at Heathrow and discovered his luggage had landed at Gatwick.

Review

The three elements of the service extension to the marketing mix have been outlined: people, physical evidence and process. The application of the cultural web to analysis of the nature organisations has been explored. The role of key stakeholders in the provision of services has been analysed within people and process. The way in which physical evidence can be used to signal service quality has been reviewed. The issues to be considered in establishing the right process for a service situation have been presented.

Further reading

Chelsom, J., Payne, A. & Reavill, L. (2005) *Management for Engineers, Scientists and Technologists*, 2nd edn, John Wiley & Sons.

Hunsaker, P. (2005) *Management: A Skills Approach*, 2nd edn, Prentice Hall.

Johnson, G. & Scholes, K. (2005) *Exploring Corporate Strategy*, 7th edn, Prentice Hall.

Lynch, R. (2005) *Corporate Strategy*, 4th edn, Pearson.

Peters, T. & Waterman, R. (1982) *In Search of Excellence*, Harper & Row.

Wilson, R. & Gilligan, C. (2005) *Strategic Marketing Management: Planning Implementation and Control*, 3rd edn, Elsevier.

PART THREE

Skills for Implementation

CHAPTER 9

The collection and management of marketing information

Learning objectives

After studying this chapter you will be able to:

■ Review the range of information required for the marketing decisions confronting the company
■ Explain the types of data that need to be collected
■ Illustrate how a marketing information system works in the collection of data and its conversion to useful marketing information
■ Describe the range of secondary research sources and the options available for primary research

Introduction

Before making a flight, a pilot will engage in research. Information will be sought on weather conditions along the flight path and at the destination. During the flight, a vast array of instrumentation monitors the position of the aircraft, the condition of the engines, amount of fuel, etc. The same should be true of marketing and business plans. A four-step process is involved:

1. What are the business decisions to be made?
2. What are the areas that need to be investigated for the decisions?
3. What type of data is required?
4. How can the data be collected and converted into decision-making information?

Information will be needed on market sectors and the changing marketing environment (there is the equivalent of clear air turbulence in the business environment). Information is needed to front-end the feedback and control system. Without this, the company is flying with no GPS data and no idea of the engine conditions or the amount of fuel remaining. The types of business decisions that require information are given in Figure 9.1. The complete system for collection of data, analysis of data and communication of information to decision makers is known as the marketing information management system (MkIS).

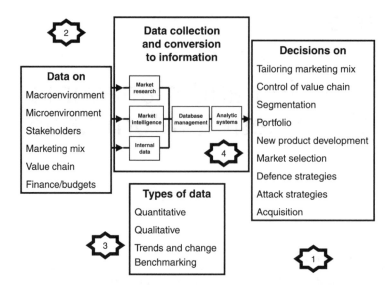

Figure 9.1 The marketing information system. Adapted from: Curtis, T., *Marketing in Practice*, figure 8.1, page 183, © Elsevier 2006. Reproduced by permission.

Data is required on the macro- and microenvironment. The nature of stakeholders and their needs and wants can change (e.g. changes in the competitive environment). It is not only important to know the state of play but also how quickly conditions may be changing (a pilot not only wants information on the aircraft's altitude and position but also on the speed of travel). Part of the art of marketing is making decisions now about what the market requires in the future; continually adapting and adjusting the product portfolio and other elements of the marketing mix. As with any system, the overall performance and stresses in individual elements must be monitored. All elements of the value chain must be considered and the budgets constructed.

Quantitative data is required about issues such as number of people purchasing the product, frequency of purchase and amounts purchased each time. Qualitative data is required about issues such as why people prefer one product to another (e.g. what influences the decision to buy a liquid crystal flat screen or a plasma screen). It is important to not only estimate the rate of change of parameters but to make judgements on how trends will continue; a forecast of the future has to be constructed. There was much celebration when the first person ran a mile in under four minutes. Such performance is routine now. In a competitive environment it is necessary to know the relative performance of the organisation against the performance of the competition. There tend to be no silver medals in business; you either win or you lose. Just as with any scientific or technical problems, the data is evidence. Judgment and creative synthesis is needed to convert raw data into decision-making information.

Why collect data?

There are a number of important questions in business:

1. Where are we? *Situation analysis*
2. What are the options? *Development of strategy alternatives*

3. Where do we want to be? *Formulation of business mission and objectives*
4. How do we get there? *Detailed formulation of strategy (e.g. marketing mix decisions)*
5. Are we on course/have we arrived? *Feedback and control systems*

For the technical staff, the management of the product portfolio is a major activity. In the past, point-of-sales terminals would take a customer's cheque and print out the details. Many major supermarkets are now refusing to accept cheques. Chip and pin is the current technology. Point-of-sale systems manufacturers need to continually develop their systems to match the needs of their clients (the supermarkets, etc.) and the customers' needs and wants in making the transaction. Decisions need to be made on what old products to drop, what new products to develop, what market segments to exit, what new segments to enter and what integrated mixes need to be developed for success.

What data?

In Chapter 2, the tools of environmental and stakeholder analysis were presented. To complete this analysis, data is required on the past and present conditions. The internal performance of the company needs to be appraised as part of the feedback and control systems. It is also part of the question of, 'Where are we?' The implications of the external environment depend on the shape the organisation is in. That wonderful market opportunity is of no value unless we know that we have the resources and competence to accept the challenge. In Chapters 4 to 8 the architectural structures of the marketing mix were developed. These pose the marketer a set of questions. For example, what is the benefit set required by customers in this particular market segment? Again, data is required to develop answers to these mix questions.

What type of data?

Both quantitative and qualitative data is required to develop business plans. Buyer behaviour is a complex process and people are not computers in the sense that they appear to make irrational decisions. A simple pay-off table will indicate that only a fool would bet on the National Lottery; the odds are against you (even when a double rollover makes it more interesting). There is an emotional context to our actions. The young person buying a motorbike is not only purchasing a mode of transport but is also making a lifestyle statement and joining a group (becoming a biker). The Ford Ka may cost the same but it does not make the same statement. Two wheels are more exciting.

Quantitative data tends to focus on what people do. This is the essential hard black-and-white outline that is needed. Qualitative data provides the additional information on why people do things; this provides the additional colour and dimensionality required for making the correct business decision. What are the intangible benefits people are looking for from the product?

Is it safe to stand in front of a car? With the handbrake on and the engine off, this is no problem. Knowing the position or value of a parameter is not enough. With a car we need to know both the velocity and the acceleration to make driving decisions. With the business environment we need to know the trends and changes, the velocity and acceleration of parameters such as size of the market. In some cases the absolute value does not tell the whole story. If the organisation has increased sales by 10%, that may be good or bad performance. If the competition has failed to grow in the market, it may indicate success. However, if the competition has grown market share by 25%, it may be an indication of less spectacular performance. Benchmarking allows the firm not only to consider how it is developing but also to know if it is winning or losing the competitive race.

Data collection

There are two types of data collection activity. There is the systematic continual collection of data monitoring the macroenvironment, microenvironment and internal environment for the organisation. This provides the necessary day-to-day information to run the firm but can also be analysed later for specific needs. The second type of data collection is research for a specific given purpose (e.g. researching the characteristics of a new market segment for the development and launch of a new product). Confusingly, the first research to be done is secondary research where existing (internal and external) sources of data are searched for useful information. This process will identify gaps and indicate areas where further data may be required and this will need new research activity: primary research. The data may be quantitative (how many units sold in a segment) or qualitative (how people feel about the brand and the product).

Internal data

A key source of data is the sales system. For production, the sales projection forms the basis of the forward production planning, including the materials resource planning (MRP) activity. Declining sales may indicate that products are nearing the end of their life cycles. In day-to-day management, cost control is vital. For marketing, analysis of individual customer's accounts is important to identify changing customer demands (e.g. new purchases as the customer moves into new products). Sales and technical visit reports add to the fund of knowledge on clients. In relationship marketing terms, getting to know the customer decision-making unit (DMU) better helps to build tighter relationships. Technical marketing people will be greatly interested in failure reports (e.g. customer complaints, returns and breakdown records). These can indicate where a product needs to be improved. In some cases, clients may be using the product for an unintended purpose and this may flag up a new market opportunity for a new product. Table 9.1 looks at internal data sources.

Market intelligence

In a market leading company, a significant technical activity is the retro-engineering of competitors' products. Formulated products such as perfumes and cosmetics can be analysed to determine their make-up. Electrical and electronic products can be disassembled and components identified and design approaches noted. This not only provides technical information but, with general market knowledge, should also allow an estimate to be made of the likely component and assembly costs. One of the major problems of test marketing is it provides the competition with all the samples required to complete this retro-engineering. A similar activity can be undertaken with services (e.g. mystery shopping in consumer markets, mystery travellers in airlines, etc.).

Competitor activity can be tracked by analysing their publications (website, company reports, sales and marketing literature, etc.). Exhibitions are not only a place to present

Table 9.1 Selected sources of internal data

Internal sources of data	Comments
Financial and accountancy figures such as costs, sales, etc.	Figures collected for formal accounts may not be appropriate for future decisions (e.g. accountancy figures may give historical costs whereas, for future marketing decisions, projected costs are needed)
Customer records including visit reports for B2B context	In the B2C context, loyalty cards can provide information on patterns of purchases. In the B2B context, sales analysis by product and period provide the black-and-white outline. Visit reports and other customer records provide the colouration
Quality assurance records, including returns and customer complaints	Quality assurance records provide additional information to sales records. Of particular importance to technical management is the analysis of returns and customer complaints. Sometimes customer complaints highlight weakness in the design or formulation of the product, thus providing crucial information for product improvement. In other cases, the product may have been used for purposes not intended by the design team, and this may indicate the potential to create a new product
Production records	Needed for inventory management and to maintain customer service. This is vital for the day-to-day running of the business

the firm's products and services but also to investigate competitive new launches and promotions. The financial and trade press exist to provide more general market intelligence about major new trends in the marketplace (e.g. uptake of broadband, new trends in fragrances for consumer products, new colours or materials for clothes and accessories, etc.). A review of sources of market intelligence is given in Table 9.2.

Table 9.2 Selected sources of market intelligence

Sources of intelligence	Comments
Retro-engineering of products	Analysis of formulated products and retro-engineering of products can yield key information on competitive product performance, source of ingredients/components and form the basis of estimates for manufacturing costs
Competitor sources	Annual reports, data sheets and websites can all provide useful competitive intelligence
Published sources (e.g. trade, financial and general press)	This can provide general information about brand re-launches, etc. and financial information
Field research	Checking on products in the field (e.g. visiting outlets to see how competitors' products are marketed). Exhibitions can be a rich source of knowledge
Technical data sources	Tracking publications (e.g. patents) can give information about developments in the market and technology

Market research

Market research is the systematic collection of data for a given purpose such as the launch of a new product. The collection of new data can be expensive so the first stage is to search for useful data that has already been collected and is available in internal or external sources such as published trade statistics, web sources, etc. Primary research is the systematic design of research approaches (e.g. sampling strategies), collection and analysis of data and reporting of findings to decision makers. Market research can be exploratory (to get a feel for the market) or (conclusive) to test a specific hypothesis. Exploratory research and market intelligence are critical as the most difficult aspect of marketing and business is not getting answers but knowing the right questions to ask in the first place.

Secondary research

Internal data can be a rich source of secondary data. In the B2C context, analysis of data collected from EPOS systems from customers' use of store loyalty cards helps retailers to better target offers and marketing communications. This can be linked to geodemographic and other external data. An indicator of lifestyle and product needs is the type of home that a person lives in. In the UK, each small section of the country where people live is assigned a postcode. Commercial databases have classified the typical type of dwelling in each postcode area. Garden products are not going to be of much use in an area where the majority of dwellings are apartments with no gardens.

Published information sources may be free (e.g. government statistics). Then there are many trade directories. Commercial research organisations conduct regular surveys and produce market research for given sectors. Table 9.3 outlines sources of secondary research data.

Table 9.3 Selected secondary research sources

Secondary source	Comments
Market research reports	E.g. Euromonitor, Mintel, Keynote, etc.
Government statistics	E.g. export/import data, RPI data, etc.
Databases	Various databases available, often on a subscription/fee basis. A variety of mailing lists can be purchased
Internet	Very valuable source of information. However, care must be taken as, unlike sources such as the *Financial Times*, the accuracy of some data can be suspect
Yearbooks and directories	Can provide general information when moving into new markets
Geodemographic sources	E.g. ACORN
Note: Internal sources and market intelligence sources can also be appropriate areas for secondary research	E.g. in launching a new line, a specific project of retro-engineering all the major competitor products might be initiated

Primary research

For the engineer or technologist working on new product development, three types of primary research are important. The process is parallel to the normal scientific process of discovery (e.g. discovery of superconductivity), exploration (e.g. search for high temperature superconductors) and application (e.g. high-performance electromagnets).

1. *Exploratory* How do people lead their lives and what 'problems' are there that might provide an opportunity for a new product or service offering?
2. *Descriptive* This may be quantitative, such as how many people might want the product and how much they might use. It is the information needed to assess the financial viability of the business case. It can also be qualitative: just how do people feel about the product and how should the product be positioned? This is the type of information needed to assess design and colour options in the product's development and the messages that might be employed in the marketing communications.
3. *Experimental* Does the product work under the customers' use situations? Does it actually do what the customer wants? Does it meet the needs and wants of the target market? For formulated products in the food and perfume industry, this may involve preference tests. (More consideration of this is given in Chapter 14.)

Two popular research methods are focus groups and questionnaires. Conducting focus groups is a specialist skill. This may be the time to consider the use of full-time marketing experts. However, it is vital that they are fully briefed as to the insights that are needed by the development team. If this is not done, vital aspects of the issues may not be explored. In the insight section below some of the key aspects of questionnaire design are outlined. Again, it is vital to know precisely what the object of the research is so that the right questions can be explored in the right way.

INSIGHT

HOW TO WRITE AN EFFECTIVE QUESTIONNAIRE

Keep to the basics. The researcher should make questions easy to understand and unambiguous. Make the format easy to respond to and make certain that the question areas are relevant to the respondent. Do not use unfamiliar technical words or concepts. Keep to the rules of clear English (e.g. few qualifying clauses and no multiple questions – one question at a time).

Possibly one of the most difficult traps to avoid is the leading question. The outrageous tabloid newspaper question is easy to spot: 'Do you want to buy cosmetics from companies that torture animals in their research laboratories?' However, it is all too easy to inadvertently pose a leading question. Care must also be taken with questions that may be considered too personal or embarrassing. A question along the lines 'Are people offended by your body odour?' in research for antiperspirants is not likely to get an honest answer.

Closed questions with a specific response lend themselves to easier analysis. Open-ended questions may capture detail and colouration that might otherwise be lost, but at some cost because they are more difficult to analyse. Here are some simple ways to pose questions:

Semantic differential scale
The performance of the product is:

Very good   [ ]   [ ]   [ ]   [ ]   [ ]   Extremely poor

Marks out of five
Please rate the performance of the product:

Very good   ☐   5
Good   ☐   4
Acceptable   ☐   3
Poor   ☐   2
Very poor   ☐   1

As already mentioned, open-ended questions can be difficult to analyse so sometimes a 'half-way house' can be appropriate. The respondent can be given a set of adjectives that could be used to describe the product and then invited to select those that they think apply to the product (i.e. more than one selection can be made).

It is important to pilot the questionnaire on a small sample of 20 to 30 respondents. This will allow you to pick up any problems with questions and double check the spreadsheet coding system is working well.

In international marketing it is important to get a native speaker to check the questions. Some international students were comparing the buyer behaviour of US bikers (where they had done extensive research on the purchase of accessories) with UK bikers. They did take care to pilot the questions, which was just as well because two of them were not appropriate in the UK. 'Do you wear suspenders?' and 'Do you carry a gun?' may be fine in the USA but not in Britain. The UK equivalent of the first question is 'Do you wear braces?' The second question is not relevant in the UK culture.

Some primary research approaches are discussed in Table 9.4.

A major problem in business research is also common to many scientific experiments. The results are no better than the sampling. No amount of analysis will be of help if the sample is not appropriately representative of the population. In a postal survey, a low response may be obtained so a key question is: 'Are the respondents typical of the non-respondents?' Follow up with a selection of non-respondents may be needed to check that there is no bias in a sample.

Database management

There are many excellent texts on the 'bits and bytes' of database management (selected references are given at the end of the chapter). This section focuses on the issues of the management of the database. Marketers talk about data warehouses and data mining. This is parallel to the processes in a technical library. Lots of information needs to go in but it is not piled up in any old fashion. Key words, for instance, provide ways to retrieve the information required for the specific question. The problem is, at the time the data is obtained and stored, some of the potential questions that researchers may need to ask in the future may not be known. Flexibility is needed to enable further analysis of the raw data when it is required. There is one major difference between marketing databases and

Table 9.4   Selected primary research approaches

Research method	Comments
Questionnaires	Need to be well devised and can provide quantitative and qualitative data. Key issues are to get correct population sampling to avoid bias. These can be administered online, by post, by telephone interview, etc.
Focus and other group interviews	Helpful to gain market feel and to gain more insight into issues such as purchase motivation
Mall intercept interviews	No Saturday high street worth its salt is without a couple of market researchers administering questionnaires
Observation	Traffic flows through an airport can be observed. A mobile telephone manufacturer used this technique to research how children used mobile telephones
Experiments	A prototype product may be used by target customers to evaluate absolute and perceived product performance. In the food and perfume industry a key type of experiment is preference testing of product variants (often against the market leader) to evaluate the formulation most liked by consumers. Even new recipes of cat food are trialled on test populations

physical sciences databases. Marketing databases hold information on people and use of the data must be ethical and compliant with the relevant data protection legislation.

The basic laws of data management still apply. GIGO (garbage in; garbage out) is just as relevant in marketing as in engineering. Data entry must be accurate and data must be maintained. If data changes, the database must be updated. Setting up a database in the first place is a sprint; then the maintenance of it is an everlasting marathon. Security is essential. Access to data may need to be restricted. Industrial espionage is real and appropriate care should be taken to prevent unauthorised access. Loss of data is expensive so back-up routines and virus protection is vital.

Analytic systems

As with scientific investigations, two activities may be needed. The first is to 'clean up' the data. In technical investigations this might be the removal of bias or noise in the sampling process. The same needs apply to marketing data. One key parameter may be sales figures to feed into a sales forecast. Monthly figures may be distorted by having a different number of trading days in the month. It should be noted that this process is very different to just rejecting inconvenient figures or results.

INSIGHT

PERILS OF SALES FORECASTING

Consider the simple case of a company making one product with a cycle in the demand. The peak demand is greater than the production capacity. The minimum demand is less than the production capacity.

After a period of high demand, there are no stocks and the sales volume will be the production volume. However, given that the demand is higher than production there will be a build-up of back orders. When the down part of the cycle begins to cut in and demand is below production level, the sales still remain constant. There is the fat of the back orders to still hold up the sales figures that will appear to be consistently good. That is, until all the back orders are fulfilled and then sales fall to the much lower level of the actual demand. The back order buffer has masked the actual change in the marketplace.

A forecasting system that just relies on actual shipped sales could run a company into big trouble. It is not enough to just feed the numbers into some statistical package. It is vital that the story behind the numbers, the meaning of the numbers, is understood.

The answer looks simple. All you have to do is not look at actual sales but look at the value of sales orders received. Job done! Well, no. In times of high demand and shortages, companies may over-order on the basis that they might get $x\%$ of what they asked for. They may also place orders with several suppliers to hedge their supply risks. Statistical forecasting packages do have their place in predicting the future. However, they have to be used with expert knowledge of the market.

An example of blind statistical data analysis, occasionally seen in the marketing and business press, is the misuse of regression. Over a fairly short period of time, the growth phase of product life cycle is approximately linear and a linear regression can look a fair fit with a good correlation indicated. Extrapolate this for a couple of years and every person in the UK will have two or three mobile telephones. Over-extrapolation from limited results can provide false estimates in both marketing and physical science. Moreover, the old rule applies: correlation does not imply causation. When a room gets warmer the mercury in the thermometer rises. All we need for air conditioning is a device to force the mercury down and the room will get colder. This is clearly nonsense. However, in marketing situations people can get carried away by the numbers and forget these two golden rules: *correlation does not imply causation* and *over-extrapolate at your peril*.

The research process

The market research process is parallel in process to the normal process of scientific research. There is a preliminary review of the topic area(s). This is then followed by generalised research to get the feel of the subject area. Once this investigative work is complete the researcher can define the issues/hypotheses that need further research. The actual research process is conducted (proceeded by research design), followed by the analysis of the results. Then, depending on the outcome (the final answers and the insights that are obtained), further work may be conducted as required (the research design–research–analysis loop).

Identification of the research aims and objectives

This often falls into distinct phases. The first question might be: 'Is there a market opportunity in market x?' The next phase might be: 'What type of new product is needed?' The final phase in the new product development (NPD) process is: 'Is this the right/best product for the market?' To conduct research without careful consideration of the aims and objectives can be interesting but it is not likely to provide a commercially useful outcome.

Review of market intelligence and preliminary secondary exploration

The major problem in research is often not getting the answers but in asking the right questions in the first place. To do effective research it is necessary to have a 'feel' for the market. Often the organisation will have had an ongoing market intelligence process in place. If so, a good starting point is to review this and, if necessary, do some preliminary secondary research. Having gained a 'feel' for the market and the problem, it is then possible to define the information required and proceed to the next phase. Some writers describe this process as 'explorative' research.

Research (planning, conduct and analysis)

With some definition of the issues to be addressed, a series of questions and hypotheses can be framed. Where these can be answered or refined by secondary research, this should be conducted. Secondary research is not cheap but primary research can be eye-wateringly expensive (even a limited questionnaire survey can easily run up a bill of £10 000).

With a firm idea of the information needed, the primary research approaches can be decided and detailed design of the research completed (e.g. sampling method, sample sizes required, etc.). After conducting the research, the results can then be analysed and the results reported. Often this will be a loop process where an outcome of the research processes is to throw up additional issues that need to be further investigated.

MICRO CASE STUDY　　　　**CADBURY'S 2007 CHALLENGE TO WRIGLEY**

In 2006, Wrigley dominated the UK market for chewing gum. This is a lively and profitable market sector, with a move into positioning some products more in the oral hygiene market (a toothbrush on the move) than just confectionery. In 2006, some market analysts predicted that the market might be given an uplift in the middle of 2007 when the UK ban on smoking in public places came into force. Cadbury entered the market in early in 2007 with its 'Trident' brand. Below is an outline of some of the research that a product development manager in this type of position might undertake. The four-stage process is used.

Stage one: the key business decisions
The key questions are: 'Is there an opportunity for another brand presence in this market?' 'What type of product(s) might be successful?' 'What integrated marketing mix would be needed to support the new product(s)?'

Stage two: what data?
The types of information needed would include the following. Macroenvironment: 'What are the trends in consumer preferences (e.g. just as with cola there is a trend for consumers to want sugar-free products)?' 'Would the change to smoking laws provide an opportunity by expanding the demand for gum?' Microenvironment: competition structure. What is the strength of Wrigley in the market? How might supermarkets and other outlets react to the launch of another brand? Would they be prepared to stock it? A company such as Cadbury would be familiar with the stakeholders for standard confectionery products but a move into the oral hygiene sector would bring in some new stakeholders (e.g. dental profession). Another

special area for gum is the 'Keep Britain Tidy' movement. Walk through any city centre and count the number of spots on the floor from discarded gum. It is important when moving into any new market to check which new stakeholder group(s) may be important. Marketing mix: 'What are the present marketing mixes employed?' 'What new approaches could be adopted?'

Stage three: types of data?

Quantitative: 'Who uses gum; what are the demographics of gum usage?' 'How much gum do people consume?' Qualitative: 'How do consumers feel about the existing brands?' 'Why do people use gum?' Trends and change: 'What are the growing market segments that might provide potential opportunities for a new entrant?'

Stage four: data collection

Internal data Since this is a new product, there may be little direct data. However, general market research in the past in the total confectionery market may have some useful background information.

Market intelligence Walk the ground and see where gum is sold and how it is sold (point-of-sale display is an important issue for gum sales). Buy all the key variants and send them into the laboratory for retro-engineering (e.g. analysis of the flavour, etc.).

Secondary research Search of major commercial databases and surveys for work conducted on the sector and the collection of relevant trade statistics. Review of competitors' advertisements (e.g. positioning claims, etc.), including web as well as traditional media. An international company might also briefly review activities in this sector in other major markets – sometimes this can yield ideas that can be adapted.

Primary research Pre-product development collection of data on users (e.g. when they buy, where they buy, how much they buy, etc.) and focus groups to probe feelings towards the use of the product and existing brands. This enables the product development team to draw up a definition of the product(s) to be developed (sometimes called the product innovation charter in NPD texts). During development of the product, there will be ongoing consumer preference tests for the product being developed (e.g. consumer reactions to new flavour approaches). Parallel research should be undertaken to develop the rest of the integrated marketing mix (e.g. branding imagery and packaging design). Test marketing might be used to trial the full mix before a full market launch. Tracking research should be conducted during the launch to check progress in areas such as brand awareness, repeat purchases, etc.

Review

In this chapter, the four-stage process for data collection and information creation has been outlined. The range of decisions confronting the company has been reviewed together with areas where data is required. Both quantitative and qualitative data are required. Changes in the data (e.g. growth of markets) must be considered as must benchmarking against competitors. The five elements of the marketing information system have been presented: market research, market intelligence, internal data, database management and analytic systems. A selected range of options for primary and secondary research have been described.

Further reading

Chelsom, J., Payne, A. & Reavill, L. (2005) *Management for Engineers, Scientists and Technologists*, 2nd edn, John Wiley & Sons.

Malhotra, N. & Birks, D. (2003) *Marketing Research: An Applied Approach*, Prentice Hall.

Swift, L. (2001) *Quantitative Methods for Business, Management and Finance*, Palgrave.

Wilson, R. & Gilligan, C. (2005) *Strategic Marketing Management: Planning Implementation and Control*, 3rd edn, Elsevier.

CHAPTER 10

Finance for marketing

Learning objectives

After studying this chapter you will be able to:

- Appreciate the importance of cash flow as well as profitability in the management of an organisation and the issues to be considered in costing a product
- Develop a budget and construct a basic spreadsheet financial model for specific situations such as new product launches
- Explain the time value of money, be able to calculate net present values and internal rates of return for projects and explain how these assist technical managers with investment decisions
- Explain how sensitivity analysis, break-even analysis, pay-back periods and internal rates of return can act as pointers to potential risk levels in a project

Introduction

Money is the energy of business: no money, no business. Tax accountancy is best left to the expert accountant, but managers making financial decisions in industrial contexts need the ability to assess the financial implications of the technical issues. The technical manager in a customer service or new product development (NPD) role needs to be financially literate.

The balance sheet

In mechanics, there is a theory that to every action there is an equal and opposite reaction. Accountancy has its own form of action and reaction, the principle of double entry. If a company spends £100 on raw materials, its cash account at the bank is reduced but its working assets (raw materials for production) are increased by £100.

$$\Sigma \text{Assets} = \Sigma \text{Liabilities}$$

Assets are the things (expressed in money terms) a company owns such as the buildings, equipment, stock, intellectual property, etc. Liabilities are the amounts of money the firm owes, including to the owners of the company and to people from whom the firm has purchased goods or services, such as raw materials for production. Revenues are the sums of money that the company receives from the sale of its products.

The situation is best considered with a simple practical example. If J. Smith, a Chartered Engineer, sets up his own business – 'Gold Connections' – to make small special electrical contacts for specific applications with a machine that uses gold plating to provide the best quality. A simple scenario for this business might look something like this:

J. Smith rents a small enterprise unit, which comes with basic insurance, services, etc. for £5 000 a year. The business is started with £11 000 of personal money and a long-term bank loan of £9 000 (at 10%, repayment in full at the end of five years, interest only during the loan period). There is a need to buy some general office equipment (computer, furniture, etc.) and this costs £4 000. The special manufacturing equipment was purchased second-hand for £10 000. The starting stock of gold contacts and other materials for manufacture cost £1 000.

During the course of the year, it is found necessary to hold stocks of finished contacts and business is good. Additional raw materials are purchased to build up raw material stock from £1 000 to £2 000 in the middle of the year and £2 000 of finished stock is being held to provide good service. Sales for the first year are £60 000. Customers are allowed one month to pay, so at any one time Gold Connections is owed £5 000. Also, the suppliers of parts and materials allow one month for payment. At any one time the business owes £1 000.

At this start-up stage of the business, no other staff are employed. Products are dispatched by post and with packaging and insurance this costs £1 000 a month. J. Smith pays himself a salary of £2 000 per month. Other odd expenses such as supplies for the computer, telephone, etc. cost £200 per month. The cost of components for production is £1 000 a month. The spreadsheets show the balance sheet at the start of the business (Spreadsheet 10.1), the cash flow for the year (Spreadsheet 10.2) and the balance sheet at the end of the year's trading (Spreadsheet 10.3).

Further reading references on the preparation of balance sheets are given at the end of the chapter. However, one key feature in the very simple case given above is of fundamental importance: you can be profitable and go out of business. Gold Connections has been trading profitably yet the amount of free cash has decreased. Profit is not cash flow. You need money in the bank to pay suppliers (no money = no supplies for manufacture). In the simple Gold Connections case, more money was needed to increase raw materials stock and to build a stock of finished products to provide good service. Growing businesses are usually cash hungry. It is vital to monitor both profitability and cash flow.

Spreadsheet 10.1   Balance sheet of Gold Connections at start of trading

FIXED ASSETS	£	CAPITAL	£
Office equipment	4,000	Personal money	11,000
Production equipment	10,000	Long-term loan	9,000
CURRENT ASSETS		**CURRENT LIABILITIES**	
Starting stock	1,000	Creditors	1,000
Debtor	0		
Cash	6,000		
TOTAL	**21,000**		**21,000**

Spreadsheet 10.2   Gold Connections' cash flow statement for the first year of trading

REVENUE	£
Sales	60,000
Total	**60,000**
EXPENSES	
Opening stock	1,000
Raw materials purchased in year	13,000
Less closing stock (materials and finished product)	−4,000
Total materials	10,000
Salary	24,000
Rent and service charge	5,000
Post	12,000
Other expenses	2,400
Bank interest on loan	1,500
Total	**54,900**
PROFIT	**5,100**

Spreadsheet 10.3   Balance sheet of Gold Connections at end of year

FIXED ASSETS	£	CAPITAL	£
Office equipment	4,000	Personal money	11,000
Production equipment	10,000	Long-term loan	9,000
		Retained profit	5,100
CURRENT ASSETS		**CURRENT LIABILITIES**	
Stock (materials and product)	4,000	Creditors	1,000
Debtor	5,000		
Cash	3,100		
TOTAL	**26,100**		**26,100**

NORTHERN ROCK

In 2007, there was the first run on a UK bank for a hundred years. Northern Rock was borrowing money, on a fairly short-term basis, to aggressively expand its mortgage business. When the 2007 US sub-prime loan crisis caused a freeze in interbank lending in the UK, Northern Rock was left with a profitable business and a sound balance sheet but no free money. It was forced to borrow billions of pounds from the Bank of England.

Profit

The aim of organisations is to make a profit. In not-for-profit organisations this might be called an 'operating surplus'. No organisation can continue in the long term paying out more than it receives in income. Suppliers and staff expect to be paid. The practising engineer and technologist, at an operational level, is not likely to be involved in complex hedging and finance deals; they come later in life, after the MBA. In this chapter, the focus is on how to develop products and market them to generate a profit. Profit is easy to define:

$$\text{Profit} = \text{Total income} - \text{Total expenses}$$

One of the key questions to be asked of the technical department is: 'What will it cost to make the product?' This is best answered by a financially literate engineer or technologist who understands the detail of the issues. In Chapter 5, three types of costs were introduced: fixed costs, variable costs and semi-variable costs. The basis on which these costs can be calculated depends on the nature of the question being addressed. To calculate the profit for taxation purposes, actual historical costs are required. To calculate replacement costs, it may not be appropriate to use actual past costs. In an inflationary world, costs may have increased. In this case, the current costs of replacing the raw materials would be the appropriate figure to use to calculate costs. Often the question is posed: 'What will the costs be for this product when we launch next year?' Here, best estimates of future costs have to be made. All estimates are subject to potential error and the sensitivity of projections to errors is covered in a later section of this chapter.

Fixed costs

Fixed costs are defined as costs that do not change with the level of production activity. If one more object is produced the managing director's salary is the same; rates, rent and insurance do not change. The margin over variable costs must first pay off all the fixed costs before the organisation makes a profit. If the organisation fails to do this it will go bankrupt in the long term. The key issue is to contain fixed costs and to ensure that longer term investments in research and training are carefully directed.

Variable costs

The simplest way to conceptualise variable costs is the difference case. If we make one more item by how much will our actual physical costs increase? In the fabrication of exotic catalysts with metals such as platinum and palladium most of the cost may be in the raw material costs of the metal. The variable costs are the greater part of the costs. The costs to an internet service provider of a customer sending one more e-mail is almost zero. Most of the costs are associated with the hardware and network costs. This has a profound effect on the development of the business model. The cost of producing just one more unit with no consideration of fixed costs is known as the marginal cost. The concepts of break-even analysis were covered in Chapter 5.

In a typical engineering shop, labour and machine time is used in the manufacture of a product. Often organisations want to arrive at a cost that includes 'direct labour costs' – the actual labour costs of manufacturing one item. This area is fraught with ambiguity. At first sight the answer is simple. If the skilled operator earns £20 per hour and can make 10 items in an hour, the cost is clearly £2 per item. However, this assumes that all operator time is productive. How does the company take account of training time, sickness and holiday absence? Should account be taken of employment overheads such as the personnel department and health insurance costs? The firm may then come up with an effective hourly rate for actual productive hours of £30. In most countries, staff cannot be hired and fired by the hour. In fact, production staff are more like a fixed cost. The key issue is that the

Table 10.1   Selected approaches to allocation of fixed costs

Method of allocation	Comments
Time	Machine time in manufacture, R&D hours for development, PR activity in hours committed to project. Person's costs divided by the hours available to give an hourly rate. Then hours used charged to the project
Space	Exhibition stand space, shop sales by department. Total costs divided by available space gives the cost for unit of space in the given period. Space occupied multiplied by this unit area cost gives the cost allocation for the period
Ratio	Staff overheads (e.g. personal administration) might be split according to the number of staff in the various departments

engineer and technologist, in calculating costs, should take account of the foundations of the cost. In using statistics, care is taken to ensure the sampling is correct. Often the statistical model assumes a normal distribution. If the assumption is violated (i.e. the distribution is not normal) the statistical model may come up with the wrong answer. The same is true in financial analysis. It is imperative that there is an understanding of assumptions made to arrive at an allocated cost (e.g. the £30 per hour effective hourly rate discussed above). Table 10.1 provides an overview of some of the ways that fixed costs may be allocated.

INSIGHT

DANGERS OF FIXED COST ALLOCATION

Consider the case of a young entrepreneur opening an internet café. A simple calculation might take this form. Cost of provision of a terminal and connection is £10 a day and the café is open 10 hours per day. So, the cost is £1 per hour. So, if a person pays £0.50 per hour, the business has lost £0.50 an hour. However, in Chapter 3 we noted that a key characteristic of services is perishability. That unsold hour in mid-morning is of no value in the afternoon. Moreover, in the evening there may be more demand than terminals. One strategy might be to charge more in the evening and accept lower prices in the morning. Some people will move from peak rate to lower rate. The overall effect will be to make more money in total, even when simple (over-simple) analysis would indicate that a loss was being made in the morning.

The implication is that clear insight is needed as to the make-up and behaviour of costs along with an appreciation of the relevant business questions. Sometimes a marginal costing with marginal pricing may make sense for a particular period. Clearly if all the costs are not fully recovered in the long term, there will be no future for the business. When it is hot, we wear a short-sleeved shirt; when it is cold, we wear an overcoat. We dress appropriately for the weather conditions. The same is true of costs: they are not absolutes; they are estimates and the appropriate framework may change with the question, the business climate and the challenges facing the firm.

Sunk costs

In the calculation of profit for taxation, the tax rules introduce the concept of depreciation. If a company buys a machine tool with five year's life, one fifth of the value may be taken into the profit calculations for each of the five working years. For tax calculations, the precise framework and way in which this must be done will be covered by the current taxation laws and regulations. The key issue is that this is 'funny money' – it does not exist in reality. It is a convention of accountancy and a guide to costing and pricing to recover the sunk capital cost of the machine tool over its useful life, to ensure funds are being recovered to replace it at the end of its useful life. The 'book value', the undepreciated value left on the company's assets register, has no relation to the real value. Usually the second-hand value of a machine, computer, etc. is less than the book value (although at the end of its useful life, the book value will be zero). There may be a small residual income to come from the scrap value of the asset. The point to remember is that there is no cash reality on depreciation; it exists to spread the cost of a capital item over a number of years. Depreciation has no effect on the company's cash flow; the money for the machine tool has to be found 'up front'.

In some texts, marketing expenses are given as variable costs. In some cases this is true: the redemption rate for a 'money off' voucher will vary with the number of items sold. This year's advertising campaign is another example of a 'sunk cost'. Once the contracts have been placed the money is committed and does not change with the number of units sold. R&D investment and pre-launch costs are the same. The money has to be committed before the actual sales are achieved. If sales are less than predicted, there will not be the recovery of the investment to fund future investments. If sales are above plan then you might be able to break out the 'bubbly'. R&D and new product development always have an element of risk.

Just as with fixed costs the company may elect to allocate 'sunk costs' in the costing and pricing models. Here again, care must be taken to consider if the approach taken is right for the business decisions being made. Costing and pricing is not an arithmetic game for the accountants. It is at the heart of the company's strategy implementation.

Semi-variable costs

The division of costs into fixed and variable costs is convenient but can be over-simplistic. The cost of raw materials may vary with quantity purchased. Often that may imply bulk discounts but if material is in short supply additional quantities may have to be purchased at premium prices. Maintenance may be calculated as a fixed cost but, in fact, if machines are worked to full capacity 24/7 then additional maintenance may be required. Spreadsheet packages can have such variable estimates built into them and become cash flow models.

Multiple outputs

A common problem in the chemical industry is the multiple output situation. In a sense, costing a washing machine is easy. The marginal cost is the total of all the component costs and the direct costs of assembly. This is often not the case in the chemical industry. Turpentine is a by-product of the manufacture of paper. In the USA the two major hydrocarbons are α and β pinene. The ratio is approximately 80% α pinene and 20% β pinene. Both products have commercial uses. However, as there is more α pinene, this tends to command a lesser price in the marketplace than β pinene. The manufacturing process is to fractionally distil the crude turpentine, under reduced pressure, and this yields commercially pure α and β pinene. How are the costs to be assigned to the two products? A first approach might be by relative mass of the two products produced. A second could be to use the relative volumes of the two materials. A third would be to ratio the costs on the relative values of the two products produced. As with the allocation of fixed costs, it is important that the approach should be rational and appropriate to the business decision. As discussed earlier in Chapter 5, the situation is even more complex with an oil refinery processing different grades of crude oil into a plethora of products, from ethylene gas to heavy bunker oil. Here complex models using techniques such as linear programming have to be used. However, these must not be just black box models and there must be a sound understanding of the assumptions and rules built in. Again this requires a deep technical understanding of the issues and financial literacy. It is not just a case of feeding in the numbers and the correct answer will come out of the accountancy sausage machine.

Budgets and spreadsheet models

For all their complexity, the organisation's budgets and spreadsheet models rely on much the same principles as drawing up a 'back of the envelope' budget for the family holiday. The business analyst collects data and makes a series of judgments (e.g. the cost of aluminium in X months time, etc.) and the spreadsheet makes the calculation. Figures 10.1 and 10.2 show a typical launch budget in schematic outline. The summary spreadsheet may be fed from a number of supporting spreadsheets which contain the working detail (e.g. the total sales may be made up of sales estimates from a range of sales territories, these individual sales estimates having been made by the local sales managers). The creation and updating of launch budgets is a key activity in the NPD process and is a vital element of project management. It is all too easy to have an unexpected budget overrun as cost estimates have not been updated as the project progresses.

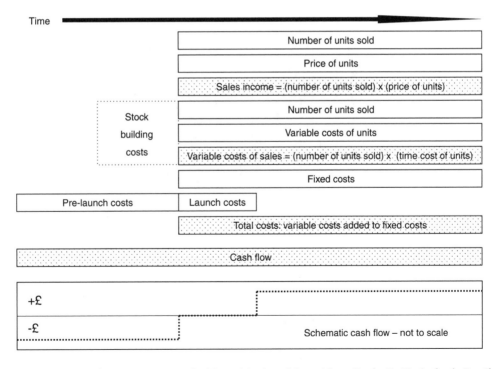

Figure 10.1 Schematic structure for a typical launch budget. Adapted from: Curtis, T., *Marketing in Practice*, figure 10.3, page 250, © Elsevier 2006. Reproduced by permission.

Cash flow element	Pre-launch Week 1	.....	Launch	.....	Steady state	.....	Comment
	Sales income						
1 Sales volume in units			#####	#####	#####	#####	
2 Selling price			#####	#####	#####	#####	
3 Sales income			^^^^^	^^^^^	^^^^^	^^^^^	Line 1 multiplied by line 2
	Variable costs						
4 Sales volume in units			#####	#####	#####	#####	Same as line 1
5 Variable cost of unit			#####	#####	#####	#####	
6 Variable costs			^^^^^	^^^^^	^^^^^	^^^^^	Line 4 multiplied by line 5
	Fixed/non-variable costs						
7 Stock building	#####	#####					
8 Pre-launch costs	#####	#####					
9 Launch costs			#####	#####			
10 Fixed costs			#####	#####	#####	#####	
11 Non-variable expenses	^^^^^	^^^^^	^^^^^	^^^^^	^^^^^	^^^^^	Lines from 7 to 10 added together
12 Total costs	^^^^^	^^^^^	^^^^^	^^^^^	^^^^^	^^^^^	Line 6 added to line 11
13 Cash flow	^^^^^	^^^^^	^^^^^	^^^^^	^^^^^	^^^^^	Line 12 minus line 3 (income – total expenses)

Estimated figure

^^^^^ Calculated figure

Figure 10.2 Schematic summary spreadsheet for a typical launch budget. Adapted from: Curtis, T., *Marketing in Practice*, figure 10.4, page 251, © Elsevier 2006. Reproduced by permission.

In field artillery, the gunners will use past calculations to set the aim and elevation of the gun. However, these are not necessarily going to give a metre-accurate delivery. The fall of the shell is noted to be over, under, etc. and small adjustments made to get right on target. A properly constructed budget is a best estimate of the future performance. Actual figures against budget are the message that adjustments are needed. Just as with the adjustments to get the shell on target, adjustments to launch plans need to be made. This process is often called 'variance analysis'. If a product is not achieving plan profitability, what is the reason? Typical possibilities include: prices gained were lower than expected, prices were OK but sales volume was down, production costs were higher than estimated, there were more product returns as a result of a design flaw. This is the normal technical/engineering approach of asking 'why? why? why?' until the cause is identified. Then relevant management action can be taken.

Management metrics

In Chapter 9, one of the key elements of the MkIS system was identified as 'analysis'. The raw data does not give the full information. On a global scale, the actual profit figure given may not be the complete information. A profit of £1 million may sound impressive but it needs to be viewed in context: a firm's profit of £1 million on sales of £10 million is very different to an organisation with the same profit on £100 million. A financial analyst comparing the relative performance of the two organisations would calculate the profitability as a percentage: 10% profit on sales is much more impressive than 1% profit on sales.

The financial analyst may be comparing two companies both of which have profits of £1 million on £10 million of sales. One company may have this profit on capital employed of £10 million and the other on £100 million. In this case, the analyst would compare the profit on capital employed as a percentage. Again 10% return on capital employed is much more impressive than 1% return on capital employed. Financial analysts have a number of ratios (metrics) that they use to measure the financial effectiveness of an organisation. A selection of the more important ones is given in Table 10.2.

COMPARE LIKE WITH LIKE

A supermarket has massive sales and less than one week's stock in the store. Stock is a form of working capital. From the business analysts' view, the firm should make as much profit on as little stock as possible. In this light the supermarket looks good.

In the food and perfume industry, many natural products are used. In Argentina there is a large lemon industry producing lemon juice and lemon oil. The industry uses a variety of lemon trees to spread the harvest season. Even so, the lemon season only lasts for a few months. The product is in demand all year. To satisfy its clients a lemon processor will have to hold stocks (e.g. frozen juice) to supply 12 months' demand from a few months' production during the harvest season. This type of company has to hold many months' stock for much of the year.

If no account is taken of the physical realities of these two situations, the supermarket will be seen as super efficient and the lemon processor grossly inefficient. Different industries have different operating characteristics and when comparing relative performance (sometimes called benchmarking) care must be taken to ensure that like is compared with like.

Table 10.2 Some selected general financial ratios

Ratio	Calculation	Comments
% return on investment (ROI)	100 × (net profit/capital employed)	Provides an overall measure of how well the organisation is using its resources
% profit on sales	100 × (operating profit/sales revenue)	Provides a measure of profit margin in terms of sales. Lower margins are unattractive
Stock turnover ratio	Cost of goods sold in year/stock @ cost	Low values may indicate overstocking to cover inefficient management
Assets and liabilities, current ratio	Current assets/current liabilities	Values less than 1 may indicate that company is exposed to short-term problems as liabilities exceed assets
Collection period	Debtors/(credit sales/365)	Measure of how efficient the firm is in collecting its money
Acid ratio or quick ratio	(Current assets – stock)/current liabilities	A measure of ability to meet short-term requirements and run the business
Gearing	Total debt/total assets	If loans are cheap there are high returns to the owners; however, if long-term debt becomes expensive, then there can be problems

The standard metrics do not tell the complete story and do not provide the full range of feedback inputs to run an organisation. An important skill for the technical manager is to have a range of appropriate metrics. In a manufacturing situation, key metrics might be minimising scrap and re-work as part of the quality assurance programme. In a service situation it might be the ratio of unsold to sold capacity. Again care must be taken to compare like with like. The cost structure of producing free-range chickens is different to the cost structures for intensive farming. Direct comparison of the metrics would not be appropriate in comparing the efficiencies of the two operations; they are producing different products for different market segments. A selection of some selected metrics for different situations is given in Table 10.3.

Project financial appraisal

Engineers and technologists are often involved in projects involving the development of a product (investment) which is then sold and produces a cash inflow. The product might be an investment in infrastructure (e.g. a new communications network) and customers' use of the infrastructure (e.g. tolls on a bridge) will produce an income. There may be internal projects. If we replace that obsolete boiler will we save enough energy (money) to make the investment appropriate? The general form of the project is to make an up-front investment

Table 10.3 Some selected marketing and management ratios

Ratio	Comments
Sales per salesperson	Used as a measure of sales effectiveness. However, it may encourage sales people to give more discounts
Sales per square metre	Used as a measure of sales efficiency in retail environments
Percentage returns	Used as a measure of quality and customer satisfaction
Percentage of new sales	The percentage of new sales (e.g. of products not made five years ago). This can be used as a measure of innovation
Marketing and sales	The ratio of marketing spend to sales can be used as a measure of marketing efficiency and/or used to benchmark marketing activity investment with industry average

(R&D, design and construction, etc.) and gain a cash flow and finally close the project. How does the technical business analyst decide if a project is financially viable? If there are funds for only one project and there are two options, how does the technical business analyst decide which option should be selected?

A key concept is that not all money is the same – some money is worth more than other money. Take the situation where two people win a prize of £1 000. The first person is told: 'The money is in the box.' The second is told they will get the money in two years' time. Who is happier? This is, in colloquial terms, a 'no brainer'. However, the second person has a fixed contract to receive £1 000 in two years. This person could sell this right to £1 000 in two years to a bank. The actual sum that the bank would be prepared to pay would depend on the interest rates operating at the time. If this were 10% the calculation would be:

$$\text{Value of £1 000 in 2 years} = £1 000 \times [100/(100 + 10)]^2$$

$$= £1 000 \times 0.826\,45 = £826.45$$

The figure 0.826 45 is known as the 'discount factor' for payment in two years' time with an interest rate of 10%. The general discount factor for N years at a discount rate of $X\%$ is $[100/(100 + X)]^N$.

There is no need to calculate these factors because a range of important financial functions are already built into spreadsheet packages. Just key in the estimates to the spreadsheet and the inbuilt functions will take care of the rest.

Consider a very simple project where a new product is developed. New equipment is needed and, with R&D added in, the total costs are £100 000. The cost of raw materials, work in progress, finished stock, etc. (i.e. working capital) needed in this very simple case is £10 000. Sales for each year are expected to be £40 000 and direct costs (manufacturing, distribution logistics, etc.) are expected to be £20 000. The project is expected to run for 10 years and the scrap value of the plant is expected to be £5 000.

Spreadsheet 10.4 DCF analysis for a simple investment project

Cash flow	Year 0 £	Year 1 £	Year 2 £	Year 3 £	Year 4 £	Year 5 £	Year 6 £	Year 7 £	Year 8 £	Year 9 £	Year 10 £	Notes
Investment	−100,000	0	0	0	0	0	0	0	0	0	0	
Sales	0	40,000	40,000	40,000	40,000	40,000	40,000	40,000	40,000	40,000	40,000	
Direct costs	0	−20,000	−20,000	−20,000	−20,000	−20,000	−20,000	−20,000	−20,000	−20,000	−20,000	
Working capital	0	−10,000	0	0	0	0	0	0	0	0	10,000	
Scrap value	0	0	0	0	0	0	0	0	0	0	5,000	
Total cash flow	−100,000	10,000	20,000	20,000	20,000	20,000	20,000	20,000	20,000	20,000	35,000	105,000 Cash no discounting
Discount factor (@10%)	1	0.90909	0.82645	0.75131	0.68301	0.62092	0.56447	0.51316	0.46651	0.42410	0.38554	
Discounted cash flow	−100,000	9,091	16,529	15,026	13,660	12,418	11,289	10,263	9,330	8,482	13,494	19,584 Cash flow 10% discount rate
Discounted cash flow @ 5%	−100,000	9,524	18,141	17,277	16,454	15,671	14,924	14,214	13,537	12,892	21,487	54,120 Cash flow 5% discount rate
Discounted cash flow @ 10%	−100,000	9,091	16,529	15,026	13,660	12,418	11,289	10,263	9,330	8,482	13,494	19,584 Cash flow 10% discount rate
Discounted cash flow @ 15%	−100,000	8,696	15,123	13,150	11,435	9,944	8,647	7,519	6,538	5,685	8,651	−4,613 Cash flow 15% discount rate
Discounted cash flow @ 20%	−100,000	8,333	13,889	11,574	9,645	8,038	6,698	5,582	4,651	3,876	5,653	−22,061 Cash flow 20% discount rate
Discounted cash flow @ 13.9075%	−100,000	8,779	15,414	13,532	11,880	10,430	9,156	8,038	7,057	6,195	9,518	0 Cash flow 13.9% discount rate
Pay-back	−100,000	−90,000	−70,000	−50,000	−30,000	−10,000	10,000					
10% increased costs	−100,000	8,000	18,000	18,000	18,000	18,000	18,000	18,000	18,000	18,000	33,000	Direct costs increase by 10%
Discounted cash flow @ 5%	−100,000	7,619	16,327	15,549	14,809	14,103	13,432	12,792	12,183	11,603	20,259	38,676 Cash flow 5% discount rate
Discounted cash flow @ 10%	−100,000	7,273	14,876	13,524	12,294	11,177	10,161	9,237	8,397	7,634	12,723	7,294 Cash flow 10% discount rate
Discounted cash flow @ 15%	−100,000	6,957	13,611	11,835	10,292	8,949	7,782	6,767	5,884	5,117	8,157	−14,650 Cash flow 15% discount rate
Discounted cash flow @ 20%	−100,000	6,667	12,500	10,417	8,681	7,234	6,028	5,023	4,186	3,489	5,330	−30,446 Cash flow 20% discount rate
Discounted cash flow @ 11.4790%	−100,000	7,176	14,484	12,993	11,655	10,455	9,378	8,412	7,546	6,769	11,132	0 Cash flow 11.5% discount rate

As noted above, the costs of financing the raw material stock, work in progress and finished product stock is £10 000. These costs occur in year one (the first year of operation) but then remain constant for the project (i.e. no further cash outflow). At the end of the 10 years, all the raw material stock, work in progress and finished product stock will be recovered (i.e. the working capital will be recovered, a cash inflow). The simple spreadsheet is given above (Spreadsheet 10.4).

Consider that the analyst regards the time value of money to be 10%. The actual cash flow can be converted into the discounted cash flow where future cash flows are discounted according to how far they are in the future. This gives the future value of the cash flows as £19 584. This figure is called the net present value (NPV) of the cash flow. If the company demands a return on investments of 10% this project is attractive as it has a positive NPV.

If we increase the discount rate, the future cash flows become less and less valuable (they are discounted more). At high rates of discount rate the NPV becomes negative. In this simple case the NPV at 20% is –£22 061. The point at which the NPV is zero is known as the internal rate of return of the project (IRR). The IRR is easy to calculate because it is one of the standard spreadsheet financial functions. In this case the IRR is 13.9075%. This metric allows the technical financial analyst to analyse different projects with completely different cash flows and initial investments. Higher IRRs indicate more profitable and attractive projects. IRRs below the company's objective rate of return are too unprofitable to be considered. An alternative way to evaluate different projects is to calculate the pay-back period. How long must the project run before the profits have paid off all the capital investment? In our simple case this is around five years.

To arrive at the figures a whole range of estimates must be made: sales volume and price, manufacturing costs, development costs, etc. As with all estimates, there is a margin of error; there is risk. In Chapter 5, we saw that break-even analysis provides one approach. Projects with a high break-even point are more likely to be risky. Projects with high IRRs and short pay-back periods should be less risky (the further into the future estimates are projected, the more likelihood there is of errors). Another approach for both break-even and discounted cash flow analysis is to conduct a sensitivity analysis. In our simple example this is shown in Spreadsheet 10.4 for a 10% increase in direct production costs. The NPV at 10% falls to £7 294 and the IRR to 11.4790%. If the project is highly sensitive to modest forecasting errors, this indicates that estimates must be refined and/or new approaches are needed. For example, if raw material costs are proving very sensitive then could less material be used (i.e. redesign the product) or could a cheaper substitute be found (e.g. composites for aluminium)? The use of 'what if?' analysis can bring more insight into the potential financial dangers in the project. The maintenance of a sound set of financial models and budgets enables the impact on existing and future projects to be evaluated. Alternative sources of energy become more and more attractive as oil and gas prices escalate. Projects that were not profitable with oil at $25 a barrel may look very attractive at $100 a barrel. Conversely, the manufacture of ethyl alcohol from oil might be attractive at $25 a barrel but natural fermentation alcohol may substitute at higher prices, demanding different processes and plants.

Review

In this chapter the balance sheet and cash flow statement were considered. Profit is important, but cash flow problems can be as big a danger to company success as low profitability. The profit for a product is the sales figure achieved less the costs of production. In this chapter the various issues in costing have been explored and some of the potential pitfalls of over simple analysis signposted.

The development of budgets and spreadsheet financial models was outlined. In the evaluation of investment projects operating over a period of years, the time value of money was discussed. The nature and use of internal rate of return (IRR) and net present value (NPV) have been discussed. New product launches and other investment projects have elements of risk. The use of sensitivity analysis, break-even analysis, IRR and pay-back periods as indicators of potential risk were presented. The use of ratios to monitor, track and benchmark performance has been explained.

Further reading

Atrill, P. & McLaney, E. (2000) *Accounting and Finance for Non-specialists*, 3rd edn, Pearson Higher Education.

Chelsom, J., Payne, A. & Reavill, L. (2005) *Management for Engineers, Scientists and Technologists*, 2nd edn, John Wiley & Sons.

Drury, C. (1997) *Management Accounting for Business Decisions*, Thomson Business Press.

Wilson, R. & Gilligan, C. (2005) *Strategic Marketing Management: Planning Implementation and Control*, 3rd edn, Elsevier.

CHAPTER 11

Managing people

Learning objectives

After studying this chapter you will be able to:

- Explain selected key theories of motivation and personality and understand their importance to individuals' workplace performance
- Formulate and implement plans for the recruitment and professional development of staff
- Describe the sources of resistance to change and plan actions to identify and overcome resistance to change
- Understand the need to manage self when managing others and formulate a strategy for improved personal effectiveness

Introduction

A marketing manager being asked what the most important stakeholder group was would be likely to respond 'Customers'. The response to the same question posed to a manager in personnel and development would most likely be 'Our staff'. Both answers are right. If the firm has no customers, it has no business. If the staff are poorly motivated and inefficient, customers will take their business elsewhere. People are a key element of the service-extended marketing mix. In Chapter 8, the complexity of people was outlined. Most project managers when asked 'What is the most challenging aspect of your role?' will respond 'Managing and motivating the team'.

Motivation

People are more than engineers, scientists and technologists. They have skills (their technical hardware), but they also come bundled with software (human emotions, desires and their own individual personalities). Every person is a one-off individual. To get the best out of people you have to not only satisfy their general needs, but also understand the individual person's specific needs.

There is no simple rule that states that 10% more motivation provides 20% more success. However, the evidence does show that for the best performance in teams, a high level of commitment and motivation is needed. The relationship may be too complex for a single

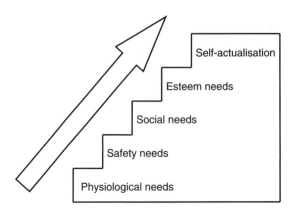

Figure 11.1 Maslow's hierarchy of needs. Adapted from: Chelsom, J., Payne, A. & Reavill, A. (2005) *Management for Engineers, Scientists and Technologists*, 2nd edn, John Wiley & Sons Ltd, page 161.

simple formula but here is a generalisation in mathematical form:

$$\text{Performance} = f(\text{ability, motivation})$$

Maslow's theory of motivation

In his book *Motivation and Personality* (1954), Abraham Maslow proposed a hierarchy of needs as a theory of human motivation. The basis of the theory is that people have a number of steps in their motivation pattern. When people have satisfied a given level they move on and the next step becomes important. When a young person gets their first full driving licence and goes to university their desire is to have a car. A couple of years into a professional career it is to have a good new car. The platform for motivation has risen up a step. The five steps in the theory are physiological needs, safety needs, social needs, esteem needs and self-actualisation needs (Figure 11.1).

Physiological needs

These needs relate to physical survival and are considered to include hunger, thirst and shelter. In current working conditions, where appropriate health and safety rules are observed, these should not be major issues for motivation in the workplace. Management does not usually say 'No drinks until you have finished that report'. However, under extreme conditions – like the 2007 UK floods that resulted in the loss of potable water supply to over 100 000 people – these survival needs can suddenly reappear.

Safety needs

In some ways, these can be best considered in the context of the negative. If people feel insecure, they do not feel well. In normal working conditions, people should not be exposed to extreme hazards. There should be appropriate training and safety provisions. However, if people are not properly trained, their work situation can be perceived as threatening.

A key concern for many people is financial security which, in the work context, involves issues such as job security, sickness benefits and pension rights. The theory indicates that management by fear introduces insecurity and will be de-motivating.

Social needs

Work is not just a mechanical, functional process; it is also a social activity. A key aspect of good team building is to realise that team leadership and good team performance requires social skills. The experience of going to university is intended to be a broad education in the art of life for students, not just force-feeding them with knowledge. The popularity of social websites such as Friends Reunited, My Space and Facebook demonstrates how important social links are to most people. An important factor in the induction programme for a new team member is to get past the wall of faces of people that they do not know; to bring people into the social network of the team. Many retired people undertake voluntary work and part of the motivation is that it provides a social network to replace the one they lost on retirement. The office vending machine is more than a human drinking trough, it is a social hub where people interact and gossip.

Esteem needs

An individual's self-esteem results in them being self-confident and having a sense of independence. Professionals often have the need for other professionals to appreciate their competence. Employee-of-the-month schemes may be a little too American for European cultural tastes, but this is an example of providing recognition for exceptional contribution and performance. This is the positive side. The lack of independence can cause loss of motivation; excessive micromanagement is not often appreciated.

Self-actualisation needs

These encompass the ability to become one's complete self through expressing creativity and developing competence. World-class professionals want a platform to grow from; they already have their recognition and are likely to already have a high salary. For this reason, creative people can be difficult to manage; they want to be creative, not get the report in by 17.00 on Friday. Leadership and interpersonal skills are required. Some managers working at this level in creative hot houses describe their jobs as 'attempting to herd cats'.

Herzberg theory

In 1959, Frederick Herzberg's book *The Motivation to Work* was published. This was based on research with professionals. After analysis of the findings, recognition, nature of work (job satisfaction), responsibility and achievement were considered to be motivators. Things that become important at a lower level when the situation turned bad were company administration, supervision, salary, relations with colleagues and actual working conditions. These are termed hygiene factors; they aren't motivators in themselves but they will demotivate if they are wrong. This theory appears to parallel Maslow's theory if one considers the average professional hovers around the social and esteem levels of the hierarchy of needs.

McClelland

In *The Achieving Society* (1976), D. C. McClelland identified three categories of human need that have to be satisfied within the working environment.

1. *Need for affiliation* This is the need to have scope to develop and maintain interpersonal relationships.
2. *Need for power* This is the need to have scope to control and influence events and control others.
3. *Need for achievement* This is the need for personal responsibility and to be able to demonstrate successful task results.

Having considered the general need for motivation and recognised the need for some understanding of how people differ, the technical manager needs some tools for assessing how people work and how they interact in teams. Theories of personality and team role styles assist here.

Personality and team roles

When we want to bring some order into an apparently disordered, heterogeneous marketplace, we look for segmentation variables that might help us. The marketer is seeking hidden structure. In personality and team roles, some parallel approaches have been developed. One approach used for this is the Myers-Briggs type indicator, which was developed from Jung's personality typology. This provides us with a framework to explore an individual's personality. The assertion is that people have preferences and favour one type of functioning over another type. For instance, some people are extroverts; others are introverts. The Myers-Briggs approach has four preference factors (summarised in Table 11.1).

The four dimensions give 16 (2^4) Myers-Briggs types, which are usually expressed in shorthand by the capital letters indicated. If a person has all the right-hand preferences they would be described as an INFP. The test questionnaire may only be administered and analysed by accredited practitioners. The outcome is enlightening for technical managers. A considerable amount of research work has been done on professions and personality types. The base hypothesis one might have is that there would be a more or less even distribution of personality types (e.g. 25% ST, 25% SF, 25% NF and 25% NT, considering just these preference parameters). The outcome is most revealing. Most managers are ST types (53%) and very few are NF (10%). Creative artists and other creative professions tend to have more people with NF preference types.

The reaction to this is interesting, but what has it got to do with practical technical management of a new product development team? Broadly speaking: accountancy managers will want to 'know the facts' and 'see what the figures tell us'; the creative engineer and designer will want to explore their imaginations and the possibilities opened up by the concepts, being more concerned about the aesthetics than the costs. It should be emphasised that there is no one 'right' personality. Each strength has its mirror image reflection of a

Table 11.1   Myers-Briggs preference factors

Extrovert (E)	or	Introvert (I)
A preference to live in contact with others and things		More self-contained and works things out inside themselves
Sensing (S)	or	Intuition (N)
Fact, details and concrete knowledge are preferred		Imagination, possibilities, creativity and sensing the whole are preferred
Thinking (T)	or	Feeling (F)
Rationality, logic, analyses are the preferred approaches		Beliefs and dislikes and human values and personal friendships are preferred approaches
Judging (J)	or	Perceiving (P)
Order though reaching decisions and resolving issues preferred		As much data and research as possible is preferred

Adapted from Myers, Isabel B. with Myers Peter B. (1980) *Gifts Differing: Understanding Personality Type*, Consulting Psychologists Press.

potential weakness. The creative engineer or designer may be a genius but may have their 'head in the clouds' and never deliver on time.

The first implication of this theoretical approach to personality and working is that self-awareness is important. We should be aware of what our natural preference states are. When we have a work situation that fits our natural preference, things are great. However, from time to time, it will be necessary to work in situations that are not so comfortable for our preferred state. An individual in the work situation needs to be self-aware; know their strengths and weaknesses. The second is that a good manager should understand and respect that other team members have their own preferred states and may have a different view of the world. Successful teams need different roles and contributions to provide balance.

People in teams

Meredith Belbin has, over a number of years, experimented with teams to explore whether there is an 'ideal' team make-up. If there is, then the next question is: what is the composition of that ideal team? The first finding was that, in general, teams with a monoculture (all the same types) are not outstandingly successful. As we might expect if we learn from nature, what is needed is a mixture of contributions. In simple terms, the weakness of one team-role type is compensated for by the strengths of other team members. Out of this work, Belbin has distilled a mix of people useful to have in teams (Table 11.2). For each of the contributing qualities there is a weakness. The plant has imagination, knowledge and intellect. However, once the grand vision has been completed, there may be little interest in writing up the report; the plant is already exploring the next interest.

The implication for team building is that each of the team members should be aware of their own preference for team working and the implications, (i.e. their strengths and weaknesses in the team role). Team members should also note the team-role preferences of the other participants in the team. In successful teams, there are hard management skills

Table 11.2 Types of contribution from people in teams

Type	Shorthand	Positive contribution qualities
Chairman	CH	A good chair welcomes all contributions. A strong sense of direction for the project team
Company worker	CW	Common sense with hard work and an ability to organise and get things done
Resource investigator	RI	Is able to respond to challenges, able to build new links and explore new challenges
Shaper	SH	Has drive and energy to confront inertia and complacency
Team worker	TW	Responds to people and can promote team cohesiveness
Completer-finisher	CF	Able to hang in and follow through and get that report written
Monitor-evaluator	ME	Can objectively assess issues and has an ability to make firm judgments
Plant	PL	Can bring knowledge, intellect and imagination to the project

Adapted from: Belbin, R. M. (1981 in spreadsheet) *Management Teams: Why they Succeed or Fail*, Butterworth Heinemann, page 74.

(e.g. setting up budgets), but just as important are the softer skills of managing the team's dynamics and interpersonal relationships.

Organisational structures

In the small start-up, it can be all hands to the pumps when things are difficult. As organisations grow, roles and responsibilities need to be more structured and formalised. This is not just some abstract management debating point. In many major accidents (e.g. the *Challenger* disaster), the technical problems were compounded by failings in management systems. In this section, just two structures are considered. There are many variations and further reading is given at the end of the chapter. Figure 11.2 shows the simple functional structure adopted by many organisations. The advantage is that it does provide clarity of

Figure 11.2 Functional structure (marketing focus).

responsibility and a clear sense of who is responsible for what. However, if there are not good cross-functional communications, the senior management can become bogged down in the detailed co-ordination of the functions.

In larger organisations with complex new product development (NPD) needs, a simple functional structure may not suffice. In this context matrix models of management have been used. Matrix management has had a 'bad press'. One major problem is that the manager in the heart of the matrix has more than one manager. This puts conflicting demands on the manager and can result in role ambiguity. However, the need to manage along several vectors simultaneously is a reality of business life in technologically advanced organisations. Figure 11.3 shows the type of matrix structure that might be used in a major creative perfumery house. The technical needs of fine perfumes are very different to those required in creating a bleach fragrance. No person can have all the knowledge and skills for all the markets.

There needs to be a focus on market types (e.g. personal care). The company needs to develop certain technological skills (e.g. in advanced instrumental analysis). This analytical skill vector needs to be managed to ensure, among other things, that analytical technologies are not only applied to existing issues, but also to the leading-edge technical development required for tomorrow's technical challenges. The market needs of India are significantly different to the market needs in the USA. Such a global organisation needs to ensure that the separate markets are serviced, so there needs to be a global extension of the matrix. This multidimensional management framework needs rapid information flows and clear communications. Fortunately, intranets and shared databases can support the weight of information flows.

The employment time line

The company needs to identify its needs and identify potential future employees. These people have to be attracted to the company and the most appropriate ones selected. After selection, new staff have to be inducted into their roles in the organisation. For technical staff, there needs to be continual professional development of the individuals. Just as with the product portfolio, there needs to be consideration of succession: people do move on. What will the future skill mix of the organisation be? What does the organisation need to do? Should it recruit new staff or re-skill and train existing staff? There is extensive legislation surrounding employment activities and detailed implementation should be left to the personnel and development specialists. However, good working knowledge of the processes is needed for the technical manager to participate fully. If the skill make-up is not properly communicated then the wrong person might be recruited. Relevant stages include:

- job analysis
- role definition
- marketing the post
- selection
- induction
- continuing professional development

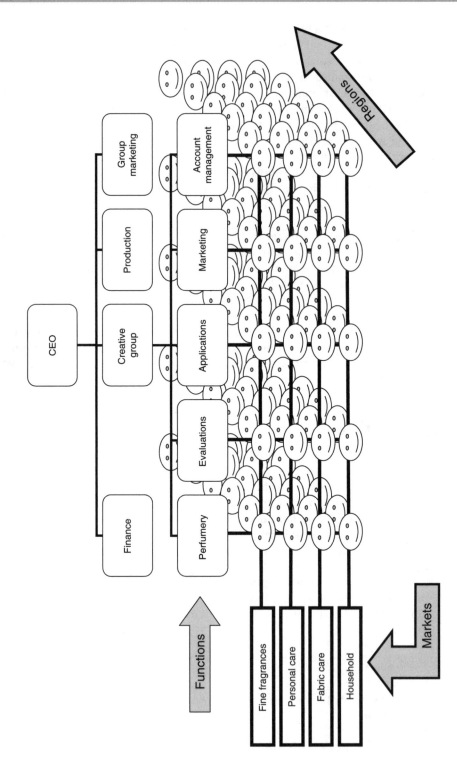

Figure 11.3 International matrix structure for fragrance creation (functions, markets and regions).

Job analysis

This is the definition of why the role exists and a person is needed. Staff are expensive and there needs to be a business justification as to why the person is required. The general nature of the role and the fit into the organisation should be defined and the results of the investigation fed into the role definition.

Role definition

There are two key documents to be developed. The first is the job description; the second is the person specification. The job description sets out who the person is responsible to and who will report to the new member of staff. Key duties and accountabilities should be specified. The insight below gives a typical schematic generic outline for a new product development manager. The second document is the person specification. Some attributes may be mandatory (e.g. for a quality assurance role in a chemical company the person might need to be a chartered chemist for regulatory reasons); others may be desirable (e.g. foreign language skills). Again, a generic outline is provided in the insight. Adaptation and detailed development is needed for each specific role. However, the framework provides a starting point.

INSIGHT

GENERIC OUTLINE JOB DESCRIPTION FOR A NEW PRODUCT DEVELOPMENT MANAGER

Job title	New Product Development Manager
Responsible to	Technical Director
Responsible for	New Product Development team members
Aim	To produce a range of new products as demanded by the company strategy and manage the NPD team
Duties:	
Staff	To train, appraise and manage NPD staff
	To project manage NPD projects
	To take the lead role in developing new technical skills where they are needed for future product developments
	To co-ordinate the external inputs to the NPD processes and NPD team from other departments and external resources
Health and safety	To ensure the safe conduct of all operations and ensure all staff observe company health and safety policies, including contractors
Security	To ensure the security of new intellectual property
Administration	To develop and agree NPD projects. To ensure that projects are completed to budget and on time
	To prepare and agree capital proposals for new equipment and facilities needed for NPD development
	To ensure that all NPD activities are fully and properly documented
Communication	To ensure good communication within the NPD team and other relevant NPD stakeholders
Legal	To liaise with company legal staff and consultants in the filing of patents and other activities to protect the company's intellectual property
General	To advise the board and participate in the formulation of NPD strategy

---

OUTLINE GENERIC PERSON SPECIFICATION FOR NEW PRODUCT DEVELOPMENT MANAGER

(Using seven-point plan and five-fold grading system)

Physical make-up	Some roles have specific issues (e.g. colour blindness with electronic engineers). However, it important that account be taken of equal opportunity legislation
Attainment	Proven track record in management of NPD Senior membership of relevant professional organisation (e.g. IET, RSC, etc.)
General intelligence	High level of problem-solving ability
Special aptitudes	Good communications capability in a multidisciplinary, multicultural context
Interests	Proven interest not only in the technologies but also the management of technological innovation
Disposition	Self-reliant to manage projects under budget and time pressures
Circumstances	In a multinational company the ability to travel may be important. However, care must be taken to observe the requirements of equal opportunity legislation
Impact on others	Sound negotiator and good assertiveness and team leadership skills
Acquired qualifications	Evidence of wider managerial skills development (e.g. Professional Postgraduate Diploma in Marketing of the Chartered Institute of Marketing)
Innate abilities	Ability to adapt to new developments and creative approaches to problem solving
Motivation	Determination to achieve challenging project objectives
Adjustment	Ability to get on with a wide variety of people in a multidisciplinary, multicultural context

---

Marketing the post

Experienced field staff know that 'cold calling' (appearing before a new client without prior communications) is daunting and often ineffective. In relationship marketing, part of the process needs to start before the sales call. The same is true in recruitment. In most of the developed world, able and qualified engineers, scientists and technologists are in short supply. There is never enough of the best. The marketing of the post starts before any recruitment. Sponsorship of university prizes and the provision of work-experience opportunities can help develop the brand image that says this is a good employer giving good prospects for career advancement (i.e. what the theories of motivation tell us). Most companies have a section on their web page about 'working with us' and list information on current vacancies. If these are to be offered only to internal candidates, the information can be posted on the internal intranet.

A little market sense is needed to consider where potential target prospects are and how to communicate with them. This can be fairly simple for new graduates: advertising and university visits can be effective. Life is more difficult for skilled and experienced staff. Often these people are in employment and are not actively searching for a new job. Here the use of a recruitment specialist may be useful. Informal network contacts may provide useful information. With continuing professional development, the company may already have some suitable internal prospects. The techniques of communication outlined in Chapter 7 can be used; there is just a different set of stakeholders.

Preliminary communications should make clear the basics:

- requirements of the job
- location
- employment type (e.g. full time, term, etc.)
- indication of reward package
- application procedure

Interested applicants can be sent full information packs, which would include the job description and person specification, or directed to the company website. Applicants may be asked to submit a standard application form and include a copy of their CV. Some employers use online systems and adopt a competency-based orientation.

Selection

The first stage is a preliminary screening. This is why the person specification is useful. All candidates who do not satisfy the 'must have' criteria can be rejected. In some circumstances there may be an early screening test (e.g. as part of the online process). The next stage is that the remaining CVs and application forms have to be ranked and an overall decision made as to which candidates should be involved in the next stage(s) of the selection process. Three common selection processes are interviews, assessment centres and tests.

Interviews

Interviews should be conducted in a friendly and professional manner with every opportunity for the candidates to present themselves well. Where several people are involved in the interview process, the chair should ensure that the range of questions is fair and appropriate.

Assessment centres

Earlier in this chapter, issues of personality and team working have been discussed. Professional assessment centres have accredited practitioners to administer psychometric and other tests. Team games and other techniques can be used to provide data for making the selection decision. Staff are very expensive and it is imperative that good decisions are made. For candidates that are appointed, the results of these assessments may be fed into induction and initial continuing professional development.

Tests

For operational roles, specific tests may be given (e.g. for word processing and computer operators, a keyboard skill test may be administered). For marketing positions, where presentation skills are important, the candidates may be asked to give a presentation to a selected group. Teachers and lecturers may be asked to give a mini-lecture. Tests are useful to back up assertions on the application form and verify the actual ability to deliver performance promised in the CV.

The selection team can then evaluate all the input data and make a group decision on who to appoint. The formalities of this are usually completed by the personnel and development specialists. However, the technical line manager will be involved in the induction process.

Induction

The purpose of induction is to integrate the new employee into the organisation and to develop full motivation and performance. There are organisational and legal aspects. These include how people are paid, disciplinary procedures, codes of acceptable conduct (e.g. what personal use of e-mail is permitted) and general health and safety issues. The normal process will include a formal induction session and the new employee will normally be given a written induction package. Full and complete cover of the issues is important. As certain issues have legal implications, a formal record of the induction process should be kept. At the departmental level the process can be considered to fall into two aspects. Functional issues should cover detailed training for specific duties and local amplification of health and safety issues (e.g. location of fire exits, etc.). The second aim is the social integration of the new employee. As highlighted earlier in this chapter, work has a social dimension and joining a new group is stressful. The aim of the social aspect of induction is for the new recruit to feel part of the team quickly and with the minimum of stress. After a short time, there should be some follow-up meetings to make certain all the issues have been assimilated.

Continuing professional development

The appraisal process provides an opportunity to evaluate the gap between what the employee skills are and what they should be in the future. For professional staff this will involve some consideration of skills for promotion as well as tracking the changing technologies in a fast-moving world. A range of techniques and approaches can be used. To become chartered and/or gain senior membership of a professional organisation, after gaining academic qualifications, may involve mentoring by a senior member of staff. Job rotation and field secondments can be useful to broaden the specialists' understanding. For instance, a new product development engineer or scientist might be seconded for a while to work in production and field service to get a practical feel for the product range. Crashing a jumbo jet is expensive and simulation can assist here. Lectures and company training sessions can have their part to play. Distance learning packages may be made available. For senior technical staff, links to universities may be maintained to develop technical skills (e.g. MSc qualifications) or managerial competence (e.g. an MBA). These senior staff may also attend and deliver papers at scientific events sponsored by the learned institutions. This not only provides recognition (part of the motivation package discussed earlier in the chapter) but also provides a way of keeping people at the leading edge of the company's technologies. The only certain aspect of management and technology is that it is continually changing to adapt to the turbulent business environment so continual skills development is needed.

Management of change

The role of the engineer, scientist and technologist in organisations is to create and manage the future with the development of new methods of production, new product development, etc. They are change agents and change has its challenges. In the past, models of change were based on the view that the change was a transition from one steady state to another steady state. The current rate of turbulence in the business environment is such that this no longer represents the case. Managers now work with a continual succession of changes. Change has ceased to be occasional and is now a permanent feature of life. In general, people may have three attitudes to change: positive, apathetic and negative. The first stage of overcoming negative attitudes is to understand why people may wish to resist change. In marketing terms, internal marketing initiatives are needed.

Resistance to change

People may be concerned about potential threats to security and rewards. There may be good reason for this if the new system involves lower staffing levels (i.e. job losses). During the change period, people may become less secure. From the earlier discussion of motivation, they may be concerned about threats to status, values, group and personal role relationships. There may be shifts in power. These may be welcomed by people gaining power but are likely to be resented by the people losing influence. There is, of course, simple in-built inertia in some people: we like it this way, it has worked in the past, why should we change? The UK government has initiated several massive change programmes based on the application of computer technology. Most of them have come in late, over budget and performed poorly at first. The first reaction of people may be 'Here we go again'. If there is no proper information, the rumour-mongers will work overtime to fill the void. In the earlier discussion of motivation, the need for people to feel some level of control over their destiny was discussed. The suspicion that something bad is going to happen, but having no idea when it will happen and what it might be, is deeply de-motivating.

Overcoming resistance to change

The first and most important facet is to ensure that there is clear communication on the nature of the change and the reasons for the change. In marketing terms, this is internal marketing communications and a complete mix of approaches from personal briefings to intranet can be used. As part of the change-planning process, there should be some consideration of the facilitation and support that people may need. This may often involve re-skilling and training for the new systems. For staff who have lost their jobs, this may involve assistance with job search as well as compensation. In a unionised context, there may be outright resistance and negotiation and agreement may be needed (e.g. loyalty bonus to people who will lose their jobs to help in the transition). Change has some of the characteristics of general project management. Good leadership to encourage ownership and participation in the change process is needed. People tend to go through four stages over the course of the change process:

1. denial
2. anger and resistance
3. exploration and acceptance
4. commitment

The role of the change-management team is to understand this and with a planned internal marketing programme take the internal stakeholders through the stages. The technical staff may well be in the front line as change champions (e.g. commissioning a new automated production line) and need to be aware of change-management issues and the importance of interpersonal and communications skills for a change champion. Changes may be technological but they have organisational and sociological implications. Technology-qualified change champions need to embrace the social as well as the technological aspects of change management. If they do not, the resistance to change issues may bog down the change process, leading to time and cost overruns.

Managing self and communications skills

The practising technical manager needs to have a sound range of interpersonal skills. If he or she is not able to manage themselves, they may well have problems managing teams. A sense of balance is needed. Too lax an approach and things will not get done. Aggressive behaviour will de-motivate the team. Good time management is essential or the 'urgent' will crowd out the 'important' and the manager can be left working in a perpetual state of crisis. Teams operate in a broader context and it is important to develop a good network. Both networking and team management need good listening and communications skills.

Assertiveness skills

In approaching a potential conflict situation, there are three strategies. You could avoid the problem or just pretend it does not exist: 'If I keep out of the way, the problem will disappear.' You could become aggressive: 'I know my rights; I will go in and stand up for them!' Assertiveness is the third (middle) way between submission and aggression. This framework of thinking declares that we have basic rights such as:

- the right to ask for what we do want and do not want
- the right to be listened to and respected
- the right not to know something and not to understand
- the right to make mistakes
- the right to change our minds
- the right to judge our own behaviour and take responsibility for the results
- a responsibility to respect the assertion rights of others

Good assertiveness skills can be seen as part of the make-up of the skilled negotiator.

Time management

There is one management resource that we all have as much of as Bill Gates or the President of the USA – *time*. Complex personal organizers or software packages are available for this. They are not necessary: paper and pencil can be fine. Use a framework that works for you. Set aside a few minutes each working day to time plan. Learn to develop good time-management skills and avoid time-wasters. An interactive 'to-do' list can be run on any spreadsheet package such as Excel. Setting one up only takes a few minutes and updating is quick and simple. The sort function allows the list to be reordered to reflect changing priorities.

Here are some selected practical tips for good time management.

- *Delegate* You do not have to do everything. Pass work on. If the staff do not have the skills, arrange for training
- *Say 'no'* A key assertiveness skill is to learn how to say 'no' when your work in-tray is full. Learn how to close interruptions and appointments
- *Stop doing things* Why have that monthly meeting if it is not effective?
- *Meeting to attend* Prepare: read agenda and minutes beforehand. Don't contribute to time wasting. If you have nothing to say, that's fine. Delegate attendance if you can and it is appropriate
- *Meeting to hold* Don't! Much can be achieved by e-networking and virtual conferencing. Only hold a meeting for a defined purpose. Fix start and end times. Do not wait for late arrivals. End at 17.35 means just that. Circulate minutes/action plans immediately after meeting. Get a person at the meeting to draft the minutes for you directly onto a laptop during the meeting. Then you only have to edit and e-mail it off. If you have lots of contributions to make to the meeting, possibly get someone else to chair
- *Don't panic* Check with people what deadlines are fixed and may not be changed and those which may be flexible and can be adjusted
- *Learn to work effectively* Develop good IT skills. Learn to speed read. Keep communications short and focused. Control the electronic 'inbox' and snail mail in-tray. Handle each item only once: action it, delegate it, file it, or dispose of it – and try to keep the pending file small (empty is good). Maintain good filing disciplines for physical and computer files (back up these regularly onto DVD or flash memory)
- *Organize work space* Keep your desk top clear – there should be nothing on it when you leave at night
- *Control time* Control appointments: 'We will meet at 15.20 for 15 minutes'
- *Know your good and bad times* Know when you are good. Are you a morning person, for instance? You should schedule complex work into the time when you work well
- *Focus* Work on one thing at a time and allocate enough time to make an impact
- *Control interruptions* There is no such thing as a one-minute interruption – concentration is destroyed and takes many minutes to be recovered. Control your telephone when you are working on something complex – that is what voicemail is for. Control your e-mail – set aside a part of the day for electronic and physical mail correspondence
- *Diary and 'to-do' list* The 'to-do' list has been discussed above where we noted electronic diaries are helpful. However, group disciplines need to be observed. For example, agree 'meeting-clear' times – times of the day when meetings may not be booked – so people can focus on project activities. (Some colleges do not schedule lectures on Wednesday afternoons to allow time for sporting and other group activities.)
- *Steal time* For longer business journeys, take the train rather than drive. It's a good time to catch up with background reading and many long-distance trains now have laptop power points. Book ahead and reserve a seat with a table

Business communications

In the management of teams and projects, clear communications with stakeholders are necessary. Business e-mails are different to private e-mails; they are formal legal communications. The use of text-speak should be avoided in business e-mails. Business and marketing reports are different to academic project reports. For the technical manager involved in marketing activities such as new product launches, presentations and press releases are important.

The first stage in communications is to decide who the target audiences are. Who are the other relevant stakeholders? What is being achieved and what is the message? It is important to write in accessible language and the 'plain English' rules are invaluable in this:

- keep sentences short
- use active verbs and positive language
- use 'you' and 'we'
- choose words appropriate for the reader
- don't be afraid to give instructions
- avoid nominalisations
- use lists where appropriate

These tips are given by the Plain English Campaign (available from www.plainenglish. co.uk/guides.html). There are many other guides that are also available from the same site, such as: How to write in plain English, The A–Z of alternative words, CVs, Design and Layout, Forms, Letters, Proofreading, Reports and Websites.

Proofreading your own work is never easy. Here you need a good friend or colleague who has the skill to know when a semi-colon rather than a comma is required and to spot the spelling errors (the 'spell check' on your PC does not pick up all errors). A spelling mistake on the front page of a report is not the best way to impress a client.

INSIGHT

PROBLEMS IN COMMUNICATION

Words do not always mean the same in 'American' English and 'British' English. That great joke about rubbers, which broke the ice in the home sales conference, may cause profound offence in a presentation to export customers with a different linguistic background.

Different cultures put different weights on the simple content of the text and the emotional and non-verbal communications used in the delivery. In some cultures, a direct 'no' might be considered offensive and coded language may be used.

Knowing the knowledge level of the group is also important. There is a communications 'window'. Go in and 'baby talk' to a technical audience and they will not be impressed, even though they fully understand. Use lots of technical jargon with a general audience and they simply will not understand (even if they stay awake during the presentation).

Business e-mails

Figure 11.4 gives the general outline structure of a business e-mail. Contrary to many people's expectations, e-mails are much more permanent than a paper-based letter. Once the hard copy (copies) of a letter are shredded, it is destroyed. E-mails go through systems with back-up security (in the sending organisation, in transmission and in the receiving organisation) and there can be 'stray' copies around that you have no knowledge of and no control over. For this reason, and with the implications of data protection legislation, every

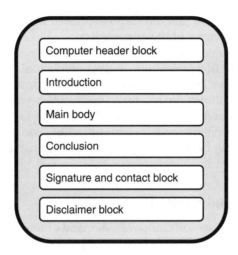

Figure 11.4 General outline structure of a business e-mail. Adapted from: Curtis, T., *Marketing in Practice*, figure 9.4, page 211, © Elsevier 2006. Reproduced by permission.

care should be taken over e-mails, just as you would with letters. That clever suggestion or lively joke could take on a different implication when examined in the cold light of day. Remember, there is no such thing as a private communication in business (leaks and data protection legislation ensure this).

The computer address block gives your name and e-mail contact information. The 'to' block is for the target stakeholders (publics/audience). The 'cc' is to copy in people who may need to be kept informed. The 'bcc' block allows you to circulate the e-mail to other people without the other recipients ('to' or 'cc') knowing. The subject (title) block should give a one-line overview of the content. With busy in-boxes, people often only display the 'from', 'date' and 'subject' fields. A meaningless subject (e.g. Re: as default from the software setting) might only get your message quickly clicked into the deleted-box. The date and time is automatically picked up. In most software, the heading block will also give the file names and type (e.g. PowerPoint, Word, etc.) of any attached files. Remember, people with dial-up access and small-capacity in-boxes do not appreciate large picture files.

The body of an e-mail follows the rules of: introduction, main body and conclusion. The introduction and conclusion may be very brief or completely missed for a simple e-mail. For professional business communications, text-speak and colloquial expressions should not be used. Good English should be used with appropriate capitalisation, spelling and grammar.

The signature block is best set up by customising your software. The associated contact address block normally gives your name, e-mail address, website, telephone contact numbers and postal address.

Normally, the disclaimer block will be set up by the organisation and will be written by the legal department. It may cover such issues as to non-disclosure of content if received in error, declaration of non-liability for virus damage, statement of the organisation's communications policy (offensive content) and in some organisations (e.g. journalists working for

TV, radio or press) that the views expressed are those of the sender and do not necessarily represent the views of the organisation.

For all their ease and speed, e-mails are part of the permanent record. The implications of data protection legislation are that only a fool will commit to an e-mail something that they would not like to defend in the media or in court. Some software enables tracking options that allows the sender to know when you have received the message, when you have read it and when you have deleted it. It is more like an instant 'recorded delivery' than an informal method of communication! Some organisations (sending, transmitting or receiving) may be monitoring content for offensive words. Be warned: an e-mail is not an electronic Post-it.

Business and marketing reports

Different contexts and companies demand different house styles and the general framework given below should be adapted as required.

- *Title page* Title of project and date
- *Executive summary* Focused and brief (200–500 words). This provides senior management with an overview and directs further selective reading
- *Acknowledgments* Assistance may have been given through resources or other support. It is good manners to acknowledge support
- *Contents* This helps people find their way around a project. Longer projects might include page numbers of main topic headings, appendices and lists of diagrams, figures, tables and illustrations. Reports should be page numbered
- *Brief introduction* A clear definition of the hypothesis, issue(s) or problems covered in the report
- *Body of the report* Make full use of headings and subheadings to break down the issues into a logical sequence of sections
- *Conclusion* This section should summarise the findings and, if appropriate, give recommended courses of action
- *References* In business reports, full referencing (according to the Harvard or Vancouver system) is generally not required but an indication where information has been obtained from is usually good practice (e.g. the source of statistical data in a table)
- *Appendices* These provide essential supporting material while not impeding the flow of the text

Most organisations have their own house styles and conventions, which may be contained in a company style manual. If not, when you come to write your first business report, talk to your manager and ask for the report that is considered to have been the best in the recent past. This will give you an indication of the company style.

Press releases that get published

In small organisations, the product development or project manager may be involved with press releases and launch events. In marketing communications terms, a press release is the same as a typical 'push and pull' strategy: you have to write a copy that will attract the attention of the editor and then lead on to an article, TV or radio feature (push aspect) that will also appeal to your ultimate audience (pull element). Again, the secret is to understand what the two target audiences need. Many press releases (possibly most) fail at the first test: they aren't newsworthy enough. Being 'newsy' is rather like beauty or an elephant; it is easy to recognise but not easy to define. 'Newsy' articles get printed and the ultimate target audience also reads them.

The skill in successful press releases is to remain focused on the longer term communications objectives and not just get carried away. Yet, at the same time, by its very nature, news is transient and when the opportunity presents itself, it has to be grasped. Having found a framework that will carry the desired message and be newsy, how do we get it written up as a press release that gets printed? Think of the editor's agenda. Give them a good story and make it simple for them to use it. Many organisations now send out their press releases by e-mail as an attached file. The editor can then simply download the file and edit (no need to waste time in re-keying and reduced possibility of errors). Many journalists use the WHAT model and it is a good framework for your press release:

- **W**: Who? What? Why? Where? When?
- **H**: How did it happen? How will the implications have an impact?
- **A**: Additional information
- **T**: Tie up loose ends

Figure 11.5 gives an outline of a suitable structure for an 'electronic' press release. This allows all the points in this model to be covered.

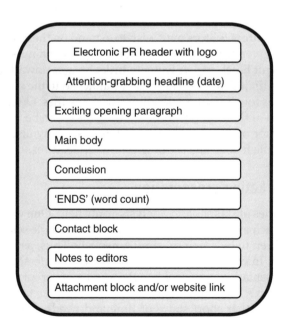

Figure 11.5 General outline structure of an electronic press release. Adapted from: Curtis, T., *Marketing in Practice*, figure 9.8, page 218, © Elsevier 2006. Reproduced by permission.

Electronic PR header with logo Press releases are a front-line communication to key people in the media and so should look both attractive and professional. The press release template can convey the organisation's logo and other image features, just as with a paper letterhead.

Attention-grabbing headline This can be repeated in the title block of the e-mail. An editor is faced with a very busy e-mail in-box and letter tray, so it is essential to have something to grab attention from the screen full of e-mails and from the overflowing in-tray on the desk. In the attachment, the heading is usually in bold and in a larger font size than the body text.

Exciting opening paragraph The secret is in a fairly short paragraph to make the key points and to provide the editor (and, later, the ultimate reader/listener/viewer) with a reason to stay with the story. Often this will be in bold, but in the same font size as the body text.

Main body Contains the detail of the story but, for most press releases, needs to be fairly short – 200–600 words would be typical.

Conclusion The 'wrap-up' paragraph to the story. A good punchy quotation from a key person is one way to do this.

ENDS (word count) It is a common practice to indicate where the 'story' has ended, and it can be useful for editors to know the word count.

Contact block This shows information for contacting the person who is going to manage the story. It should typically include office telephone number, 'office' mobile – in the 24/7/365 world, a major organisation will have a PR rota so that the press can get information at any time (e.g. when a story goes international and is followed up through various time zones) – and, of course, e-mail contact address. In the instant communication age, this is important because news editors may be scanning their screens for stories, so the first call can come in seconds.

Notes to editors Editors may wish to expand on the story so more background information can be given here, without cluttering up the main focused story.

Attachment block and or website links Images nowadays will most often be held in high-quality digital format. These can be attached to the e-mail, but not all recipients may have facilities for easily downloading very large files. Often the image files will be held on the PR area of the organisation's website; these can be downloaded as and when needed by the editor or journalist. Past press releases may also be archived here, so that they are accessible to journalists doing follow-up features.

The marketing presentation

All the rules of stakeholder analysis apply here. One way to view the process is to regard it not so much as a mass communication, but a whole series of 'one-to-one' communications that happen to be going on simultaneously. Thus, as with personal selling, start with the audience. In one-to-one contact, you have a single agenda and personality. In a technical sales presentation, you will be talking to a group of different people with different roles in the client's decision-making unit. Therefore, the task is a little more complex, as it takes place in a rather short space of time and needs careful presentation. Some simple rules apply.

As with one-to-one interactions, know your agenda and the probable agendas of the target audience. Decide on the media. Most often it will be computer-based, so check that your software is compatible with the systems at the venue you will be using. At a conference in Hong Kong, there was considerable confusion with several different versions of the same presentation software in circulation. Not all of them worked on the residents' hotel computers and there were some late-night file conversions necessitated. The rule is: check what facilities will be at the venue before you prepare your material.

Prepare the material (including any supporting documentation and samples, etc.) and get another person to proof it (do not just rely on the spell checker). More than one PR manager has stood up to talk about 'pubic' rather than 'public' relations! If possible, carry out a run-through to make sure that it works and to check timings. At the venue, arrive early and check all the last-minute details (e.g. will you have a radio microphone, a fixed microphone or can you choose?). Remember that in the actual presentation, you are building many one-to-one relationships. Try not to look at your script too much (prompt cards treasury tagged together so they stay in order are a popular option) and sweep the audience with your eyes. Then people in the back row will feel that they have not been forgotten.

POWERPOINT CAN HAVE QUIRKS

PowerPoint files do not always travel well. All the information is there but sometimes there can be little hiccups. In arriving at a destination the local computer may have different operating system (e.g. Vista rather than XP) and may have different release dates of PowerPoint. Take care because Vista/PowerPoint 2007 is not backwards compatible. If you suspect that you will not be using a Vista system at your destination, save in a compatible mode.

A common hiccup is reversal of an embedded image (top becomes bottom or left becomes right). The suggested good practice is to have the presentation loaded on the hard drive the night before and then run through on the actual computer and projection system to be used. Any reversal gremlins can be quickly corrected using the appropriate flip command and the debugged file saved.

Remember housekeeping points. Is the presentation informal (so you are happy to take questions at any time) or is it more formal so questions will only be taken at the end? Make certain you have agreed to these points with the chairperson if it is a formal meeting. Prepare your 'deliverable' handouts, brochures and the like well in advance. Make certain they are sent by secure means if you are not taking them yourself. In international meetings, take special care; there can be problems with, for example, customs clearance.

As always in management, reflect on the process. This is not your last presentation so think of it as a continual learning experience from which you gain more and more skills. This is important for the practising marketer.

Review

People are not machines and there is more to motivation than just changing a gear. Theories of personality have been outlined, which enable managers to appreciate people's differences, and relevant theories presented to help to develop approaches to motivating staff. The Belbin approach to the analysis of team performance has been summarised. This allows a manager to appreciate team-working styles of individual team members and the need for balance in the team. Organisations need to have role definitions and organisational structures – the functional and matrix approaches to organisation structure have been covered.

Staff are very expensive. The timeline for staff selection, recruitment, induction and professional development have been discussed and management approaches outlined. The first stage of effective management is the management of self. Approaches to assertiveness, time management and business communications have been given.

Further reading

Belbin, R. M. (2002), *Management Teams: Why they Succeed or Fail*, Butterworth Heinemann reprint of original 1981 edition.

Boddy, D. (2002) *Management: An Introduction*, 2nd edn, Prentice Hall.

Hunsaker, P. (2005) *Management: A Skills Approach*, 2nd edn, Prentice Hall.

Johnson, G. & Scholes, K. (2005) *Exploring Corporate Strategy*, 7th edn, Prentice Hall.

Lee-Davies, L. (2007) *Developing Work and Study Skills*, Thomson Learning.

Lynch, R. (2005) *Corporate Strategy*, 4th edn, Pearson.

Wilson, R. & Gilligan, C. (2005) *Strategic Marketing Management: Planning Implementation and Control*, 3rd edn, Elsevier.

CHAPTER 12

Project management

Learning objectives

After studying this chapter you will be able to:

- Describe the stages of a project and describe the activities that take place
- Explain how network analysis and charts can assist in the management of projects
- Understand the human side of project management, the stages of project team formation and break-up, and explain the need for a balanced leadership style from the project manager
- Plan a marketing event, such as a launch or exhibition, and explain the additional issues to be considered in the planning of international events

Introduction

Projects come in a wide variety of types and sizes. A simple process change or computer system upgrade may take only a few days. Major construction projects may take years. Projects have a start and an end. After the project is completed the project team will disperse. Figure 12.1 shows the project stages.

Project stages

It is important that the early stages are completed with care. Poor consideration of the pre-initiation, initiation and planning stages will manifest itself as problems in the later stages.

Pre-initiation

The management team considers what needs to be done and why the project is needed. Pre-planning and feasibility are undertaken. Why do we need this project? What are our aims and objectives? What is needed to complete the project? What are the costs and time issues? Will the proposed project deliver the required benefits? What resources will be required (e.g. staff time)? How will it integrate with other activities? The broad definition needs to be firmed up into the detailed project charter. A common scenario is that the project

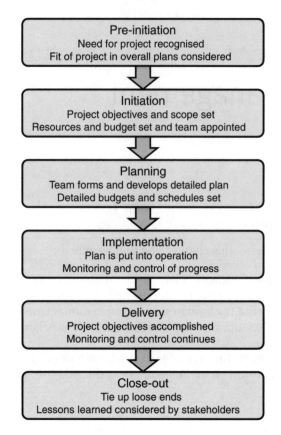

Figure 12.1 The stages of a project. Adapted from: Curtis, T., *Marketing in Practice*, figure 9.9, page 222, © Elsevier 2006. Reproduced by permission.

sponsor(s) should be responsible for this phase and the project manager involved in the next phase.

Initiation

This is the stage where the project is defined including the objectives, scope, what is to be delivered/achieved, any constraints, any assumptions (e.g. delivery dates promised by suppliers), resources, outline schedule and project team (including responsibilities). Team selection should ensure that all skills are included and that, apart from functional contributions (e.g. computer knowledge), team roles are filled (e.g. Belbin team roles: chairperson, shaper, plant, company worker, team worker, monitor-evaluator, resource evaluator and completer finisher). Some writers call this project definition the project 'charter'. For new product development (NPD) projects the charter should consider the value chain issues (e.g. procurement, production, etc.) and a provisional view should be taken of the full marketing mix with more detailed definition of the product. Chapters 4 to 8 provide the overview of the issues that need to be considered.

The outcome of this phase should be the full detailed project charter. Most often the project leader will prepare this with appropriate support. It is important that the sponsor(s) agree and 'sign off' the charter and the budget.

Planning and planning tools

The core team formulates the detailed plans for implementing the project charter, including the assignment of responsibilities and scheduling of activities, with appropriate costing(s) and budget(s). Some consideration of contingencies should be made. There are some excellent planning software packages available for use where appropriate. However, for uncomplicated projects, a simple chart may be all that is required. Care should be taken to communicate with all the relevant project stakeholders who will be involved. This is particularly important where aspects of the project are being subcontracted (e.g. use of design consultants or advertising agencies). At this stage, detailed consideration should be given to ensure that the project 'deliverables' are clearly specified and communicated. For instance, if your team has to conduct a major customer demonstration, you must all be clear about what documentation will be needed, what samples need to be prepared, etc.

Gantt chart

These are easy to construct. For simple projects, pro-forma wall charts can be purchased or a simple Excel spreadsheet set up. Figure 12.2 shows a simplified schematic outline of a

Activity	W1	W2	W3	W4	W5	W6	W7	W8	W9	W10	W11	W12
Agree general content	▓											
Get information		▓	▓									
Write copy			▓	▓								
Agree deadlines with printer	▓											
Agree images to be used		▓										
Clear copyright file images				▓								
Clear images/copy with authorities					▓							
Final sign-off of total copy							▓					
Dispatch files to printers							▓					
Printer typesets								▓				
Receive proofs and proofread									▓			
Get final sign-offs of copy									▓			
Amendments sent to printer									▓			
Brochure printed										▓		
Delivery from printer										▓		
Distribution of brochure to agents												▓

Figure 12.2 Outline time plan for printing a product brochure. Adapted from: Tony Curtis, *Marketing in Practice*, figure 9.10, page 223, © Elsevier 2006.

chart for a project to print a product brochure. The time axis is set in suitable time periods (in the example, weeks). The task activities, often with the person(s) responsible, are listed on the other axis. The period of the activity can be indicated by blocking in the cells during which the activity can take place. Though simple, such charts are powerful and effective for simple projects. The planner has to formulate a clear, logical view of the sequence of activities. This logical flow of events is clearly communicated to the project team members by the chart and the consequences of any missed deadlines can be clearly seen. Milestones for project reviews can be indicated.

Network analysis (PERT and CPM)

The first stage of network analysis is to define the project (from the project charter) and identify all the individual activities and tasks that will be needed to complete the project. The next step is to spell out the relationships between the activities and ensure all the precedencies have been identified (e.g. foundations must be completed before walls of a building can be built). For each task, the time needed should be estimated. The flow chart (network chart) can then be drawn (usually with one of the specialist computer packages). A schematic flow chart is shown in Figure 12.3 for the launch of a new product in 'activity on node' representation. The longest time path through the network chart is the 'critical path'. This is the minimum time in which the project can be completed if all the tasks along the critical path are completed on time. If this is longer than the time period given in the

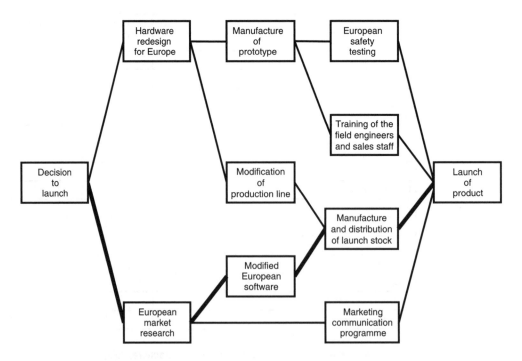

Figure 12.3 Basic network for launch of new oven.

original project charter (often the case) then the individual tasks along the critical path need to be examined.

In completing the analysis times are calculated for:

- EST (earliest start time) This is the earliest time that an activity can start and it depends on all the preceding tasks having been completed. For an activity on the critical path, it is the sum of the preceding task times.
- LST (latest start time) This is the latest time that an activity can be started without delaying the project.
- EFT (earliest finish time) The earliest time at which an activity can be completed.
- AT (activity time) This is the estimated time required to complete the activity.
- LFT (latest finish time) This is the latest time that an activity can be finished without delaying the project.
- ZS (activity slack time) This is the amount of slippage (start or duration) that can be accepted without the project being delayed. On the critical path through the network, this is zero.

This allows the construction of some simple rules:

$$EFT = EST + AT.$$

EST equals the maximum of all the EFTs of the immediately preceding activities.

$$LST = LFT - AT.$$

LFT equals the minimum of all the LSTs of the immediately following activities. Figure 12.4 shows the structure for 'activity on node' network analysis.

A typical problem is that there may not be enough resources in one of the departments for a key activity. The team leader can then decide if temporary staff might be recruited or some of the work contracted out. The network provides a powerful tool to identify project 'pinch points' that can be given special attention. Activities not on the critical path have some slack time and a measure of time drift, provided it is less than the slack time, will not delay the project. We will now look at an example of a simple project.

Consider the case of a project manager who is in the position of European product manager (responsible for marketing as well as production co-ordination) for a company manufacturing advanced food-processing equipment for catering establishments. The parent

Earliest start time [EST]	Activity label	Earliest finish time [EFT]
Latest start time [LST]	Estimated activity time [AT]	Latest finish time [LFT]

Figure 12.4 Activity on node structure.

Table 12.1   Activity times and tasks for combination oven launch in Europe

Label	Time (weeks)	Task
	0	Decision to launch
A	12	Hardware redesign for Europe (e.g. metric rather than imperial dimensions)
B	18	Market research (e.g. new applications for European recipes, such as Cornish pasties in the UK, plus installation issues such as electrical voltages and electrical connection requirements in the various EU countries)
C	6	Manufacture of prototype
D	4	Modification of production line
E	6	Modified European software for controls, etc. (metric/centigrade)
F	8	EU safety testing in an independent laboratory
G	12	Training of the field engineers and sales staff
H	8	Manufacture and distribution of launch stock to agents
I	6	Development of marketing communications programme
		Final launch

company is US-based and has successfully launched a new range of 'combination' ovens (conventional and microwave capabilities). The product manger has been given project management responsibility for the project to launch the new oven in Europe. The US company has manufacturing facilities in Poland to service its European customers.

The objective of this chapter is to present the basic concepts, so a very simple outline is used. In real life, any of the excellent computer packages such as Microsoft Project would be used. Even in a simple project such as this, there may be well over 100 individual activities. The amendment of a single activity can have a significant impact and the calculation of this, with hundreds of potential interactions, could take hours – just what computers were made for. An outline of the necessary operations that might be included (with estimates of the required times for completion) is shown in Table 12.1.

This set of activities can be set out in a simple network. It is not possible to start the modification of the production line or the manufacture of the prototype until the design work has been completed. If we lay these out simply, we end up with an outline network as shown in Figure 12.3.

There are several conventions for the construction of these networks and for full details, the applications notes should be consulted for the particular software package being used. The form used here is the so-called 'activity on node'. We construct the network using the six-cell node structure shown in Figure 12.4.

To calculate the earliest times, we begin at the start of the project and calculate the set of ESTs. For activities A and B these are 0. The EFTs for A and B are the ESTs = ATs. The EST of a succeeding activity is the latest EFT of all the preceding activities. For activity H, there are two preceding activities – D (EFT 16) and E (EFT 24) – so the EST for H is 24. This set of calculations is continued until we have the entire EFTs to the finish of the project. The reverse calculation can be completed, starting from the finish time. The LST is the LFT – AT. Where an activity has two or more later activities, the LFT for the earlier activity is the lower

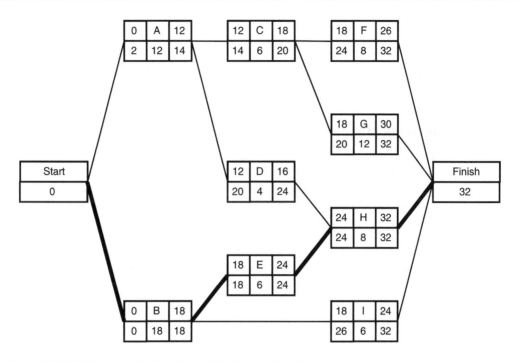

Figure 12.5 Activity on node network analysis for oven launch.

LST for the latter activities. Activity C has two succeeding activities – F (LST 24) and G (LST 20) – so the LFT for activity C is 20. The rest of the calculations are completed working back to the start of the project. The overall calculations for this simple project outline are given in Figure 12.5.

It can be seen that there are some nodes where the EST and the LST are the same. The path linking these nodes is called the critical path. Any delay in these activities will result in an overall delay to the project. Other activities can be seen to have some 'float'. That is to say we have a time buffer that allows for some delay or activity time extension without delaying the whole project.

$$\text{Float} = \text{LFT} - \text{EST} - \text{AT}.$$

The network can be converted into a bar chart where the activities can be set out and any float times indicated.

In CPM/CPA (critical path method/critical path analysis), only one estimate of the task is made. All estimates are subject to error. In the PERT approach (programme evaluation and review technique), account is taken of estimation error. In the PERT analysis of a building project, some of the building activities may be weather dependent. Three estimates are made: optimistic, probable and pessimistic (in this example, ideal good weather, normal weather, poor weather). The PERT software will then calculate out an expected completion time and its potential variance.

As the project progresses, actual progress against plan can be compared and the impact of delays noted on the expected completion time. Management can be informed of any potential slippage of completion date. If this is unacceptable, the revised estimate of the critical path can be examined to see where extra resources might shorten an activity to bring the project back on target. These various approaches provide powerful tools for the planning of projects and their subsequent control. Further reading references are given at the end of this chapter.

Implementation

The team leader ensures that there is continual tracking of the activities against plan. The charts and/or computer packages provide the management framework for this. Where key activities are slipping (e.g. late delivery of copy), then corrective action can be taken. Monitoring of costs (both invoiced and committed) against the agreed budget is essential because cost overruns are a major problem. Good communication within the project team and with key stakeholders is essential and here again the charts and/or computer printouts can assist in keeping all people in the picture. A careful balance must be struck in maintaining control but without micromanaging too much. Excessive reporting requirements and meetings slow progress.

Delivery

For a new product development project, this is the product launch. For a construction project, this is completion of the building. In marketing activities, typical project deliverables are customer presentations and exhibitions. The full delivery inventory should have been defined earlier at the planning stage and confirmed during the implementation stage.

Close-out

After the project has drawn to a close, the project manager should check all expenses have been paid and close down budgets. Any final project reports should be written and other final documentation completed (e.g. final hand-over documentation). Every project is a learning experience. What went well? What did not go so well? How can we do it better next time? Close-out should not only consider the hard issues (e.g. performance of the PERT software), but also the performance of the project team.

The performance of project teams

In chapter 11, key issues in team management (such as motivation, personality and preferred team roles) were explored. However, there is one additional dimension for managing project teams. A departmental manager in their normal role is managing a 'steady state' team. The operations manager ensures that production continues in the factory. The project manager's role is slightly different as the team's sole reason for existence is the project and projects are time bound. A simple project may last a few days, major ones for years, but at the end of the project the team members disperse. This transient nature of project teams is important. In general, teams tend to go through five stages: forming, storming, norming, performing and mourning (Figure 12.6).

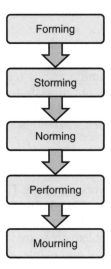

Figure 12.6 Life cycle of a team.

Forming

The team assembles for the first time often in a strange room and often with people that have not worked together before. A new member of staff starting in a new department may ask quietly: 'What is the boss like?' In projects, the team leader may be unknown to the entire group and may have been appointed or seconded just to manage this project. At this stage, only the team leader may have been fully briefed on the full details of the project (often having been involved in writing up the project charter). 'How will I get along with the team leader and all these new people?' 'What is my contribution expected to be?' 'What are my personal project objectives and responsibilities?' People are polite but will have mixed feelings: excitement about new challenges, but apprehensions about the unknown as well. In a stable department, formal and informal power structures become established (see Chapter 8). For the project team, their mini cultural web needs to be established.

Storming

At this stage, people have become a bit more knowledgeable about what is demanded of them and are becoming a little more assertive. However, the ground rules of the cultural web still have not been established. There may be some friction and conflict as different people or sub-groups in the project team have differing views of how things should be done. For simple projects, this may last for a short time. For complex projects with difficult technical decisions to be made in the planning phase, the conflict may be extended. The implication is that the team leader needs to be a skilled manager and have good interpersonal skills. A healthy debate about various technical approaches for the project is essential. However, without good management, this can develop into a mire of destructive personal power feuds. A strong participative management style should hold the ring, but take a tin hat along, just in case.

Norming

Once the major 'difficult' planning issues have become settled, people begin to know each other better, what they have to achieve and what the total project objectives are. The team begins to 'norm'. Communications tend to be good, with active listening and effective meetings. Constructive, appropriate feedback should be given to individual team members. Project team decisions should be clearly articulated and any remaining interpersonal conflicts resolved. The team is now beginning to buzz.

Performing

This is the true team-working stage. The team members have come to know and respect the other team members. They know their roles and responsibilities and communications channels are open. Sound project management control systems (e.g. PERT) provide feedback on project progress; problem areas are identified promptly and effective actions taken. This is just like surfing – great and exhilarating – but care has to be taken. When things move fast, 100% concentration and focus is required.

Mourning

This is the bitter-sweet taste of success. For the young, professional graduate, in some ways the feelings are similar to those experienced at graduation. The final end-of-course party (not just end of year) and the realisation, walking past empty lecture theatres, that you will never meet some of these people again as you disperse around the world. The bridge construction engineer will have celebrated the topping out and formal opening, but walking through the now almost empty site office and past the last few people completing the landscaping, there is a feeling of achievement but also of personal loss: 'That was my team.' The formal bridge opening event is a celebration for the local community and the team but it is also a formal closing ritual for the construction team.

Good interpersonal and leadership skills are needed to take the team through these stages. This involves more than just a single-minded focus on the project objectives.

Action-centred leadership for project team management

In his 1988 book *Effective Leadership*, John Adair suggested that there were three components to successful leadership. The leader has to have a balance between three needs: the needs of task, team and individual (Figure 12.7). Exclusive focus on any single element will leave the needs unbalanced and lead to project problems.

Task needs

The team leader needs to monitor the project/task environment. The tools for this (e.g. STEEPLE, five forces of competition, extended value chain, etc.) have been presented in earlier chapters. The team leader is a key decision-maker and must be promptly and properly fed relevant decision-making information from the MkIS (Chapter 9). On the basis of the changing contexts, the team leader should share objectives and targets and any necessary

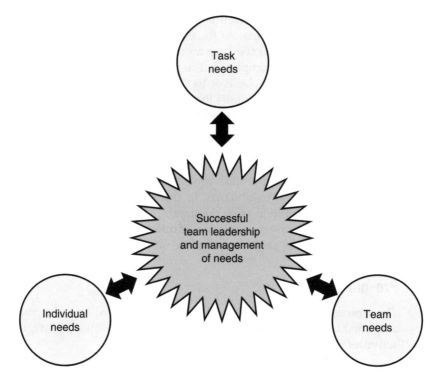

Figure 12.7 Management of needs. Adapted from: Adair, John (1984) *Action-Centred Leadership,* **McGraw-Hill.**

adjustments in response to environmental factors. The team leader has the responsibility to see that appropriate resources are given to the team members to complete the tasks and objectives they have been assigned.

Team needs

A key responsibility during the storming and norming stages of the project team is to recognise and resolve destructive conflicts within the team. Skilled leaders offer public praise (recognition is a motivator) and offer constructive criticism in private. The team leader should orchestrate the development of the mini cultural web for the team. At all times, the team leader should ensure that the team understands the significance of the project and the assigned tasks' contributions.

Individual needs

In Chapter 11, the issue of individual motivation and potential sources of de-motivation were presented. Tasks should be delegated with appropriate feedback channels, not micro-managed. The team leader should ensure that all the Herzberg hygiene factors are satisfied. During the forming and norming stages, there may be emotional security issues affecting individual team member's well-being. Recognition by consultation and acknowledgment of good ideas is motivating. At the end of the project the team will dissolve; team members should not feel that they are no more than disposable units to be binned once their contribution has been completed. The best leaders accept a type of psychological contract with their team members. Deliver 100% contribution to the team and the team member will be rewarded with 100% support for personal and professional development, enabling the individual team members to progress to more senior roles in their next project.

Event management

A technical manager in a NPD project role may be responsible for event management, such as launches and exhibitions. In this section, the generic issues of successful event management are outlined using the standard project management format. There are specific additional issues in the management of international events and some of the more common ones are given at the end this section in an Insight box.

Pre-initiation

The reasons for holding the event need to be defined and objectives set. These should be amplified to cover all the major stakeholders and issues of integration into other project activities considered.

- *Why*? Why have an event? How does this fit in with the stakeholder analysis and stakeholder objectives? How does this fit in with the rest of the launch communications plan, which, in itself, fits within the overall marketing plan?
- *What*? What type of event (e.g. a 'sales launch')? Do we want a separate event? Would it be beneficial to link it to an exhibition?
- *Where*? Where is the geographical location going to be and what other details are associated with that location? This can be very important for international conferences, where travel connections and visa requirements may be significant issues.
- *Who*? Who among the general stakeholders will be involved? Do we need/want additional stakeholders for this particular event?
- *When*? Timing of the event may be vital (e.g. to fit in with the overall plans for a product launch).
- *How much*? How much of the overall budget can be allocated to the event?

Having established some general boundary conditions in the pre-initiation phase, the actual project initiation can start. The above questions can be asked in a more detailed fashion.

Initiation

The type of event has been defined from pre-initiation and more detailed issues of 'what' is physically required can be considered. This includes a whole range of detailed issues that will feed into the venue selection criteria. Issues can include: food (e.g. international clients' special dietary needs), electrical supply (in international contexts, supply may be different; e.g. 120 V, 60 Hz in the US), internet access, computer projection systems, water, drainage and so on. A detailed set of criteria for the venue selection needs to be drawn up (this aspect is considered in more detail in the next section).

The project team should be assigned and decisions made about speakers, VIP guests, etc. The overall budget should be agreed and communicated to the project team.

Planning and venue selection

One of the key tasks in the planning phase and one of the early actions is to select and book the event location. Care is needed to ensure all the facilities required are available. Access for heavy items (e.g. boats, cars, etc.) may require specialist venues designed for this type of access.

Access

Is the venue in the right regional location? Is the venue going to be available at the time required (popular venues may be booked years in advance)? Is the venue easily accessible for delegates using various forms of transport (e.g. roads, rail links and airports)? Is the venue suitable/accessible for disabled delegates? Remember exhibition stands may need heavy vehicle access. What are the conditions for set-up/take-down access before and after the event and the like? How long will it take to set up and dismantle the stand?

Size

Is there enough room for the event? Are delegates going to be comfortable? Health and safety issues need to be addressed. What is the official capacity of the venue? Will that be exceeded with delegates and service staff within the venue? Are there enough rooms of the right type and quality?

Facilities

What facilities do you need for your event? Seating: how many delegates? Can the venue provide the required seating plan? Is presentation equipment readily available (e.g. projection screens)? What accommodation is needed? Are delegates bringing partners who need to be accommodated? Is the accommodation comfortable, with suitable facilities to meet delegates' needs (e.g. internet access, disabled access)? What are the technical requirements such as: broadband/communications facilities, power supply, special services (e.g. extraction, water, drainage, etc.) and is computer software/hardware compatible?

Appropriateness

The right ambience is required (exciting and original for new perfume launch or just professional for a routine sales meeting). Types of venues include hotel, conference/exhibition centre, other (theatre, concert hall, museum, art gallery, etc.), unusual (e.g. sailing training ship). Is the venue going to attract the right audience? Does it have appropriate entertainment facilities?

Exhibition checklist

- Has the budget been agreed and authorised?
- Have the aims and objectives been agreed and approved?
- Have all the relevant contracts been obtained and checked (including subcontractors – catering, photography, etc.). Contracts must be in detail and cover all the relevant issues (e.g. water supply, power, communications, cleaning, security, insurance, refuse disposal, etc.)?
- Have payment terms been agreed?
- Has stand design been finalised and agreed? Has stand fabrication been completed? Are all components on order (including fittings such as displays, lighting, signage, etc.)?
- Have the safety arrangements been checked and any necessary permits obtained?
- Has all the promotional material been designed, copy cleared and material printed (and checked)? Do not forget press releases and briefings.
- Have guest lists been approved and invitations dispatched? Do not forget other stakeholders such as the media.
- Have all staff been briefed?
- Have all accommodation and travel arrangements been made for staff and guest presenters?
- Have all transport arrangements been made for stand, fittings, promotional material, demonstration equipment and promotional literature?
- Have all the arrangements for erecting and dismantling of the stand been agreed and checked?
- Has a rota for manning of the stand been agreed and all relevant staff briefed? This should include all guest speakers and others.
- Have events been arranged and guest presenters briefed (e.g. press conference)?
- Have all the integration aspects been agreed and checked (e.g. links with general advertising)?

Implementation (execution)

In the planning process, all the team members and key participants (e.g. speakers) should know their roles, responsibilities and deadlines. Good communications are essential alongside good relationships with the location's event management staff. The basics sound simple: make certain everything is running to plan and adjust the programme if unexpected issues arise (e.g. sickness of a speaker). In reality, event managers can expect a busy and eventful time. Good planning, along with a motivated team and efficient communications, should ensure the event is successful. It is important to maintain discipline, or that sudden idea for an addition to the venue's requirements may take you over budget with an unplanned expense.

Close-out

All invoices and expense claims should be checked to ensure only what has been agreed is being paid. Once all expenses have been cleared, then the relevant budget can be closed. One of the last actions of the event team leader is to ensure that follow-up is completed.

This can be administrative (e.g. courtesy letter of thanks to speakers) or more aligned with marketing management (e.g. checking sales have got all the new contact information and are progressing with the new leads; issuing of conference proceedings, etc.). Issues to be considered in the de-brief include:

- *Venue* Was access, parking, catering, support (e.g. direction signs) acceptable? Were the rooms large enough? Were the rooms well serviced and not too hot/cold? Did all the equipment work properly? Were all the required services and equipment available? Did delegates and speakers feel the ambience was appropriate? Were there any complaints about the facilities? Were rooms arranged (e.g. horseshoe seating) as required? Was there enough time and support for setting up/taking down?
- *Speakers* How was their contribution received? Were they well prepared? Did they arrive on time?
- *Administration* How effective was pre-event publicity? Was all event material delivered on time? Were there errors or gaps in the documentation (e.g. missing name badges)? How did registration proceed?
- *Costs* Were there any cost overruns on the budget?
- *PR* Were arrangements for the media satisfactory? Was the eventual media coverage satisfactory in tone and quantity?
- *Stand* How did it compare in quality and impact with the competition? Was it erected and taken down on schedule? Did it and all the services function satisfactorily?
- *Objectives* How many new contacts were made? What was the cost per new contact made? Did we gain any useful knowledge about the competition? Was overall attendance satisfactory in numbers and quality?

INSIGHT

INTERNATIONAL EVENTS

The general issues of international marketing have been covered in Chapter 3. Issues to be considered for international events include:

Language
Will translation of proceedings be needed? Not all venues have the facilities for simultaneous interpreting to participants.

Religion and culture
Does the date clash with religious or national holidays for key delegates or speakers? Does the venue cater for the range of dietary needs that may be required? Different cultures have different attitudes to dress, (e.g. in the USA, a conference dress code is likely to be 'business casual' in daytime sessions; in the UK, formal business attire, i.e. a business suit, may be expected). Indicative comments on dress codes may be appreciated to avoid embarrassment. For a major international event, it may be appropriate to appoint an official travel agent who will provide general support (e.g. arranging transport for long-haul delegates from the international airport). Alcohol consumption is not universally appreciated, so a suitable range of non-alcoholic options should be available. Remember the reverse: a hard-drinking sales team may not appreciate a 'location' within a culture where alcohol is not readily available.

Political/legal

Visa requirements have become much stricter since 9/11. Visas may take some time to obtain (sometimes months), so early planning is needed. Visas may need supporting documentation from the organisers (e.g. formal letter of invitation). Event documentation should make visa issues clear. In general, it is the delegates' responsibility to ensure compliance with passport/visa requirements.

Payment

If there is a payment for the event, how will payment be accepted (e.g. what currency, what form of payment, etc.)?

Access

International air travel can be disrupted and schedules may involve arrivals in the middle of the night. Can delegates check in 24/7? Flight patterns may dictate that international delegates may have to arrive at an earlier and/or depart at a later date. Are the costs of additional days reasonable and are the rooms available?

Insurance

Travel, health and other insurance are normally the delegates' responsibility and this should be made clear in the event documentation. Many overseas locations have health requirements (e.g. inoculations and anti-malaria medication).

Accompanying persons

International delegates may wish to take advantage of the trip for a holiday stopover and may bring partners. A social programme for such accompanying persons might be appropriate for a major event. Note there may be visa problems with accompanying persons. In some circumstances, the accompanying person will not be considered to be a delegate (conference visa) and may need a holiday visa.

Review

In this chapter, the stages through which a project progresses were discussed. The specific requirements of the various stages were reviewed.

A number of tools have been introduced to assist project managers, including charts and network approaches. Scheduling tools can be considered as the firmware of project management; the people management issues are the software. In Chapter 11, the general issues of team management were presented. In this chapter, additional elements, including the stages of team life cycle and project team leadership, have been introduced.

A particular type of marketing project that involves technical staff is event management. The general issues to be considered in event management have been presented using the context of exhibitions events as an example. The additional management needs of international events have been discussed.

Further reading

Chelsom, J., Payne, A. & Reavill, L. (2005) *Management for Engineers, Scientists and Technologists*, 2nd edn, John Wiley & Sons.

Mantel, S., Meredith, J., Shafer, S. & Sutton, M. (2005) *Project Management in Practice*, John Wiley & Sons.

Martin, P. & Tate, K. (2001) *Getting Started in Project Management*, John Wiley & Sons.

Meredith, J. & Mantel, S. (2006) *Project Management: A Managerial Approach*, John Wiley & Sons.

Newton, R. (2005) *The Project Manager: Mastering the Art of Delivery*, FT-Prentice Hall.

Wilson, R. & Gilligan, C. (2005) *Strategic Marketing Management: Planning Implementation and Control*, 3rd edn, Elsevier.

CHAPTER 13

Consultancy

Learning objectives

After studying this chapter you will be able to:

- List the issues to consider in setting up at home as a self-employed consultant
- Apply the concepts of the service-extended marketing mix to marketing yourself as a consultant
- Describe the mix of skills needed for successful networking and negotiation
- Write a consultancy CV as part of an integrated consultancy communications package

The consultancy role

In the departmental manager relationship with team members, the programme of work is agreed with the individual and the manager may be responsible for appraisal and staff progression issues. In the normal consultancy role, the consultant is not a member of the organisation and is usually paid a fee, not a salary. The manager does not have the mentoring responsibilities for the consultant in the same way as for a new member of staff. The consultant completes the contract, supplies the deliverables (report, etc.) and is paid. If the delivery was good, the consultant may get more contracts. The consultant as part of his/her contract is expected to adhere to certain general company rules (e.g. health and safety issues) but is not subject to normal internal company disciplinary procedures. Moreover, in his/her work, the consultant does not have executive power. The consultant often needs considerable interpersonal skills to win support.

Consultants are normally used when the organisation does not have specialist skills (e.g. expert witness), where an external perspective is needed (e.g. consultancy assistance in an ISO 9000 or ISO 14000 implementation), where a resource is only occasionally needed (e.g. specialist training), or where there is an overload situation.

Sole-trader consultancy

In the mid-twentieth century, people joined organisations thinking they would be working there for the whole of their working lives. This expectation now no longer exists with either the employer or employee. People move on, either for better opportunities or because their role is no longer required. A significant proportion of professional jobs are now term appointments (e.g. construction and plant commissioning work). Many professionals now have a portfolio business life. This may be as a life choice or because no suitable full-time opportunity exists. The downside of sole-trader consultancy is that with no contract, there is no money. There is an element of risk. The upside is that there is considerable flexibility, which can provide a better life/work balance. There is no 'typical' consultancy – each person builds up their own unique skills profile. When considering going into consultancy/portfolio working as a sole trader, certain issues need to be considered.

Finance

Setting up as a consultant does not involve massive sums of money but, nonetheless, significant start-up finance is required. This can come from several sources – a severance payment is a common catalyst.

In general, a bank overdraft is not a good idea because banks have the short-term option to withdraw this facility. Some other form of medium-term loan is better. Part of this decision process may involve choosing the most appropriate financial structure: remain as a sole trader or set up as a limited company. Most often, lenders will not lend to a new limited company with no trading record or assets. In obtaining loans, some form of collateral is often required. A related issue in Europe is whether to register for VAT or not. These are complex financial decisions.

Many professional institutions have special interest groups to promote networking. Talking to other consultants can be most useful and networking costs a lot less than accountancy charges. By talking to your network, you get the chance to think through the issues, which means you can make decisions more quickly (i.e. less expensively) when you seek professional advice. As always, get professional help when you need it. In buying a house, a professional survey is a good idea. It is best to get advice up-front rather than get the accounts into a pickle and then have an expensive accountancy fee to pay after a professional sorts things out. There are good sources of information on self-employment generally available: you might want to refer to some of these.

It is important to keep records of all income and allowable expenditure. In the UK, current information is available from the HM Revenue & Customs website. It is normally prudent not to mix private and business finance and to set up a business bank account. Many banks offer free consultancy services for new commercial customers and their advice can be invaluable.

Insurance is an important issue. When in full-time employment the employee is covered by his/her employer's insurance. Often a condition for tendering for a consultancy contract is to produce appropriate evidence of professional indemnity insurance. The evidence should indicate the nature of work and amount that is covered. Networking with other consultants can help identify suitable providers who give competitive rates. Checks should be made with other insurance policies in case there need to be amendments (e.g. some car insurance policies exclude 'professional' use and provide cover only for 'normal domestic use'). Similar issues may apply to a home working base. This is not normally a problem for a home office but a home test laboratory for pyrotechnics might be a different issue.

A compact desk unit in the corner of the living room to dock a laptop may be fine for the one day a month hot-desking at home but it is not suitable for the full-time, sole-trader consultant. There are two problems with the 'desk in a corner' solution. The first is that it is not a solution. For example, the dog barking when you are taking an important call from a client is not professional. The second is that it merges home life and business life, to the detriment of both. Separation, both physical and in terms of time, of business and personal life tends to provide better quality time for both in the end. It is not suggested that the new consultant should go out and spend thousands on new furniture, etc. Most towns have second-hand office furniture stores and second-hand office furniture may provide better functionality (being built for full-time office use) than a flat-pack office kit as well as being cheaper. What is required is a good, functional home base at an affordable cost.

A box room is fine; just take a little time to maximise the use of space. Lateral filing may be better than a large drawer filing cabinet. It is good to use shelving to keep things off the floor. The basic needs are for a sound computer system, with legitimate software, and a good quality printer. Broadband access is essential for research and e-mail. It is suggested, given the comparatively low line cost, that a separate land-line for business use is maintained. Little Johnny (five years old) may sound cute to family members when he answers the telephone but not to a client. A separate line with answer-phone is a better solution. It may be worth considering a separate mobile telephone for business use. Moreover, this keeps a clear distinction between personal telephone expenses and business communications expenses. The fax is much less used today. However, a scanner, printer/fax combination is not vastly expensive. Having considered the home base logistics, the marketing issues can be addressed.

Marketing information system

General market intelligence is vital. Where are the opportunities? Often they may not be formally advertised. Later in the chapter, networking is considered. Your network is a crucial source of market intelligence. The professional societies provide frameworks to assist their members operating as consultants with networking support and other facilities. It may be useful to subscribe to key industry journals, but these can be very expensive so make sure they offer you value. The internet provides a good platform for market intelligence and market research (e.g. researching a client's website). A key part of the system is maintaining a contact index.

Product

The product is the consultant and his/her skills, knowledge and experience. However, for the portfolio consultant, they can be focused into different product areas. Some typical examples are:

- part-time teaching at a local university or college and tutoring students on national distance learning programmes as a regional tutor
- in-house delivery of training
- technical writing (e.g. books, articles, training materials, instruction manuals, etc.)
- auditing (e.g. hazard and quality assurance audits)
- expert witness and arbitration
- technical consultancy (e.g. environmental impact reviews)
- assessments (e.g. part-time marking of professional exams)

The first reaction from people is that being a sole-trader consultant is a simple business. This is generally not true. The business may not turn over a million pounds but there are a series of sub-business and market segments to be considered. A personal audit is useful to help decide the areas in which to operate and, just as important, the areas not to enter.

Price

'Wow, you charge £750 a day! You'll be into your first million in no time.' This is sometimes the comment you will get. However, life is not that simple. Not all time is billable time (e.g. travelling time as well as travel costs can sometimes be billed, but not always). There are expenses and time involved in preparing a pitch for a consultancy contract. If you apply for a job most employers will pay reasonable travel expenses; not so for the consultancy sales pitch. This is a double whammy because not only is this an overhead on the successful pitch, but the 'wins' also have to pay for the 'losts' (where there were pitching costs but no income).

What price to charge? In Chapter 10, the dangers of over-simplistic costing and pricing were discussed. The same rules run for the consultancy business. Teaching, regional tutoring or professional exam marking may only pay £20 to £50 an hour. However, the income can be steady and often the timing can be a flexible. When you have unique skills and the client has a deep pocket (e.g. acting as an expert witness in the High Court), the question is, what would be an appropriate charge? The opposite now applies. Ask not how much it costs to run the business and what your standard margin is. The key question is: what is the 'going rate' (the market valuation) of that type of consultancy? This is where the professional societies and professional networks can be of assistance.

It is important that appropriate contracts are developed. Here again, the professional societies and networks can be helpful with pro-forma style contracts and invoices for different types of contexts. A few specific points to be considered are:

- What is being paid for? If a training package is developed for a company, who owns the copyright? In the training situation, is the consultant required to provide the course manuals or just supply the master copies for the company to reproduce and bind?
- What are the allowable expenses and what evidence is required?
- Are stage payments to be made?
- How is payment to be made (e.g. cheque, electronic transfer)?
- How long will it take from invoice to payment? (This is often typically four to six weeks.)

KNOW WHAT THE DELIVERABLES ARE IN FULL

A training consultant developed a large training package for a major international company. The contract specified that the company would own the copyright and that WP files would be required. These were provided in Microsoft Word format. The consultant was informed that the company did not use this and needed the files in WordPerfect format. The conversion caused some formatting and pagination problems and another week's work was required to provide the files in the required form. The contract specified that the files were required but not the format. When writing a book, the publisher's contract will specify the nature of the files to be delivered and their format.

Place

What are your selected travel options? The use of a car is great in that you can pile any amount of junk (e.g. training manuals) in the back. However, driving time is dead time. Rail and air travel can be reading and working time (just what the laptop was made for).

What is the working pattern that the consultancy package will demand? Does this involve 100% attendance at the client's premises (e.g. delivery of a training package in the client's training facilities) or is it substantially home office-based (e.g. preparation of an expert witness report for a court case). What dates are mandatory (e.g. attendance at court as an expert witness) or more discretionary (e.g. post-course review meeting). How easy is the travelling? Are parking facilities, etc. available? In the pricing structure, are travel and accommodation expenses part of the allowable contract expenses?

Promotion

The general issues covered in Chapter 7 apply, but expensive advertising and very costly printing of brochures is not generally advisable. The key targets are the decision makers in the target organisation's DMUs. Networking can be useful to get your name known in your industry sector. Conference presentations and articles in the trade journals can also be helpful. The professional societies and trade journals often hold directories of consultants so ensure you are listed in them all.

Mass snail-mail activities can be expensive in terms of printing and postage costs (however, top-quality business cards are a good investment). Spam e-mails are not well received. Targeted communications are needed. If you are considering some post-graduate part-time teaching, then the local university website will identify the relevant programme leader(s) who can be targeted with context-specific e-mail(s) with CV attached (the consultant's CV is covered later in this chapter).

A good basic website is a better investment than an expensive printed brochure. It can be updated and can be accessed 24/7. What to include is specific to the context. Just research the websites of some consultants in your selected area and this will point you in the direction of the content that will be appropriate.

Word of mouth and networking are important. The skills needed for successful networking are covered later in this chapter.

People

You are the person and you need to project your qualifications, skills (e.g. project management), work experience, professional memberships and past achievements. Past successful contracts with blue-chip organisations are a powerful indicator of your professional competence.

Physical evidence

All your documentation should be in a professional, personal house style. All deliverables, such as training manuals, should be professionally presented.

Process

Your consultancy business may be relatively modest in terms of turnover but sound administrative procedures must be set in place. Customer communications must be answered promptly. However, care must be taken to not become a slave to e-mail. One technique is to set aside two or three times a day for administration and work through the e-mail in-box. In writing a complex report there is no such thing as a two-minute interruption. It can take many minutes to regain concentration and focus.

The internal consultant

In Chapters 11 and 12, the nature of teams and individuals' roles and team participation styles were discussed. However, one facet of involvement was not fully discussed, that of the internal consultant. The role of the consultant is not to make executive management decisions but to provide know-how, knowledge and advice. Although the internal consultant may be a senior member of staff, he or she should take care not to interfere or damage the team leader's authority.

A special internal consultant role is the internal audit. This may be done as a normal facet of management or as a 'dry run' in preparation for a major external audit for external accreditation. The audit should be done professionally and supportively. A heavy-handed approach is often counter-productive. People become defensive and problems become buried rather than brought out into the open. Better the internal audit (e.g. safety) highlights the issue than an external audit after a systems failure. As always, the consultancy role demands a high level of interpersonal and communications skills; knowing the technology is not enough. Most industrial systems failures have 'people' and managerial aspects as well. A highly skilled technologist without interpersonal and communication skills may be an inept internal consultant.

INSIGHT

SECONDMENT VS INTERNAL CONSULTANT

In this text, the role of the internal consultant is considered to be different to the role of an employee seconded into a project team. In the secondment situation, the person becomes a full member of the team (even if part time) and is expected to participate fully and be responsible for executive actions in the project plan.

Networking – relationship marketing in action

It is easy to collect vast numbers of cards at exhibitions and conferences. This is not successful networking. The first stage of successful networking is to understand your own objectives and use the concepts of segmentation and stakeholder analysis. It is important to understand that networking involves more than an exchange of addresses – computers can do this. There needs to be a relationship and that implies you must be sensitive to the other person's agenda and make the relationship work in both directions (win–win relationships). An analysis of the networks that a professional might wish to build could include:

- *Social* Meeting new people and making new friends, including social networks such as boat clubs and so on.
- *Customers* Use events such as exhibitions to strengthen network links with existing customers and develop new links with potential customers.
- *Suppliers* Good relationships with suppliers (e.g. printers, marketing agencies, etc.) are valuable and should be developed.
- *Competitors* The consultant should remain on good professional terms with competitors. You may be competing in the marketplace but in other areas you may collaborate (e.g. in staging continuing professional development events for consultants with the local branch of a professional society).
- *Local business community* Consultants should network to develop a range of contacts through the various types of associations that exist at local (e.g. local Chamber of Commerce) or national level as appropriate.
- *Professional* Good network relationships with other professionals are vital to the marketer. Topics such as 'project management' and 'time management' are of interest to many professionals and interesting local events are often hosted by professional groups such as the Institution of Engineering and Technology. Many institutes post their local diaries on their websites and most are very welcoming to guests from other institutes. E-mail contacts are usually given on the website to check that a meeting is open (guests welcome) or closed (strictly for members only).

Day-to-day events, such as meetings, provide a rich variety of networking opportunities. These opportunities should be exploited. However, your network plan above will imply the need to create new networking opportunities to extend your range and level of network contacts. Seek out new networking opportunities – the professional equivalent of speed dating. Events can include seminars, conferences, trade exhibitions, professional meetings and training courses (internal and external to the organisation).

Networking can be viewed as personal selling: you are the product and the outcome is a successful network relationship. Apply prospecting and evaluating routines,as stated above, your concern is with building up relevant contacts, not filling up a card index system. Apply the 80:20 rule, only a minority of people at the event are likely to be valuable networking contacts. Be selective: politely close and move on if it is clear this person is not likely to be a relevant member of your network. Prepare: many conferences will post the list of delegates on the conference website and this can help you identify key prospects before you arrive. Most conference organisers will ask participants to wear their name badges. If you do not spot a prime contact, remember many events will have a participant's message board where you can post a message requesting a meeting.

Networking is a lot less formal than a sales presentation, so the 'approach and presentation' is not so tightly structured. However, you should always introduce yourself briefly. The objective of the conversation is to explore if a network relationship is appropriate for both parties and then to start to establish this. Active listening is as important as talking in a productive conversation. Barriers to communication include:

- *Premature judgment* People can jump to conclusions without hearing the full story
- *Poor listening skills* If a message conflicts with what the hearer is expecting then selective listening may occur. After the discussion of a product with a customer, only the good comments may be remembered
- *Culture* Different cultures have different emphasis on forms of verbal and non-verbal communication
- *Filtering in transmission* It can appear to be an easy option to only communicate positive messages to avoid friction. Thus, a customer may comment on the positive aspects of a presentation. However, they may have sufficient reservations that they do not intend to buy, but do not communicate these to avoid an embarrassing situation

There are a number of strategies to help in ensuring clear, interpersonal communications. Take care to use appropriate language. If the person is not an expert do not use technical words. Try to give the context and complete information or the recipient may only get half the picture. In person-to-person contacts, take possession of your opinions. Say 'I think' rather than 'It is thought that'. Remember that your non-verbal communications will also help. Gestures and facial expressions are all part of person-to-person communications. Ensure that your actions reflect your statements. For instance, if you say you will follow up with an e-mail, ensure that is it is sent. Failure to do so is unprofessional and will damage credibility.

Good networkers develop the skills of remembering faces and names. Remember that people like to be treated as people. Closing the sale is the next step to establishing the network relationship. This may be a simple exchange of business cards (note for some national cultures this is a serious matter to be done with due dignity) or a diary appointment for a meeting and so on. Notes for follow-up can be made on the back of the card. Follow-up is important. Network relationships require maintenance; increasingly, this may be electronic. The objective is not to see how big a collection of business cards you can develop. You want quality network relationships. Part of the follow-up should be filing and indexing. Physical systems are on sale for this and can be seen on many executive desks. However, your contacts are too valuable to leave in the office; you want them with you 24/7/365. Good e-mail software systems (e.g. Outlook) will include an electronic diary. Card information should be added to this as part of the networking event follow-up.

The marketing-orientated CV

The CV is not a document to tell them everything about yourself. The purpose of the CV for a consultancy marketing package is to tell the truth well. The CV for a consultancy role is a significant marketing communications tool, advancing the message: 'I am the solution to your consultancy problems'. There is no single right way to write a CV, any more than there is one right way to word an advertisement. The right way is the one that gets you the interview and the contract. The view advanced here is that a similar approach should be taken with the CV as suggested for a press release. There is a debate as to how long a CV should be and some people assert that readers do not get past the first page. That is simply untrue. What is true is that if the reader does not become interested while scanning the first page, they are likely to move the CV into the reject tray. With the press release, a five-part structure was suggested: eye catching headline; attention grabbing first paragraph; well focused body; full contact information and supporting evidence.

A single template is not provided as different situations and contexts need varied responses. Whenever possible, the boilerplate basic CV should be customised for the given context. In personal selling, it is important to establish the buyer's needs and then use the sales dialogue to address those needs. For a fixed-term project contract, the employers' process follows the steps for recruitment given in Chapter 11, with a job description and a person specification. With a short-term consultancy project, with little interaction with the full-time employees, the process may not be so formal, but the principle remains the same. Understand what the buyer wants and then tell them the truth that you are the best person. Consultancy is a service so, rather than adopting a typical personnel and development view, this review is structured around the service-extended marketing mix. It is not suggested this is used to structure the CV; rather, it is a pre-writing research document if you are writing a new CV from scratch, or to be used to check all points are covered in your existing CV. It may also be used to identify points that may need to be customised for a given situation.

Product

The first stage is to analyse what the benefit need is. If the client or employer has provided a job description and person specification, the job is largely done. If such background is not provided, spend a few minutes considering what these might look like if they had been provided. The next stage is to see the fit with your profile. In terms of the marketing view of product, do you have the 'features' (qualifications, experience, etc.)?

Price

Check that the financial package is acceptable. Have you priced yourself appropriately? As mentioned earlier in this chapter, unless the work is subject to regular payment schedules (e.g. marking exam papers), you should find out what the acceptable 'going rate' is for your services and charge accordingly.

Distribution

Can you deliver to the working pattern required and has this been indicated in the CV or covering letter? Your potential clients will be looking for reassurance on this issue.

People

You are the person. How do you match up to the needs of the contract in terms of education, qualifications, additional languages spoken, training, transferable skills (e.g. project management), work experience and professional memberships? What have been your past achievements with other clients or employers? Remember hygiene factors, such as a clean driving licence: if they are missing, it may be easier for the client to reject your CV rather than to go back for clarification.

Physical evidence

For the successful CV, part of the overall process is maximising the production quality. If the CV contains errors and is badly formatted, this suggests the quality of your future work may be suspect. If the CV is submitted electronically, then the covering e-mail should be professional and free of grammatical errors. Text-speak is not acceptable here; this is an electronic cover letter. If the submission is in hard copy, use good-quality paper and a high-definition printer. Use a full-size (A4) envelope so that the documentation arrives unfolded. This is not only better looking but it makes your CV easier to copy if photocopying is necessary.

Process

Check the required details of the submission process, particularly if electronic submission is preferred. If you get too clever with the software usage, you can't be certain your CV will appear as you wished at the other end.

Promotion

This has been left to last. Before writing or updating the CV, the client organisation should be researched. Check their website. If it is permitted, engage in pre-submission discussions. Complete all the analysis and reviews suggested above. Then check that the CV is not only complete, attractively presented and easy to read, but is also comprehensive relative to all the issues that will be relevant to the client. Follow-up is essential, so ensure that you have 24/7 contactability (e.g. e-mail and voice-mail, and check these frequently).

Negotiations

A key aspect of consultancy and project management is to be able to negotiate with team members and with other project stakeholders. The issues might be major (the need to delay the launch because of major technical problems) or minor ('where shall we have the team away-day?'). Negotiations go through five stages:

1. context evaluation
2. preliminaries
3. negotiation
4. closing
5. follow-up

Evaluation of context

For major negotiations, this may involve a thorough review of the environment surrounding the issue. For an internal negotiation, it may involve consideration of the office politics, pressures on the individuals and their personalities (e.g. leadership style of a manager). The need is to evaluate the stakeholder expectations, objectives and agenda. This includes an objective analysis of your own situation and agenda.

Preliminaries

For a major programme of negotiation, this may involve fact-finding sessions and agreement of the negotiation process (e.g. scheduling negotiation meetings). For internal negotiations, the process may be much less formal, such as a brief e-mail: 'Smith is away for a month with a broken leg, we need to re-negotiate workload allocations. Can we meet tomorrow?'

The need is that there should be a shared, agreed understanding of ground rules and roles by all relevant stakeholders.

Negotiation

- *Exploration* The objective of this phase is not to negotiate. This phase is for the stakeholders to state their position and agenda. This stage is not about countering or bidding but parties seeking utmost clarity of the full range of relevant stakeholder issues.
- *Solutions* Here the relationship management (RM) and interpersonal issues are most important. If the stakeholders do not have trust, there will be a barrier to free exchange of ideas. One side may go for a killer-win strategy (which, in the long-run, normally results in a lose–lose situation). Good relationships come from building long-term relationships. Creative problem solving is needed.
- *Deal* Failure to maintain focus and clarity on detail is an area where negotiations may fail. Detailed bargaining and negotiation is needed to finally come to a solution that is fair and acceptable to both parties.
- *Bidding* This is the detailed bargaining discussed above. There may be several rounds of give-and-take in reaching the final settlement area.
- *Bargaining* This is the stage at which final agreement is reached. The bidding exploration might have taken place with a small working party. However, more senior executives may need to be involved in the final stages for a major issue.

Closing

Once the final framework is agreed, the outcome should be clearly stated and summarised. Both parties must clearly understand what is being agreed. In simple cases, the agreement may be confirmed in writing; for major contracts, a formal agreement may need to be drawn up and signed by all parties.

Follow-up

As always in business, evaluation and control must be exercised so follow-up activities are essential.

CONFRONTATION OR CO-OPERATION?

A food manufacturer in a specific region, far-distant from London, supplies a major supermarket distribution centre in the London area. Chilled transport delivers the processed foods to London and return empty to the regional factory. In the continual war on costs the supermarket is pressing to reduce its purchasing costs. A brief overview of the potential negotiations is given below.

Context evaluation

The need here is for both sides to appreciate the commercial imperatives in a harsh business environment. There are no second prizes; you have the contract or you do not. The 'thank you' letter for a nice presentation does not pay the rent.

The imperative for the supermarket is to obtain its products at the best possible price – if it does not, the one just down the road will. The imperative for the food manufacturer is to maintain margins.

Preliminaries

One of the criticisms of the Porter competition model is that it can suggest, to some strategists, that this is a simple 'win–lose' situation. In relationship marketing, a counterpoising view is advanced – that for long-term success, trust is needed to build up supply chain relationships to the benefit of all in the vertical industry value chain. The preliminaries here should reveal that the key issue is to reduce the supplier costs in some way, with the supermarket assisting in achieving these cost reductions. The focus should be: 'Let us lower costs and split the gains to both party's advantage'.

Negotiation

The preliminary exploration will state the supermarket's need for cost reduction and the supplier's need to maintain margins in the face of increasing energy costs.

A consultant is employed to consider some potential options. Only one solution is presented here: this is reduction in the cost of deliveries. Fifty per cent of the mileage clocked up by the regional food manufacturer's deliveries is wasted (returning empty vehicles to the regional factory). At the same time, transport delivering to the regional supermarket outlets would be returning to the London distribution centre empty. Wasted 'food miles' are of no use to either party.

The solution: use one vehicle to deliver the processed foods to the distribution centre and for the same vehicle then to take the mix of food products for delivery to the supermarket's outlets in the food manufacturer's region, thereby reducing costs, reducing food miles, reducing CO_2 emissions and creating a truly win–win situation.

The deal situation is just a little complicated. The supplier saves one journey but the supermarket not only saves the long-haul journey but a fair number of miles and time is involved in several drop-offs in the regions to the individual regional supermarkets. The gains for the two parties are not equally 100%. Detailed negotiation is needed to finally come to an outcome that is satisfactory to both parties.

Both sides may overbid somewhat and then to go though several rounds of give-and-take to reach a final settlement. Then the bargain can be struck and the proposed contract passed on for senior management agreement.

Closing

The new contract agreement should clearly state the rights and obligations of the parties including standards of service.

Follow-up

Both sides will want to know that the new system is operating as agreed. Are drops-offs to the supermarket's outlets being made to schedule? Are the drop-offs being assisted appropriately by the supermarket's staff so that the food manufacturer's driver time is not being wasted?

This consultant's solution has provided both parties with what they needed – namely, to be able to maintain margins. However, it has the added bonus of strengthening, in relationship marketing terms, the supplier–buyer value chain links.

Review

In this chapter, the differences between a normal management role and a consultancy role have been noted. The financial and physical issues in setting up a home office base have been presented. The consultant is in a service sector and the service-extended marketing mix for the consultancy role has been developed. Communications, negotiation and networking skills are important to a successful career in consultancy. Approaches to developing these skills have been outlined. The nature and role of the CV as part of the communications package for a consultant have been outlined.

Further reading

Cameron, S. (2005) *The Business Student's Handbook: Learning Skills for Study and Employment*, 3rd edn, FT-Prentice Hall.

Holtz, H. & and Zahn, D. (2004) *How to Succeed as an Independent Consultant*, 4th edn, John Wiley & Sons.

PART FOUR

Bringing it all Together

CHAPTER 14

New product development

Learning objectives

After studying this chapter you will be able to:

■ Describe the different types of new products and the stages of the new product development (NPD) process

■ Apply a number of different techniques for the collection and generation of new product ideas

■ Describe the different types of intellectual property and understand the value of intellectual property

■ Formulate appropriate approaches for new product development for different products and market situations

Introduction

Organisations need to innovate to survive. As existing products become obsolete, new products must be added to the portfolio. Not all new products are the same: Figure 14.1 shows the spectrum of new products. It is sometimes possible to simply reposition a product by changing other elements of the marketing mix and directing the effort to new market sectors. Minor incremental improvements can rejuvenate a product and extend its life.

New technologies can be applied to existing product types (e.g. more use of composites to replace metal in cars and aircraft). Developing technologies can be focused to create new products to meet benefit needs that were previously unmet. From time to time, totally new products burst onto the marketplace. Totally new product innovations can take some time to come to full potential. The internet would not be possible without the development of fibre optics and lasers which were 'blue sky' developments at first. The more innovative the product, the more likely that it will need more marketing support. For totally new products, customers need to be educated about the benefits of and how to use the product.

It has been said that invention and new product development is 1% inspiration and 99% perspiration. Just as great trees grow from small seeds, these sparks of inspiration have to be gathered and nurtured to provide a pool of concepts and innovative ideas. Figure 14.2 shows the stages of the new product development process.

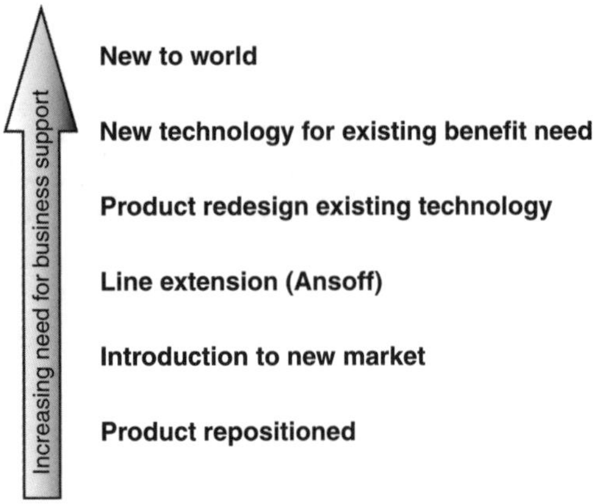

Figure 14.1 How 'new' is a product?

Generation and collection of concepts and new ideas

Some major advances appear to have been the result of lucky accidents (e.g. the discovery of penicillin). However, this is not entirely true. Happy accidents only happen to the inquisitive, imaginative and alert mind that can creatively interpret the implications. It would have been so easy to throw away that 'spoilt' culture. Major companies cannot just wait for happy accidents; they have to systematically explore various approaches to harvesting creative concepts.

Suppliers

In the B2B market, one source of competitive advantage is to provide superior technical service. Chip manufacturers design faster and more powerful graphics capabilities, which can then be exploited by games console manufacturers and software houses to produce more lifelike graphics for computer games. In developing countries, suppliers can be agents of technology transfer, providing design and training to grow new industries.

Competitors

One legitimate business strategy is to be a market follower. The art of innovation for this type of organisation is to copy technology, fast. In Chapter 9, the role of market intelligence in retro-engineering products was outlined. The distributor's own brands are largely 'me too' countertypes of the market leader's products.

Channels and customers

Channels are close to the ultimate consumers and can spot trends. Staying close to channels and agents can help in identifying changes in the marketplace needing product development. Customer complaints can be indicative of where product improvement is needed. In some cases, the customers are using the product in a way never intended by the NPD team. Exploration of this can lead to new product development.

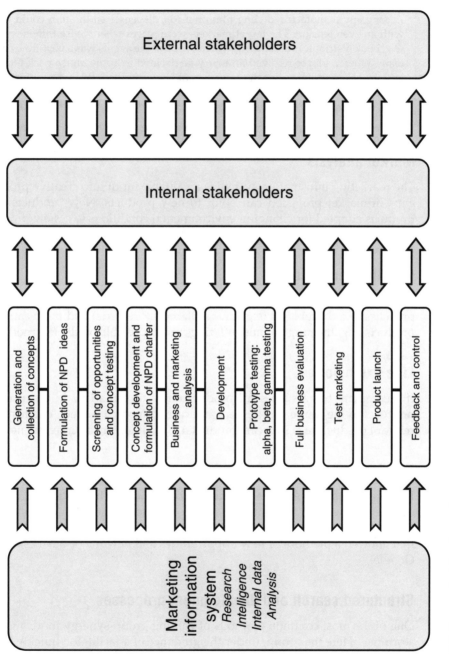

Figure 14.2 New product development process.

MICRO CASE STUDY

MEDICAL CLING FILM

A company manufactured cling film on a roll dispenser so the film could be applied easily with an even tension. The target markets were places where loose things were being packed (e.g. book distributors assembling orders). One of the agents was a part-time coach to a football team. When a player received an injury he decided to apply an ice pack to it with cling film and it worked well because the tension could be controlled. When this information came back to the parent company, they developed a new version of the product. They coloured it medical blue, registered the product as a medical device and promoted it to the sports market.

Market analysis

The marketing information system is a valuable input into creative processes. Identifying gaps in market provision can point to new products. New products can be created or products adapted for changing environmental conditions (e.g. new products aimed at the 'grey' pound as people live longer, have higher incomes and property values appreciate).

Enabling technologies

New materials and new technologies provide platforms for the development of new approaches to old problems (e.g. CDs replaced LP records) and the creation of entirely new products (e.g. the range of new offerings made possible by the internet).

Line extension

If a company has a successful product range, it can add additional related companion products to the range. In the personal care industry, cosmetic chemists will formulate a range of products (e.g. skin care products) to complement a successful new fragrance brand.

Problem solving

In solving an old problem, solutions can be found that have additional characteristics that can then allow the development of new applications. The internet was originally conceived as a solution to a military communications problem. It then was found to have characteristics that allowed a plethora of new opportunities and new major businesses grew from it (e.g. Google).

Structured search and development processes

One of the most common methods of gaining group synergy in idea generation is 'brain storming'. Here the group, under the guidance of a facilitator, quickly develop wild ideas with suspension of judgment. At a later stage a review of the wild ideas can point the way to innovative breakthroughs. Another approach is to review all the negative features of a product and see if re-engineering it could solve the deficiencies and move it into a new generation of products (e.g. appreciating that the QWERTY keyboard is not a totally efficient way of person–computer interaction gave birth to the mouse). The 'ideation' stimulation checklist throws a range of questions at the team to consider about the product. For instance 'Can the product be made smaller? (e.g. microelectronics), 'Can the time element be changed? (e.g. quick-drying ink). The key questions that can be asked are:

- Can the dimensions be changed?
- Can the quality be changed?
- Can the order be changed?
- Can the time element be changed?
- Can the effect be changed?
- Can there be a change of character?
- Can the form be changed?
- Can the state be changed?
- Can the use be adapted to a new market (Ansoff matrix application)?

Crawford & Di Benedetto (2006) provide an extensive review of the ideation stimulation checklist and other creative approaches. The full conduct of attribute analysis (Chapter 4) also provides insights to aid the development of new approaches (e.g. new features to support intangible benefits).

Creative inspiration

All of the above is not to suggest that there is not a place for pure creative genius. There is, but the great pressure for a continual stream of innovation demands that the structured approaches given above are needed to feed raw ideas into the innovation activity.

Formulation of new product ideas

The above activities, with a continual flow of information, feed ideas and concepts into the creative pool. The next stage is to build a bridge between the market benefit needs and the technological possibilities. The process of attribute analysis provides a framework to assist in this process. The golden rule is that there must be a cost-effective technical solution and there must be a genuine market need. Just because you **can** do does not imply that you **should** do. With a full outline definition of the product in both dimensions (benefit sets to consumer and technical approaches), the development team can take the concept into the screening process.

Ansoff analysis as a tool in structuring new product development

Ansoff is a model used for evolving strategy alternatives. It is often presented as a four-cell matrix (Figure 14.3a). This gives four strategies: market penetration, market development, product development and diversification. With market penetration, both the market and the products are known and this is the least risky strategy. With market development and product development one element is new and some increased risk is involved. With product diversification both the product and the market are new and this adds even more risk.

However, this form of the Ansoff matrix suggests a '0' or '1' type of situation. Either a product or market is old or new. The 2008 re-launch of the Ford 'Ka' involved some innovation but it was very different to launching the first commercial hydrogen car. The matrix is best

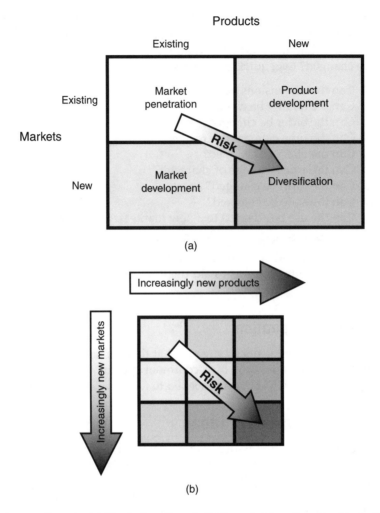

Figure 14.3 The Ansoff matrix. (a) Simple Ansoff matrix (b) Extended Ansoff matrix. Adapted from: Ansoff H. (1957) Strategies for Diversification, _Harvard Business Review_, 25 (5), September–October, pp. 113–24.

considered as a continuum of present products/markets to new products/markets to very different products/markets (Figure 14.3(b)).

The practical way to use the Ansoff matrix in new product development is to set up a matrix in a spreadsheet package (a schematic example is given in Figure 14.4). Potential new products/markets can be listed with a score indicating increasing newness (existing products/markets are assigned a score of zero). When the analysts think they have listed the potential new products and markets, the sort function can be used to arrange the new products/markets along two dimensions. The outcome can be reviewed and weightings changed after discussion. Then the real debate occurs. Each cell where the conjunction of product and market is viable indicates a new market opportunity. Used in this way the model becomes a powerful form of product/market analysis.

	Newness	Product A	Product B	Product C	Product D	Product E	Product F	Product G	Product H
Newness		0	0	0	0	1	2	3	4
Market A	0				■				
Market B	0						■		
Market C	0								■
Market D	0	■							
Market E	0								■
Market F	1					■			
Market G	2						■		
Market H	3								■
Market I	4		■						
Market J	5					■			
Market K	6							■	
Market L	7			■					

Figure 14.4 Schematic outline of Ansoff working spreadsheet.

However, some skill is needed to provide the appropriate input into the model. If a single product has two very different uses (i.e. satisfies two or more different benefit needs), then the separate benefit needs should be listed. The deceptively simple word 'market' hides complexity. The model is only fully effective if care is given to complete a full analysis to understand the market's segmentation structure(s). Moreover, the development of new ideas for products/markets is a creative process – there is no mathematical algorithm that provides the answer. The creative application of market and technical product knowledge is required. Overall, the usual result of this process is to create more business opportunities and a process is needed to pick out the best.

MICRO CASE STUDY   **ANSOFF ANALYSIS: 'MANE 'N' TAIL' HORSE SHAMPOO AND CONDITIONER**

Just as with new product ideas, the new product development manager must be alert to potential new markets. 'Mane 'n' tail' horse shampoo was formulated for horses. However, internet and word-of-mouth has also positioned it with some people as just the product for healthy hair on the basis that it is 'Not animal tested – it is animal proven'.

In the reverse direction, a whole range of human personal care products have been tailored for various pet needs. Pet personal care (e.g. shampoos) is a specialist but lucrative market. Pampered pets are profitable.

Screening of opportunities and concept testing

At this stage, the two issues above should be retested. Is there a real market need and will the technical approach yield a cost-effective product offering? However, a third aspect should be brought into the equation: the fit with the business mission, aims and objectives.

Products that might be viable but not fit with the overall business plans (e.g. taking the business into markets it does not want to enter or using technologies where the organisation does not have a competitive advantage) need not be wasted. Innovative ideas can be sold on to other organisations where there is a better business fit.

This preliminary screening process is possibly the most difficult NPD management area. At this stage there is limited information. It is easy to make type-one or type-two errors. There were some mainframe manufacturers who thought PCs were but a passing fad. It is all too easy to say 'That won't catch on!'. The second problem is developing products that fail to gain acceptance in the marketplace. New product development history is littered with the wreckage of failed projects. Both Concorde and the Channel Tunnel were brilliant feats of engineering but in commercial terms they were gaping money-hungry holes, never attaining profitable operation. Up front, realistic estimates must be made of costs and time scales. Good project management is needed at the start. It is not a fix when the budget and launch time are under pressure. More consideration of product selection with portfolio approaches is given in Chapter 16.

Concept development and formulation of the NPD charter

At this stage, the new product development project plan should be developed by considering more general business issues. Will new components or raw materials be needed? What will they cost and will they be available in sufficient quantities in good time for the launch? The Sony Playstation launch in 2007 was slowed down with supply problems affecting the new laser system. Full consideration should be given to the development of the full marketing mix, addressing the issues outlined in Chapters 4 to 8. All the key project stakeholders should be identified and plans and frameworks put in place to manage their contributions.

Business and marketing analysis

There is a problem with the two-dimensional representation of the NPD process. The process appears to be rather linear and orderly. In fact, there are many feedback and feed-forward loops with a continual flow of additional information needed from the marketing information system. As the product is being developed, parallel work needs to be undertaken on the development of the business and marketing plans. Where will the product be made? Will this need new equipment and investment? Are there partner organisations that need to be informed and relationships managed? The introduction of catalytic converters in cars would not have been possible without the concurrent development of non-poisoning grades of petrol. All the implications for the other elements of the marketing mix need to be considered and plans formulated. What field support might be needed for installation and/or maintenance? At this stage, the financial model should be refined and checks continually made to see that cost overruns do not occur.

Development

For formulated products such as foods, cosmetics, personal care and household products, test formulations will be evolved to perfect the optimal solution. Parallel processes take place in other types of products (e.g. computers, cars, home entertainment, etc.). The detail of each project is specific to the mix of technologies that are needed and outside the scope of this book. However, appropriate testing of the product is key.

Alpha, beta and gamma testing

The 'α' test is: 'Does the product work in the laboratory?' Great care will be taken in the laboratory to ensure that tests are reproducible and conditions are ideal. This might not be the case with the consumers' in-use situation. Therefore, 'β' tests need to be conducted to ensure the product will perform and survive in the real in-use environment (e.g. drop tests for mobile telephones to ensure that they have reasonable resistance to accidental damage). The final aspect is the 'γ' test: 'Does the product really do what the consumer wants and provide real benefits?'

MICRO CASE STUDY

PERSIL POWER

In 1994, Unilever launched Persil Power. To obtain whiter effects, detergents incorporated bleaches to deal with stains and discoloration of fabrics. However, these were only effective at elevated temperatures whereas the trend was for washing at lower temperatures to be less harsh on the fabrics and to conserve electrical energy, a major element of running costs. The solution was to incorporate a bleach activator, which would work with the bleaching ingredient, to provide the desired effects at lower temperatures. However, under certain conditions of use, the product was so effective that it not only washed the clothes but also destroyed them. Unilever's archrivals, Procter & Gamble, were able to show two halves of a garment washed in the competing products. The damage was self-evident. Persil were forced to withdraw the product and lost market share. Product testing had not highlighted a beta problem that was only discovered after the product had been fully launched. Total costs of the problem, including lost market share, were estimated to be in excess of £100 million.

Over a decade later, it is interesting that the market has moved on into new areas – colour care and easy iron are the contemporary platforms.

This need for rigorous testing often involves the technologist devising laboratory-based in-use simulations of how the product will be used by the consumer. Sometimes the results can be evaluated by instrumental means (e.g. stain removal in testing a detergent system). In other cases, the results are more subjective (e.g. taste and texture of a food product or the smell and softness of a fabric after a wash cycle). Here, the use of trained panels may be required to develop the product. In the final stages of product development, additional panel testing to select the best product for the market may be needed.

In all stages, care will have been taken to ensure the safety and legal conformance of the product. At this stage, final tests (e.g. EMC for electrical products; stability test for formulated products) must be made and all the relevant information collected for hazard assessments and quality assurance needs (e.g. labelling requirements and hazard warnings).

PRODUCT TESTING

Product testing can be objective or subjective. The colour of a product or the intensity of its odour are objective tests. Colours can be ranked according to intensity of the hue. If possible, instrumental methods should be devised for such testing. Colour matching of products is now largely an instrumental process. However, odour is more difficult to instrument and here well-trained panels are still the order of the day. Such panel testing is costly (highly trained staff time is expensive) and takes time and effort to organise and conduct. The selection, training and motivation of panels are significant overheads.

A more difficult problem area is subjective odour assessments, where the question is entirely subjective (e.g. which sample smells fresher?) Skilled panels are more consistent but become 'house trained' and fall into 'company group-think', which makes them less representative of the real consumers. The use of semi-trained panels (non-technical staff taken from commercial departments with no technical connection to the project) can provide a partial solution. Full consumer testing is better but is slow and expensive to administer. In addition, because the participants are less well trained (i.e. produce more variable results), a larger panel is often needed. Tests can be undertaken *in vitro* or *in vivo*. For instance the testing of a hair conditioner can be undertaken on standardised hair swatches. Final benchmark testing against the action standard can be undertaken with half-head tests on volunteers (half the head is treated with the test preparation; the other half with the action standard).

There is no point in designing performance into a product unless you have a test procedure to evaluate the success (or the lack of it). Good quality laboratory facilities are required to simulate the in-use situations and provide acceptable conditions for assessments. For odour assessments, this requires temperature and humidity control and minimal background odours (e.g. care should be taken to avoid porous surfaces where odours can linger and provide cross-contamination between tests).

There is interaction between our senses and appearance can affect flavour perception. Wine tasters with white wine tend to use 'white fruit' descriptions such as gooseberry. Given the same wine with a tasteless and odourless red dye and the descriptions tend to come out with red fruit descriptors such as blackberry and plum. It is not that the people are not skilled. In *nouvelle cuisine*, the food should look as good as it tastes. People perceive patterns and we use all our senses to build a picture. The formulation scientist uses this in building the range of signal attributes into a product. However, the same effects can cause problems during the development phase. In the case of food tasting, one partial solution is to conduct the tasting under monochromatic light (e.g. sodium light) so that colour differences may not be perceived.

The analysis of sensory tests needs some degree of skill (additional reading references are given at the end of this chapter). Many sensory experiences – e.g. perception of sound, perception of odour or flavour intensity – are non-linear. Moreover, different subjects may have different sensitivities (e.g. people become less able to hear higher sound frequencies as they grow older).

This insight has been written in the context of sensory tests but the principle remains the same for other situations; it is only the technologies that differ. In devising tests to monitor performance of air bags and seat belts, test rigs have been built and sophisticated test dummies evolved to provide vital data for product improvement. At the time the engineer or technologist is designing performance into a product, consideration should be given to how performance can be evaluated. As always in technology, to manage you first have to measure.

Full business evaluation

Pilot production provides good, firm estimates for costs. The marketing mix approaches have been investigated. Consumer trials have proved the acceptability of the product. Now is the time to firm-up the outline plan into the full launch with cash flow projections. All the detail of the launch must be considered, from the development of the advertising copy to the training of the field staff. However, will it work?

Test marketing

The advantage of test marketing is that it gives the firm an opportunity to test the mix and estimate the likely success of the launch. The disadvantage is that it takes time and delays the launch, increasing the time to market. Moreover, it showcases the firm's intentions, giving weeks of notice for the competitors to consider their responses.

Care must be taken to select a suitable test market area. The town should be fairly representative of the overall market it is intended to test. Slightly isolated cities, such as Plymouth in the UK, are useful. There are problems if people outside the test area buy the product because this gives a false result. The full mix should be tested, including TV if it is to be used in the full launch. (If you live in one of these test market areas, you can tell when this is happening because the advertisement will state: 'Only available in xxxxx'.)

Product launch

When all the planning is completed, the advertisements should be booked, the creative work finalised and stocks built up in the channels. As with the completion of most projects, there must be meticulous attention to detail. The big picture is fine but just one small oversight can cause major problems.

Feedback and control

The only certain thing about a launch plan is it will need some modification. Estimation of market size is not a precise science and anticipating the competition's response is problematic. The marketing information system should be used to track the progress of the launch. Some contingency needs to be built into the plan. If sales are 20% greater than predicted, can the additional product be manufactured?

The management of intellectual property

Great care must be taken in the research and development process to protect the intellectual property developed. Necessary evidence of invention must be collected to support patent applications. Commercial secrecy is not only important to prevent signalling developments to the competition but also as inappropriate disclosure may invalidate a later patent application (the information having been put into the public domain then becomes part of the 'prior art' and is no longer patentable). When working in collaboration with suppliers, this becomes even more important and there should be a clear understanding about the ownership of any jointly developed intellectual property.

In the information age much of the value of the organisation does not exist in physical things but in intellectual property rights. J.K. Rowling owns nothing but the intellectual property rights to the 'Harry Potter' series, yet this has made her one of the richest women in the UK. Google and Microsoft's business value is not in their buildings but in their software rights. A jeweller keeps gemstones in a safe. Intellectual property is the modern gemstone of the service-industry age. Just as much care should be taken in the management and protection of intellectual property as with physical assets. Table 14.1 provides an overview of intellectual property.

If a person takes money from a company by fraud, a criminal act has been committed. If there is obvious 'passing off' with the intent to deceive customers, then trading standards officers may intervene. However, issues such as patent and trademark infringement are

Table 14.1   Types of intellectual property

Type of intellectual property	Comments
Patents	Must be a novel, non-obvious invention that has not been disclosed (reported or patented) in the past. To gain a patent, the nature of the invention has to be disclosed in the patent. Patents are issued on a regional basis and a European company wanting protection in USA, China, India, etc. will have to file applications in all the areas where cover is required. This process is expensive. Patents have a defined period of validity and may not be extended. Once the patent has expired the competition have full right to make use of the invention
Trademarks	Any sign capable of being represented graphically that is capable of distinguishing goods or services of one undertaking from those of other undertakings. More recent legislation can allow packaging to be registered (e.g. the classic Coke bottle). Registration is required and, again, multiple registrations are needed for worldwide cover. Trademark protection, unlike patents, can be extended
Brands	Brand names are intellectual property
Registered designs	A problem occurs in areas such as fabric design, which may not be patented. This provides some protection
Design right	This does not require registration and runs along the lines of copyright
Copyright	Copyright is automatic and covers original literary, dramatic, musical and artistic work. Importantly it also includes sound recordings, films, etc. A major area is computer software. Copyright infringement has to be enforced through civil action and that can be costly. A key issue is for people in employment. Many contracts will involve the employer having rights over intellectual property developed during the period of employment. In working with agencies (e.g. creative advertising agencies), contracts should clearly state who owns the resulting intellectual property generated (e.g. advertising images and text copy)

often rather technical. Here, the remedy is in civil law and the firm is out on its own with no state support. The company in effect has to police its intellectual property rights. One reason to retro-engineer competitors' products is to check that they have not infringed the firm's own patents. Part of the MkIS activity in companies with intellectual property rights is to monitor the global environment for infringement of those rights. Intellectual property rights disputes can be vastly expensive in terms of legal costs. Good specialist advice from experts is advised at all key stages (e.g. use of good patent agents familiar with the firm's technology).

MICRO CASE STUDY   **THE LIGHTING MARKET**

This case study has not been titled 'Create the perfect light bulb'. New technologies are emerging, such as LEDs, which may give us new options paralleled in the past with fluorescent technologies. Lighting has become one of the hot beds of environmental concern. The vast majority of electrical energy consumed by a traditional tungsten coil bulb is wasted as heat. The conversion of all such bulbs to low energy would save a significant proportion of total electricity usage. The two pillars of NPD development are explored here: (1) What is the state of the market? (2) What are the available and developing technologies? No final solution is proposed, as the products have yet to be invented. This is work in progress.

Brief historical introduction
The campfire might have been adequate for cave dwellers but more advanced peoples needed something better. Candles and lamps provided an effective solution. A key part of the systems was in wick technology. The wick of a modern candle slightly curves as the wax burns down exposing more wick. When the wick curves enough to reach the edge of the flame it burns away. Candles thus have self-trimming wicks. If this did not happen, the wick would get longer and the flame bigger. One of the original reasons for piping town gas (made from coal in the nineteenth century) to houses was to provide gaslight. This was originally with just a 'bats wing' burner but later with much more efficient incandescent mantles. This, in effect, was material made very hot by the flame and one way of defining the electric bulb is to say we have replaced gas with electricity for making things hot. In theatres, much more intense light was needed and rather dangerous systems were devised to produce 'lime light'.

Selected segmentation variables for lighting
Intensity of light required In domestic situations, relatively modest. For other purposes (e.g. film/TV studios, floodlighting, vehicle headlights) high-intensity light is needed.
Colour of light required It may not be of major importance (e.g. sodium light acceptable to road lighting situation); it may be not too distracting (e.g. normal domestic lighting, where some deviation from 'natural' is tolerated); critical (e.g. for artwork and laboratories describing colour and appearance, where 'natural daylight' bulbs are required); special colour effects (TV screens, video projectors, neon advertisements, traffic signals, warning lights, etc.).
Environmental conditions Normal domestic. Exposed to the elements (street lighting, flood lights, etc.). Immersion (e.g. remote controlled submarines). Dangerous environments (e.g. potentially explosive environments such as mines, oil rigs and chemical plants).
Speed of start up Extremely fast (e.g. laser for optic communication). Fraction of a second (e.g. normal domestic tungsten light). Some seconds can be tolerated (e.g. sodium street lights).

Control Remote control (e.g. photo-cell control for street lighting, whereas in the early twentieth century, clocks were used because cost-effective technology did not exist). Simple on/off switch (normal domestic use). Variable intensity (e.g. lecture theatre).

Power supply Low voltage (e.g. car headlights). Normal mains AC voltage (domestic lighting). Uninterruptible supply required (e.g. emergency lighting in public buildings).

Type of fitting Existing (screw, bayonet, etc.). New build, where new fittings could be devised.

Aesthetic issues Floodlights for a football ground are designed more for function than style. Lighting for the home must look good as well as perform.

Developing technologies

These include better construction of fluorescent technologies to make smaller and more attractive low-energy bulbs and new technologies such as LEDs.

There are also companion technologies. Efficiencies could come from increased use 'environmental power scavenging' technologies to make power sources independent of the mains supply (e.g. garden lights powered by photo-cells, sailing boats' electronics powered with photocell and micro wind generation).

Review

The approach is to scan the environment for the market segment under consideration and then, using the concepts of the ultimate product, draw up the perfect product characteristics (the marketing leg of NPD). Then the creative process of scanning the existing and developing technologies can be applied. The aim is to develop a new synthesis; to make a product as close to the dream product as economics and technology allows. Intimate knowledge of the customers' use of the product is needed concurrently with expert knowledge of the technologies needed to realise the near-dream product.

Review

In this chapter, the different types of new products have been presented. New-to-the-world products need much more support than more modest product repositionings. The new product process is not a simple linear process. However, there are distinct activities (e.g. structured collection and generation of new product ideas). These elements have been identified and a range of approaches suggested that can be applied to a variety of new product development situations. The process of new product development is a considerable investment. The nature of intellectual property has been described and the need for its protection explained. The need for feedback systems has been emphasised and some issues in evaluating the performance new products considered (e.g. α, β and γ testing approaches).

Further reading

BS 7667: Part 1 (1993) *Assessors for Sensory Analysis: Part 1 Guide to the Selection, Training and Monitoring of Selected Assessors*, British Standards Institution.

Crawford, M. & Di Benedetto, A. (2006) *New Products Management*, 8th edn, McGraw-Hill.

Curtis, T. & Williams, D. (2001) *An introduction to Perfumery*, 2nd edn, Micelle Press.

IFSCC Monograph Number 1 (1978) *Principles of Product Evaluation: Objective Sensory Methods*, Micelle Press.

Trott, P. (2002), *Innovation Management and New Product Development*, 2nd edn, FT-Prentice Hall.

CHAPTER 15

Market driven quality

Learning objectives

After studying this chapter you will be able to:

▪ Define the concept of market driven quality and describe a range of tools used in market driven quality management
▪ Explain the differences in delivering service quality programmes and outline the five-gap approach to service quality
▪ Outline the structure of the European Foundation for Quality Management (EFQM) model and explain how this differs from the ISO 9000 series.
▪ Review the major points to be considered in a quality assurance disaster plan, including product recall

Introduction

Quality is central to customer satisfaction. Commitment to quality should not be seen as an expense, but more as part of the investment in customer satisfaction. Not a year goes by without a major quality scare. A mishandled quality situation can do long-term damage to a brand. In the mid-twentieth century, much of the treatment of quality management centred on acceptable defect levels and sampling strategies. With automated production, in-line test equipment and six-sigma policies, zero-defect levels are the objective, with customer satisfaction the aim. 'Conformance' is not so much the game as 'customer satisfaction'. Quality control can be said to be about conformance and is still needed as part of quality assurance and total quality management where a holistic view is taken of quality. Quality may be defined as:

> Quality is the fitness for the intended purpose of customers and users, subject to the legitimate expectations of other relevant quality stakeholders.

The implication of this definition is far-reaching. The span of interest of a quality assurance manager is the whole value chain of the organisation, with consideration of all the players in the supply and distribution chains, customers, users and the satisfaction of other relevant quality stakeholders (e.g. consumer pressure groups, industry regulators, etc.).

INFORMAL DEFINITION OF MARKET DRIVEN QUALITY

An effective market driven company makes and sells products that do not come back, to customers who do come back.

Using the Plymouth model of 'product' (Chapter 4), the key characteristics of performance and features can be developed. For each parameter a specification must be developed. In consumer goods an important part of the labelling is the bar code. Under certain conditions the actual final printed bar element can thicken. If the bar elements thicken up too much, the bar code becomes unreadable. This slows the checkout process because the code then has to be manually keyed into the till. All the key quality characteristics must be specified and methods of measurement or assessment devised.

The quality stakeholders should be identified and an audit conducted to check that the product and its quality specification are appropriate to their demands. An increasingly important issue is the history of the product. Some products (e.g. wine or olive oil) are perceived to be of higher value if they come from a specific, favoured location. In the supply chain, an unscrupulous person can make large sums of money by adulterating a high-value oil or substituting an oil from another location. Corn-fed chicken and free-range organic eggs command a premium price. Fair trade and organic do not provide physical 'tell tale' signs in a product. Passing off farmed salmon as wild salmon is potentially profitable. Shoplifting is not the only type of illegal activity that a retailer must guard against. In some cases, there is no physical process of testing or analysis that can provide protection against abuse (e.g. guaranteeing accordance with fair trade employment policies). Here, consumers must rely on certification and audit along the supply chain. This is not fully satisfactory and, wherever feasible, comprehensive methods of detection should be developed. At this level, quality control becomes almost forensic in its application. Indeed, in some cases, very similar approaches are used. For instance, genetic profiling and isotope ratios can be used in quality control; techniques also used in forensic science.

Quality assurance is an important aspect of the technical marketing manager's role. The specification forms part of the contract of sale; it defines the acceptable quality between the supplier and the buyer. Additional quality demands imply additional costs and these must be recovered in the price charged to the buyer. Moreover, the technical marketing manager must understand soft issues of quality assurance (e.g. technical advice) and the hard aspects in defining methods of testing to measure parameters that form part of the product specification and, hence, part of the terms and conditions in the sales contract between seller and buyer.

The tools of total quality management (TQM)

The precise methods of testing and measurement depend on the industries involved – food is different to electronics in test procedures. For specific approaches to given test or measurement problems, reference should be made to specialist texts. However, there are some generic issues that apply to the management of quality across all businesses and disciplines.

Statistical process control

A general problem is the dispensing of product in a filling line. It is illegal to sell underweight/under volume products. In the pharmaceutical industry, too large a dose could be dangerous. In short, the filling process needs to be under complete control. Before in-line testing procedures (e.g. for product weight) became feasible, sample packs would be taken from the production line and the quantity filled measured. This took time and considerable 'off-standard' packs could have been produced before deviation in the filling process was detected.

In an ideal world, what is required is 100% testing – which is now often possible with new technologies that can be applied on the production line – with a degree of accuracy and reproducibility that is significantly less than the tolerance limit for the finished product. With that in place, corrective action can be taken before a defective product makes it off the production line. The normal rules of control apply. A system is needed that provides an alarm when there is a real problem, but does not flag up alarms when there is no problem. Control charts are one approach and these can be computerised. Two common versions are Shewhart charts and Cu-Sum charts.

With a Shewhart chart, the inherent variability of the process and test procedure is estimated (i.e. the standard deviation, σ, of the process calculated). The measurements are plotted in terms of their deviation from the desired target standard. Two sets of lines are drawn. The two lines at plus-or-minus two standard deviations are known as warning limits and the two lines at plus-or-minus three standard deviations are known as action limits. If the standard deviation of the process and its measurement is significantly less than the tolerance limits, then deviations can be picked up before defect products are produced. A schematic outline of a Shewhart chart is given in Figure 15.1. Additional comments on Shewhart chart characteristics are given in the 'insight' panel below.

In a Cu-Sum, chart the cumulative sum (hence, Cu-Sum) of the differences from the set point are plotted. When the process is running at around the set point, then the long-run average of the Cu-Sum will be zero. The Cu-Sum line runs horizontally with some slight statistical noise around zero. If the process starts to run above the set point, the line starts to rise. If the process starts to run below the set point, the line will drop. The slope is a measure of the amount of the deviation from the set point.

The Shewhart action and warning lines are replaced by a so-called 'V-mask' etched into transparent plastic. The front of the V-mask is placed on the latest observation plotted. If the Cu-Sum plot touches or runs outside the V-mask, then an action is signalled. The method and calculations for the V-mask are given in British Standard 5703. A schematic outline of a Cu-Sum chart is given in Figure 15.2. The slope of the line provides a measure of the degree of drift from the set point in terms of standard deviations.

These two methods provide approaches that are not only statistically rigorous, but, given the simple nature of the charts, can also be easily understood by operators who are not mathematically literate.

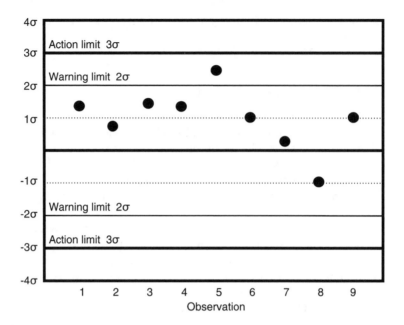

Figure 15.1 Shewhart chart.

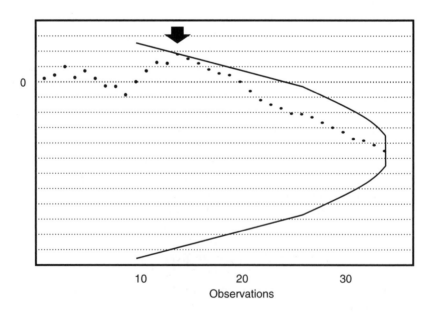

Figure 15.2 Cu-Sum chart.

THE OPERATING CHARACTERISTIC CURVE

In some circumstances, total sampling is not feasible and/or not economically justifiable (e.g. with the delivery of raw materials in drums). In these situations, classical quality assurance theory focuses on the sampling strategy. A simple, robust strategy is to sample the square root of the number of objects, rounded upwards.

In classical theory, an acceptable percentage of defective items is set as part of the quality specification. For example, a 2% defective rate might be set as acceptable. If there is no sampling, there is 0% chance of detecting the 2% defective items in the batch. If there is 100% sampling, there is 100% chance of detecting the 2% defective items in the batch. Between these two extremes, there is a variation in the probability. This is often referred to as the operating characteristic curve. The producer's risk is the risk of a 'type-one error' (rejection of the null hypothesis when it is true, called alpha-risk). That is, the rejection of a batch when the percentage of defective items is within the specification limits. The buyer's risk is the risk of a 'type-two error' (acceptance of the null hypothesis when it is untrue, sometimes called beta-risk). That is, the acceptance of a batch when the percentage of defective items is outside the specification percentage defective limit. Figure 15.3 shows a schematic operating characteristic curve.

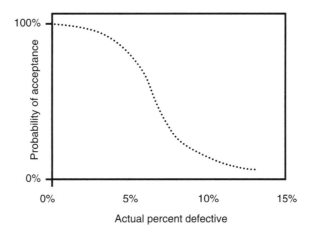

Figure 15.3 Generalised operating characteristic curve showing level of risk.

Details on calculating these curves for various lot sizes, percent defective and sampling strategies are given in the further reading sources at the end of this chapter. These references also give details for constructing 'V-masks' (Cu-Sum charts) and action limits (Shewhart charts) to give appropriate operating characteristic curves for different quality situations.

Fishbone approach

This is a particular form of the 'what and why?' approach. It is a graphical representation of a structured process to set out the factors and sub-factors that contribute to the potential quality outcome. Figure 15.4 shows an Isikawa or fishbone diagram for a technical course at a university.

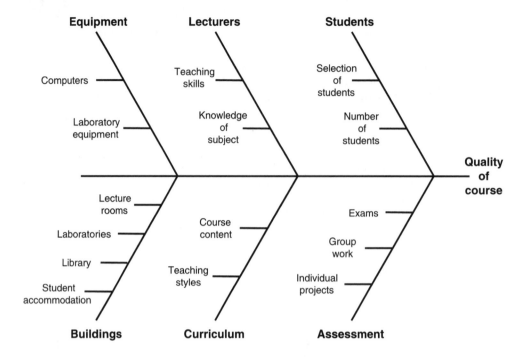

Figure 15.4 Adapted Isikawa or fishbone diagram for a technical course. Adapted from: Curtis, T., *Business and Marketing for Engineers and Scientists* p.156, McGraw-Hill, 1994. © Tony Curtis. Reproduced by permission.

The quality of the course could be affected by the quality of students, lecturers, equipment, buildings, curriculum and assessment processes. For lecturers, the sub-elements may be teaching skills and knowledge of the technical specialism they are teaching. The value of the process is that it is simple and communicates to a range of people in the team, yet it is rigorous if applied with care.

Continuous quality improvement

Deming's 'quality wheel' takes the view that the improvement of quality is a continuous process, with continual efforts needed to incrementally improve quality. The four stages of the Deming wheel are plan, do, verify and measure.

- *Plan* Plan what are the next actions for the next stage of quality improvement.
- *Do* Implement the actions that have been planned.
- *Verify* This is the first part of the feedback and control system: check that all the actions have been implemented.
- *Measure* This is the second part of feedback and control. Now the actions have been fully implemented, what are the measurable outputs in quality improvements?
- *Plan* Go round the cycle again.

The Deming cycle is shown in Figure 15.5.

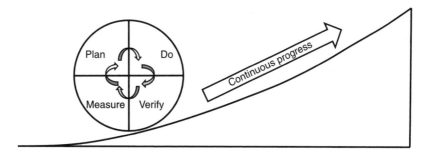

Figure 15.5 Deming cycle.

Kaizen is another approach to continuous quality improvement. In the *Kaizen* approach, the search is not for the next big quality breakthrough, but the continual search by all involved in the business for incremental quality improvement. Although the contribution of each individual action may be modest, the total effect over a period of time can be dramatic and transformational.

A key aspect of many of these approaches to total quality management is the involvement of all people in the organisation. Errors in order input can be just as big a quality issue as defects in production (perfect production of the wrong product).

Pareto analysis – the 80:20 rule

This rule may be expressed as: 'The majority of problems are caused by a minority of potential sources'. For example, 80% of defective deliveries come from 20% of suppliers, 80% of complaints come from 20% of customers, etc. The implication is that a greater proportion of management action should be focused on the 20% that causes 80% of the problems. Figure 15.6 shows a schematic Pareto analysis.

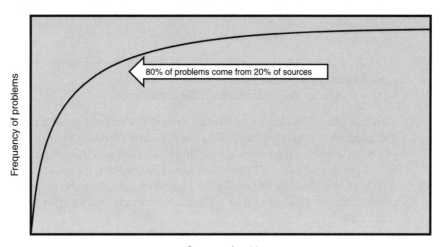

Figure 15.6 Schematic Pareto distribution.

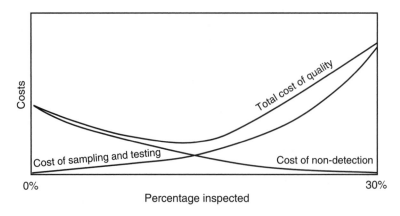

Figure 15.7 Cost of quality.

Cost of quality and PONC

At times in business it is difficult to estimate the cost of doing something. Sometimes the solution is to ask the question in the negative: what is the cost of not doing something? One input in the financial consideration of quality management is estimating the price of non-conformance (PONC) – i.e. the cost of poor quality. Some aspects of this are relatively easy (e.g. estimating the loss of raw materials and the costs of re-working defective product). More difficult are the soft issues, such as the damage to brand value from a quality failure (e.g. in the case of Cadbury when microbiological contamination of chocolate resulted in a product recall).

The cost of perfect quality is infinite. Just as with service quality and optimal stock control, there is a balance to be chosen between the costs of quality programmes and the costs of non-conformance (Figure 15.7). The concept is simple but the application is difficult. As noted, a major problem is the estimation of 'soft' costs of product failure (damage to brand value). This involves two difficult estimates:

- an estimate of the cost of a quality failure in the marketplace (e.g. product recall costs and damage to brand value)
- an estimate of the probability of the occurrence

In traditional stock control theory, the set-up time/costs of a product change-over were accepted as a given input. With a just-in-time philosophy, management attention is directed to lowering the set-up costs/times. The same is true of quality control. In traditional twentieth-century quality control theory, 100% testing (often with destructive testing methods) was an economic impossibility. However, continual developments in sensors and data processing are making in-line 100% non-destructive testing increasingly possible at economic cost.

The cost-effective management of quality needs hard technical skills (e.g. the development of highly accurate, low-cost, automated in-line testing with 100% sampling) and soft skills (e.g. the ability to estimate the costs and probability of product failure). Some of the theories of quality were developed in military procurement, with military specifications for NATO customers. BS 5750 was developed for the commercial sector. BS 5750 became the ISO 9000 series. However, much of the focus and concentration was on physical products. In the commercial world today, services are at least as important as physical products and methods that are simple to apply to nuts and bolts are not applicable to service. This is because of the intangible nature of services. Customer perceptions of service quality necessitate a different approach.

Service quality

It is easy to measure the amount of food in a pack or the thickness of paint on a car. It may take some ingenuity, but assessing the quality of a product is about measurement and evaluation. The perceived quality of a service involves intangibles and a different approach is needed. A model for this has been developed by Parsuraman, Zeithami and Berry (1988): the SERVQUAL model. As a result of their research, they propose that there are five potential gaps between what is intended and what is actually delivered and perceived. The five gaps are shown in Figure 15.8.

Gap 1 This is the gap between what the organisation considers should be the service (the intended service) and what the customers want. In Chapter 14, the concept of α ('does it work in the laboratory, does it do what is intended?'), β ('does it work in the customer's situation?'), γ ('does it do what the customer wants?') testing was

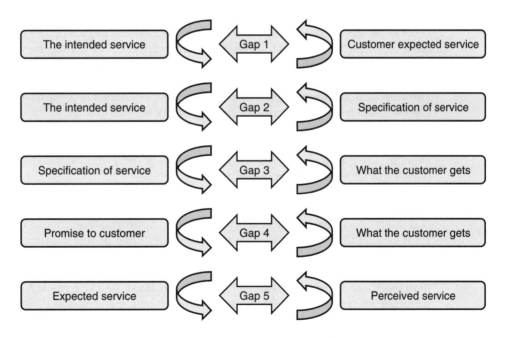

Figure 15.8 SERVQUAL gaps. Adapted from: Parasuraman, A., Zeithaml, V. & Berry, L., SERVQUAL: A Multiple-Item Scale for Measuring Consumer Perceptions of Service Quality, *Journal of Retailing*, 64 (1), 12–40.

presented. The issue here is the same as in new product development: the team developing and managing the product or service must be close to their customers.

Gap 2 This is the gap between the intended service and what is actually specified. In common language, this is one of the universal laws of life, the law of unintended consequences. As services are intangible, it is often difficult to find appropriate metrics. The temptation is to specify what can be measured and this need not necessarily correlate with what is intended. The problem is then similar to that encountered in computer programming: the computer will do what you tell it to do, but it is easy whilst writing the code to make a small error so that what actually happens is not what was wanted.

Gap 3 This is the gap between the specification and what is actually delivered. If the logistics are inferior and the staff training poor, the actual delivery is not likely to hit specification levels. Targets are fine but they must be realistic and the staff empowered to be able to achieve them.

Gap 4 This is the gap between the promise communicated to the customer and what the customer actually gets. Is what you see what you get? The picture of the hotel in the advertisement looks fine, but it said nothing about the eight-lane motorway running alongside the hotel or mention it was under the flight path to the local airport. Overselling the service will only end in customer disappointment.

Gap 5 Here, the gap is between what the customer expected and the customer's perceptions of what was delivered. Customers want to be surprised and delighted. However, in too many cases, expectations are not met and the customer is disappointed.

The first stage in the delivering service quality is to recognise that these gaps can exist. It takes good, open management and a sound MkIS system to pick up the gaps and recognise the issues. The final stage is to close the gap with appropriate management action. Research into this area has identified five dimensions that are important in the customer's perception and evaluation of service quality. These are: tangibles, reliability, responsiveness, assurance and empathy. The service-extended marketing mix (Chapter 8) is the tool that management can use to address these customer perceptions of service quality.

Tangibles are one element of the service extension of the marketing mix that is specifically aimed at this dimension of customer-service perceptions: physical evidence. The three key elements are physical environment, tangible clues and facilitating goods. Full coverage of these mix elements is given in Chapter 8.

A one-hour delay can cost days if that international flight is lost. In Europe, we expect 100% service in areas such as utility services (gas, electricity, water, communications, etc.). Reliability is a hygiene factor. People expect the appropriate service to be delivered at the right time. If this does not happen (a gap 5 issue), then people are unhappy and they tell other customers and potential customers.

Services are more complex than products. Accidents and breakdowns are not pre-planned. Each incident is a one-off and well-trained staff are needed to provide an appropriate response. Often the perception of the responsiveness is down to the front-line staff in customer contact. This has an implication for management policy: not only must staff be well trained, they must also have the resources and discretion to take effective action.

DISRUPTION OF SERVICE

Accidents and extreme weather conditions can cause cancellations, delays and disruption in travel networks. In the 2007 UK floods, only a very restricted number of trains ran from London Paddington to the West Country on a holiday weekend. The train manager could not change the weather but the train was declassified, making it single class. The empty first-class seats were occupied by standard class passengers, easing the overcrowding. The manager had reacted with an effective response.

Often services can be disrupted by forces outside the control of the service provider. Customers can understand this and, in general, will be more forgiving so long as the service provider keeps them informed and appears to be taking responsive action. Such disruptions are stressful to the customers and if they are not kept informed and responsive actions are not taken, considerable damage is done to the reputation of the service provider.

Beyond ISO 9000

ISO 9001 (the most complete version of the ISO 9000 series) covers the whole cycle of new product development and manufacturing (thus also covering supply chain issues). Major sections in the standard include management responsibility, quality systems, contract review, design control, document control, purchasing, purchased products, traceability, process control, inspection and testing, inspection equipment (including measuring and test equipment), inspection status, control of non-conforming products, corrective action, outbound logistics (including handling, packaging, storage and delivery), quality records, quality audit procedures, training, servicing and statistical techniques. The European Foundation for Quality Management (EFQM) quality model takes this further with a division between 'enablers' and 'results'. In simplistic terms, ISO 9000 covers the 'enablers', but does not provide as much coverage of the customer-orientated aspects of 'results'. Some progressive companies are building on ISO 9000 and reaching for the higher levels of customer satisfaction that the European Foundation for Quality Management focuses on. The components of the EFQM model are given in Table 15.1.

Negative distribution – the product recall plan

In Chapter 6, the issue of having a negative distribution system was considered in the context of recycling of products. In the quality assurance disaster plan, there needs to be provision for a product recall. This will involve informing the ultimate customers and users by mass advertising and having arrangements for the return of defective goods via the distributors or direct to the company. In 2007, major product recalls ranged from laptop batteries to contaminated food products.

Table 15.1   European Foundation for Quality Management (EFQM) quality model

Enablers

Leadership	100	
People management	90	
Policy and strategy	80	
Resources	90	
Processes	140	
Total		**500**

Results

People satisfaction	90	
Customer satisfaction	200	
Impact on society	60	
Business results	150	
Total		**500**
Total EFQM		**1 000**

Source: European Foundation for Quality Management (EFQM) quality model. Copyright © 1999–2003 EFQM.

QUALITY ASSURANCE DISASTER PLAN

In the majority of cases, the information about the nature of defective products will come from the technical quality assurance staff. This may be from test results from the production line (e.g. detection of microbiological contamination of a food processing plant) or from customer complaints (e.g. overheating of laptop batteries). Here, it is vital that front-line staff are well trained to recognise the potential implications of the discovery. Given the potential costs (in extreme cases, this may involve many hundreds of millions of pounds), there must be rapid (minutes rather than hours) communications 24/7/365 to the key decision makers. In a matter of hours (certainly not days), the quality assurance/product recall plan must swing into operation.

The contingency plan should clearly identify, in principle, the disaster stakeholders (by its nature, full definition is not possible until the event actually occurs). The core members of the disaster management team should be defined (additional members will be drawn in, depending on the nature of the issue) and frameworks set out for technical investigation of the problem and communications with key stakeholders.

The contingency plan should outline the decision-making process and the senior management that must be involved. How is the precise company position to be decided? With millions of pounds potentially at stake, this is a top management decision. The decision involves the company's assessment of the technical nature of the failure and its marketplace and financial implications.

The disaster plan should cover how communications to the key stakeholders (e.g. channels, suppliers, employees) should be conducted. A key aspect is communication with the media. It is recommended that a sole authorised source should be part of the plan. All other employees should not talk to the media but refer them to the appointed media contact channel. This channel must be responsive and with BBC News 24, CNN, etc. must be able to operate 24/7/365. If information is not freely given out, the media are likely to assume that the company is hiding something. Here again, the technical marketing manager is likely to be in the hot chair. The major papers and TV news channels have expert correspondents, capable of asking penetrating technical questions, backed by armies of well-trained researchers. Technical managers must not only be highly expert in their company's operations and its associated technologies (e.g. potential eco-effects of a transport spillage) but must also be well trained in dealing with the media. It is common practice in major companies to have a disaster simulation from time to time to test the robustness and responsiveness of the quality assurance recall plan.

The same issues apply to other incidents such as a factory fire.

Review

In this chapter, the concept of market driven quality has been defined and a range of tools used in market driven quality management presented. The differences in delivering service quality programmes have been discussed. The five-gap approach to service quality, with the use of the service-extended marketing mix, provides a management approach for the quality delivery of market driven services.

The differences between the ISO 9000 series and the European Foundation for Quality Management model have been explained, with the increased customer focus provide by the EFQM model. The major points to be considered in a quality assurance disaster plan, including product recall, have been reviewed.

Further reading

Brassington, F. & Pettitt, S. (2003) *Principles of Marketing*, 3rd edn, Prentice Hall.

BS 5703, *Guide to Data Analysis and Quality Control Using Cu-Sum Techniques*, British Standards Institution.

Chelsom, J., Payne, A. & Reavill, L. (2005) *Management for Engineers, Scientists and Technologists*, 2nd edn, John Wiley & Sons.

Curtis, T. & Williams, D. (2001) *An Introduction to Perfumery*, 2nd edn, Micelle Press.

Parasuraman, A., Zeithaml, V. & Berry, L. (1988) SERVQUAL: A Multiple-Item Scale for Measuring Consumer Perceptions of Service Quality, *Journal of Retailing*, **64** (1), 12–40.

Swift, L. (2001) *Quantitative Methods for Business, Management and Finance*, Palgrave.

Waller, D. (2003) *Operations Management: A Supply Chain Approach*, 2nd edn, Thomson.

CHAPTER 16

The marketing plan

Learning objectives

After studying this chapter you will be able to:

- Describe the various elements of the marketing plan
- Explain the differences between mission aims and objectives and be able to formulate SMART objectives
- Review the elements of the balanced scorecard approach to an organisation's objectives
- Outline the processes to formulate strategy alternatives and explain how portfolio methods can aid strategy selection

Introduction

Figure 16.1 shows the business planning cycle. The first stage of the process is to complete the macroeconomic analysis, microeconomic analysis and internal audit, (Chapter 2). As part of this process, the existing segmentation structure and marketing mix should be audited. This situation audit involves the consideration of a wide range of information and it can become easy not to see the wood for the individual trees. Just what is the bigger picture and what are the critical issues? The SWOT analysis provides the tool to focus all the diverse information into a coherent set of factors – the key imperatives that face the organisation (e.g. when existing products are in the decline phase of the product life cycle phase, new product development must be a priority).

The next phase is the search for strategy alternatives (e.g. by Ansoff analysis) and strategy selection (e.g. portfolio analysis). The brand strategy is then developed into the full detail required (e.g. detailed formulation of marketing mix). The plan is then implemented and progress monitored by the feedback and control system. The MkIS system feeds the data into all stages of the planning process. Overall, the process can be seen to have four elements:

1. *Where are we?* The environmental audit.
2. *Where do we want to be?* How do we bridge the strategic planning gap?
3. *How do we get there?* Strategy formulation, selection and implementation.
4. *How do we control this process?* MkIS and control systems.

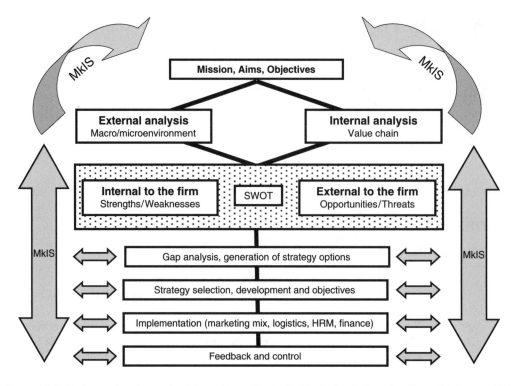

Figure 16.1 Business planning cycle. Adapted from: Curtis, T., *Marketing in Practice*, figure 11.1, page 265, © Elsevier 2006. Reproduced by permission.

Mission

The mission is the long-term expression of what the organisation is, an expression of why it exists. It should focus on the value the organisation delivers to its major stockholders, not just that the company wants to make loads of money. The mission statement or vision should be expressed in customer-orientated benefit terms. Though it may need amendment and adjustment from time to time, the mission should be on a longer time scale and transcend year-to-year strategy. It should be inspiring and motivational to the internal stakeholders and reflect the values of the key stakeholders, (e.g. owners, employees, agents, etc.). It should acknowledge the organisation's resources and capability in its environment and focus on the firm's distinctive competitive advantage. It should signal the company's strategic stance (e.g. market leader, market follower, etc.).

Definition of business scope

The served markets are important to the definition of the business scope. Should the company be regionally focused or globally focused? What are the company's key market segments and what represents value and service to them? A second dimension is to define the scope of the businesses operations. Is it to be focused or more vertically integrated? The

UK Co-operative movement also engages in manufacture to supply its consumer outlets. Other organisations contract out manufacture (e.g. Tesco, Marks & Spencer, etc.).

CHANGE IN BUSINESS PHILOSOPHY

At the start of the twenty-first century, Boeing came under intense competitive pressure from the Airbus consortium and some economists forecast the long-term demise of Boeing.

However, Boeing's Dreamliner has since become a major market success with record forward orders. Part of the success was because Boeing had been prepared to change the scope of its operations. Much of the Dreamliner is not made by Boeing but is outsourced to best-placed suppliers around the world. A major business scope decision is to decide what is the core competency and competitive advantage of the organisation and what aspects may be appropriately outsourced.

Technology can be another dimension that a firm may use to define its scope. A firm may be engaged in the transport of people across the English Channel. Possible options are tunnel, ship, hovercraft and air. Often companies elect to limit their scope, operating in one selected area and attempting to build distinctive competitive advantage into their offering. Eurostar, with its 2 hours 15 minutes service from London to Paris, believes that it has a competitive advantage over the airlines with its city centre to city centre service. It has no plans to go into the car ferry or airline business.

Competitive stance

Some organisations seek to be the market leaders and make heavy investments in research and development to keep ahead of the following pack of competitors. Companies such as IBM and Philips attempt to be in the technological lead in their selected markets. However, the implication may be that, from time to time, market exit may be indicated (e.g. IBM's withdrawal from the PC market when PCs became commoditised). Other companies are happy to follow different competitive strategies (e.g. low-cost providers of consumer electronics from China).

The pharmaceutical giants invest billions in new blockbuster drug technologies but there is a very profitable second tier of low-cost producers that make generic versions once the patents have expired.

Firm's capability

The mission must be appropriately resourced. Setting unattainable objectives is demotivating. The senior managers who develop the mission must satisfy the internal stakeholders who have to deliver the vision. The mission should be relevant to the internal situation and take due account of the changing pressures in the business environment. It should help internal stakeholders appreciate the distinctive competitive advantage of the organisation.

Values of key stakeholders

The UK Co-operative movement and the Body Shop pioneered attitudes to fair trade and corporate social responsibility. Changing attitudes and values has been a major challenge for the privatised public utilities (gas, electricity, water and telecommunications) as they moved from a public service orientation to a commercial context.

Time scale

Mission statements change, but not with the seasons. The value of mission is to give some continuity to the organisation. IBM may no longer make tabulation machines or typewriters but it is still in the business of office efficiency. The technologies of broadcasting are fast changing but the mission of CNN and BBC World Service to bring the news to people is still core.

Aims

The mission sets the long-term direction of the organisation; the aims set the direction of action. For a company that is expanding, it might include aims to penetrate new markets and develop new products. It gives a sense of direction but has no dimensions. Objectives have dimensions.

Objectives

Objectives have the characteristics of vectors; they have both direction and scale – the organisation wants to launch that new product in nine months, with a budget of £100 000. The character of objectives is summarised in the acronym SMART:

- **Specific** Objectives should be focused and specify clearly the outcomes to be obtained.
- **Measurable** Objectives should have dimensions or standards of attainment. For a launch plan the metrics might include the sales volumes and other budget objectives (e.g. costs and profit levels).
- **Aspirational** Objectives should be motivational; the objectives should be challenging but not so ambitious as to be unachievable. Unrealistic objectives are demotivating.
- **Realistic** This is the continuation of the above point. If the objectives are to be challenging, then the team implementing the plan must be properly briefed, trained and resourced.
- **Time-bound** The plan schedule should set time targets for completion and for major milestones in the plans. For a launch this might include the dates for launch and key dates such as completion of prototype testing, etc.

There can be confusion with the term objective being used at several levels; there is a cascade of objectives. The business objective might be to increase profitability by $X\%$ next year. The global marketing objective might be to increase market share in existing markets by $Y\%$ and $Z\%$ in a specified new market, maintaining profitability and with attainment in the next financial year. There then would be a full set of sub-objectives for all the elements of the marketing mix right down to the full detail of individual product launches.

Figure 16.2 The Kaplan and Norton scorecard. Adapted from: Kaplan, R. & Norton, D. (1992) The Balanced Scorecard – Measures that Drive Performance, *Harvard Business Review*, 70 (1), January–February, 71–9.

The balanced scorecard

Kaplan and Norton's balanced scorecard approach (Figure 16.2) asserts that the single-minded pursuit of short-term profits will lead to a long-term disaster. What is required is a balance of the four elements: financial, internal, learning and customer.

- **Financial** How does the organisation look to the owners? Is the cash flow and profitability satisfactory and stable? Chapters 5 and 10 give a range of financial tools such as ratio analysis to audit this aspect of the balanced scorecard.
- **Internal** How, within our internal business, do processes work? Chapter 2 illustrated how Porter's value chain can be used to audit the organisation's capability. Just how effectively and efficiently are the various elements of the primary value chain working? How well does our value chain support systems function?
- **Learning and innovation** How efficient and effective is the organisation's new product development process? Is the organisation first to market with its innovations? In the 'internal' audit, the effectiveness and efficiency of the current operations was examined. However, how well is innovation being applied to logistics and other elements of the value chain? Chapters 14 and 15 provide some approaches for exploring this aspect of the firm's balanced scorecard.
- **Customers** What is the customer's perspective of the organisation? What the customers experience is the offering provided by the firm's marketing mix. Full treatment of the marketing mix is given in Chapters 4 to 8.

The use of balanced scorecard requires a free flow of timely information on the macro-environment, microenvironment and internal environment of the organisation. Chapter 11 provides an overview of the processes to achieve this.

The environmental audit and SWOT

The tools of the environmental audit were discussed in full in Chapter 2. STEEPLE analysis provides the insight into the general macroenvironment. In the microenvironment audit, the Porter five forces of competition model provides a framework to evaluate the competitive environment facing the organisation. This analysis should embrace the full vertical extent up and down the industry supply chain. The augmented value chain provides an approach to assess the internal capabilities of the organisation.

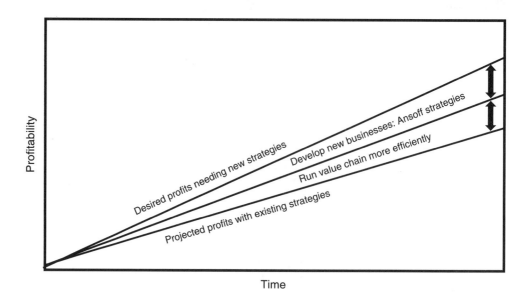

Figure 16.3 Gap analysis. Adapted from: Tony Curtis, *Marketing in Practice*, figure 3.6, page 92, © Elsevier 2006.

A dynamic SWOT analysis (Chapter 2) distils the great range of environmental forces to be aggregated into key imperatives facing the organisation (e.g. new product range is needed, with a refreshed marketing mix). Sometimes the environmental audit reveals a step-change in the environment that forces a complete review of the core mission, aims and objectives. This situation confronted Kodak's traditional 'wet' film business as the development of digital imaging technologies gathered momentum.

Gap analysis

The next stage of the planning process is to ask: where do we want to be? Figure 16.3 shows the strategic planning gap. On the projections of present policies the organisation will attain less than desired profitability. There are two generic ways in which the profitability gap can be bridged. The company can be run better (make the value chain more efficient) and/or the company can expand sales (Ansoff strategies of market, penetration, product development, market development and diversification).

Generic competitive strategies

Porter advances the view that if you are everything to everyone, you are, in effect, nothing special to anyone – the so-called 'stuck in the middle marketing wilderness'. Three options are advanced: cost leadership, differentiation and focus (Figure 16.4). In the cost leadership strategy, the imperative is to be the lowest cost provider. With their low-cost structures and abundant labour, this is a strategy being implemented with outstanding success by India and China. Consumer electronics products can be made in

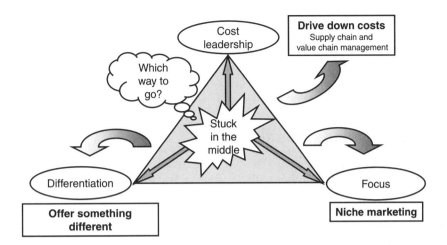

Figure 16.4 Generic strategy alternatives. Adapted from: Porter, Michael E. (1985) *Competitive Advantage: Creating and Sustaining Superior Performance*, **Free Press, figure 1.3, page 12.**

China, then delivered and sold in Europe for a fraction of the cost of manufacture in the high-cost structures of Europe.

With differentiation, the strategy is to offer something significantly different to the normal competition. This could be aesthetics (e.g. Bang & Olufsen's hi-fi is not only leading-edge quality, but also has a design flair that makes the equipment more of a contemporary work of art than just functional furniture). Celebrity endorsement is one way of a brand differentiating itself from the crowd by aligning with the distinctive qualities of the endorsing personality. Branding provides a strategy to differentiate the product in the mindset of the consumers when there may be relatively little scope in the differentiation of the physical product.

GREEN ELECTRONS

The physical delivery of electricity to homes is generic and is not under the control of each individual electricity supply company. However, this does not stop the electricity supply companies attempting to brand position themselves. When you buy 'green' electricity from the 'eco-friendly' brand, they do not ship special electrons painted green down the cable. The delivery is generic; the market positioning and communications attempt to differentiate providers. Other elements of the mix can be used (e.g. British Gas with providing a range of other services, such as boiler maintenance agreements). One company can position on 'total home care' with another focusing on green credentials.

With the focus strategy, a company makes a specific differentiated offering to a market segment with special needs. The PC and Windows have swept the office clear of most other competition but Apple still is the preferred choice in the graphic design studio. In the depth of the B2B context of the industry value chain specialist, niche companies provide specialist solutions for their clients. For instance, oil rigs, oil refineries and chemical plants are hazardous areas where potential explosive atmospheres can occur (e.g. valve burst). In such situations, 'flame proof' electronics and electrical equipment is needed (one spark could cause a massive explosion). This is a highly specialised, high-value area. Here, exceptional performance under demanding conditions is required: the question is 'how good?' not 'how cheap?' Focus and differentiation can still offer business opportunities to high-technology companies operating in higher cost development markets such as Europe.

Strategy generation and selection

In Chapter 14, the use of the extended Ansoff matrix to develop new business ideas was presented. Taken together with the internal and external audits and consideration of the generic strategy alternatives, the technical strategist is faced with more options than the organisation has resources to pursue. To maintain a balanced portfolio some products/business need to be dropped and new ventures started. One approach is the Boston matrix (Figure 16.5). The two key parameters are rate of market growth and relative market share. The market share is expressed in percentage annual growth. The relative market share is plotted on a logarithmic scale (base 10). The benchmark company is taken to be the competitive company with the largest market share. If the company completing the analysis is the market leader, the relative market share will be over one. If another company has a larger market share then the figure is less than one.

There are some difficulties with this model because it depends critically on using an appropriate segmentation approach and obtaining market share information in sufficient detail can be difficult. This model is fairly helpful for certain FMCG products such as cola. Here, the competitive advantage is derived from the number of outlets stocking the product. Healthy (low sugar/sugar free) versions are gaining market share and are thus

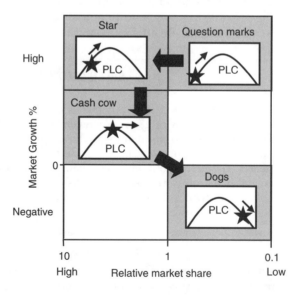

Figure 16.5 Adapted Boston (BCG) matrix. Adapted from: Hedley, B. (1977) Stategy and the business portfolio, *Long Range Planning*, 10, Elsevier.

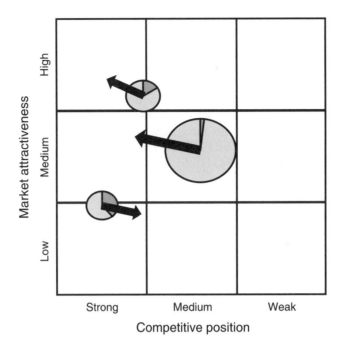

Figure 16.6 The General Electric (GE) multifactor approach. Adapted from: Day, George (1986) *Analysis for Strategic Market Decisions*, **West Publishing Company.**

more attractive than traditional high-sugar formulations. However, for many B2B products and high-technology consumer products, other factors – such as technical superiority rather than crude market share – can be more important.

The so called 'nine cell' models provide a more general solution. The General Electric multifactor type of approach is shown in Figure 16.6. The size of the circles can be used to provide some indication of the size of the market under consideration. The pie segment indicates the present market share held by the company. The arrow shows the best judgement by the analyst as to how the market is developing. The two axes are attractiveness and competitive advantage. Rather than use a single variable, the strategist considers a basket of several relevant factors and produces a weighted average of scores against these parameters to position the product in the matrix (e.g. technical superiority, field service and low manufacturing costs may factor into competitive position for comparing various consumer electronics products). The information for this analysis is taken from the organisation's MkIS activities.

Products in the top left-hand corner are attractive. Products in the bottom right-hand corner are unattractive. The company should devote more resources to those products that will stay in the high and/or strong and/or medium cells. Consideration should be given to withdrawing from products in or entering the low/weak cells.

If market attraction is considered to be solely market growth and competitive position considered to be solely relative market share, then the General Electric model will cover the same ground as the Boston matrix. The safe option at all times is to use the GE type of approach because it provides more flexibility and, where appropriate, will provide the same result as the Boston matrix.

Implementation

The planning team can now draw up the detailed market plans. The marketing mixes to be implemented can be developed (the marketing mix is covered in Chapters 4 to 8). The logistics, human resource and financial issues should be determined and the series of projects forming the detailed implementation plan agreed with management. Appropriate budgets and schedules should also be developed.

Feedback and control

The MkIS system provides the information to compare actual performance with plan performance. Relevant tools for this have been discussed in Chapters 9, 10 and 12. Where deviation from the plan is identified, the cause should be investigated by such techniques as variance analysis. Once the critical cause is identified, relevant action can be decided to bring things back to plan. It is good practice to allow some flexibility in budgets to allow for the need for such contingency action.

Review

The differences between mission, aims and objectives have been discussed and the nature of SMART objectives discussed. The need for a balanced approach in formulating objectives was reviewed and the Kaplan and Norton scorecard approach described. The various stages of the marketing plan were summarised. The nature of competitive strategies was reviewed and process for generating alternatives described. Portfolio methods evaluating the best options for the organisation to focus on have been presented.

Further reading

McDonald, M. (2007) *Marketing Plans: How to prepare them, how to use them*, 6th edn, Elsevier.
McDonald, M. & Morris, P. (2004) *Marketing: A Complete Guide in Pictures*, 2nd edn, Elsevier.
Wilson, R. & Gilligan, C. (2005) *Strategic Marketing Management: Planning Implementation and Control*, 3rd edn, Elsevier.

Glossary

7-S	See McKinsey 7-S
Action-centred leadership	A balanced framework for successful team leadership proposed by John Adair in his 1988 book *Effective Leadership*.
Aims	The general direction the organisation wants to take (e.g. expand the business).
Assets	The things of value that are owned by a company such as stock, plant and intellectual property.
Augmented product	The augmented products are those aspects or elements of a product that add value to and improve or support the core and actual features.
B2B	Marketing by business to other business, sometimes called organisational selling.
B2C	The marketing of goods or services by a company to general consumers.
Balanced scorecard	An approach developed by Kaplan and Norton for balancing the owner's profit objective for an organisation with other needs (e.g. longer term development and customer satisfaction).
Belbin types	A framework for exploring the roles people fulfil in teams.
Benchmarking	Often it is not the absolute value that is important but the relative value. If one company saves 10% on costs, it is doing badly if the competition is saving 25% on costs. Organisations often 'benchmark' themselves with best operators in their business sector.
Boston matrix	A 2 × 2 matrix approach to portfolio analysis for an organisation.
Break-even analysis	Analysis of how a business venture's profitability changes with sales volume.

Break-even point	In business situations where there are fixed and variable expenses, this is the sales volume at which the total sales income just equals the total of fixed and variable expenses.
Complementary products	Many products are part of a system and can only be utilised with other products, equipment and so on (e.g. cars need fuel).
Core benefit	The main primary benefit that a product provides for the user (e.g. for a car, this is transport).
Cost drivers	Those expenses that account for a substantial proportion of the company's expenses.
Cost-based price	A method of pricing based on taking a percentage of costs and 'marking up'.
CPM	Critical path method: a framework of network analysis to manage projects.
Cu-Sum chart	A chart for signalling when a process may be drifting out of statistical process control.
Decline	A phase of product life cycle where consumer preferences may have changed or innovative new products may have displaced existing products.
Deming cycle	The cycle of plan, do, verify and measure for the continuous development of quality.
Depreciation	Items of capital equipment have a productive life of a number of years. Depreciation is the accountancy process where only part of the value is assigned to a given production period. Depreciation affects profits but is a non-cash expense and so it does not affect cash flow and thus does not enter discounted cash flow calculations.
Derived demand	When a company makes components or raw materials for a final product, the ultimate demand for the product or service depends on the demand for the final product (e.g. demand for disk drives depends on the sales of computers, etc.).
Discretionary costs	Consumers have some mandatory costs (e.g. if you do not pay the mortgage, you will lose the house). Other items of expenditure are discretionary (if money is tight, then that Caribbean cruise holiday may have to wait for another year).
DMU	Decision-making unit: the group of people who may be involved in the purchase of an item (note that the company buyer may not be the key decision maker).

EFQM	European Foundation for Quality Management.
Elasticity of demand	The way in which consumer demand varies with price. For example, fuel prices are relatively inelastic: motorists continue to use fuel even if the price rises by a sizeable amount (you still have to get to work). On the other hand, with some other goods, a price rise can result in a significant drop in demand.
Environmental/life cycle	Not to be confused with product life cycle. Analysis of the environmental impact of the product from cradle to grave (manufacture, distribution, use, disposal and recycling).
EOQ	Economic order quantity: the amount of material to be purchased or manufactured which provides minimum cost.
EPOS	Electronic point of sale.
Expected product	This is the level and quality of product attributes that the buyers normally accept and agree to when they purchase the product. When the attributes exceed the buyers' expectations, we have satisfied customers; when they fall short, we have dissatisfied customers.
Feature attributes	These are the features that make up the product. Using the example of a car, this could be low-profile tyres, powerful engine, aerodynamic design and quality of construction materials.
Fishbone diagram	A structured approach to the identification of the key factors for delivering quality products or services.
Fixed costs	These are costs that do not change with production volume (e.g. rent for a factory).
Gantt chart	A chart that shows how various activities are scheduled to complete a project.
Gap analysis	A model for evaluating strategies for moving a company from where might go with existing strategies to new strategies to achieve better goals.
GE matrix	Named after General Electric, this is a 3×3 matrix approach to portfolio analysis for an organisation.
Generic strategies	Strategy alternatives proposed by Porter: cost leadership, focus and differentiation.
Growth	A phase in the product life cycle. This is where most products enter the market and there is less product distinctiveness. Rising sales generally mean more profitable returns at this stage.

Intangible benefits	Benefits that cannot be measured (e.g. love, security, passion, etc.) that a user may gain from the product or service. For example, mobile phones can create a sense of security for the lone female traveller.
Internal marketing	The activities undertaken to 'market' to the internal stakeholders in the organisation.
Introduction	A phase in the product life cycle. This is when a new product is launched and the goal at this stage is to create awareness and communicate the product's benefits to the consumers.
JIT	Just-in-time delivery: goods are delivered within a narrow time-window (and the goods are not accepted if they are either too early or too late).
Kennedy rights	The four components of consumer rights: to be safe, to be able to choose, to be informed and to be heard.
Liabilities	In simple terms, the money owed by the organisation (e.g. raw materials that have been delivered but not paid for).
Life cycle	See product life cycle (PLC).
Limited life cycle	Some products are only launched for a season (e.g. 'Olympic Games 2008' sweatshirt).
Macroenvironment	The general business conditions within which an organisation has to operate analysed in this text with the STEEPLE model. Other models include PEST an SLEPT.
Market intelligence	The collection of general market information to keep decision makers informed about developments in the business environment, not for a specific single marketing purpose.
Market research	The collection of information for a specific marketing purpose.
Market segmentation	The way marketers break up (segment) a diverse market into groups of similar customers.
Marketing mix	The seven levers of power for marketers: product, price, place, promotion, people, physical evidence and process.
Maturity	A phase in the product life cycle. This is where most products are situated. Profitability carries on growing but at a reduced rate.
McKinsey 7-S	A model used to appraise the internal environment, focusing on soft issues: structure, systems, style, staff, skills, strategy and shared values. Key aspects of this model are taken into the augmented value chain in this text.

Microenvironment	The immediate business conditions within which the business operates, including the competition environment.
MkIS	Marketing information management system. A marketing information system is a continuing and interacting structure of people, equipment, and procedures to gather, sort, analyse, evaluate and distribute pertinent, timely and accurate information. The information is used by marketing decision makers to improve their marketing planning, implementation and control.
Myers-Briggs factors	A framework for exploring a person's personality.
Pareto's principle	The rule proving that a minority of the issues drive the majority of the effects (e.g. often around 20% of the customers provide 80% of sales income).
Penetration pricing	A strategy of low prices to buy market share from competitors.
PERT	Programme evaluation and review technique: a framework of network analysis to manage projects.
PEST	An analysis of political, environmental, social and technological issues to conceptualise the macroenvironment.
PONC	Price of non-conformance: this is an estimate of the cost of product quality failure.
Potential product	This is the form of a product that encompasses all the augmentations and transformations that the product might ultimately undergo in the future. These could be future improvements that might keep the product competitive within the market.
Product life cycle (PLC)	The stages of a product's life: introduction, growth, maturity and decline. The actual timescales and shape of the life cycle curve depend on the product and the macro- and microenvironments.
Profit contribution	The sales revenue of a unit minus the variable cost of production of that unit. This ignores fixed costs, including depreciation, and is used in the calculation of the break-even point. Fixed costs divided by profit contribution give the break-even point.
Qualitative data	Key data for developing deep plans. It involves more difficult but crucial questions, such as: 'How do people view my brand and why do they view it that way?'
Quantitative data	Information that is easy to convey in numbers (e.g. how many people buy a product and how much they use).

Range and depth	The range is the number of product types. Ford makes a broad range of cars, from small run-arounds to off-road 4 × 4s. The depth is the variety within each individual type or range. So, with cars they might include automatic versions, diesel engine option, colour, paint finish and so on.
Rejuvenation	After a number of years on the market, a product (e.g. an existing model of car) might be re-thought and updated using a facelift and re-launch.
Relationship marketing (RM)	A view of marketing where success is seen to come from building long-term relationships and networks and not simply focusing on short-term profits from a single transaction.
Segmentation	See market segmentation.
Semi-variable costs	These are generally taken to be costs that vary with production volume but not in a simple linear relationship. For instance, energy costs for heating and lighting a factory are relatively fixed but the amount of energy used in production machinery will vary with the level of production. The overall energy cost function is thus not a simple linear function of the production volume.
Sequential skimming strategy	This is a process where several markets of different benefit and value are skimmed in turn. For example, advanced braking systems were first introduced into luxury cars; now they are standard in all production cars. This is an example of both sequential skimming and learning curve effect.
SERVQUAL	A model for appraising the issues relevant to the delivery of quality services to customers.
Shewhart chart	A chart for signalling when a process may be drifting out of statistical process control.
Signal attributes	Those aspects of a product that do not necessarily directly contribute to tangible benefits but communicate to the user (e.g. texture, sound, smell and design).
Skimming strategy	A strategy of entering the market with a high unit price to maximise the profit per unit. This is typical for luxury products during the introduction phase.
SMART objectives	Objectives provide dimensions to aims. They are said to be SMART: specific, measurable, aspirational, realistic and time-bound.

Stakeholder	Stakeholders are groups of people or organisations that have an interest in and/or may affect the organisation (e.g. owners, employees, suppliers, customers, pressure groups, etc.).
STEEPLE	In this model, social, technological, economic, educational, political, legal and environmental issues are analysed to give a picture of the overall business conditions (macroenvironment) in which the organisation is operating.
Strategic pricing gap	The gap between a customer's perceived value and production costs.
Sunk cost	In some textbooks, advertising is given as a variable expense. However, this is not so. A perfume company may spend many millions of pounds launching a new perfume; this money is committed or 'sunk' before any perfume is sold and thus is entirely independent of sales achieved.
SWOT	An analytical technique to distil the key factors out of an extended macro- and microenvironment analysis: strengths, weakness, opportunities and threats.
Tangible benefits	These are measurable benefits the user gains from the ownership or use of the product or service.
TQM	Total quality management: a holistic view of quality, which involves all quality stakeholders, both internal and external (e.g. suppliers).
Value	This is the amount of money people are prepared to pay for an object or service. This need not have any relationship to the physical costs of delivering the product or service. A first edition Harry Potter has a value far in excess of its original production cost.
Value chain	A model developed by Michael Porter to analyse the internal environment of an organisation. An adapted (augmented) form of the value chain is used in this text.
Variable costs	This is generally taken to be costs that vary directly with the volume of production (e.g. raw material costs).

Index

Note: Page references in *italics* refer to Figures and Tables